WHERE TO SKI in France

Edited by
Chris Gill

Consultant Editor
Dave Watts

LAGRANGE

SKI 2018-2019

SELF-CATERING APARTMENTS | CHALETS | HOTELS

FRENCH ALPS & PYRENEES

WEEK STAYS | SHORT BREAKS | WEEKENDS

*Valid from 17-11-18 to 04-05-19 *(departure dates)* on Lagrange branded properties only.

Contents

About this book

by the editor

If you're a skier, you probably know *Where to Ski and Snowboard* – the annual guide to all the resorts that matter to a British skier, published from 1994 to 2015.

Or maybe you don't. WTSS, edited by me and Dave Watts, set the standard for ski resort guides for those 20-odd years, seeing off various rival books (including *The Good Skiing Guide*, which I started back in the 1980s while editor of *Holiday Which?* magazine). WTSS was widely recognised as the British skier's bible.

Based on the same foundations of thorough research, impartial evaluation, warts-and-all text and reader-friendly layout, the book you're reading is the second in a new series of smaller resort guides launched in 2017, each dealing with a single country. *Where to Ski in Austria* was published first; Italy, Switzerland and other countries will follow. Various ebook versions are planned, too.

These books are all-new: they have been written from scratch, and have a new structure – an improved one, I hope. As you might expect, this volume covers more resorts in France than WTSS did – check out Espace Diamant, for example.

You might expect this book to cover the resorts in more detail, too. Well, it does and it doesn't. A book covering 100 resorts rather than 350 has room for more detailed analysis of the skiing. In these new books, beginners get more attention, and the broad church of intermediate skiers is split: the needs of cautious 'true blue' skiers are considered separately from those of confident red-run skiers.

But some of the detail that seemed necessary in 1994 (or even 2004) is now made largely redundant by comprehensive resort websites and feedback sites such as TripAdvisor. So, some of that detail (on hotels, for example) has gone.

Much of the redundant detail that has disappeared was also quick to go out of date. With that detail gone, annual revision looks extravagant; so these new books will stay on sale for about three years before they are revised.

Where to Ski and Snowboard started life as *Where to Ski*. The 'Snowboard' was added in year three, after Dave and I decided to get to grips with boarding, and sent ourselves off to Colorado to take a course strictly for grown-ups. Twenty years on, ski resorts are still called ski resorts; so the 'Snowboard' has gone.

My WTSS co-editor Dave is acting as consultant editor to this series, which means he is making contributions to some chapters based on his resort visits, and bringing his vast experience to bear by reviewing others. But I carry the can: comments and contradictions to me, please – or compliments, if you like.

Creating this book has been hard work, but I've really enjoyed the process; I hope you enjoy reading the result, and find it helps you decide ... where to ski in France.

Chris Gill
Exeter, 13 November 2018
editor@wheretoski.uk

◀ In some ways, the ultimate French ski resort – Val Thorens, in the 3 Vallées

France: an introduction

by the editor **Chris Gill**

Most British skiers take their holidays in Austria or France – together, they have around 60% of the UK market, with France currently taking the slightly bigger share. Some 30 or 40 years ago it was Austria that dominated – until France was propelled to the top of the league in the mid-1990s by the big lift systems and reliable snow of its high, purpose-built resorts.

The appeal of France remains essentially unchanged: big ski areas (including the world's biggest) at high altitude, where you can expect or at least hope for good snow conditions, and plenty of resort villages with ski-in/ski-out lodgings.

There was a time when to get these benefits you had to accept some negatives: stark, soulless villages and a blanket absence of après-ski (except in Dick's Tea Bar in Val d'Isère). But things have changed. Many purpose-built resorts have been improved in atmosphere and appearance over the last decade or three, partly by expanding them in a more appealing style and partly by retro-fitting traditional elements such as pitched roofs and stone or wood cladding.

And après-ski has been transformed, with at least one or two throbbing bars in most resorts, and multiple ones in some. In a few resorts there is even life on the mountain in the late afternoon, as in Austria, thanks to the half-dozen branches of the Folie Douce chain (another Val d'Isère institution).

La mouche dans la pommade

French resorts have a reputation for high prices, and with some justification. Bar and restaurant prices, in particular, are noticeably higher than in Austria and Italy, France's eurozone rivals. In the big, internationally famous resorts – Courchevel, Méribel and Val d'Isère – prices can be painfully high. But other prices – lift passes, equipment hire, ski school lessons – are not so high, with the result that your total on-the-spot spending in most resorts does not need to be particularly painful. And of course there is a spectrum, and there are resorts at the cheaper end. In our Shortlists chapter we pick out places for a budget holiday.

And there are strategies for keeping your spend in bars and restaurants down. Staying in a catered chalet (read the relevant feature chapter, if the term means nothing to you) means your pre-dinner drinks will be at shop prices, more or less

– and your wine with dinner will be included in the holiday price. Choose where you stay with care. Lodgings in Les Menuires may seem a good way to cut costs in the 3 Vallées, but think about where you'll be having lunch – you certainly don't want to be skiing over to Courchevel to pay its mountain restaurant prices. A base in Courchevel, on the other hand, means that you can do most of your lunching in Les Menuires and St-Martin-de-Belleville.

Times to avoid

More than most parts of the Alps, France is affected by local school holidays. The country is split into three zones, each having a fortnight off over a four-week period. Easter is late in 2019, and the French holidays are quite late, too – from 10 February to 10 March, with the important Paris fortnight falling in the second half of the period. So the peak week will be 24 February to 3 March, when Paris overlaps with Zone A, including Lyon; the week before that will also very busy.

Lots of websites carry these dates. To be sure you're getting the real deal, go to the French government website, www.education.gouv.fr, and search for 'calendrier scolaire'.

Mountain quirks

France remains unusual in using four piste classifications, with green identifying really easy runs in addition to the usual blue, red and black. This is an entirely excellent scheme that helps beginners move off the nursery slopes with confidence, and it is amazing that it has not been more widely adopted. In my

Val Thorens, on p6, represents one extreme form of French skiing; here, Megève represents the other

Look after yourself

In these new guides I have tried to give direct guidance to specific groups of skiers about which resorts and even which runs will suit them. In particular, I have tried to help a group that we perhaps neglected slightly in the many editions of *Where to Ski and Snowboard*: the inexperienced, not entirely competent or confident early intermediate skier.

Obviously, giving clear guidance of this kind is problematic. I don't know your individual abilities or how well equipped you are, or the conditions you'll meet; I can't guarantee that the judgements Dave and I have made are consistent from day to day, or year to year, however hard we try.

So I have to say that you should not plan your week, and still less your day, solely on the basis of what you read here. Treat this book as a starting point. If you haven't reached the stage where you can get down any intermediate slope (given time), you should be skiing with someone who knows the slopes and understands the conditions. This might mean an instructor.

At the other end of the scale, this book also spells out the opportunities in each resort for off-piste skiing – or freeriding, as it is now branded. Off-piste skiing is inherently dangerous; it requires specialised skills, equipment and – crucially – knowledge, some of it general and some of it very local. For most people, the only safe way to do it is with professional guidance.

experience the green label is a reliable guide to scare-free pistes, except in Val d'Isère where the Verte to La Daille is infamously challenging.

Some resorts make little use of the green classification, and some don't use it at all – notably Les Arcs; linked La Plagne doesn't use it much, either. They surely have winding easy pistes that could be made into greens. At the other extreme, a resort that makes wide use of the green is Val Cenis. I particularly like the long Escargot from the Col du Mont Cenis to the valley, which is adorned by all kinds of road signs; in summer it is revealed to be the Route Départmentale 1006.

The piste classification we devote most attention to in these pages is blue. We've made a determined attempt to spell out in each chapter how the piste network suits a 'true blue' skier – someone who is simply not comfortable, yet, on slopes that are even slightly challenging.

It's worth emphasising that you can't judge a resort in this respect on the basis of how much blue is visible on the piste map, or on numerical summaries of the skiing on offer – the number of blue runs, or the percentage of runs that are blue. First, you need to know how the blue runs connect (or not); second, you need to know whether the blue runs are truly of blue-run difficulty. Look through the book, and in the sections headed 'The mountains in brief' you'll see a range of verdicts for true blue skiers. We hope you find them helpful.

As any French Alps visitor who likes to stray from the piste will have noticed, in recent years France has done away with what was an excellent feature of its mountains, the *itinéraire* – a marked but otherwise unprepared and unpatrolled

Practicalities: getting to French resorts

French resorts are about the easiest Alpine resorts to reach from the UK. The airports serving the French Alps are the best served by EasyJet and its rivals, while the drive to the northern French Alps is the shortest on offer.

By road it's 820km/510mi from Calais to Geneva, gateway to the northern Alps, which can be done in only seven hours. Chambéry and Grenoble, gateways to the central and southern Alps, are a bit further. Bear in mind that the tolls on the autoroutes are non-trivial.

Once upon a time, those with no respect for the law could get to Geneva in under seven hours by ignoring the permitted maximum of 130kph (80mph), but now ... now the French authorities are able to interrogate other national licencing databases and thus pursue foreign car drivers who break the law – and there are more speed cameras on the *autoroutes* than you might think. Oh, and it's illegal to use a satnav that shows where the cameras are.

There are no blanket rules about equipment (as there are in Austria), but you may well encounter conditions (and roadside signs) requiring winter tyres or chains – so in practice you need to be equipped with one or the other, or ideally both. Winter tyres plus traction control form a surprisingly effective combination. Check what you need to carry in the car – currently a hi-vis jacket, warning triangle and breathalysers.

The best-served **airport** is Geneva (for all practical purposes in Switzerland, although it does have a door into France). But Chambéry, Lyon and Grenoble are worth considering for all except the northern resorts. Geneva airport and the Geneva border crossing can be jammed on Saturdays.

The boom in independently organised travel has spawned a thriving industry of minibus operators from Geneva to the northern resorts, in particular, operating shared or private services. The costs are non-trivial.

With the notable exception of Chamonix (reached by narrow-gauge railway from St-Gervais), French resorts aren't served by **railways –** unless you count Bourg-St-Maurice (connected to Arc 1600 by funicular railway) as a resort. But the Tarentaise resorts can be reached using Eurostar services from south-east England – an attractive option if you can easily get to the departure points – London St Pancras and Ashford.

In season there are direct day trains on Saturdays and direct night trains on Friday evenings, returning on Saturday night – allowing eight days on the slopes. The night service is not a proper sleeper train, with anything resembling beds – you spend the night in your (slightly) reclining seat. The terminus is Bourg-St-Maurice, with stops at Moûtiers for the 3 Vallées etc and Aime for La Plagne. There's no charge for taking skis or a snowboard.

On weekdays, you have to change trains in Paris (which means crossing the city, not crossing the platform). There are various daily services from there, with extra services at the weekend in season.

route. Mr Watts and I cannot ski the pistes from Val Thorens down the head of the Méribel valley without recalling the days, [cough] years ago, when there was just a series of markers every half mile down the valley – a great adventure at the time.

At least that *itinéraire* has been replaced by pistes. Most (such as the excellent ones from La Masse, at Les Menuires) have simply been dropped. It's a shame.

What sort of lodgings?

Whereas practically all Austrian resorts offer a wide range of styles of accommodation – smart hotels, simple hotels, apartment buildings large and small, guest houses, private houses with rooms to rent – many French resorts offer much less variety. The situation is improving all the time, but some purpose-built resorts consist almost entirely of apartment blocks (these days often cunningly disguised as chalets), with just one or two hotel options and maybe a few catered chalets.

Those original apartment blocks were dreary to behold and miserable to inhabit, particularly if you took their specified capacity at face value. As a general rule, to accommodate x people you needed an apartment nominally able to sleep 2x people. These days, things are much better. There are now apartment residences all over the French Alps offering reasonable space, comfort and style. There is more about this in another feature chapter.

For the major resorts in this book, we've invited our friends at the twin French holiday specialists Peak Retreats and Ski Collection to summarise the top apartment options. These guys have a unique French perspective and know the best residences better than we do – and as well as anyone we know.

France is the spiritual home of the catered chalet, a British institution explained in another feature chapter. Méribel and Val d'Isère, in particular, are Chalet Central, each with scores of operators and hundreds of chalets to choose from. But there are countless other resorts with chalets available, from super-low Samoëns to super-high Val Thorens. Our resort chapters make it clear whether you'll find many chalets in each resort.

A few years back the French tourist trade woke up to the fact that it was underselling its hotels. Its star ratings, unlike those of its rivals, topped out at four stars. In 2009 this was put right, with the introduction of a 5-star rating (followed a bit later by the even more elevated Palace designation). Half a dozen hotels in Courchevel were among the first very small batch to earn promotion.

Since then, a ratings race has taken a grip on French ski resorts. Courchevel now has an astonishing 20 5-star hotels. Even places like Arc 2000 have acquired one. Meanwhile, the 4-star category has become the 'very comfortable without being swanky' category, as in Austria, and naturally many 3-star places have sought and got promotion.

More modest hotels are not always easy to find – we try to pick out resorts such as Les Deux-Alpes and La Clusaz that have lots. And it must be said that finding a 3-star hotel doesn't necessarily mean you have found one you can afford. Some hoteliers prefer to retain their middle-ground rating while actually offering quite luxurious accommodation, and charging for it.

Resorts with altitude

The stereotypical French resort is high, purpose-built in the years after World War 2, and lacking charm. There many variations on this theme, and plenty of exceptions, but it does have a foundation in fact.

In general, higher altitude means more snowfall, and a longer shelf life for the snow that falls. Fans of low-altitude resorts rightly point out that higher altitude also means rockier terrain, which requires deeper snow-cover to be safely skiable. But there is another angle to consider: the quality of the skiing surface. As spring approaches, the snow in low resorts is more likely to become slushy in the afternoon and therefore rock-hard in the morning.

The highest major resort village in Europe is in France – Val Thorens, in the famous 3 Vallées, at 2300m. Its skiing goes up to 3230m (and includes some patches of glacier). The top heights of nearby Les Arcs and La Plagne are much the same. With resort villages at around the 2000m mark, you can hope for good snow conditions for a long season in all these places

Val Thorens is higher than the mountaintops of some other areas further north. Megève has one lift to 2350m, but most of its high-points are in the 1800-2000m region. Nearby Espace Diamant tops out at a modest 2069m, and most of its high-points are below 1900m. With the conspicuous exception of its Balme sector, practically all the skiing in La Clusaz is below 2000m.

The altitude coin has another side, though: trees. Trees are the key to enjoyable skiing in falling snow – not so much because they provide shelter from the storm but because they give some direction to the light, and so to a surprising degree make the ground and its contours easier to see. The treeline varies from place to place, but in general you don't get many trees above 1900m.

And resorts with charm

Related to resort altitude is the matter of the character of the village. Roughly speaking, the higher you go the more likely it is you are going to a village that has been developed for skiers, usually without much regard for style, tradition or human scale. This is subjective territory, of course, but some of the monstrous original buildings in resorts such as Les Menuires, Les Arcs, La Plagne, Flaine and Tignes were just mistakes, to our eyes.

Many purpose-built resorts have been improved over recent years. And some were originally designed with more flair than others – Avoriaz, Val Thorens and Arc 1950, for example. Views differ on Valmorel, the core of which was built in the 1970s in cute mountain-town style around a narrow pedestrian street; for some, it feels like Disneyland Savoie.

The most appealing major resort villages in France, for our money, are Megève and La Clusaz, both at about 1100m. Then there is the lively, characterful mountaineering town of Chamonix, at 1035m. Among smaller resorts, about the most cute is Samoëns (in the Grand Massif area), which is so low the lift company doesn't dare to give the figure on the piste map – it's at 720m.

Le weekend starts ... where?

Since the market in flights to the Alps was radically expanded by 'budget' airlines, we've all been freed from the tyranny of the weekend charter flight – we've been able to organise shorter trips, over weekends or whatever. But flights are only half the battle: what about lodgings for three- or four-night stays?

In a business dominated by week-long stays, it can be tricky to find places to take a shorter booking. The resort that has long been different in this respect is Chamonix – a big town with lots of accommodation, where the real high season is the summer. In winter, it's not difficult to make a short-break booking – and the resort is quickly reached from Geneva airport; just the ticket.

There are niche operators specialising in short breaks, of course, particularly for corporate clients. Ski Weekend uses hotels throughout the Chamonix valley and also operates its own chalet on a flexible basis. But the firm has spread its wings too; marketing manager Doug Newman says: 'Whilst our home is Chamonix, where our proprietors Gavin Foster and Sue Greenslade are based year-round, we organise fully tailor-made, action-packed corporate events all over the Alps.'

Alpine Weekends, run by Tony Steward, offers much the same tailor-made approach, without the slight Chamonix emphasis. 'We concentrate on corporate trips mainly in hotels,' says Tony, 'drawing on an extensive hotel database built up over many years and covering all major resorts. We can then organise whatever extras the client wants, from flights to tuition.'

Another operator geared to short breaks is Stanford Skiing, in Megève (another resort not much more than an hour from Geneva airport). To minimise empty rooms in its two chalet hotels, Stanford offers a slightly more regimented deal. 'Our short breaks are primarily for three or four days beginning and ending on Wednesday, Thursday or Sunday,' says manager Elizabeth Kinnear. 'Ideally, fly out Sunday and go home Wednesday or Thursday – flights are cheaper, as is the accommodation.' The company runs its own good-value minibus transfers, which is a real bonus.

STC Ski offers tailored holidays in a handful of French resorts (alongside other countries), and in a handy web-page guide to their top 10 weekend resorts lists Chamonix and Megève first and second – so you can see a bit of a pattern emerging here. Third, as it happens, is very much in the same part of the French Alps – Morzine, in the Portes du Soleil.

Convenience truths

Purpose-built resorts introduced the idea of skiing from your door, and many skiers have come to attach importance to this luxury. It has great attractions for families, in particular – parents are freed from the nightmare choice of insisting the kids carry their skis or spoiling them by shouldering the burden. But don't run away with the idea that booking an apartment in a high, purpose-built resort will automatically mean ski-in/ski-out convenience.

If you find yourself at the wrong end of an apartment block in Les Arcs or Tignes, you may have quite a way to walk within the building before you emerge into the light. And then you may have more walking to get across the snow to the lift you want to ride – an arrangement we will often refer to as ski-in/plod-out. For really convenient skiing, you generally want small buildings on a slope.

That slope needs to be a piste, of course. Méribel is prettily laid out on a slope, but those who conceived it failed to incorporate multiple pistes – if your chalet is at the south end, you may be able to ski from the door, but if it's not, you have no chance. It's a shuttle-ride to the lifts.

Reliance on ski-buses at the start and end of the day is quite common in resorts that have grown out of valley towns and villages – Val d'Isère is the classic example. The key thing then is that the service is up to scratch (Val d'Isère's is one of the best, happily – a bus every five minutes).

Size matters, to most of us

For many British skiers, a properly enjoyable ski holiday requires a big ski area, where you can travel around from one resort village to another, mostly skiing new terrain every day. France is the place to find such areas. It has five areas in our 4-star size category, meaning they have over 175km of pistes: Alpe-d'Huez, Espace Diamant, Grand Massif, Megève (taking its two separate sectors together) and Val d'Isère-Tignes. And it has three in the 5-star category with over 400km – Portes du Soleil, Paradiski and (well in the lead) the 3 Vallées. No other country comes close to matching this range of mega-resorts.

At the opposite extreme, there are resorts an order of magnitude smaller – for example, we'd be surprised if the pistes of Ste-Foy, down the valley from Val d'Isère, amounts to 40km (we can't find any evidence of a measurement). To be happy spending a week in one of these small resorts you need to be content with very little variation in what you do from day to day – in fact, very little variation from hour to hour.

Or you need to be prepared to go on outings to other resorts. France doesn't have the vast regional lift passes of Austria, which allow you to cruise around wide areas visiting many resorts at essentially no extra costs. But there are some passes that allow outings to nearby resorts, and we aim to mention these in the Pass notes section on the first page of each resort chapter.

There is still immense confusion in the ski resort business over piste extent. Some resorts like to inflate their assets by taking the length of their pistes and applying a multiplier, on the basis that skiers don't go straight down the run – they make turns, and therefore travel further. Faithful readers of *Where to Ski and Snowboard* will be aware of the campaign we ran about this nonsense.

This mess has been illuminated by the work of a dedicated German consultant, Christoph Schrahe, who has digitally measured the runs of the world's top 100 resorts (and more). He has published his findings, and you'll find many references to them in these pages. Naturally, he uses no multiplier.

We understand that the French national association of lift companies recommends that resorts should publish centre-line figures even if they choose to publish other figures too. Some follow this recommendation, but most ignore it. Some resorts have responded by publishing area figures alongside length figures or, as in Serre-Chevalier, by publishing only area figures. This also is nuts. Who knows how to interpret area figures and how to relate them to km?

Catered chalet holidays

For many British skiers, a ski holiday means a chalet holiday. This chapter provides a quick tour of the catered chalet market – which resorts have them, who offers them – and includes a basic beginner's guide to what to expect, and some tips on finding the right chalet for your party.

Although the catered chalet first saw the light of day in Switzerland (read our beginner's guide), France has become its spiritual home. Many firms operate nowhere else.

Where to find them

It's no surprise that the greatest concentration of chalet holidays is to be found in Méribel – a British-founded resort built entirely in chalet style in the centre of the world's largest ski area. All the big-name operators are here; there are mid-sized operators specialising in the resort (notably Meriski) and countless small firms running anything from one chalet to a handful. There are lots of very luxurious places to be found.

Méribel's neighbours can't match it for numbers, but Courchevel can certainly match it for the range of properties; swanky Courchevel 1850 in particular has some glorious places – though the best properties here are those let privately. The other parts of Courchevel – Moriond, Village, Le Praz and La Tania – cater for the likes of you and us, with plenty of affordable but comfortable chalets.

In the Belleville valley, neither Les Menuires nor Val Thorens comes near matching the best luxury chalet offerings in Méribel and Courchevel, but there are plenty of more affordable options in both.

Chalet Lea – a Ski Amis Premium Service chalet in La Tania (next to Courchevel in the 3 Vallées)

The chalet holiday – a beginner's guide

Legend has it that the catered chalet holiday was invented by one Colin Murison Small in 1958, when he rented a bit of a chalet in Grindelwald and installed in it the first British chalet girl, briefed to keep house for those who responded to his small ad in (reportedly) the *Telegraph*. That was the beginning of Colin's business, Small World, and of an industry.

In some respects, the chalet formula is unchanged in the intervening 60 years. You still get breakfast and dinner prepared by a more-or-less resident, more-or-less English-speaking person, served at a communal table shared with fellow inmates. It is very much a house party, and that remains at the core of its appeal – you get the privacy and informality of a home-from-home, with no restaurant bills, and without having to cook.

In other ways, it has changed a lot.

The legend tells us that bread and jam was served at teatime; the industry long ago standardised on cakes, too. Wine with dinner is included in the price (although it's increasingly common to offer upgrades to meet more demanding tastes), and there is almost always a system for acquiring pre-dinner drinks at well under resort bar prices. These features are really helpful in keeping your holiday outgoings under control.

The housekeeping is now quite likely to be done by a chalet boy, or even by a grown-up couple. The cook will have had some training in cookery; the menus may be dictated by head office, or the cook may be in control. In bigger, smarter chalets, he/she is likely to be a professional.

The chalet holiday started out as a budget option – a way to avoid the costs of a hotel. The accommodation was basic. Twenty years down the line, when we started taking chalet holidays, you still had to accept bedrooms divided by paper-thin walls to cram in more guests, primitive shared bathrooms and hot-water systems designed for four serving a chalet for 16.

Now, en suite bathrooms and powerful boilers are the norm. Regrettably, most chalet bedrooms are still appreciably smaller than hotel rooms (the space priority tends to be given to the living room, and the logic of that is understandable). But there are plenty of pricey chalets to be had where the master bedroom, at least, is spacious. Spa facilities of some sort are common – the hot tub, preferably outdoors, has become a key feature.

Really plush chalets tend to be let as a whole property (costing £20k to £150k, depending on the season and chalet, flights not included), but in most chalets you can still book a room or two and share the chalet with a bunch of strangers. Obviously, this presents risks, but for many people, it's a key feature – ready-made, like-minded ski-buddies, and sociable evenings.

At a point now lost in the mists of time, someone had the bright idea of running a hotel along chalet lines, and thus conceived the chalet hotel. It will have hotel-sized bedrooms (good), a bar (bad – higher prices) and may have a pool (good, obviously). Chalet hotels are now widely offered.

Méribel's close rival in the chalet business is Val d'Isère, where again you have a very wide choice of operators and properties, including some lovely places with high-ceilinged living rooms and pools in the basement. A highly unusual feature here is that a central 5-star hotel was recently taken over to be run as a catered chalet hotel by the Inghams/Total/Esprit group.

Moving over the ridge from Val to next-door Tignes you are leaving super-chalet territory, but there is a good range of attractive cheaper options. The same is true of most other big, high, international resorts. Move to lower altitude, and in Morzine and Les Gets you'll find another major concentration of chalets, including some lovely pricey ones.

You can't assume you'll find a choice of chalets everywhere – in the Grand Massif resorts of Les Carroz and Flaine, for example, they seem to be rare, though there are more in Samoëns. Although there are plenty of glamorous chalets in and around Megève, very few find their way on to the UK catered chalet market.

Le Ski's uber-desirable Scalottas lodge, in the modern suburb below the centre of Courchevel Moriond

Finding a chalet that suits you

If you've taken chalet holidays before, you're quite likely to start the search for your next chalet by looking at the firm(s) you've used before. If you haven't ... well, we're happy to recommend all the firms who advertise in this book. Most of them have been in business for decades, and we've got to know them well in that time. But many of them are focused on just one or two resorts, which may not be the resorts you had in mind. What you probably need then is an agent.

Do some googling and you'll unearth both general ski travel agencies and sites specialising in chalets. In the case of specialist chalet sites, you'll often find yourself unsure as whether you are looking at the site of an operator, offering just that operator's chalets, or the site of an agent, dealing with multiple operators.

Agents' sites are not always very helpful. One with a very promising web address is of little use in practice because it offers only one way of filtering the impressive lists of chalets on offer in a given resort, which is by size. More powerful shortlist-builders offer the ability to filter on price, facilities, even departure airport.

But how do such agents work in practice? One good holiday-finder site is run by Skiline, one of the UK's major ski travel agencies. We asked boss Angus Kinloch about its *modus operandi*. His answers in summary:

Who's covered? Skiline lists holidays from 200 different suppliers, including nearly all the main British tour operators (and the odd exception is being rectified); and we list many smaller operations, including single-chalet businesses.
(Editor's note: Skiline does not list three of our chalet-holiday advertisers – Host Savoie in Morzine, Powder N Shine in Les Menuires and Stanford Skiing in Megève. So you'd need to check out their offerings separately.)
Live availability? Almost ... 90% of the prices and availability of our holidays are updated every day, some twice a day. Not all our smaller suppliers are up to speed with technology, so their availability is updated manually every few days.
Online booking? Not yet – it's something we are looking at, but we find that in most cases the clients book something quite different from what they initially enquired about. Our clients find our informed, personal advice very helpful.
Identity of chalet operators? Once we are talking to clients, we are entirely upfront with them about who operates the chalets they are looking at – and we always try to match our clients with the most suitable tour operator.
Price matching? We will always offer prices that match those available through the tour operator directly; if online discounts are available, we match those. And we can always save clients money on equipment rental – often as much as 50% off.

Apartment holidays

With the arrival recently of a 5-star hotel in Arc 2000 and a fourth one opening in Val Thorens, is the era of apartment domination of high French resorts over? *Au contraire!* Apartments in France are enjoying a full-blown renaissance. The quantity of self-catering accommodation available in purpose-built resorts is enormous, and staying that way. The important change, as these resorts have matured, is in quality: there are now many excellent alternatives to the cheap-and-not-very-cheerful formula on which they were founded, and every year more come to market. And it's all down to a very few companies.

Both of your editors try to fit in a proper ski holiday each season. Well, we need a break from the rigours of press trips and resort inspection tours, and it's good to keep in touch with the way real holidays work. And what accommodation do we choose for these week-long stays in one resort? Apartments.

We stay in apartments because apartment life is so flexible and relaxed. There is no timetable; you can eat what you like, when you like; your booze is bought at shop prices (in valley towns, ideally); and you get your own living room in which to do your own things – you don't even have to dress properly while playing Bananagrams and binge-watching *The Trip*. Catered chalets, by comparison, seem the very essence of regimentation.

In France, though, we used to have a problem: the great bulk of apartments on the market in the UK were, frankly, shoddy and cramped. You had to do your own

Like most CGH-managed, MGM-built residences, the Cimes Blanches in La Rosière has a lovely pool

research and book direct to find good places. But then, about 20 years ago, things started to change. In 1999, after three editions in which we assiduously tried to sift out the best of a mediocre bunch of apartments, the chapter on Les Arcs in *Where to Ski and Snowboard 2000* noted that 'New for 1999-2000 are the luxury Alpages du Chantel apartments, above Charvet'.

Well, 'luxury' turned out to be something of an exaggeration. But the next year we were able to pronounce them the best in town and then, after an opportunity to stay in the apartments, to describe them as 'exceptionally attractive, comfortable and spacious by French standards, with a pool, sauna and gym'. Also part of the appeal was that the residence was on a human scale; most residences in Les Arcs were not.

A construction company called MGM was behind the development, and had in fact opened its first residence in Argentière in 1996. Over the 20+ years since then, the successful MGM model has been used repeatedly across the French Alps, and developed considerably.

The residence Kalinda, a key component of the newly developed Tignes 1800 (pka Tignes les Boisses) marked a step up in scale, with the first phase completed in 2013. The 2016-17 season saw completion of Kalinda, and the opening of the 5-star residence Le Cristal de Jade in central Chamonix, marking another step up in quality.

A small number of MGM developments are managed by a division of MGM, but most, including Kalinda in Tignes, are run by management company CGH, founded by MGM but now independent. CGH has over 30 residences in its portfolio, spread over 20 resorts. Others are now managed by Pierre & Vacances (Alpages de Chantel, where we started this story, is one), or by Lagrange.

It is surely no coincidence that one of the great success stories of the British ski travel trade has followed a very similar trajectory. In 2002 two highly experienced French travel professionals who had been working in the UK for many years set up a tour operation called Peak Retreats. Their plan was to promote holidays in smaller, traditional French resorts, many of which offered an alternative 'back door' into larger ski areas. Many also were able to offer new, second-generation apartment residences.

The plan worked. And the continuing growth in supply of high-standard apartments led to the development in 2005 of a second company, Ski Collection, to offer hand-picked, high-quality apartments in bigger, high-altitude French resorts that didn't fit the Peak Retreats model.

Of course, other developers have plugged in to the demand for relatively smart apartments. 2003 saw the opening of the first phase of Arc 1950 (effectively a suburb of Arc 2000), built with characteristic thoroughness by the Canadian company Intrawest, developers of Whistler. It is composed entirely of comfortable apartments. Intrawest went on to build Flaine Montsoleil, just outside Flaine, and initiated Edenarc above Arc 1800.

Edenarc is now managed by Odalys, a company started in the late 1990s which in recent years has greatly expanded its upscale portfolio to include places such as Isatis in Chamonix, Panoramic in Flaine and Fermes de Châtel.

Montagnettes is another developer that caught on to the need for bigger and better apartments in the 1990s and built a series of upmarket residences through the 2000s. More recently it opened the Hameau du Kashmir in Val Thorens in 2012, and most recently the Taos in Tignes le Lac, opened in 2015.

Village Montana also deserves a mention as one of the pioneering developers of upscale properties in Val Thorens and Tignes, now adding the brand new Chalet Skadi in Val d'Isère.

The huge development and management company Pierre & Vacances has played its part in promoting higher standards. In 2010 it began branding its best properties with the Premium label, reinforcing that with the opening in 2011 of the very smart Amara residence in Avoriaz, the purpose-built resort that it (or its owner) created in the late 1960s. It now has over a dozen Alpine properties in its Premium portfolio, including a large part of Arc 1950.

Smaller Lagrange – mainly an agent, although it does have properties under direct management – similarly flags its best properties with the Prestige label. You'll find these in over a dozen resorts across the French Alps.

MMV is a more recent competitor for the big players in the self-catering market, especially with its recent upscale developments in Tignes 1800 and Les Saisies in the Espace Diamant (and the less well known Arêches-Beaufort): very family-friendly, typically with kids'/teens' clubs and on-site family restaurant.

The list goes on. 'More and more companies are coming in and growing this market,' says Xavier Schouller, one of those two founders of Peak Retreats. 'Developments in Arc 2000 and then the beautiful Koh-I Nor residence in Val Thorens have been followed by the equally impressive Daria-I Nor in Alpe-d'Huez.

'And then there are smaller companies operating locally, whose properties we are able to bring to the UK market because of our unique knowledge of the Alpine development scene. We are particularly excited about Les Fermes du Mont Blanc apartments in Combloux (in the Megève ski area), new to our programme in 2018-19. Santa Terra in Tignes les Brévières is an example of a one-off, privately owned development.

'Demand for high-standard apartments continues to grow,' says Xavier. 'This is evidenced by the new properties opening each year, and we are proud to continue to be the operator at the forefront of bringing these properties to the UK market.'

All of which means that your editors now have an ever-increasing range of comfortable options when we come to choose those well-earned breaks.

Buying property in France

For keen skiers with some cash in the bank, buying a property in a ski resort is a powerfully attractive idea. Quite apart from fun for the family, a ski property can make sound financial sense.

But what's involved? What are the pitfalls? Simon Malster of specialist agents Investors in Property guides us through the maze française.

Who can buy?

In France, anyone can buy anywhere. Although in both Switzerland and Austria certain areas are off limits to foreign buyers, there are no restrictions in France.

Can I use a company to buy?

Yes, you can – there are no restrictions in France. You should take expert advice, though, as there are several possible forms of company.

The most commonly used vehicle is an SCI, a *Société Civile Immobilière*. However, this has drawbacks if you are letting a furnished property as a commercial activity: an SCI does not allow you to depreciate the asset – so it may be better to buy in a SARL, a *Société A Responsabilité Limitée*. A 'SARL de Famille' would also be a more suitable method of obtaining joint ownership.

Buying in a company or a SARL may give you tax benefits such as tax-free transfer to your children, a reduction of wealth tax and legitimate negation of inheritance taxes. Buyers should take advice, as the savings depend on your country of residence and other factors.

The set-up costs for an SCI start at around €1,000, and you will be required to pay a yearly maintenance fee of around €800; there are also formalities to attend to.

High-quality development right on the slopes of Les Arcs, with full spa and wellness facilities, from €315,000

What is the purchase process?

You start by simply securing an option to purchase, blocking sale of the property to others – but you must soon follow this up by signing a reservation contract and paying a deposit. This is usually 5% of the purchase price. All deposits are held in escrow by the appointed notary – a government officer who is the official third party in every property transaction, ensuring safe transfer of ownership.

You will then have a 10-day cooling-off period when you can withdraw. Even after that you still have the right to cancel and get your deposit back if your mortgage application is refused.

Finally the notary's contract must be signed in the notary's office; but most buyers sign a power of attorney in favour of the notary's secretary or another responsible person who can then sign on their behalf.

What are the purchase costs?

As a tax incentive, to stimulate construction, the purchase costs for a new property (including notary fees, land registration fees and taxes) will be kept down to about 2.5% of the price. For resale properties the total purchase costs will be 6% to 8%.

Can I buy with a mortgage?

Yes – to EU citizens French banks will lend up to 85% of the purchase price for a classic freehold and 80% for a leaseback (explained later). US citizens will find France is their best option in the Alps for borrowing.

The repayment period is usually 15 or 20 years and French banks are able to offer fixed and variable rates. Rates vary continually, but currently they are at almost the lowest level they have been for the last ten years; long-term fixed rates are very attractive at around 2.15%.

Luxury ski-in/ski-out apartments in Val d'Isère from €2,990,000

What will a mortgage cost?

The notary will charge an additional 1% of the loan to register the mortgage.

How do I pay if I buy property that isn't yet built?

New-build properties are paid for by stage payments as the construction work progresses. If you are taking a mortgage, you will pay the first stage payments, and then the bank will pay the remaining instalments. When you receive the keys you have one month in which to take possession of your property and report any faults to the developer.

Are there construction guarantees?

Yes. Buyers are extremely well protected in France by strict laws. All deposits paid by the buyer are held by the notary in escrow and must be returned to the buyer if the developer becomes bankrupt or some other major delay occurs. Only when the developer has obtained a bank guarantee can the notary sign the title deeds for the transfer of ownership and transfer monies to the developer. Usually the developer must pre-sell 50% of the apartments in a given development before a bank will provide this guarantee.

Can I specify how a new-build property is fitted out?

Yes – the developers of most new chalets and apartments will allow you to tailor the design and finish of your property. Some will even let you alter the layout. A few come with furniture included, though most offer this as an optional extra.

Do I have to let my property?

Most properties in France are 'classic freehold', which means you are not obliged to let your property. But units in some of the larger developments (often with a reception, pool, restaurants etc) are sold on a 'leaseback' basis. You still own the freehold, but you are required to let your apartment on a basis chosen when you buy the property. Usually you have four to eight weeks' personal use each year, and the management company will let your apartment when you are not using it.

Are there tax breaks for letting my property?

Yes. If you buy a new 'classic freehold' property and you let it on a commercial basis, you can still reclaim the VAT and effectively get 20% off the price. You must let your property to a specialist company (we can introduce you to one) on a long lease, but you can block out periods for your own use, making it quite flexible. If you later decide that you do not want to let the property any more, you can pay back a part of the TVA you reclaimed, and cancel the rental agreement.

How much rental income can I expect?

Rental yields tend to vary between 3% and 5% depending on a variety of factors such as the resort, the location of the property within the resort (ski-in/ski-out properties command a premium), the property itself and the facilities. Some larger leaseback developments even come with a guaranteed rental income, so you know exactly what you will be earning each year.

What are the running costs likely to be?

Apart from the obvious utility bills and maintenance costs, there are two local property taxes, the *taxe foncière* and the *taxe d'habitation*. Each is around 10 to 20 euros per m^2 per year – however, as another incentive to purchase a new property you are exempt from the *taxe foncière* for the first two years.

Family holidays

Skiing is a great way to spend holidays with your kids – at least during the small window of time from when they can keep up with you to the moment when they start to get bored waiting for you to catch up with them. So it's worth going through the preliminary stages of taking them to ski resorts as toddlers and then as infants capable of learning. Editor Chris Gill gives some advice.

For about 15 years I took my kids, now more grown-up than me, to the Alps pretty regularly. Every year I learned something. Here's a summary. It's all obvious, I know, but I wish someone had written it all down for me 25 years back.

1 Accept that there's a culture gap with the French

... and plug in to the services of British tour operators, who employ endlessly patient nannies to give your spoilt brats the care and attention they have come to expect. Most such services are connected to catered chalet holidays, but some operators offer crèches for hotel guests.

2 Disappear quickly in the morning

Don't loiter at crèche handover time – the kids will guess (rightly) that you're feeling guilty about going skiing and that there is a chance you'll cave in to emotional blackmail.

3 Be prepared to find they're too young for skiing

Kids can be taught to ski as soon as they can stand, but a crash one-week course of the kind a British kid is given isn't likely to work before the age of four, and with some kids may not work until six, or ... insert number of your choosing.

Awww – could almost be the editorial daughter Laura, about 23 years ago

4 If you like chalets, consider chalet hotels

With more families in the same gaff, you increase the chance that your kids will find compatible buddies, taking the amusement burden off you in that vital evening phase leading up to bedtime.

5 Buy general outdoor jackets, not special skiing jackets

You might need to buy special insulated salopettes, but skiing jackets are no better than cheaper insulated jackets from outdoors suppliers.

6 Make them go to ski school – for years

If you don't, there's a chance they will never develop the skills needed to go fast enough to get a thrill from skiing, and will lose interest. I allowed my daughter Laura to fall into this trap. I don't think she regrets it, but I do.

7 If school trips are on offer, say yes

Son Alex did several school trips, and did a lot of learning in the process – much more than he did on the more frequent family trips we indulged him in. Peer pressure, and all that.

8 Don't obsess about the choice of resort

Choosing a resort that has evolved or been designed to suit families increases the chances of a successful holiday, but in the end it's the details that matter.

9 But do avoid the key pitfalls

A key factor if the kids are going into the resort ski school (and you don't have the assistance of your tour operator) is that you don't want a long schlepp to get them there in the morning.

10 Think about the travel out and back

Depending on how you plan to go, this might mean thinking about breaking your drive to the Alps with an overnight stop, or avoiding very long airport transfers.

11 Think more about après-skiing than skiing

What activity grabs your kids (or might)? Is it available? What does it cost? Alpine aquatic centres, skating rinks and toboggan runs can cost very little, or a great deal. Should you look for lodgings with a pool?

12 Bear in mind that skiing from the door can have other benefits

Lodgings offering skiing from the door are quite likely to provide sledging from the door, too, which can work brilliantly if the other circumstances are right. Our most successful apartment in this respect had a terrace level with the snow.

13 Go late in the season rather than early

As spring approaches, the early-evening sledging window lengthens, creating an opportunity for at least some in your party to enjoy an aperitif; or to cook supper.

14 Be aware that lift pass deals vary widely

Once the kids are out of the free pass age group, you'll find French resorts are relatively mean with their child discounts. This is when the different family deals offered by resorts become important. Be prepared to get a bit cross when you find that the best deal is for two parents and two kids, and you don't qualify.

15 And that free lift/beginner lift provision varies widely too

In some resorts, even kids who don't qualify for a free pass can ski free because there are free lifts. In others, there are cheap passes for a limited range of lifts.

Resort shortlists

To get you started down the road towards the choice of your perfect resort, here are a few shortlists. Each list is in alphabetical order, we hope. If you're new to skiing and therefore don't have a clear picture of how resorts vary, take a look at the photos on p6 and p9, and read relevant parts of the Introduction to France.

Most charming

La Clusaz
Les Gets
Megève
Samoëns

Best back doors to major areas

Tignes 1800 / Les Brévières (Tignes)
Champagny (La Plagne)
St-Martin-de-Belleville (3 Vallées)
Les Carroz (Grand Massif)
Vaujany (Alpe-d'Huez)

Biggest areas

3 Vallées (you know …)
Portes du Soleil (Châtel, Morzine etc)
Paradiski (Les Arcs, La Plagne etc)
Val d'Isère-Tignes
Megève (including Le Jaillet)
Grand Massif (Les Carroz, Flaine etc)
Espace Diamant (Les Saisies etc)

Best for lively après/nightlife

Alpe-d'Huez
Chamonix
Méribel
Val d'Isère
Val Thorens

Most reliable snow conditions

Chamonix
Courchevel
Les Deux-Alpes
Val d'Isère-Tignes
Val Thorens

Best off-piste

3 Vallées
Alpe-d'Huez
Chamonix
La Grave
Paradiski
Val d'Isère-Tignes

The favourite resort of many keen, competent skiers, and one of ours for sure – Val d'Isère

Best woodland skiing

Les Carroz
Courchevel / La Tania
Peisey-Vallandry (Les Arcs)
Serre-Chevalier

Best for beginners

Courchevel
Flaine
Les Menuires
Montgenèvre
La Rosière
Valmorel
Val d'Isère

Best mountain restaurants

Alpe-d'Huez
Megève
La Plagne
Val Thorens

Best for families

Les Arcs
Avoriaz / Ardent
Courchevel / La Tania
Flaine
Les Gets
Les Menuires
La Plagne / Montchavin-Les Coches
La Rosière
Ste-Foy
Valmorel

Best for slope-side lodgings

Les Arcs
Avoriaz
Flaine
Les Menuires
La Plagne
Valmorel

Best for tight budgets

Maurienne valley
Montgenèvre
La Rosière
Serre-Chevalier
Ste-Foy
Val Cenis
Valmorel

... and worst for tight budgets

Courchevel
Méribel
Val d'Isère
Val Thorens

Best toboggan runs

Courchevel
La Plagne
Val Thorens

Simply ... the best

Courchevel
Val d'Isère
Val Thorens

Les 3 Vallées

Courchevel / La Tania / Méribel / Les Menuires / St-Martin-de-Belleville / Val Thorens / Orelle

The world's biggest ski area, and one of the best

There are other areas that can match the 3 Vallées in overall dimensions (although it measures an impressive 21km across), and there are regional lift passes in Austria and Italy that cover more lifts and more km of piste. But for quantity of connected skiing, there is nowhere like it. The claim of 600km of pistes may be an exaggeration, but it is not a huge one. The next-door Paradiski area (linking Les Arcs and La Plagne) and the northerly Portes du Soleil (Morzine, Les Gets, Avoriaz, Châtel) are way behind.

We give separate chapters to the four major resorts – Courchevel in the easternmost valley, Méribel in the central one, Les Menuires and Val Thorens in the westerly one. Then there are smaller satellite resorts: we treat La Tania as an outpost of Courchevel, St-Martin-de-Belleville as an outpost of Les Menuires and Orelle (in the fourth valley, opened up many years after the area was created and the 3 Vallées brand well established) as an outpost of Val Thorens.

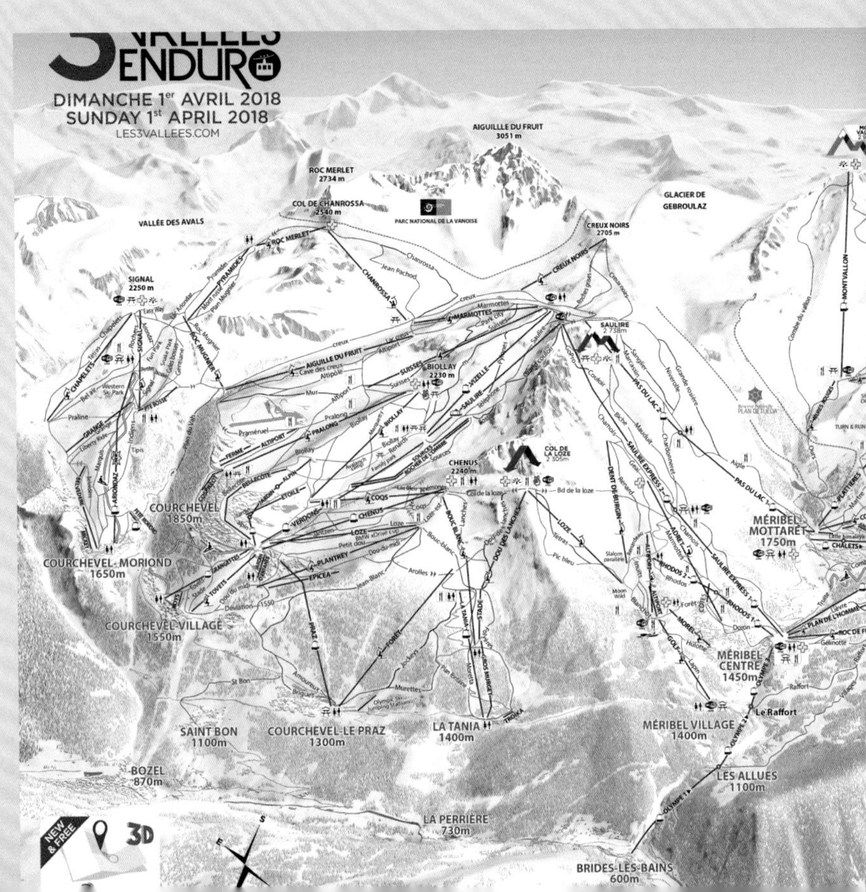

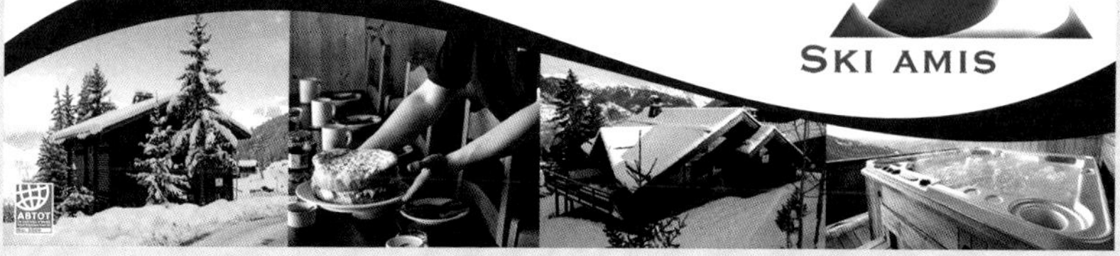

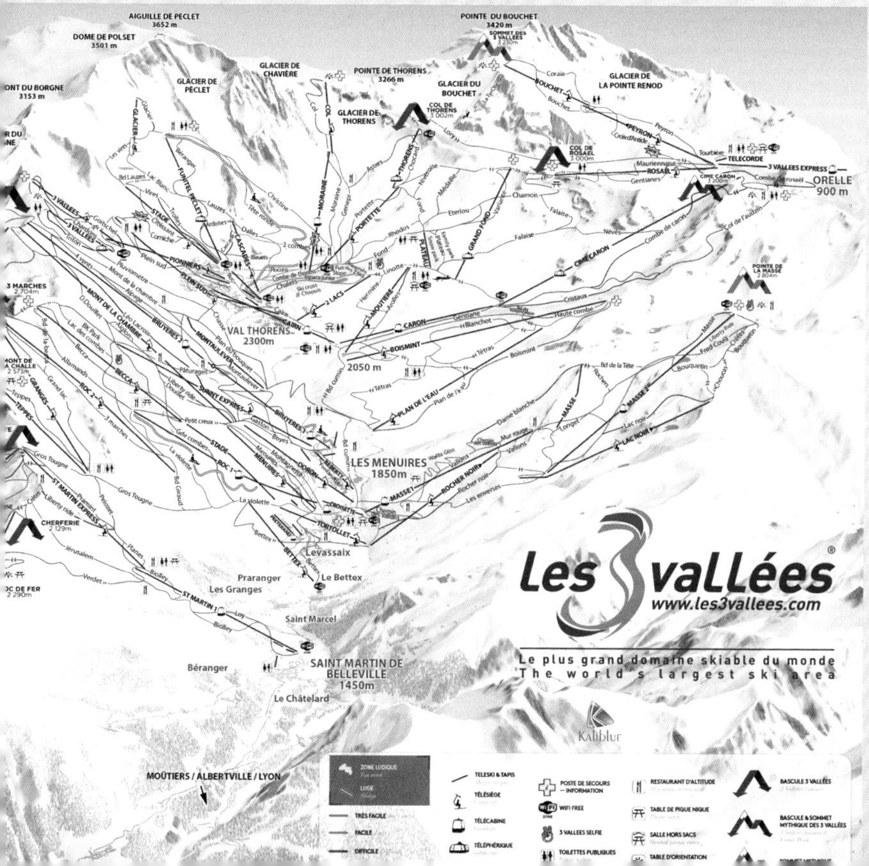
AIGUILLE DE PECLET 3652 m
DOME DE POLSET 3501 m
POINTE DU BOUCHET 3420 m
GLACIER DE CHAVIÈRE
POINTE DE THORENS 3266 m
GLACIER DE PÉCLET
GLACIER DU BOUCHET
GLACIER DE THORENS
GLACIER DE LA POINTE RENOD
COL DE THORENS 3 002m
COL DE ROSAEL 3 000m
CIME CARON 3 200m
ORELLE 900 m
POINTE DE LA MASSE 2 804m
VAL THORENS 2300m
2050 m
LES MENUIRES 1850m
Levassaix
Le Bettex
Praranger
Les Granges
Saint Marcel
Béranger
SAINT MARTIN DE BELLEVILLE 1450m
Le Châtelard
MOÛTIERS / ALBERTVILLE / LYON
CHERFERIE 2 129m
Les 3 vallées
www.les3vallees.com
Le plus grand domaine skiable du monde
The world's largest ski area
Kaliblue
ZONE LUDIQUE
LUGE
TRÈS FACILE
FACILE
DIFFICILE
TELESKI & TAPIS
TÉLÉSIÈGE
TÉLÉCABINE
TÉLÉPHÉRIQUE
POSTE DE SECOURS — INFORMATION
WIFI FREE
3 VALLEES SELFIE
TOILETTES PUBLIQUES
RESTAURANT D'ALTITUDE
TABLE DE PIQUE NIQUE
SALLE HORS SACS
TABLE D'ORIENTATION
BASCULE 3 VALLÉES
BASCULE & SOMMET MYTHIQUE DES 3 VALLÉES

Courchevel

Several varieties of Courchevel, strangely named / La Tania

Courchevel attracts two kinds of visitor. Those (mainly French and Russian) who have money to burn, and like to burn it ostentatiously; and those who have worked out that this is the best base from which to enjoy the world's biggest ski area. Its local slopes are excellent, access to the distant Belleville valley is adequately convenient and – worth noting – it is the only 3V resort to offer worthwhile skiing in a snowstorm.

The resort has several separate parts; none is particularly attractive as a village. The major part previously known as 1850 is the best placed for skiing; but it goes for the moneyed visitors, and is accordingly pricey. Happily, the other parts cater very well for the rest of us.

The mountains in brief

Size A sizeable area, even if you ignore the rest of the vast 3 Vallées

Slopes Varied and interesting, with the bonus of a good woodland sector

Snow Pretty good, thanks to height, northerly orientation and TLC

System, Lift Generally efficient, without being overtly slick

Sustenance Too pricey: do lunch above Les Menuires, or plan picnics

For beginners Good slopes; pity you need a lift pass to use the 1850 ones

For true blue skiers A good network of runs, though some are challenging

For the confident A superb resort, with the rest of the 3V awaiting ...

For experts Lots to do, on- and off-piste, here and further afield

Fancy stuff The park here is aimed at families; tougher stuff in Méribel

Courchevel (pka 1850) – the resort in brief

Convenience Skiing from the door is possible, if you pick your spot

Lodgings A wide choice for money-burners, enough choice for you and us

Bars and restaurants Some good affordable places to be found

Off the slopes Fab out-of-town pool complex very welcome

For families Worth considering – superb kids' nursery slope area

Pass notes

In 2018 a 3V six-day pass was only €44 more than the local one. A one-day 3V extension cost almost as much.

There are several free drag-lifts – not including the 1850 nursery lifts, for which you need the half-price Easy Rider day pass, also covering several major lifts serving long green runs.

Key facts

Altitude	1260–1850m
Range	1260–3230m
Slopes (see text)	600km

Where to stay, ideally

A stroll from the Croisette, the lift base at the heart of the skiing.

Websites

courchevel.com
latania.com
les3vallees.com

Key ratings

Size	*****
Snow	****
Fast lifts	*****
Mountain rest's	***
Beginner	****
True blue	****
Confident	*****
Expert	****
Convenience	****
Families	****
Village charm	**

The mountains in detail

Courchevel occupies the easternmost of the 3 Vallées, but it is not a simple single valley. The main feature of the slopes above 1850 is in fact a minor peak, Vizelle, with runs on several sides; the Verdons gondola out of 1850's Croisette lift base accesses the Vizelle gondola and the big Saulire cable car, either of which will get you to the col that is the main link to Méribel. To spectator's left of Vizelle, the valley of Praméruel separates it from the gentler slopes of Moriond pka 1650, with links at two points.

Riding the Chenus gondola from Croisette takes you to the Chenus ridge separating the main resort from the slopes of La Tania. From here you can also ski down to Le Praz, or to Courchevel Village pka 1550 or back to 1850. Beyond Chenus, and reached by chair-lift from mid-mountain above La Tania, is Col de la Loze, the less popular route to Méribel.

Size

The local slopes are claimed to amount to 150km – big enough to amuse some visitors for a week. You can buy 3V day extensions to the local pass, but a 3V pass usually makes better sense – read Pass notes in the blue panel.

The 3 Vallées as a whole is amazingly extensive – well over 500km and not far short of the claimed 600km.

Slopes

The slopes of Courchevel (including those of La Tania) have something for everyone, from glorious motorways on which turns are optional to proper blacks, and access to good off-piste terrain.

The slopes above Courchevel pka 1850, on Vizelle and Saulire, follow the text-book pattern of easy runs low down and more serious stuff high up. The low-altitude slopes above Le Praz and La Tania are different – generally steep.

These low slopes are also key to one of the attractions of staying here rather than elsewhere in the 3V – they are heavily wooded, and skiable in even the worst weather. Most of the rest of the skiing is open; there are wooded sections directly above Courchevel pka 1850 and at Praméruel in the valley that separates Moriond pka 1650 from the rest of the area, but most of the lifts deposit you above the trees.

This combination of high open slopes (Saulire peaks at 2738m) and extensive wooded lower slopes of all colours is not just rare in the 3V – it's rare.

Snow

Courchevel's altitude and north-east orientation help to make the best of the snow, and conditions here are almost always appreciably better than in most of the adjacent Méribel valley or on the main slopes of Les Menuires. Naturally, Courchevel can't rival super-high Val Thorens in this department.

And today, today we have naming of parts

Courchevel has always had a problem with names. For decades its main high-altitude parts were called Courchevel 1850, Courchevel 1650 and Courchevel 1550. The numbers related only vaguely to altitude (the centre of 1850 is at about 1740m), so the decision in 2011 to rebrand the villages 'to emphasise their different identities' was to be welcomed in principle. And Courchevel Moriond and Courchevel Village are acceptable replacements for 1650 and 1550 respectively. But 1850 is now ... plain Courchevel.

Using the same name for the whole resort and a village within it is simply not workable – for us, for you or for the resort itself: on the right is a screen grab from the resort's hotel booking screen.

VILLAGES

Saint Bon | Courchevel Le Praz
Courchevel Village | Courchevel Moriond
Courchevel 1850

ONLINE BOOKING

Here and in Méribel a selection of red and black pistes, labelled Peuf Expérience on the map, are left ungroomed for a while after snowfalls; obviously, these are worth seeking out or avoiding, according to your appetites.

System, Lift

The lift system is not conspicuously state of the art – the four-seat Chenus gondola, for example, is beginning to look a bit of an antique – but in practice it works very well, and there is a steady flow of upgrades. As we write in 2018, a six-seat chair-lift is being built on a new line from La Tania to the start of the Bouc Blanc chair to Chenus, thus creating an alternative route to 1850 and easing pressure on the village gondola. (Sadly the updated map was not ready when we went to press.) At the same time, the gondola between 1550 and 1850 is being upgraded in speed and capacity.

You may find queues at Croisette as the ski school gets going, and the Biollay chair-lift can be over-busy, despite upgrades. But queues are not generally a problem. There are still two slow triple chair-lifts; sadly, one of these, Creux Noirs, will be out of action for 2018/19, pending repairs/replacement.

Sustenance

All the restaurants above Courchevel are simply too expensive. Even one of the most reasonable, Les Chenus, was charging €20 for its pdj in 2018. Many people like the Bel Air above Moriond, and so do we – it offers a splendid tiered terrace, friendly and efficient service, good food, cheap house wine. But we won't pay €22 for a potato and cheese confection, even if it is called tartiflette.

The good news is that above La Tania is a more affordable option – the reliable Bouc Blanc, where we have enjoyed countless satisfactory meals served efficiently and with good humour. But even here, regrettably, the pdj seems to be edging up towards the €20 mark.

Of course, the natural thing in good weather is to head to the Menuires valley, where it isn't hard to eat for €15.

Restaurants are marked on the piste map, but not named. Why?

More on the slopes

For beginners

The main nursery area at 1850 is at Pralong, at the top of the village, near the Altiport – there is a not-very-frequent

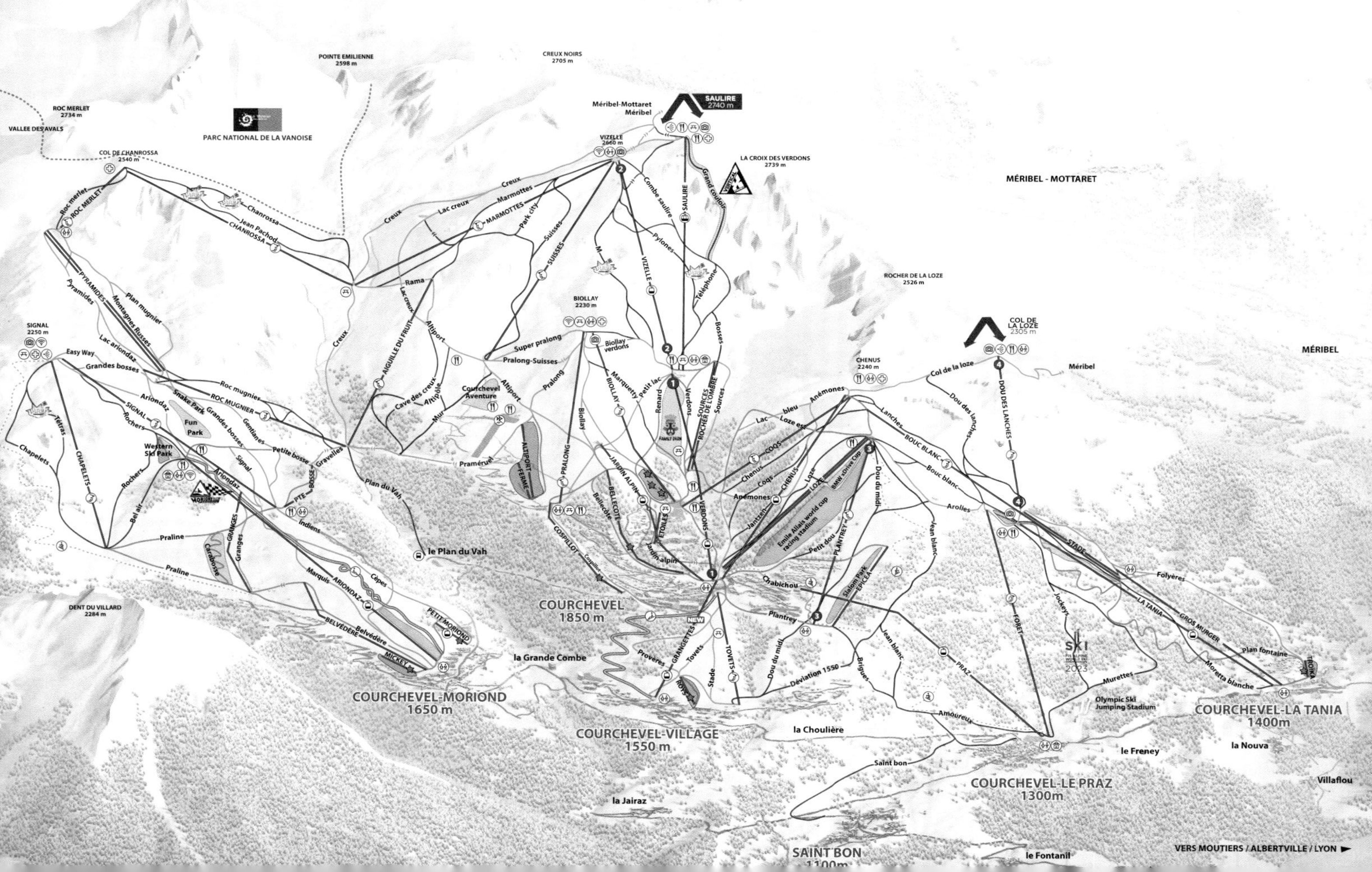

POINTE EMILIENNE 2598 m
CREUX NOIRS 2705 m
ROC MERLET 2734 m
VALLEE DES AVALS
PARC NATIONAL DE LA VANOISE
COL DE CHANROSSA 2540 m
Méribel-Mottaret
Méribel
SAULIRE 2740 m
VIZELLE 2660 m
LA CROIX DES VERDONS 2739 m
MÉRIBEL - MOTTARET
ROCHER DE LA LOZE 2526 m
BIOLLAY 2230 m
SIGNAL 2250 m
COL DE LA LOZE 2305 m
MÉRIBEL
Méribel
CHENUS 2240 m
DENT DU VILLARD 2284 m
COURCHEVEL 1850 m
la Grande Combe
le Plan du Vah
COURCHEVEL-MORIOND 1650 m
COURCHEVEL-VILLAGE 1550 m
la Choulière
COURCHEVEL-LA TANIA 1400m
la Nouva
le Freney
COURCHEVEL-LE PRAZ 1300m
Villaflou
la Jairaz
SAINT BON
le Fontanil
VERS MOUTIERS / ALBERTVILLE / LYON
Olympic Ski Jumping Stadium
Roc merlet
ROC MERLET
Chanrossa
Jean Pachod
CHANROSSA
Creux
Lac creux
Marmottes
MARMOTTES
Park city
Suisses
SUISSES
Combe saulire
SAULIRE
Grand couloir
Pylones
Téléphone
VIZELLE
Bosses
PYRAMIDES
Pyramides
Plan mugnier
Montagnes Russes
Rama
AIGUILLE DU FRUIT
Altiport
Super pralong
Pralong-Suisses
Pralong
Lac ariondaz
Easy Way
Grandes bosses
Roc mugnier
ROC MUGNIER
Snake Park
Fun Park
Ariondaz
SIGNAL
Rochers
Western Ski Park
Tétras
Chapelets
CHAPELETS
Bel air
Praline
Carabosse
GRANGES
Granges
Gentianes
Petite bosse
PTE BOSSE
Gravelles
Indiens
Signal
Cave des creux
Altipôle
Mur
Courchevel Aventure
ALTIPORT FERME
Praméruel
Plan du Vah
PRALONG
Biollay
Biollay verdons
BIOLLAY
Marquetty
Petit lac
Renard
Verdons
SOURCES
ROCHER DE L'OMBRE
Sources
JARDIN ALPIN
BELLECOTE
Bellecôte
ETOILES
Jardin alpin
VERDONS
COSPILLOT
Cospillot
Marquis
ARIONDAZ
Cèpes
PETIT MORIOND
BELVÉDÈRE
Belvédère
MICKEY
GRANGETTES
Provères
Tovets
TOVETS
Stade
ROYS
Lac
bleu
Loze est
Anémones
COQS
Chenus
Coqs
CHENUS
Jantzen
LOZE
Loze
BMW xDrive Cup
Emile Allais world cup racing stadium
Petit dou
PLANTREY
Dou du midi
Slalom Park
EPICEA
Chabichou
Plantrey
Déviation 1550
Brigues
Jean blanc
Lanches
BOUC BLANC
Bouc blanc
Arolles
Col de la loze
Dou des lanches
DOU DES LANCHES
STADE
FORET
Jockeys
Folyères
LA TANIA
GROS MURGER
Plan fontaine
Moretta blanche
Murettes
TROIKA
PRAZ
Amoureux
Saint bon
NEW

ski-bus service. The splendid long, easy slope is served by drag-lifts (the 450m Ferme and 760m Altiport). Courchevel has long had some free lifts (notably the long Bellecôte drag beside the gentle green piste of the same name leading down to Croisette); but, astonishingly, you have to buy the half-price Easy Rider day passes for these nursery lifts. This is all mildly bizarre, and should be changed.

There are plenty of longer green runs to move on to, also covered by the Easy Rider pass. The step up to blues can be a bit of a challenge though.

In all the satellite villages there are small but satisfactory nursery areas near the lift bases, with free drag-lifts about 200m long. The only one we have reservations about is at Village pka 1550 – it's a tad steeper than the rest.

The French ski school has developed a special area at Pralong for introducing disabled people to sit-ski. Eight instructors have been specially trained.

For true blue skiers

There are blue runs all over the piste map, allowing a confident early-intermediate skier to get around the whole area, but quite a few present challenges. This is perhaps not surprising, given that the resort makes good use of the green piste classification to identify really easy runs.

If you are very cautious, consider starting with the Easy Rider pass; as well as a good number of runs around 1850, it covers green and blue runs at Moriond and La Tania (reachable by free ski-bus).

The blue pistes above Moriond are mostly fine, long, wide runs, a bit more testing around mid-mountain at the top of the Ariondaz gondola – as its name hints, the Grandes Bosses run is steep enough in places to get mogulled.

The long Creux run curling around Vizelle was red until a few years ago. The steepish start was smoothed out a bit at the time of the change, but it remains a testing run – the top half is quite sunny and can get bumpy.

Most of the runs lower down on and around Biollay, close to 1850, are fairly easy; Pralong is a tad steeper than most. If you're looking at a base in Village pka 1550, note that the Cospillot blue run offers a gentle and pretty way home.

Our main reservation in the blue piste department is the long Folyères run over at La Tania. This lovely woodland run is a fine thrash for a confident skier, but a real test for the nervous – right at the tough end of the blue spectrum.

Vizelle, a key feature; on the left, blue piste Creux (red in the past); down the ridge, red piste Marmottes

For confident intermediates

Courchevel is a wonderful playground for confident intermediates, with rewarding red runs all over the place – and these are supplemented by long blue runs such as Creux and Folyères that verge on red gradient, and blacks that include some barely deserving black run status – Suisses, for example.

It's hardly worth trying to identify particular red pistes – ride a lift to any of the area's half-dozen high-points and you can expect a choice of worthwhile ways down. Don't overlook the runs from the under-used Chapelets chair on Signal, above Moriond, and the runs from Creux Noirs (out of action for 2019). Down in the woods between Le Praz and La Tania, Murettes is a neglected favourite of ours.

Check the resort grooming map to find out which blacks are most likely to give you an easy ride.

Val Thorens, Les Menuires and St-Martin are all only four fast lifts away.

For experts

Most of the black pistes are towards the easy end of the spectrum, but are steep enough to offer good fun in the right conditions. And the rather neglected woodland blacks to Le Praz have the additional feature of length – Jean Blanc drops about 600m. The blacks are groomed fairly frequently – Pylones and Suisses from Vizelle, for example, are rarely mogulled for long. But most are Peuf Expérience runs – read the note under 'Snow'.

From the Saulire cable car you have immediate access to the Grand Couloir. It is the steepest piste in Courchevel, but not super-steep (and not as steep as the GoPro Couloir, on the Méribel side from the same point, directly underneath the Saulire gondola.) It's also wide as couloirs go; much the trickiest aspect of it is the access along the narrow, bumpy ridge from the cable car. Once upon a time the two gnarlier couloirs to skier's right of it were also pistes.

There is lots of off-piste terrain within the piste network. Traversing left from the Combe Saulire piste takes you behind the prominent Rocher de l'Ombre to lovely broad, easy slopes. On all sides of Vizelle there is lots of terrain between the lifts.

From Col de Chanrossa there are several options. The slopes next to the pistes down the Chanrossa chair are one; but by traversing to the left you open up a huge shady area down to the chair. A short hike south from the chair takes you to the start of a popular run down the Vallée des Avals, with a long run-out to Moriond (or Bozel when conditions permit). Another option is to hike up northward for access to the north-facing slope down to the Pyramide drag-lifts.

There is further terrain reached from the Dou des Lanches chair-lift above La Tania, some of it much steeper than the black piste nearby.

Fancy stuff

The main park here is now styled the Family Park and, as you might expect, is more of a fun affair than a serious-thrills freestyle park. Good call, we say – it gets a lot more use than many parks with big jumps. For excitement, head to Méribel.

Courchevel (pka 1850) – the resort

We were tempted to give pride of place to Moriond, but this, the glitzy bit of Courchevel, is best placed for sunny days in Val Tho and snowy days in the woods. Most of the swanky hotels enjoy lovely secluded or piste-side settings, leaving the rather plain central area for more modest lodgings. 1850 has countless bars and restaurants, some of which we can afford.

Convenience

There are plenty of hotels, chalets and apartments to be found in 1850 and in the other villages (except Le Praz) that offer ski-in/ski-out convenience, or at least ski-in/plod-out. There are more that involve walks, but generally not long ones. The tourist office publishes very clear plans that should help you figure out how much walking you're in for.

There are ski-buses linking the main resort villages, and on two routes within 1850 – to Altiport and around the Jardin Alpin area.

Lodgings

The money-burners have a wide choice of swanky hotels – no less than 20 5-star places, making up half the resort's total. Extraordinary. But there are half a dozen 3-star and even a couple of 2-star hotels. Our pick would be the 3-star Courcheneige, in a ski-in/ski-out location at the very top of the village.

There are lots of catered chalets, including some very smart ones from upmarket operators. More modest options exist, but are easier to find in the lower villages, particularly Moriond and La Tania. Inghams runs a simple, good-value chalet hotel in an amazing position a few metres from the Croisette lifts.

Ski Collection Pick of the apartments

In Courchevel (pka 1850)
There is a great range of 4-star apartments to choose from close to the central Croisette. Coeur Courchevel 1850 has four warmly welcoming, thoughtfully designed apartments with additional features from a breakfast service to champagne on arrival. Belledonne is another intimate residence with just six apartments and facilities including sauna and fitness space. All apartments have balconies with village or mountain views. The Chalets du Forum has recently been renovated, creating 55 contemporary apartments with heated ski lockers.

In Moriond
The 20 apartments at the 4-star Chalets de la Mouria are in six traditional-style chalets that form a hamlet. Facilities include hot tub, sauna and steam room.

www.skicollection.co.uk 023 9289 0960

Bars and restaurants

At close of play there are plenty of expensive piste-side places to pause in just above the village, and equally expensive places in the village to inhabit later on. We asked our man on the spot in 1850, Neal Manuel of Courchevel specialists Green to Black, for some pointers to more modest places. His suggestions: 'Le Tremplin at Croisette is lively for après-ski (but rather expensive). L'Equipe is very buzzy and fairly friendly (although renowned for French attitude); Bar à Vin is more calm but needs to be busy for an atmosphere.'

If you like Michelin-star restaurants, you'll be in clover here – there are six of them, all in top hotels. Le 1947 in the Cheval Blanc hotel was awarded its third Michelin star in 2017. Enjoy.

Carefully framed shot of the 'front de neige' at 1850, with the none-too-pretty lift base hidden on the left

Back in the real world, the 50-odd restaurants in 1850 do include some we can afford. We like the Chabotté, bargain basement (literally) of the famous 2-star Chabichou. Neal came up with three top tips: L'Arbé (French cuisine along with local specialities), La Fromagerie (yes, mainly cheese nonsense but also a few other traditional dishes) and Mamma Mia (run by Italians, so very authentic).

Off the slopes

A long-standing weakness of the resort was put right in 2015 with the opening of the big Aquamotion leisure complex, in the valley below 1850, between Village and Moriond. It is a splendid affair, with various kinds of pool and spa facilities. Gentlemen, rejoice: swim shorts are permitted. It's very pricey. The Courchevel ski pass covers use of the 'fun' part for one day, in 2018-19 at least, but there is no such deal for 3V pass buyers. In 2019 a new apartment residence will be built next door, and a lift link with 1850.

There is a floodlit 2.3km toboggan run – said to be pretty exciting – from 1850 to Village, free to use daytime and evening, and served by the Grangettes gondola (free early evening). All in all, an excellent facility. There's a longer one at Moriond too (read that section).

There's a good-sized ice rink in the central Forum complex.

There are cleared paths and snowshoe routes in the woods, all shown on a special map. There are plenty of other activities, from dog sledding to ice climbing. The tourist office Welcome booklet catalogues them all.

For families

Like the other main villages, 1850 has a child-friendly 'front de neige' area (shown in our photo), and if you choose carefully, you can find lodgings with more or less direct access to the snow.

The resort works hard to keep parents happy. Below 1850 is a huge medieval-themed 'children's village' covering 5ha (about 12 acres), with its own gondola. At mid-mountain above Moriond are several other areas designed for kids (read the Moriond section later in the chapter).

Several UK tour operators run their own nurseries here.

Other variants of Courchevel

Courchevel comes in three or four other forms, all totally unlike Courchevel pka 1850. Some 300m below 1850, but on a different planet, is inoffensive Courchevel Village, pka 1550. Down at the base of the skiing is a more villagey village, Courchevel Le Praz. For those looking for an affordable chalet holiday, or for long, gentle runs on the doorstep, there is Moriond, pka 1650, on the road up to 1850 and at the foot of its own slope sector.

Although it's now in the Courchevel commune, La Tania stubbornly retains its own identity, its own tourist office and its own website. A traffic-free village at the foot of a steepish mountain, it has its own attractions.

Courchevel Moriond (pka 1650)

For those heading to 1850, Moriond is a parade of everyday shops and apartment blocks lining the road up to their destination. But away from the road it has an old village core, and quiet suburbs of modern chalets and hotels, some of them very smart. The centre, pleasantly animated in the evening, has been improved beyond recognition in recent years, by smartening up the buildings and calming the through-traffic. But there's no calming without traffic, as they say.

There's a good little nursery slope with free lift, and the Easy Rider half-price day pass covers the gondola to mid-mountain serving long green runs.

Convenience It depends on your location. Ski-in/ski-out lodgings exist; so do places where you'll need the ski-bus. There's a three-stage covered escalator that gets most people based in the lower suburbs up to the main street and lift base.

Lodgings There are some excellent hotels; the two 4-star options are a recently created branch of the funky Fahrenheit Seven chain and the more traditional Portetta, complete with the most luxurious boot room in Europe. The catered chalet scene is dominated (as it has been for many years) by Le Ski, which now has 17 properties here, ranging in size from 2 beds to 22 and in style from the simple Bonheur to swanky Bouquetin (one of several units in the very smart Scalottas Lodge). Mountain Heaven has two mid-sized chalets. There is plenty of self-catering accommodation (read the Pick of the apartments, above).

Bars and restaurants The throbbing Boulotte attracts numbers of Brits but is not our tasse de thé. The Schuss has a more diverse clientele. There are several standard places doing pizza, pasta and cheese dishes in or near the little square above the main road. Nick Morgan of Le Ski tells us there is now a seriously good restaurant at the first stop going down the village escalator from the main street – the excellent, cool (but pricey) Bistrot le C.

Off the slopes A new 3km toboggan run was built in 2017 down the length of the new Ariondaz gondola. It's open from 11am but also in the early evening twice a week. This run, unlike the 1850-1550 one, is very definitely not free – €15 in 2018 (small children free).

Families There are several special areas on the hill for kids – a Western-themed learning park with totem poles and teepees, the Snake Park funslope and the undulating Carabosse run. The snow-front area is good for informal sledging.

Courchevel Village (pka 1550)

The original Courchevel is overlooked by many visitors. The village has no great charm, but at least it is bypassed by the traffic to the higher resorts. A short gondola gets you up to 1850, and it runs in the evening (and was upgraded in 2018, halving the travel time). There's a nursery slope with free lift, but for longer easy runs you have to go up to 1850, buying the Easy Rider half-price day pass.

Convenience The village spreads across the hillside at the bottom of the home slopes, and has developed a chalet suburb up the western side. Nowhere is more than about 300m from the lifts.

Lodgings The hotel Flocons is at one end of the snow front. There are catered chalets to be had – some owner-run, some from mid-sized operators – including some quite swanky ones.

Bars and restaurants There is some life in the village – there are half a dozen bars and restaurants clustered around the base of the gondola. L'Oeil de Boeuf is noted for excellent wood-fire grills; it changed hands in 2018 – fingers crossed.

Off the slopes The huge Aquamotion complex is close by, though we're not clear whether there's a footpath. The toboggan run from 1850 ends here.

Courchevel Le Praz 1260m

With its narrow, mostly car-free streets, Le Praz feels much more like a real village than, er, Courchevel Village. The busy road up to the higher resorts only touches the fringe of the core of the village. There is a nursery slope with free lift, but for other easy slopes you have to ride up to 1850, buying the Easy Rider day pass.

Convenience It's a small village, no more than 500m across. The lifts are about 130m from the hotel Peupliers.

Lodgings The 4-star hotel Peupliers is the focal point of Le Praz; well run by the grandson of the founder, with a good restaurant. There are catered chalets to be found; Mountain Heaven has three, including the lovely traditional Jardin d'Angele, where we have enjoyed staying. Mountain Heaven also has some self-catering places.

Bars and restaurants For a small place, Le Praz is well equipped, though this is not a place to expect riotous bar parties. The Peupliers gets some après business, L'Escorche-vel has live music, and the Cave des Lys is good for a quiet drink – a vaulted cellar bar doing tapas-style food. Le Bistrot is an old favourite for a blow-out meal. Azimut has a Michelin star, but few pretensions.

Off the slopes Not a lot to do, but 1850 is not far away.

La Tania 1350m

Built for the 1992 Olympics in the woods between Le Praz and Méribel, La Tania is probably the lowest of French purpose-built resorts. The resort centre is not pretty, but it is traffic-free. There's a good nursery slope with a free lift, and another slope at mid-mountain for which you need the half-price Easy Rider day pass. There's a green run to the village, though it's not the easiest.

Convenience It's a small place, Many of the apartments are close to the piste that runs through, past the nursery slope to the main lift, and to the few central restaurants and shops. Most of the chalets are well above the centre – you use a lift to go up and down – and at varying distances from the piste.

Lodgings Above the resort centre is a wooded chalet suburb, where many of the properties are operated by British catered chalet firms. Ski Amis has seven chalets, all in great locations close to the piste and all but one with a hot tub. 'Premium' service is available in several, including the characterful chalet Elliot, where we have enjoyed two or three excellent stays. Le Ski has five varied properties, including a rare standalone place for four. The company has its own crèche (next door to the four-bed place, as it happens). Mountain Heaven has one chalet for ten.

The Olympic apartments are available through various agencies. Ski Amis has a rather broader range of properties.

Bars and restaurants The pivotal place is the Ski Lodge, overlooking the home piste – lively, with live music, good-value food. Le Farçon, a pricey spot which must have been a risky venture at the start, seems to have a secure hold on its Michelin star; very good-value lunches. Between those extremes comes the cosy Taïga, just over the road from the centre.

Off the slopes Various activities are advertised, but the main activity seems to be sledging on the nursery slope.

Families The traffic-free resort works well for families, provided you're not expecting proper toboggan runs and pools.

Méribel

Méribels various / Les Allues / Brides-les-Bains

Méribel comes perilously close to being a British colony. It was started by a Brit, Peter Lindsay, just before WW2, and has been developed in a traditional chalet style that suits British tastes; it has more examples than anywhere else of that uniquely British institution, the catered chalet; and naturally it is full of British visitors. Great, if you like that kind of thing.

The slopes directly above the main village (which we're calling Méribel Centre – more on this later) suffer from the afternoon sun; after midwinter, they can be rock hard in the morning, heavy in the afternoon. Courchevel residents on their way to Val Thorens get the worst of the first.

Bar and restaurant prices are among the highest in the French Alps.

The mountains in brief

Size A fair size, but you stay here to explore the vast 3 Vallées

Slopes Mainly open slopes of middling steepness

Snow Two halves, with generally much better snow on one than t'other

System, Lift Impressive, and still improving, but not without flaws

Sustenance You won't starve, but lunch above Les Menuires is preferable

For beginners Good arrangements, but the best slopes are out of town

For true blue skiers Some snags – but yes, you can ski the 3 Vallées

For the confident There aren't many better places

For experts A huge amount of off-piste terrain

Fancy stuff Everything you could wish for, including a half-pipe

Méribel Centre – the resort in brief

Convenience For a purpose-built resort, a strikingly careless layout

Lodgings Catered chalets by the hundred, and some good alternatives

Bars and restaurants There's a Folie Douce ... and plenty of options

Off the slopes An impressive range of stuff, now including a toboggan run

For families A wide range of piste amusements, which may be your priority

Pass notes

In 2018 a 3V six-day pass cost €51 more than the local Méribel one. A one-day 3V extension cost €36.

For beginners, there are several free carpet- and drag-lifts, and a half-price Easy Rider day pass covering gondolas out of Centre and chair-lifts out of Mottaret accessing blue runs.

Key facts

Altitude	1400-1720m
Range	1260–3230m
Slopes (see text)	600km

Where to stay, ideally

As close as possible to the blue piste running down beside the village.

Websites

meribel.net
brides-les-bains.com
les3vallees.com

Key ratings

Size	*****
Snow	***
Fast lifts	*****
Mountain rest's	***
Beginner	****
True blue	****
Confident	*****
Expert	*****
Convenience	***
Families	****
Village charm	***

The mountains in detail

Méribel's slopes fall into three major sectors, though each of these sectors could easily be further subdivided. The main lift bases are below Méribel Centre, at the satellite of Mottaret up the valley and at the micro-satellite of Méribel Village, in the woods on the road to La Tania.

The main resort village sits on the west-facing (afternoon-sun) side of the valley. The slopes above it spread across from the minor link with Courchevel, Col de la Loze above La Tania, to the major link, Saulire.

Across the valley, the morning-sun slopes spread more widely beneath five high-points on the ridge served by lifts giving access to Les Menuires and St-Martin-de-Belleville, in the third valley.

Then, at the head of the valley, a chair-lift towards Val Thorens goes up to north-facing slopes on Mont de la Chambre, while off to spectator's left a gondola serves the valley's isolated high-point, 2952m Mont du Vallon.

Size

This is the smallest of the three valleys, in terms of pistes. By normal standards it is a decent area, probably meriting a 3-star rating for size. But you come here, more than the other valleys, to use the place as a launch-pad to ski the whole 3V area. Nowhere beats Mottaret, in particular, for that purpose.

The 3 Vallées as a whole is amazingly extensive – well over 500km and not far short of the claimed 600km.

Slopes

Although it doesn't have the extensive and challenging woodland skiing of Courchevel, Méribel does have a bit of sheltered skiing – above Méribel Village and on the Rhodos gondola on one side of the valley, and on the Tougnète gondola on the other side.

Most of the slopes have been carefully equipped with lift stations at mid-mountain. The big descents are from Saulire to Centre, a vertical of 1300m

Looking south up the valley, with Mottaret just visible in the centre; Mont Vallon off to the right

(slightly more to Village), but there are lots of others approaching the 1000m mark. But much of the best skiing is on the upper slopes, where you have to settle for more modest verticals.

It's not a resort for notably long runs in terms of distance, but you can wrap up your day in Val Thorens with a descent to Centre of 11 or 12km, and Village is over 5km as the crow flies from Saulire.

Various pistes are picked out on the map as fun zones, but don't take this to mean family fun zones: they include the serious GoPro couloir at Saulire.

Snow

Méribel has a bit of a problem with sunshine. Méribel Centre is at a modest 1450m, and the slopes down to it from the main link with Courchevel, Saulire, face only a tad north of west, so after midwinter the conditions are routinely affected by the afternoon sun, with rock-hard snow in the mornings and heavy snow in the afternoons. The runs at Altiport and down to Village get less sun. Mottaret is higher, but here the runs from Saulire face south of west – the pits. The morning-sun side of the valley is much less affected, and generally offers good conditions, although the runs from Roc de Fer get more sun than the rest.

Here, as in Courchevel, a selection of red and black pistes, labelled Peuf Expérience on the map, are left ungroomed for a while after snowfalls. Worth seeking out or avoiding, according to your appetites. Two of these, the adjacent red Lagopède and black Bartavelle, and the terrain around them, are advertised as a freeride zone with 'the best snow in the area'.

System, Lift

The lift system is pretty good, and is energetically upgraded as necessary. Hardly any slow lifts remain: there is just one slow chair left – the Morel triple – but it's only 600m long, linking the village to the Altiport slopes. As we write in 2018, the Roc de Fer/Cherferie sector is being completely remodelled. A very powerful six-seat chair-lift will replace the two chairs on the lower mountain (Plan de l'Homme and Roc de Fer), while another six-pack will replace the tricky Cherferie drag accessing the popular Jerusalem piste to St-Martin.

Queues are not entirely absent, though. Most are related to the tidal flows of skiers travelling to and from Val Thorens. You may find queues for the Côte Brune chair outbound and the Plan des Mains on the return trip. This is driven by a desire to avoid the flat start of the Ours blue run, but there are alternatives – if you have time, do a lap on Mont Vallon; if not, confident skiers can traverse off-piste just above Plan des Mains, skipping the flat bit of the Ours piste.

A bottleneck that is less tidal is the Tougnète 2 chair; although its capacity is twice that of the gondola feeding it, this lift must also cope with people coming down four attractive pistes. It doesn't.

Crowds on the pistes can be a problem, too. The blue Martre into Mottaret can be miserably crowded (and bumpy as a result) in the afternoon. Another good reason to avoid the Plan des Mains chair (see above).

Sustenance

We've never been greatly impressed by the lunch opportunities in the Méribel valley, and prefer the Belleville valley.

We generally approve of restaurants in the Fruitière (Folie Douce) chain, so the one here would be one of our preferred options. Plan des Mains at the foot of Mont Vallon, an old favourite, has had good reports of late. And the Crêtes at Tougnète, arguably on St-Martin territory, is well liked; it is being revamped and extended in 2018. Will it retain its cosy log-cabin ambience?

The Coeur de Cristal just above the village has become Le Monchu, and is reported to offer great food and a wonderful ambience, which sounds like a change for the good. Also on our agenda for next time are two places near Altiport: Le Blanchot and the Clos Bernard, which seems to arouse differing responses.

Restaurants are marked on the piste map but are not named. Why?

More on the slopes

For beginners

There are nursery slopes with free lifts at several points. At Rond Point (at the top of the village) there is a covered carpet-lift mainly used by kids and the Côtes drag. Higher up, pleasantly set in the woods

AIGUILLE DU FRUIT
3051 m
MONT DU BORGNE
3153 m
GLACIER DU BORGNE
MONT VALLON
2 952m
PARC NATIONAL DE LA VANOISE
COL DE LA CHAMBRE
2850 m
Val Thorens
Les Menuires
3 MARCHES
2704 m
Les Menuires
Saint Martin de Belleville
MONT DE LA CHALLE
2573 m
TOUGNÈTE
2437 m
CHERFERIE
2251 m
Saint Martin de Belleville
ROC DE FER
2294 m
SAULIRE
2740 m
PAS DU LAC
Courchevel
DENT DE BURGIN
2739 m
ROCHER DE LA LOZE
2527 m
COL DE LA LOZE
2305 m
Courchevel
La Tania
Boulevard de la loze
GoPro Couloir
MONT VALLON
Campagnol
Combe du vallon
Lac de la chambre
COTE BRUNE
Venturon
Alouette
PLATTIERES 3
Bouvreuil
PLAN DES MAINS
Mouflon
Jn bee
CHATELET
Sittelle
Lagopède
ROC DE TOUGNE
Bartavelle
Dahu
Combe tougnète
Ecureuil
Crêtes
Blaireau
Buse
Fouine
COMBES 2
COMBES 1
Pouillard
TOUGNETE 2
Faon
CHERFERIE
Choucas
PLAN DES MAINS
MURES ROUGES
Niverolle
Sanglier
PAS DU LAC 2
Marcassin
Grande rosière
Biche
SAULIRE EXPRESS 2
Mauduit
Chamois
Chardonneret
PAS DU LAC 1
Aigle
MÉRIBEL MOTTARET
1750 m
PLAN DE TUEDA
Ours
PLATTIERES
Martre
Little himalaya
easy way
AROLLES
INTER TOUGNETE
Coqs
Perdrix
Grive
ARPASSON
Eterlou
LEGENDS
Escargots
CAVES
Roc de Fer
SKI
FIS ALPINE WORLD SKI CHAMPIONSHIPS
2023
Face
OLYMPIC
Stade Bosses
Stade de slalom
AIGLE
CHALETS
Combe laiteiet
TOUGNETE 1
Truite
MISSION BLACK FOREST
NEW
Lièvre
Bosses
Roc de Fer
Gelinotte
Geai
Renard
DENT DE BURGIN
Renardeau
Blanchot
ALTIPORT
RHODOS
Geai
Marmotte
ADRET
SAULIRE EXPRESS 1
Chamois
Mauduit
RHODOS 2
Rhodos
Rhodos
CÔTES
RHODOS 1
Mauduit
Doron
Tétras
LOZE EXPRESS
Pic bleu
Piste des fruits
ALTIPORT
FONTANY
Forêt
ROND POINT
MOREL
Blanchot
Hulotte
GOLF
Lapin
MÉRIBEL CENTRE
1450 m
Stade de slalom
CHAUDANNE
Raffort
le Plantin
MÉRIBEL VILLAGE
1400 m
la Gittaz
OLYMPE 3
OLYMPE 2
Raffort
le Raffort
Hauteville
le Villaret
Villarnard
le Biollay
Chandon
Villages
LES ALLUES
1100 m
le Cruet
Villages
le Villard
OLYMPE 1
VERS MOUTIERS / ALBERTVILLE
BRIDES LES BAINS
600 m

at Altiport (the resort's snowy airfield), there is a better set-up – a rope-tow and the 1.2km Altiport drag serving the lovely, broad Blanchot green. These are all good arrangements in themselves (editor Watts can vouch for the Altiport slopes, where he learned to ski [cough] years ago). But it's a bit of a schlepp out to those slopes (frequent shuttle-buses).

To get off the nursery slopes, you need the Easy Rider half-price day pass, accessing various easy blue runs. The upper Rhodos gondola also accesses the Rhodos green, so that might be the place to start. The Lièvre blue from the Tougnète gondola is not super-easy.

For true blue skiers

Near-beginners needing to build confidence could start with the Easy Rider day pass described above.

For progression from the Altiport green runs, the Dent de Burgin chair is a good bet – the Geai run has better snow than on most of this mountainside. Sadly, the runs down to the main Chaudanne lift base may offer crowds verging on the absurd and tough snow conditions; added to a non-trivial gradient, this can be too much for an apprehensive skier. If so, ride the gondola down or ski the Hulotte to the northern fringes of the village and get a ski-bus from there.

The blues on the morning-sun side are generally middle-of-the-road runs, not entirely easy but not particularly tough – and this side does enjoy better snow. Ski the Roc de Fer before trickier Choucas, so that you can check out the latter as you descend the former. Similarly, the very easy Grive gives a view of Faon.

The blue Martre into Mottaret can be challenging, too, but there is a green alternative to the tricky bit.

The really good news is that there are easy ways to explore the 3 Vallées. Go to and from Courchevel over Col de la Loze. All the blue ways into the Belleville valley can be tackled, and very nice they are too. There are several viable ways back, assuming you haven't found the blues on the Méribel side of the ridge a problem. The lovely long Lac de la Chambre piste from Val Thorens is now a straightforward blue, as a result of reshaping work in 2017 to cut out the tricky bits that made it red.

For confident intermediates

There are huge amounts of worthwhile red run skiing in the valley. If you get fresh snow, hit the afternoon-sun side while you have the chance of good conditions

Méribel Centre – a sprawl of chalets big and small, on the afternoon-sun side of the valley

– ski Mauduit in one and your legs will know about it – but it has to be said the runs we've always enjoyed most are the upper slopes on the other side: Alouette, Mouflon, Lagopède, Combe Tougnète, Blaireau. Mont Vallon is of course a must.

Of course you'll want to explore the other valleys. Make sure that one day in the week you go over to Courchevel first thing, to ski Combe Saulire when it's freshly groomed and free of people.

For experts

There are black pistes dotted around the map, and most just about merit the classification. Of the 'regular' pistes, Grande Rosière from Saulire is the one with the most sustained challenge. And then there is the highly irregular GoPro Couloir, originally Couloir Tournier, directly beneath the Saulire gondola. This shady couloir will not faze real experts, but it is narrow and steep enough (37° they say) to lead us to wait for the perfect conditions, which we have so far not encountered; crying shame.

There is lots of good off-piste terrain close to the lifts and pistes all around the valley. For example, on the afternoon-sun side, there is a wide, varied area around the Tetras black run – great in fresh snow, and in falling snow you can go into the trees to skier's right of the Pic Bleu piste. From the col of Pas du Lac where Méribel meets Courchevel you can traverse south to ski the slope beyond the Grande Rosière black piste to Mottaret.

On the morning-sun side, from Roc de Fer at the north end there's a range of long descents (with great views) down to the mid-stations on the gondola from Brides-les Bains at Le Raffort and Les Allues. (There are also lovely easy descents over the ridge to St-Martin – read the Les Menuires chapter.) Further south on that same side is some of the best terrain, including lots of more challenging stuff, with runs from each of the high-points on the ridge between Tougnète and Mont de la Chambre. Short but sweet guides' favourites include the Cairn, from Roc des 3 Marches, and Le Spot, from Mont de la Challe.

From Mont Vallon there are obvious possibilities in departing from the pistes, plus the less obvious Col du Vallon run down into the Plan de Tuéda nature reserve (permitted, apparently, despite the general no-skiing rule). In the opposite direction is the popular Lacs du Borgne run to join the piste from Val Tho.

There are some good runs accessed from lifts in the other valleys. A ridge walk from Courchevel's Creux Noirs chair-lift brings you to the classic Col du Fruit run to Mottaret. Read the Val Thorens chapter for possibilities from its lifts.

Fancy stuff

Méribel has not one but two big parks. Snowpark DC Area 43 on the Chatelet chair-lift, above Mottaret, is the serious one, including big kickers and a serious half-pipe, and is apparently highly regarded by aficionados. But it does have a Rookies zone including a small pipe. There's a boardercross course here. Elements Park, at mid-mountain on the morning-sun side of Centre, is aimed at families and beginners, and also includes a boardercross and a funcross course. There's a big air bag at Mottaret.

There are countless other 'fun' features, several of which are mentioned in the families section. Add to those Turn & Run, below the DC Area 43 park, offering a gentle introduction to freestyle with banked turns, tunnels etc, and the Little Himalaya green piste at Mottaret – a funslope for beginners and families.

Méribel Centre – the resort

With its rigorous chalet-style building code, this is the most attractive of the 3V resorts – and arguably the most attractive purpose-built resort in France. Set on a slope, it could have been one of the most convenient for skiers – but in fact it's convenient only for a privileged few. It does have a more skiing-oriented outpost, up the valley at Mottaret.

Convenience

The countless chalets and chalet-style apartment buildings are set along zigzag roads that climb from the village entrance at 1400m and the central square at 1450m to Rond Point at 1650m. The main piste passes down the south side of all this (with branches to the centre and to Chaudanne, the main lift base), and of course some chalets enjoy positions beside it or close to it. Most do not. The Hulotte piste from Altiport and the Morel chair-lift at the opposite end of the village offer less valuable links to the snow.

A tunnel under the main piste goes on from Rond Point to the suburb of Belvédère and the further, more exclusive suburb of Domaine de Burgin, while another road climbs on to Altiport, the airfield and location of the main nursery slopes at 1720m. You may find all these higher parts of the main village branded as Méribel les Hauts. When it suits the resort's marketers, though, they'll refer to the whole of the main village as Centre, and that's our policy. Like Courchevel, Méribel has messed up its village names.

Upmarket chalet operators deal with the inconvenient layout by running their own shuttles, but free resort ski-buses also run on four routes, linking all the necessary points.

Lodgings

The website lists 10 hotels in Méribel (by which it means Centre), the village plan more than double that number. They range from the lone 5-star Kaïla (to be joined in 2019 by a second, Le Chirou) to the 2-star Eliova le Génépi. Surprisingly, 3-star places outnumber 4-star ones. If you can afford them, our favourites are the 4-star Allodis and Grand Coeur.

Mottaret and the afternoon-sun side of the valley at about midday, with the piste from Courchevel softening

Méribel and Val d'Isère are the two capitals of the catered chalet business. There are dozens of operators here, and hundreds of properties, including a good number of swanky places with grand living rooms, hot tubs and other spa stuff. There are several chalet hotels.

All the main chalet firms are here, and there are lots of single-chalet operations. In between are mid-sized firms focused on Méribel – including Meriski, here for 30 years and offering a wide range from traditional to very smooth and spacious.

In addition to the residences picked out below, there are adequate apartments to be had in and around Centre. The Golf at Altiport has obvious attractions if you have beginners in your party.

Bars and restaurants

We've called in a local expert here. Colin Mathews of specialist tour operator Meriski lets us in on his favourite spots.

'Many people end (or truncate) a hard day on the slopes up at mid-mountain, at Méribel's branch of the famous Folie Douce, and then head down on skis to the throbbing Rond Point des Pistes, at the very top of the village.

'Clive has completely refurbished the popular Barometer to provide a fine mix of a bar and a quality restaurant; try the new Copiña for some tapas and cocktails, L'Abreuvoir for cocktails and good snack food. In Méribel Village, the Lodge du Village is very popular. Later on, live bands of a very high standard play in many venues; for a late-night drink, head for O'Sullivans (formerly Dick's Tea Bar).

'Restaurants? My tips for classic French cuisine include Le Cèpe, the 'old faithful' Chez Kiki, Le Bistrot de L'Orée and Aux Petits Oignons. Several of the top hotels have superb restaurants, including Le Grand Coeur and the Allodis. Méribel's sole Michelin star belongs to L'Ekrin at the 5-star hotel Le Kaïla.'

Off the slopes

All the major boxes are ticked, now that there is a proper toboggan run. The 3.4km Mission Black Forest run, opened in 2017, is now open 7 days a week; served by the Tougnète 1 gondola, with a vertical of 470m, it sounds fun (which it ought to be for €12 a go in 2018). For smaller kids, there is a sledging slope with a carpet-lift at the Chaudanne lift base. At Mottaret, the Little Himalaya green piste is open for sledging in the evening.

The Parc Olympique is a big sports centre built around the ice rink used for the 1992 Olympics. The rink is open early evening, lessons are available, and there is a weekly hockey demonstration match. Other facilities: a 25m pool, kids' pools with flume, climbing wall, gym and spa.

At Mottaret there's a tubing slope – and you can do tube jumps on to the BigAirBag, open into the early evening.

You'll find cross-country loops and cleared paths in two pretty areas – around Altiport (to Courchevel), and up the valley beyond Mottaret around Lac de Tuéda. There are good map leaflets.

For families

There is a full range of childcare and associated activities, and the range of stuff listed above is compelling. But you'll need to pick your spot with care for access to snow for casual sledging etc.

The resort seems to have gone a bit wild with family-oriented piste trimmings in the Altiport area. The Blanchot green run off the first stage of the Saulire gondola is a Family Cool fun-themed area. Off that is the Eskimo-themed Piste des Inuits, with an Inuit village complete with entertainers. Across the slope a bit is Moon Wild – la Piste des Animaux, an informative trail through the forest. Up the hill off the Loze chair-lift, the Pic Bleu blue run is also branded the Altaï Dragon piste, with 'full-size dragons'. (What?)

Up at Mottaret, off the Little Himalaya funslope is the Yéti family fun park.

Alternatives to Méribel Centre

A few km up the valley, with its lift base at much the same altitude as the top of Centre, much smaller Mottaret is in pole position for exploration of the 3V, only two lift rides away from Val Thorens. In contrast, the other options are not in pole position for anything (except sheltered woodland skiing, for which Village is unrivalled). But they do offer a clear retreat from ski resort glitz – and in the case of Brides-les-Bains, much lower prices.

Méribel Mottaret 1690m

Although Mottaret retains the pitched-roof theme of the mother resort, it is much closer to purpose-built resort norms – more apartment buildings, fewer small chalets, and all the lodgings either on the snow or a short walk from it. It's a resort of two halves, both set on quite steep slopes – on the morning-sun side Le Laitelet, with the Chalets gondola to get you up to the higher lodgings; and on the opposite side Le Chatelet, a bit further up the valley, with a little funicular up to the higher residences. Each part has a good nursery slope with a carpet-lift at the base.

There are four 3-star and 4-star hotels, all but one on the Laitelet side. There are quite a few catered chalets, some occupying apartments, and there is a chalet hotel. Read 'Pick of the apartments' earlier in the chapter. At the base there are the essential shops, and here and up the slopes a reasonable range of bars and restaurants.

Méribel Village 1400m

Below Altiport, at the bottom of the Golf chair-lift and the Lapin blue run, Méribel Village might have been better called Méribel Hameau. Although it has grown to offer quite a range of catered chalets and at least one sizeable apartment residence (read 'Pick of the apartments'), it remains essentially a hamlet, offering just the essentials of life – a bakery, a grocery and couple of bar-restaurants. The Lodge du Village, the longstanding après favourite, changed hands recently; its downstairs restaurant has been rebranded La Terrasse, with a more adventurous menu.

Les Allues 1100m

Méribel is in the commune of Les Allues, and in its early days was called Méribel-les-Allues. At the first stop on the gondola ride up from Brides-les-Bains, Les Allues is a quiet, rustic sprawl of chalets. There is a red piste to this point from the Roc de Fer sector of slopes, but don't count on it being open as spring approaches. The simple old 2-star hotel Croix Jean Claude is a bit of an institution, with a cosily traditional restaurant. There are some catered chalets here, and some apartments.

Brides-les-Bains 600m

The athletes competing in the events hosted at Méribel in the 1992 Olympics were accommodated in this neat little spa town in the valley below Méribel. It now offers a budget back door to Méribel, via a long and rather slow gondola (followed by a bit of a walk to the main lifts), but it also promotes the idea of easy access to Courchevel – 15 minutes' drive to Le Praz, they say. And it's no further to Champagny, for access to La Plagne.

The key attraction, of course, is valley prices rather than resort prices; the difference is striking.

The Grand Spa Thermal, re-opened in 2018 after a 16-month makeover, claims to be the biggest in the Alps, with three pools and 2700m^2 of fitness and treatment rooms. Several hotels have spas too – notably the Mercure Grand Hôtel des Thermes, one of the two grand 4-star hotels. There are 10 3-star places and a couple of 2-stars. Two contrasting 3-stars to consider: Les Bains, with its cosy mountain decor, and the Altis, dotted with baroque furniture – and the attraction of a cool wine bar in the vaulted cellar. There are plenty of apartments, including some attractive residences with pool, such as the Cybele.

The only casino in the Tarentaise region is here, with all the usual games, and a nightclub in the basement. There are plenty of other bars and restaurants, but it's not a great party town. And don't imagine you can do your après partying up in Méribel – the gondola closes early.

Les Menuires

Les Menuires / St-Martin-de-Belleville

Les Menuires has always been worth considering for its location – quick access to Val Thorens and to the best of the Méribel skiing – and for prices that are the lowest in the 3 Vallées. Having broadened its range of lodgings and in the process improved its rather dire original looks, it is now a generally attractive base, provided you pick your spot with a bit of care (although shopping in its central bunker-mall remains a gloomy prospect).

Although considerably lower than Val Thorens at the head of the valley, Les Menuires is still more or less treeless; probably its bigger weakness, though, is that the main local slopes – a broad, gentle area of quite long runs – get excessive amounts of afternoon sun

The mountains in brief

Size A fair size, with similarly extensive Val Thorens in the same valley

Slopes Good variety, although practically treeless

Snow Reasonable; main slopes are very sunny, La Masse much less so

System, Lift Pretty good; continually improved, too

Sustenance The best area for lunch in the 3V – good places, good prices

For beginners Excellent in most respects; snow can be tricky, runs busy

For true blue skiers With fewer people around it would be perfect

For the confident Quite a bit to do locally, but you'll want to explore the 3V

For experts Huge amounts of off-piste, including a lot of gentle stuff

Fancy stuff Not quite in the Méribel league, but enough for most of us

Les Menuires – the resort in brief

Convenience Lots of lodgings that are at least ski-in, and some ski-out

Lodgings A good range, from simple apartments to smart hotels

Bars and restaurants A wide choice, from trad to cool

Off the slopes Lots to do, indoors and out

For families Pick your spot and it's near ideal

Pass notes
The local pass saves about €55 on the 3V pass but doesn't cover Val Thorens. An extension cost €37 in 2017/18.
There are free carpet-lifts on the nursery slopes.
The half-price Easy Rider day pass covers several long lifts serving longer green and easy blue runs.

Key facts

Altitude	1600–2000m
Range	1260–3230m
Slopes (see text)	600km

Where to stay, ideally
Slope-side in Reberty or Les Bruyères – suburbs of Les Menuires.

Websites
lesmenuires.com
st-martin-belleville.com
les3vallees.com

Key ratings

Size	*****
Snow	***
Fast lifts	****
Mountain rest's	****
Beginner	****
True blue	****
Confident	*****
Expert	****
Convenience	****
Families	****
Village charm	**

The mountains in detail

The slopes of Les Menuires are much more one-sided than those of Méribel. Again, the resort village sits on the afternoon-sun side; above it is a huge network of lifts and runs, mainly quite gentle, linking Mont de la Chambre above Val Thorens to St-Martin, 9km to the north. There are half a dozen points on the ridge where you can cross over into Méribel.

Then, on the facing morning-sun side of the valley, is the Pointe de la Masse, a much smaller but quite shady, tall and challenging sector.

Size

Les Menuires claims its local slopes amount to 160km, which can't be far out. What's more, the Belleville valley as a whole (ie taking in Val Thorens) amounts to about half the skiing in the 3V. Sadly, the valley pass including Val Thorens is sold only by the day. For a week, it's a Menuires pass or a 3V pass; the 3V pass is worth the premium of around €50, even if you don't leave the valley.

The 3 Vallées as a whole is amazingly extensive – well over 500km and not far short of the claimed 600km.

Slopes

As you can see from the photos, the main slopes are immensely wide and practically treeless, while the trees at the bottom of La Masse don't offer much in the way of sheltered skiing.

There are some long, gentle runs criss-crossing the main mountain, and the verticals are respectable – 1000m from Mont de la Chambre to Les Menuires, 1250m from Roc des 3 Marches to St-Martin (quite a bit lower than Menuires). La Masse is a steeper hill with more character (as well as better snow), and a maximum vertical of almost 1100m.

Three Liberty Ride zones (on the Sunny Express and St Martin Express chair-lifts and the Masse 2 gondola) are left ungroomed but are in other respects pistes. Bizarrely, the first of these appears green on the piste map – presumably resulting from a blue line overprinted by a yellow tint showing the zone.

The resort spreads about 3km from the entrance on the left to the end of Les Bruyères, on the right

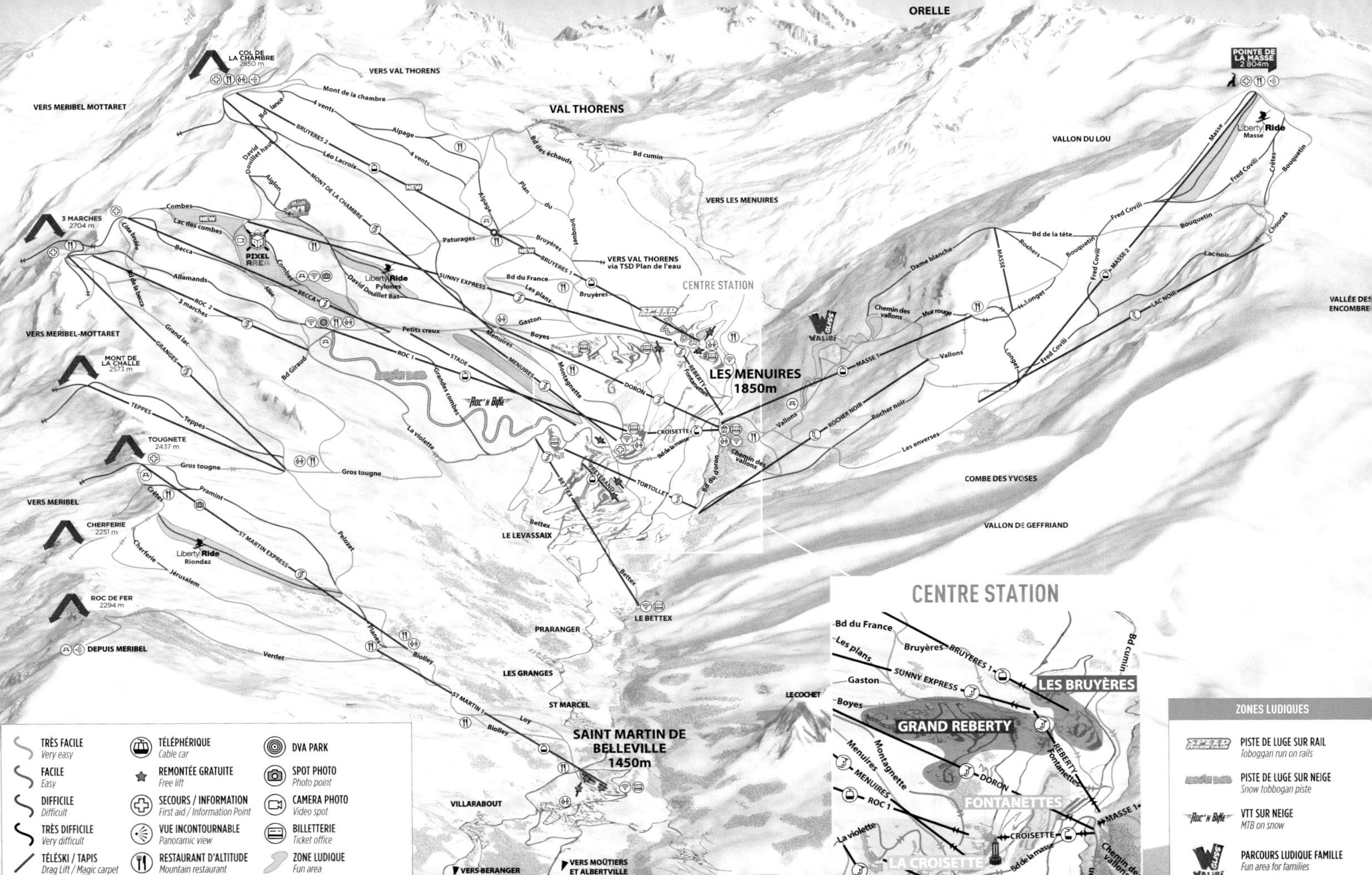

ORELLE
VAL THORENS
VERS VAL THORENS
VERS MERIBEL MOTTARET
COL DE LA CHAMBRE 2850 m
3 MARCHES 2704 m
VERS MERIBEL-MOTTARET
MONT DE LA CHALLE 2573 m
TOUGNETE 2437 m
VERS MERIBEL
CHERFERIE 2251 m
ROC DE FER 2294 m
DEPUIS MERIBEL
POINTE DE LA MASSE 2 804m
VALLON DU LOU
VALLÉE DES ENCOMBRE
VERS LES MENUIRES
VERS VAL THORENS via TSD Plan de l'eau
CENTRE STATION
LES MENUIRES 1850m
COMBE DES YVOSES
VALLON DE GEFFRIAND
LE LEVASSAIX
LE BETTEX
PRARANGER
LES GRANGES
ST MARCEL
LE COCHET
SAINT MARTIN DE BELLEVILLE 1450m
VILLARABOUT
VERS BERANGER
VERS MOÛTIERS ET ALBERTVILLE
Mont de la chambre
4 vents
Alpage
Bd lance
BRUYERES 2
Léo Lacroix
MONT DE LA CHAMBRE
David Douillet haut
Aiglon
Combes
Lac des combes
PIXEL AREA
Becca
Côte brulée
Bd de la becca
Allamands
ROC 2
3 marches
Grand lac
GRANGES
TEPPES
Teppes
Gros tougne
Crêtes
Pramint
Cherferie
Jérusalem
ST MARTIN EXPRESS
Liberty Ride Riondaz
Pelozet
Planes
Verdet
Biolley
ST MARTIN 1
Loy
Liberty Ride Pylones
David Douillet Bas
BECCA
Allée
Bd Giraud
Petits creux
ROC 1
Grandes combes
STADE
La violette
Roc'n Bike
Paturages
Plan du bouquet
Bd des échauds
Bd cumin
Bruyères
BRUYERES 1
SUNNY EXPRESS
Bd du France
Les plans
Gaston
Boyes
Menuires
MENUIRES
Montagnette
DORON
REBERTY Fontanettes
CROISETTE
Bd de la masse
PREYERAND
BETTEX
Bettex
TORTOLLET
Bd du doron
Chemin des vallons
Vallons
ROCHER NOIR
Rocher noir
Les enverses
MASSE 1
Mur rouge
Dame blanche
MASSE
Rochers
Bd de la tête
Longet
Fred Covili
Bouquetin
MASSE 2
Lac noir
LAC NOIR
Choucas
Crêtes
Masse
Liberty Ride Masse
NEW
WALIBI
CENTRE STATION
LES BRUYÈRES
GRAND REBERTY
FONTANETTES
LA CROISETTE
TRÈS FACILE Very easy
FACILE Easy
DIFFICILE Difficult
TRÈS DIFFICILE Very difficult
TÉLÉSKI / TAPIS Drag Lift / Magic carpet
TÉLÉPHÉRIQUE Cable car
REMONTÉE GRATUITE Free lift
SECOURS / INFORMATION First aid / Information Point
VUE INCONTOURNABLE Panoramic view
RESTAURANT D'ALTITUDE Mountain restaurant
DVA PARK
SPOT PHOTO Photo point
CAMERA PHOTO Video spot
BILLETTERIE Ticket office
ZONE LUDIQUE Fun area
ZONES LUDIQUES
PISTE DE LUGE SUR RAIL Toboggan run on rails
PISTE DE LUGE SUR NEIGE Snow tobbogan piste
VTT SUR NEIGE MTB on snow
PARCOURS LUDIQUE FAMILLE Fun area for families

Snow

The main slopes on the afternoon-sun side, like those in Méribel, are affected by the sun, so in late season particularly you may have to contend with ice in the mornings and slush in the afternoons. La Masse is quite different – essentially facing north-east, it keeps its snow well. Of course, the premium-quality snow of Val Thorens is easily reached.

System, Lift

The lift system is generally excellent, with continual upgrades. As we write in 2018, three upgrades are taking place. On the upper mountain, the Granges chair-lift is getting a boost in capacity. At village level, both the Bruyères and Roc gondolas are getting a boost to a state-of-the-art speed of 6m/s. The few slow lifts are in one area – the Rocher Noir chair and Lac Noir above it, on La Masse; and Tortollet, for the return from those lifts to the village.

Queues are not usually a problem, but the lifts towards Mont de la Chambre for access to Val Thorens can build bearable queues at peak times, and if the afternoon-sun side is rock hard in the morning, there may be a bit of a queue to get up La Masse.

Sustenance

The mountain restaurants here mostly offer welcome relief from the prices in the other 3V resorts, while managing to serve good food in pleasant surroundings.

An old favourite doing satisfying food is the Grand Lac, a big, welcoming chalet at the bottom of the Granges chair. Well across the mountain to the south, the Alpage and Chalet du Sunny also do a good job. We stretch a point to include the excellent Ferme, down at Reberty – a resort restaurant, really, but well above the bottom of the lift system.

At Mont de la Chambre is the Bouche à Oreille, a distant relative of the famous Bouitte in St-Marcel. Views differ on whether its elevated prices are justified.

Restaurants are marked on the piste map but are not named. Why not?

More on the slopes

For beginners

There are five free carpet-lifts on gentle slopes dotted around the sprawling village, so you would be unlucky to find yourself very far from one. The carpet-lift at Les Bruyères is covered.

The arrangements for progress

The original uncompromising buildings in the centre, seen from the fringes of more traditional Reberty

from the absolute beginner slopes are excellent – the Easy Rider mini-pass is just the ticket. It covers the Doron chair and other lifts serving the gentle Montagnette green run and the Gaston blue, and the Roc 1 gondola, accessing a long green on one side, a blue the other.

We do have reservations, though, about snow quality on these sunny slopes, which can make life difficult, and crowds on some of these runs.

For true blue skiers

Near beginners wanting a gentle transition from green runs might consider starting with the half-price Easy Rider day pass (read 'For beginners' above).

There is a huge amount of blue run skiing on the main area above the village, all of it correctly classified and most of it genuinely easy. But, again, we have a reservation about crowds on popular through-routes. The trip to St-Martin via Roc des 3 Marches with the return via Tougnète is a great outing, and gives a chance to check out some slightly stiffer blues, such as 3 Marches. Mont de la Chambre is another broad, gentle blue.

La Masse is a bit steeper. There are two worthwhile runs down the lower mountain, but Vallons has to resort to a zigzag detour to avoid a tough section halfway down. A fairly recent development is the Bouquetin piste from the top; this is rightly classified blue, but is quite tough in places.

For confident intermediates

Practically all the red runs you'll see on the upper part of the main slopes are genuine reds, with stretches offering a bit of challenge; Quatre Vents is about the most testing. But you're likely to want to spend more time on La Masse, or up at Val Tho, or over in the other valleys. One of the features of this area is that the red descents from the ridge down the morning-sun slopes of Méribel are generally excellent.

On the upper part of La Masse, the Fred Covili red served by the Masse 2 gondola is a great spot for laps. As you descend check out the Lac Noir run on your left – the softest of the blacks.

For experts

La Masse, facing the village, is steep enough to give some satisfaction, and the Dame Blanche black piste is direct enough to make the most of it but isn't seriously steep, while Lac Noir follows a winding course. Both are quite short. The very short Masse piste at the top barely reaches black gradient. On the main slopes above the resort, the Léo Lacroix from Mont de la Chambre has a steep pitch that just about rates as black.

There are vast amounts of off-piste terrain. From the lift-served high-points of the ridge shared with Méribel there are lots of ways down over gentle, rolling ground – a great mountainside for off-piste novices to find their feet. The Méribel side of the ridge is steeper, so it offers more to amuse real experts.

There are more exciting possibilities on La Masse. The Lac Noir chair accesses huge amounts of terrain, including runs via the minor peak of Le Teurre. You can climb to the low peak of La Gratte for a fine descent to Les Menuires or epic gentle descents towards St Martin. From the peak of La Masse, an easy run goes south and then loops around past Lac du Lou to the resort. (This was a marked itinéraire in the past – a real shame it is no more.) As from Val Tho, there are long descents south-west from La Masse into the Maurienne valley. From any of these points you can drop into the deserted Vallée des Encombres, which meets the Belleville valley just below St-Martin.

Fancy stuff

The snow park on the Becca chair-lift got a makeover in 2018. It has three areas to suit different levels, and a new colourful chill zone. Features include multiple boardercross courses. On the Masse 1 gondola, Walibi Gliss is a fun zone for families incorporating a slalom course and boardercross.

Les Menuires – the resort

Les Menuires was first developed in the mid-1960s, when the French norm was to cram visitor beds into cramped apartment blocks and expect the occupants to do their après-skiing and shopping in claustrophobic, low-ceilinged shopping malls, possibly underground. The resort still has its main blocks and its mall, but it now also has lots of more attractive chalet-style buildings in the areas away from the centre.

Convenience

The resort is big – the whole thing measures 3km end to end and covers an exceptional altitude range of 400m. It's big enough to be divided into five pretty distinct 'quarters' – La Croisette around the main lift base, then what is now called Grand Reberty across the hillside, and then three lower suburbs – Preyerand on the down-valley side, Les Fontanettes in the middle and Les Bruyères on the up-valley side. In all these quarters there are large amounts of slope-side lodgings, and no one has to walk very far – the resort has lifts (and pistes) running through it, and shuttle-buses linking La Croisette to the other quarters.

Lodgings

There are now quite a few hotels, with at least as many 4-star as 3-star places. The 4-star Kaya and Ours Blanc have both impressed us – the Ours has an excellent restaurant. The Kaya offers all-inclusive deals. The funky, value-oriented Hostel Ho36 opened in the centre for 2017/18.

Since Les Menuires developed chalet-style suburbs, the catered chalet business has boomed here. Quite a few companies operate chalets in slope-side Reberty 2000. Family specialist Family Ski Company had seven at the last count. Powder N Shine has a handful of places sleeping 15+ people, with hot tubs etc – and, new in 2018, a place with all the trimmings down the slope in Les Bruyères, close to the gondola and next to the swimming pool. Ski Amis has nine chalets, all with hot tub, some with sauna; they're split between a ski-in/ski-out location at Les Bruyères and a peaceful setting in Bettaix, in the valley bottom.

There are lots of smart chalet-style apartment developments. The 4-star Chalet du Mont Vallon is a smart apartment residence/hotel at Les Bruyères with a good restaurant, spa and pool. Les Clarines is an MGM-built, CGH-managed residence in Preyerand. Others to check out include the Hameau de la Sapinière, the Alpages de Reberty and the Chalets du Soleil.

Bars and restaurants

The resort's *Guide pratique* has quite useful restaurant listings. But for proper guidance we called on Francesca Smith of chalet operator Powder N Shine.

In the afternoon, the local substitute for a Folie Douce is the Chalet du Sunny, high above Reberty – live music, resident DJ, great atmosphere. Down at Croisette, Skilt is a Brit favourite, with live music and a big terrace. A recent addition is Ho36, a cool bar with great wine and cocktails, and live music downstairs.

For dinner, the Ferme de Reberty is a great all-rounder – well priced, excellent service. Au Petit Rendez-Vous in Reberty 1850 is a small place doing great food – good value. Au Village is a cosy Savoyard restaurant in a galerie at Croisette – always gets good reports. Là-Haut in Preyerand is a real find: great atmosphere (live music) and delicious food.

Later on, Kube is a modern but cosy lounge doing good cocktails, with a great atmosphere (live music sometimes); open late. Challenge and Moose are bars in the Croisette mall with pool tables and live music, appealing to seasonaires etc.

As most of the skiing world knows, the star restaurant hereabouts is La Bouitte, a few km down-valley at St-Marcel.

Off the slopes

Roc'N Bob is a 4km long/450m vertical toboggan run down the length of the Roc 1 gondola, open afternoon and early evening; not cheap. There is also a sled-on-rails coaster at the base of the Bruyères gondola, open until mid-evening – and nearby, a sledging area by the carpet-lift, open some evenings. There's also a sledging/snow-fun area at La Croisette. No sign of skating, though.

There's an impressive sports centre with pool at La Croisette and an 'aquafun' pool at Les Bruyères – taken together, lots of facilities and a bewildering range of deals and prices.

In 2018, at least, a premium lift pass costing €50 extra was offered covering two toboggan rides and four entries to the sports centre or pool.

There are 28km of cross-country loops along the valley below the village, plus marked walks and snowshoe routes.

For families

The resort works well for young families, with plenty of snow to play on well away from traffic, and a good range of things to do. There's a 'fun park' in the Croisette sports centre, with trampolines and suchlike.

St-Martin-de-Belleville 1400m

St-Martin, well down the valley from its offspring Les Menuires, is an old village that has developed into a mini-resort, offering a rustic, human-scale alternative to the ten-times larger child. For a quiet time, worth a look.

The village is centred on a fine old church, there are lots of authentic old buildings, and new construction has been done (and continues) in traditional style. It has long been bypassed by the valley road, so traffic is not a problem.

There is one piste in (the amiable but excessively sunny blue Jérusalem, starting at the Méribel ridge), and one lift out – an adequate gondola to mid-mountain. The Easy Rider half-price pass covers the gondola and the short village drag-lift. All of which makes this a viable base for near-beginners. For absolute beginners there are two free carpet-lifts near the gondola. Then you have to make the step up to the long blues up the mountain, but they are very gentle – particularly the home run to St-Martin.

Convenience Although it's a small resort, and there are ski-in/ski-out lodgings to be had all around the lower slopes, the village spreads widely enough for the useful village plan to divide the place up into five quarters. The northern extremity is 400m from the central village drag-lift, which for most people is the route to the gondola, 300m away and 40m higher. Some people drive to the gondola base, and a ski-bus runs twice in the morning and twice in the afternoon. There are four buses a day to and from Les Menuires.

Lodgings There are several hotels; both the 4-star St-Martin and the 3-star Alp are on the snow. For something completely different, the Trait d'Union is a stone-built farm refuge on the home run with three rooms (it's also open as a restaurant).

The range of catered chalets continues to grow. Alpine Club (not really a club) has three luxurious chalets in different styles in the slightly higher satellite hamlet of Villarabout, a four-minute chauffeured drive from the gondola. Two (each with four bedrooms) are for whole-chalet bookings only. Sister company White Mountain Chalets also has four very smart chalets in Villarabout, and two in St-Martin – one in a central, ski-in/ski-out location.

Peak Retreats Pick of the apartments

There are some stunning options for larger parties. Top of our list is the 4-star Chalets Caseblanche, new for 2018/19. These beautiful self-catered chalets and apartments (there are 34 in total) are in one of the best locations in the resort, just 50m from the gondola. Near the top is the uber-stylish Chalets Home apartments and chalets, all of which have a contemporary fireplace to cosy up by; free shuttle service. The 4-star ski-in/ski-out Chalets du Gypse has a pool, hot tub, sauna and steam room.

www.peakretreats.co.uk 023 9283 9310

Bars and restaurants The are several attractive opportunities to pause for a quiet beer on the home run; you may find a bit more life in one of the bar-restaurants fronting on to the village slopes. A few steps away is Pourquoi Pas, a vaulted cellar bar that's an old favourite with Brits. Live music sometimes.

The influx of lunchtime visitors from other 3V resorts helps support a range of restaurants that's impressive for a place this size. La Voute is an old favourite. We like the rustic Montagnard, and its less traditional offshoot, Jardin de Joséphine. There are a couple of outlying farm restaurants where cheese may figure prominently. Just up the valley in St-Marcel is the famous multi-starred La Bouitte, which long since climbed out of our price range.

Off the slopes There's a sledging area at the main lift base. For the 2018 season a tiny token ice rink was built in the village. For a pool, stay at the Chalets du Gypse (see above). There are cleared paths along the valley, cross-country trails and snowshoe routes; dog sledding is said to be available.

Families Choose lodgings on the snow and acquire something to slide on, and you may have a fine time. For more fun, it's not too far to bus up to Les Menuires.

Val Thorens

Val Thorens / Orelle

Val Thorens is the snow guarantee for the 3 Vallées – not so much for its small fragments of glacier, more for its general altitude. At 2300m, it is the highest resort in Europe. It's very tempting for a late-season trip, in particular; but storms can make skiing unpleasant or impossible for a time, and we generally prefer to visit Val Tho from Courchevel.

The village is one of the more successful purpose-built places, with a lot of accommodation that is genuinely ski-in/ski-out, and buildings generally designed with a bit of style, using a lot of wood cladding. Its wide range of lodgings includes a striking (and continually expanding) choice of upmarket places – it now has no fewer than four 5-star hotels.

The mountains in brief

Size A fair size, but most people will want a 3 Vallées pass

Slopes High, open slopes with plenty of variety; increasingly busy, though

Snow Very high, and mostly shady: short of a proper glacier, top-notch

System, Lift Many powerful lifts, but when crowds invade, queues result

Sustenance For a high resort, a respectable number and range of options

For beginners We'd pick somewhere less bleak, but the slopes are great

For true blue skiers Plenty to do, including visits to the fourth valley

For the confident Lots to do here, on the best snow – plus 3V day trips

For experts Fabulous off-piste routes in all directions

Fancy stuff All the terrain features you could wish for – except a half-pipe

Val Thorens – the resort in brief

Convenience It's a compact place, with a lot of ski-in/ski out lodgings

Lodgings A wide choice, from budget apartments to top hotels

Bars and restaurants Lots going on from early until late, and good dining

Off the slopes An impressive range of activities; but no skating, it seems

For families Plenty of snow to play on, away from traffic

Pass notes
In 2018 a 3V six-day pass cost €50 more than the local pass, which does not cover Les Menuires. A day 3V extension cost €36. There are four long, free carpet lifts on the nursery slopes. A half-price beginner's day pass covers four lifts serving longer blue and green runs near the village (read the main text).

Key facts

Altitude	2200–2350m
Range	1260–3230m
Slopes (see text)	600km

Where to stay, ideally
Anywhere that is ski-in/ski-out, or nearly so.

Websites
valthorens.com
les3vallees.com

Key ratings

Size	*****
Snow	*****
Fast lifts	*****
Mountain rest's	****
Beginner	****
True blue	****
Confident	*****
Expert	*****
Convenience	*****
Families	***
Village charm	**

The mountains in detail

The main slopes around the resort can usefully be split into five sectors.

Approaching from Méribel or Les Menuires via Col de la Chambre, you're in the small, sunny Plein Sud sector. To spectator's right of this are slopes beneath the Aiguille de Péclet, served mainly by the Péclet gondola, with a small glacier area at the top. To the right again is a broad mountainside with lifts up to the ridge at three points, all over 3000m. Two of these three points access the 'fourth valley', where the sunny skiing includes a slow chair-lift to 3230m – the highest point in the 3 Vallées.

Back on the shady side, the fourth sector above Val Tho is the challenging Cime Caron (3200m), reached by a famously queue-prone jumbo cable car. And finally, below that is a lower but worthwhile sector served mainly by the Boismint chair-lift, peaking at a mere 2640m.

Size

Val Thorens claims its local slopes amount to 150km. Certainly, the Belleville valley as a whole (ie taking in Les Menuires) is much the biggest sector in the 3V – it would be the third largest in France if it were an isolated area. A valley pass covering Les Menuires is sold by the day. But for a week it's worth paying the 3V premium of around €50.

The 3 Vallées as a whole is amazingly extensive – well over 500km and not far short of the claimed 600km.

Slopes

High does not necessarily mean steep. This is a classic intermediate area, with abundant blue and red runs, and relatively few blacks. The slopes are entirely open – only the lowest runs, to the base of the Boismint sector, come close to any trees.

It's not a resort for notably long runs – Col de Thorens is about 4km from the village. Not that the runs are unacceptably short: from the rim of the bowl around the village, you're typically doing descents in the order of 600–900m vertical.

Spot any trees? At about 2300m, Val Thorens is the highest proper resort in the Alps, and specialises in snow

Snow

In Val Thorens you spend most of your time skiing at altitudes between 2300m and 3200m. This is exceptional – in the Alps, only the very glacial Saas-Fee in Switzerland keeps you at higher altitude run after run. Most of the slopes around the village face roughly north, but there are exceptions: the Plein Sud sector, naturally, is sunny, but so is the Péclet sector, facing roughly west. The little glacier at the top is more shady. The fourth valley is something else: most of the runs here face south-west.

The bottom line is that Val Thorens is one of four resorts in France to merit a 5-star rating for snow (Tignes, Val d'Isère and Les Deux Alpes, since you ask). The best snow of all you'll probably find on the high, shady and relatively quiet piste served by the Col slow chair.

But nothing's perfect. The off-piste needs a good depth of snow to put a safe depth over the many rocks, so it can be dodgy early in the season.

System, Lift

The system is impressive, with a higher proportion of fast lifts than anywhere else in France. These include no less than four twin-cable gondolas capable of operating in quite high winds (if you count the Thorens lift, which actually operates more like a cable car).

But the place is far from queue-free: it draws in visitors from the other 3V resorts on a big scale, especially on a fine day when snow elsewhere is dodgy, and the main access lifts can then build queues.

Then there is the Cime Caron cable car. It's big, but not big enough to meet peak demand, accessing as it does excellent black and red runs both on the front and the back, into the fourth valley.

There are three slow chairs, distinguished on the map – Glacier, Col and Bouchet (in the fourth valley). All are at the upper extremities of the slopes, on bits of glacier or at least at glacial heights, where you can skip them if they are busy.

Sustenance

Amazingly, on the local piste map (unlike the other three 3V maps), restaurants are named as well as marked. There's a good range of places – impressive, given that there are also lots of easily accessible options facing the snow in the village.

For years we have had two regular table-service haunts – the Fruitière (part of the funky Folie Douce in the Plein Sud sector), and the Marine on the Dalles blue piste in the Péclet sector. Both are pricey, but neither has ever disappointed us.

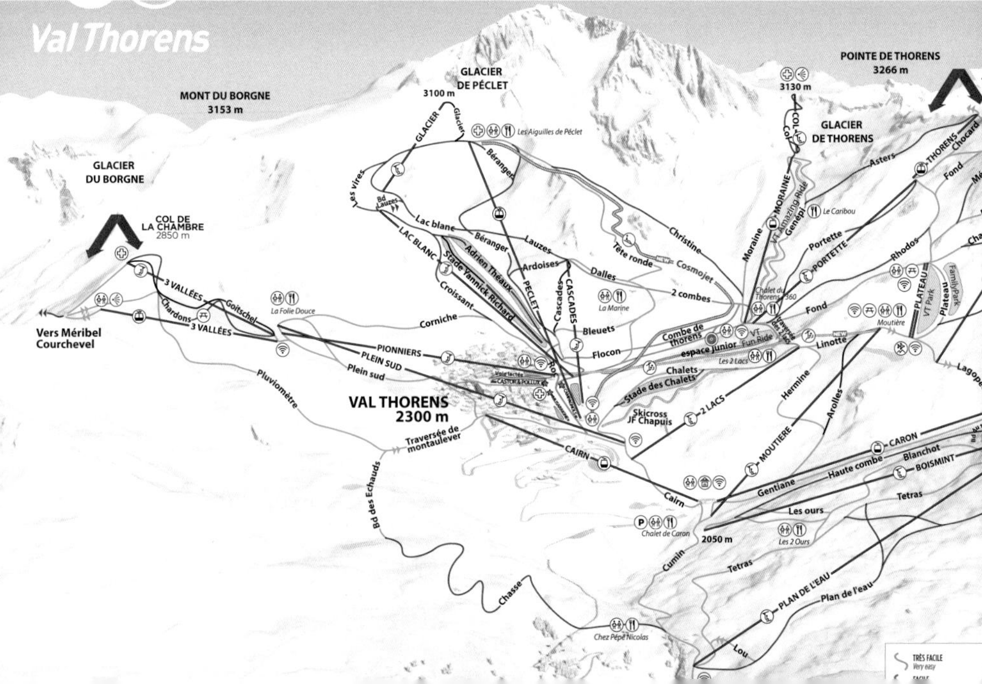

But these have been somewhat eclipsed since the emergence from off-piste obscurity of Chez Pépé Nicolas. An old stone hut, rebuilt in 2014 but still steeped in tradition, it's run by the grandchildren of Nicolas Jay who, as mayor of St-Martin, played a key part in the development of the Belleville valley. The menu is interestingly varied, and the plat du jour excellent and affordable. It's now reached via the Chasse red piste, off Pluviomètre from Col de la Chambre.

The Chalet des 2 Ours also gets good reports and is a bit cheaper than most.

More on the slopes

For beginners

There are four long, covered carpet lifts on the gentle slopes right in front of the village, with at least part of the terrain well separated from the heavy passing traffic.

Progress to longer runs is well organised, too. The half-price Easy Rider pass covers the Cascade chair-lift, serving the roundabout 2 Combes green run, and the 2 Lacs chair and Cairn and Caron gondolas, serving blues that are gentle although unfortunately very busy.

All that is mostly splendid, and might normally merit a 5-star rating. We've docked a star because of the crowds on those blue runs, and because of the bleak setting; if you hit bad weather here in your first week, you might well be put off skiing for life.

For true blue skiers

If you are seriously lacking confidence, you might want to start with the half-price pass described above.

There are blue runs all over the piste map. The Cime Caron sector has always been the exception, with only red and black runs; but as we write, in summer 2018, the new Cime piste is being created from the top, 3km long and dropping almost 600m, which will start life as a red and then be massaged to become blue in 2019. We can't wait to try it.

As ever, some blues are trickier than others, but none is of red steepness. And everything is made that bit easier by the quality of the snow, usually.

Most of the runs around village level are gentle motorways, though they are made less appealing by crowds, and fast skiers. From the Plein Sud and Pionniers chairs, there is now a welcome alternative to the crowded Plein Sud piste – the gentler Corniche running across the mountain to the bottom of the Péclet sector. The runs in the low Boismint sector

have stretches that are a tad tougher than most. From the Moraine gondola, Genépi is a bit steeper at the start than its neighbour Moraine.

From Col de la Chambre (the only route in from Méribel and Les Menuires) most people use the Pluviomètre piste, which is a fine, varied run but distinctly tough (it used to be red) and often very busy. The Val Tho piste map shows no blue alternative. But there is one, signed at the top for Les Menuires and shown on the Les Menuires piste map: the Mont de la Chambre run, which is slightly gentler, quite broad and considerably quieter. Just remember to keep left at mid-mountain, or you'll end up in Les Menuires.

On arrival in Val Tho (or on riding the Cairn gondola from the bottom of the slopes) you have to deal with a unpleasantly narrow, steep and crowded bit of blue run; this needs to be sorted out – but it's a problem of long standing.

Access to the fourth valley is easy on the lovely Lory piste from the Thorens lift – more satisfactory than the zigzag Gentianes from Col de Rosaël. From Rosaël on the way back, we reckon Niverolle is easier than Chamois, provided you keep to your right until you reach the top of the Portette chair.

For confident intermediates

The local slopes are great for the competent intermediate: there are excellent red runs from high, fast lifts in each of the five sectors listed in the intro. You'll want to ski the rest of the 3V, but the snow here will lure you back.

The Péclet gondola is good for laps when queues permit – it rises almost 700m and serves good reds and a worthwhile blue. The Cime Caron cable car is one of the great lifts of the Alps, rising about 875m and serving an excellent red run on the front (to be joined now by a blue) and blacks on the front and back that are not seriously steep. The red Mauriennaise alternative is a good long thrash with some steeper pitches.

Don't overlook the lower Boismint sector – often quieter than other parts of the area; the reds here are excellent slopes with lots of easy off-piste adjacent, and you can ski a vertical of 840m.

For experts

There isn't much black piste skiing, and it is all at the easy end of the spectrum, with difficulty depending crucially on snow conditions and grooming. In 2018 a new black run is being created in the Boismint sector, but we can't see that adding much

The village is one of the most conveniently laid out resorts, with ski-in/ski-out lodgings in abundance

in the way of challenges. The off-piste possibilities, however, are something else.

There are huge amounts of terrain between the lifts around the main bowl – from the high-points, of course, but also from lower lifts such as Cascade and 2 Lacs, and in the Boismint sector.

The Col chair-lift is a key launchpad. An easy traverse south-west (with great views across the Maurienne) takes you to the Col Pierre Lory for a gentle descent of the glacier du Bouchet, down to the fourth valley lifts. Among other options from the Col chair is to hike up for an epic descent of the glacier de Gébroulaz to Méribel Mottaret. Heading south instead, across the glacier de Chavière, opens up several routes down into the Maurienne, for a taxi ride to the gondola at Orelle; one of the more difficult ones passes close to Pointe Rénod to access a glorious bowl of 1000m vertical before you hit the forest above Le Villard. For energetic experts there are some serious descents to be undertaken on the Aiguille de Péclet.

You can also reach the glacier du Bouchet from the Bouchet chair-lift – once upon a time there was a black piste here – and there are other routes from the same point.

There is a good slope into the Bouchet valley from the top of the Grand Fond gondola, and challenging descents from Cime Caron either into the Bouchet bowl or on down into the Maurienne. Also from Cime Caron, Lac du Lou is a famous run dropping 1400m over about 8km to Les Menuires. It's not difficult – the snow is usually excellent (mostly north-facing).

The 3 Vallées chair-lift accesses some short but worthwhile, varied slopes at the head of the Méribel valley.

Fancy stuff

There is a funslope on the 2 Lacs chair-lift, with 50 bits of fun along its 900m length. Then there's the Family Park, and finally the impressive Snowpark, these two served by the Plateau drag-lifts. There's an air bag with a mid-sized jump by the Roc drag-lift, and a skicross off the Chalets blue piste.

Val Thorens – the resort

Val Tho is a second-generation purpose-built resort, with its buildings spread up a slope instead of dumped at the bottom. It has also been built with some regard to style, and from the snow doesn't look bad. Some of the streets you'll use when arriving or exploring are very dreary, though.

Convenience

It's a compact village, about 1km long and about half that wide. As you might guess from our photo, there are too many buildings to guarantee everyone doorstep skiing, but it's not difficult to find. The furthest anyone has to walk to/from a slope is about 200m, and for most people it's much less.

Lodgings

Val Tho has all the bases covered, with a wide choice of hotels, chalets and apartments – though in the end it's the apartments that dominate. Chalet Cocoon is a new concept: ten apartments for up to 12 people, each with a private wellness area and hotel services.

There's a better range of hotels than in most high, purpose-built resorts – over a dozen, more or less equally split between 3-star (our tip is the cosy Sherpa), 4-star (check out the funky Fahrenheit Seven) and 5-star (we'll take the Pashmina).

There's plenty of choice of catered chalets, but they don't include any notably swanky ones. Most occupy apartments in quite big developments – often with use of a communal pool and/or spa. Start by looking at the major operators: Crystal has nine properties, most in apartments.

If you're self-catering, heed the resort's warning: water boils here at 92°C.

Ski Collection Pick of the apartments

There's a wide choice of 4-star places.
Directors' Choice The ski-in/ski-out Hameau du Kashmir is just metres from the nearest lift and has brilliant facilities including a pool, spa and three different types of sauna.
Other options The stylish Oxalys apartments nearby are also ski-in/ski-out and have a restaurant on site. We also like Chalet Altitude, Village Montana Plein

Sud and Les Balcons de Val Thorens Platinum. For 5-star comfort, the Koh-I Nor apartments are stunning; we love the pool, the panoramic views from the sunny terrace and the choice of on-site restaurants.

www.skicollection.co.uk 023 9289 0960

Bars and restaurants

There's plenty going on here, and a good range of restaurants.

The obvious place to end your day, for those who like this sort of thing, is just above the resort in the Plein Sud sector – the Folie Douce, the first clone of the famously throbbing Val d'Isère original. You can check out the terrace from the Plein Sud chair-lift. A less ostentatious but still very lively alternative is the vast Chalets du Thorens on the main home run, and, in particular, its 360 bar.

At the top of the restaurant market, the hotel Pashmina's Les Explorateurs grabbed the Michelin star crown in 2017 after star chef Jean Sulpice closed his restaurant in the Oxalys residence to move down to Lac d'Annecy. (The residence now has a good-looking new Italian, Il Gusto.) There are countless more affordable options. La Maison on the snow front is an old favourite. Check out also the Auberge des Balcons, and Base Camp in the hotel Pashmina.

The well-liked Steak Club has become Club 72, and offers live music every evening, with the kitchen open until 11.30.

Among several bars at the top of the village, the Frog and Roastbeef is a long-established British ghetto. Malaysia is apparently the main nightclub.

Off the slopes

There is a 6km toboggan run down the Péclet gondola, variously claimed to be the longest in France (could be) or in Europe (nonsense). Anyway, it's long, said to be great fun but rather pricey (€16 in 2018). Open afternoon and early evening.

From the 3V high-point at the top of the Bouchet chair-lift (in the fourth valley), the world's highest zipline soars high above the Bouchet valley to the top of the Thorens cable car 1.3km away. Building on that success, a 1.6km twin zipline is being constructed in 2018, from the Moutière chair-lift to Place Caron in the heart of the resort.

The sports centre is open 10-to-10, with a wide range of features including pools and fitness rooms. Other diversions include snowmobiling, ice driving, footpaths and snowshoe routes, dog sledding and ice diving in the Lac du Lou. There are footpaths up into the slopes, but for cross-country loops you need to head down-valley.

For families

Provided you pick your spot, you can keep away from traffic and close to snow. The ski schools operate snow gardens, and the main nursery slopes are good. There are lots of things to do, though they have non-trivial costs.

The Orelle option

In the 1990s, the commune of Orelle, in the long, deep Maurienne valley to the south of the 3 Vallées, found itself with hydro-electric pay-offs sufficient to build a huge gondola. So it built one almost 5km long up to Plan Bouchet, with chair-lifts above it linking to Val Thorens and serving sunny slopes beneath the high-point of the 3V. No attempt was made to create a piste down to the resort.

Three categories of visitor planning to ski Val Tho might profitably look into staying in Orelle: those who can't stomach the prices even in Les Menuires; those who want to avoid the long drive up the Belleville valley from Moûtiers; and those who fancy exploring other Maurienne resorts (check out our chapters on the Maurienne valley and Val Cenis).

For exploration of the whole 3V, Orelle is far from an ideal base; but it can be done, and you can be skiing Val Thorens more quickly from here than from Méribel Centre or Courchevel.

Orelle is made up of several hamlets, some of which offer simple lodgings. At the lift base is the micro-resort of Francoz, with the bare necessities of life – a ski shop, a branch of the ESF (plus a guiding group, Maurienne Hors Piste) and a snack bar. The main lodgings are in a big apartment residence a shuttle-ride away from the lift base. We believe it has a spa, a food shop and a restaurant, but check.

There are big car parks, for day trippers from Grenoble and Turin. The result can be queues for the gondola down, especially on fine weekends.

Alpe-d'Huez

Alpe-d'Huez / Vaujany / Oz / Auris / Villard-Reculas

Alpe-d'Huez is the one southern resort that offers some direct competition to the mega-resorts of the Tarentaise region further north. It's big and high, with a good lift system. But it's also very unusual in having a lot of very sunny slopes, which reduces the area's appeal as the season wears on.

The village looks a bit of a mess, and feels neither purpose-built (which it mainly is) nor rooted in tradition, but it's not an unpleasant place to inhabit, and it offers a good range of lodging options.

The smaller satellite villages dotted around the fringes of the area range widely in scale and style, from the quite grown-up resort of Vaujany to the minuscule Villard-Reculas.

The mountains in brief

Size Big enough for most purposes, with other options on the lift pass

Slopes High, open and varied, with some great long runs to be done

Snow A distinct drawback: a lot of the slopes face the strong southern sun

System, Lift Works pretty well, and the remaining slow lifts are marginal

Sustenance As high, keen skiers' resorts go, an excellent choice

For beginners One of the best, though we quibble over the lift pass

For true blue skiers Lots to do, but you have to plan your days with care

For the confident Some excellent long runs, but you may thirst for more

For experts Rewarding black runs, and some classic off-piste descents

Fancy stuff An impressive park immediately above the village

Alpe-d'Huez – the resort in brief

Convenience For a purpose-built resort, not great; choose location carefully

Lodgings More or less every type and standard you might want

Bars and restaurants A good range of both, with après starting on the hill

Off the slopes A complete range of activities, indoor and out

For families Works well for young families, if you pick your spot with care

Pass notes

A six-day pass covers two days in Les Deux-Alpes, plus days in Serre-Chevalier, Puy-St-Vincent and Montgenèvre.
For beginners there are some short free lifts and a half-price day pass for some slightly longer ones accessing green runs.

Key facts

Altitude	1720–1860m
Range	1120–3320m
Slopes (see text)	180km

Where to stay, ideally

On the fringes of AdH, close to snow. Or close to the cable car in Vaujany.

Websites

alpedhuez.com
vaujany.com
oz-en-oisans.com
auris-en-oisans.fr

Key ratings

Size	****
Snow	***
Fast lifts	****
Mountain rest's	****
Beginner	*****
True blue	****
Confident	****
Expert	****
Convenience	***
Families	****
Village charm	**

The mountains in detail

It's quite a complex area. Alpe-d'Huez sits in the pit of a wide, sunny bowl, with lifts rising gently to several points 300–500m above it – rather less gently in the case of Signal, on the back of which is tiny Villard-Reculas. Outside the bowl are shady runs down to two more substantial satellite resorts, Vaujany and Oz; and from Alpette, in the middle of that sector, a huge cable car rises to the Dôme des Rousses, for most visitors the high-point of the area at 2800m.

The slightly lower shoulder of the Dôme is also reachable by the big DMC gondola from the top of the village. From there, a smaller cable car accesses the real high-point, Pic Blanc, the start of some famous black runs, also reachable via the top stage of a gondola from Clocher de Macle. Detached from all of this, across the steep-sided Sarenne gorge, is the skiing on Signal de l'Homme, and beyond that the mini-resort of Auris.

Size

Alpe-d'Huez Grand Domaine Ski, to employ the ludicrous brand the area adopted a few years back, prefers to focus on area rather than length of runs these days. It claims 10,000 hectares 'to be explored', which is an area 10km square – ie the size of the whole massif. The skiable area is a more modest 840ha. A length claim occasionally surfaces, though: 250km of runs. This would put the area ahead of Val d'Isère-Tignes, and looks an optimistic figure. The Schrahe report puts it at a more reasonable 180km. This is still a big area, but it only just scrapes into our 4-star size category.

If you doubt that's enough, note that a six-day pass covers other resorts (read 'Pass notes') including Les Deux-Alpes. It is only 10km away as the chopper flies, and on certain days helicopter transfers operate – a great adventure, in 2018 reasonably priced at 70€ (return).

Slopes

This really is a resort for everyone, with terrain from the blissfully flattering to seriously challenging.

With the resort at about 1800m, it's no surprise that its slopes are essentially treeless; there are some trees above the resort, and areas of forest above Oz and Vaujany, but they don't offer much scope for sheltered skiing in practice. The black run La Fuma on Signal de l'Homme is about the best spot for laps in trees.

There are some good long runs to be done. The black Sarenne run from Pic Blanc down into the gorge between the village and Signal de l'Homme is rightly famous, but its claimed length of 16km is an exaggeration. Our own measurement on topo maps came to about 10km and Christoph Schrahe's more sophisticated measurement is 10.5km. Still impressive and, with a vertical of about 1800m, a run not to be missed.

In the right conditions and with the necessary bottle, a descent of the bumpy Sarenne black piste on the front of Pic Blanc can lead to a run of about 2200m vertical to L'Enversin d'Oz, below Vaujany. This on-piste vertical is exceeded in the Alps only by the run to Mont-de-Lans at Les Deux-Alpes, nearby.

From the other high lift stations of Dôme des Rousses and Clocher de Macle, at 2800m, there are a few runs of 1000m vertical to the village, and longer ones to Oz, La Villette and L'Enversin.

There's night skiing twice a week on Signal, free with a six-day ski pass.

Snow

The area gets decent amounts of snow, but the south-west orientation of many slopes – coupled with a sunny weather record and southerly latitude – means that as the season progresses the snow conditions become less and less reliable. Heavy snow or slush develops in the afternoon, and rock-hard ice overnight. The problem is most acute on the steeper slopes, because they get the full force of the sun. (In spring the optimum angle for solar panels at this latitude is about 40° – an extremely steep black run.)

The runs towards Oz and Vaujany, facing roughly north-west, don't have this problem, but they don't add up to a lot of skiing, and they get a lot of traffic. The best place to go when the snow is sun-affected is Signal de l'Homme, on its north and east aspects.

On Pic Blanc there is a chair-lift called Glacier, and a short black run ditto. But there is very little glacier left these days.

System, Lift

The lift system is pretty efficient, with powerful, fast lifts in the key positions. You can hit queues at peak times, but most shift quickly enough. The main bottlenecks arise when snow low down is poor, and demand rises for the Pic Blanc cable car and the two slow chairs on the very high slopes it takes you to.

There are some slow chair-lifts dotted

The resort sits on a huge sunny shelf beneath Pic Blanc, with the slopes spreading in all directions

around the main slopes too, but they are mainly on the fringes of the area; the main irritant is the fairly central Lièvre Blanc.

Our main complaints about the mountain are more to do with crowded pistes than with over-busy lifts. The runs here include some of the most unpleasantly congested we've found.

The Eclose and Bergers chair-lifts on the lower edge of the village are being replaced in 2018 by a 10-seat gondola.

Sustenance

For a high, modern, middle-market resort, Alpe-d'Huez has very good mountain restaurants.

In the main area above the village (actually slightly outside it, on the cross-country trails running across to Alpette), an old favourite is the Chalet du Lac Besson – cosy, calm and welcoming, with excellent food and service. The Folie Douce, like its siblings, has a good restaurant, La Fruitière.

Further afield, our standard ports of call are: above Villard-Reculas, the woody Bergerie; at the end of the Sarenne run, the rustic Combe Haute; at Le Châtelard, below Signal de l'Homme, the little Forêt de Maronne hotel; on the way to Vaujany, the unpretentious Auberge de l'Alpette and, further down, the Airelles, built into the rock of the mountainside.

More on the slopes

For beginners

At the main lift base the Grenouilles carpet-lift and Petit Ecole drag-lift are free, as is the Petit Rifnel drag-lift at the Bergers lift base. These are both good places to start, with gentle slopes.

A glance at the piste map shows the striking quantity of green-run skiing directly above the village, and it is all genuinely green – so progress from the nursery slopes is easy. You can buy a half-price day pass covering longer lifts on these slopes – fine in principle, but the lifts concerned go only halfway up the home slopes, which strikes us as rather mean. The pass should cover the longer lifts to the mid-station of the DMC gondola and to Signal, we reckon.

For true blue skiers

There's no problem in re-building your confidence from last year here – there are easy blues beside the expanse of greens above the village, and the purple Marcel from Signal is of blue gradient.

But then, things get a bit more complicated. The first thing to think about is snow conditions: steeper slopes get more affected by the sun.

Then, there's the degree of difficulty. You should be OK on the top of Signal, but don't be tempted to ride the top section of the DMC to 2700m until you are feeling properly confident – the Couloir blue is quite tough, it gets very crowded, and it's long.

You'll need confidence, also, to ski to Oz and via there to Montfrais above Vaujany, where there are some nice cruisey blues. The route involves an easy red stretch to a point near the mid-station of the Poutran gondola; ride the short Champ Clotury drag up to the station, for access to the lovely, gentle Champclotury blue run to Oz for the gondola to Alpette and good blue runs to Montfrais.

The runs over on Signal de l'Homme don't pose any real difficulties, and have the attraction of good snow (they're shady) and a lack of crowds. But be warned: you get to them by riding a chair-lift that plunges down into the Sarenne gorge before rising up to the slopes.

For confident intermediates

This is a curious area for the keen, confident intermediate. There are some cracking red runs, but they don't add up to a huge amount of skiing. Of the available 180km of runs, we'd guess no more than a quarter, 45km, are red.

The two epic 1450m-vertical descents from Dôme des Rousses to Oz are favourites – Belvédère, Bartavelles and Alpette, or Dôme, Chamois, Poutran and Olmet. (But be warned: the section of Bartavelles that combines with Rousses can be uncomfortably busy, while the latter descent has a weak spot in Chamois, which is too sunny and too narrow/busy for comfort.)

Déversoir from Clocher de Macle is rewarding; and the short, sharp reds below it, served by the Lièvre Blanc chair, are pretty tough, verging on black. There are other worthwhile reds over on the Fontfroide chair on Signal de l'Homme.

For experts

There are some excellent black pistes here. The trouble is, they get a lot of sun.

Pic Blanc is the start of two iconic runs. As explained above, the famously long Sarenne run is not actually as long as the resort makes out, and it is very much a run of two halves, with a long run-out down the Sarenne valley that is nearly flat. The first half, facing south, has steepish pitches that justify the classification, and it adds up to a very rewarding run; apart from all else, it offers splendid views of the Meije massif. Then there is the Tunnel run on the front face under the cable car, reached as you might guess by a long tunnel through the mountain. This is a proper steep black, but its difficulty depends on the snow conditions (it faces west) and the bumps at the very start. Seek local advice if in doubt.

Lower down, there are some worthwhile runs in the Clocher de Macle sector, notably Combe Charbonnière: after a traverse across a steepish slope, this descends a beautiful lonely bowl before turning towards the resort. The two short blacks from the same point are worth a look – Balcons is a proper black, and facing north-west often has good snow. Clocher de Macle is less steep, busier and sunnier. Below them, La Balme is worth a look, though less special than the parallel Combe Charbonnière.

The main short black runs on Signal and Signal de l'Homme are branded as freeride zones; this presumably means they are not groomed, but they are not alone in that respect. Over at Vaujany, the low, sunny Fare run to L'Enversin relies heavily on artificial snow but is a good, varied run, well away from the lifts.

There is also a lot to do off-piste. You might warm up with the slopes on the back of Signal, above Villard-Reculas – some good terrain, with the option of heading instead for the lift station in Huez. There is also a lot of available terrain on Signal de l'Homme, including the sunny descent to Chapelle-St-Giraud, across the mountainside from Auris.

But mighty Pic Blanc beckons. The classic introductory run from here is the Combe du Loup, to skier's left of the Chateau Noir piste; there's a genuinely steep pitch soon after the start, but it's otherwise not difficult. On skier's right are more challenging routes towards the resort – Col de l'Herpie and the couloirs known as the Cheminées de Mascle.

Going north instead, about 1km from PIc Blanc is the slightly higher Pic de

The resort is no beauty; in the distance, Les Deux-Alpes (complete with glacier) and La Meije

la Pyramide and beyond that Col de la Pyramide, start of a classic, serious 2000m descent to the pistes of Vaujany. On the lower half of this run there are multiple options that can alternatively be tackled from the lower starting point of Dôme des Rousses.

Heading east instead of north and west from Pic Blanc you have another classic run – the 2000m descent starting on the Glacier du Grand Sablat and ending at Clavans, for a taxi back to Auris (or a chopper ride back to AdH), or traversing to your right to Col de Sarenne from which point you can ski to lifts.

Fancy stuff

In a great position directly above the village, served by multiple lifts, is the big snow park, with lines of differing difficulty and lots of features including a snowcross course and (last time we were there, at least) a half-pipe. It has a video system, and there's a big air bag at the bottom.

Alpe-d'Huez – the resort

Like so many French resorts, Alpe-d'Huez expanded to meet demand by throwing up buildings at minimum cost, but more recently it has joined the twin trends towards traditional building styles and smart upmarket lodgings. The first is to be welcomed, even if you can't afford the second.

Convenience

It's a mid-sized resort – the main part a densely developed triangle measuring about 1km on each side. Three quartiers are identified within this – Vieil Alpe at bottom left corner, Jeux bottom right and Cognet at the top, where the main lift base is located. Then there are four outlying districts adjacent to Jeux, the biggest of which is Bergers, with the secondary lift base.

There are plenty of lodgings close to snow, but also plenty that are not at all close – although this is a resort developed for skiing, and is on a sloping site, it hasn't been planned for the convenience of skiers. One piste runs through Vieil Alpe, which helps, and a bucket-lift runs slowly back up to the top lift base. Navettes run on two routes around the main village, one of them also serving the Bergers district; a third route runs down the hill to Huez.

Lodgings

There's a good range of options, including plenty of chalets to rent.

The dozen hotels are mainly 3-star; of these the Petit Prince is said to be excellent value for money. But like so many French resorts this one has edged upmarket; it now has a 5-star hotel, thanks to the elevation of the family-oriented Chamois d'Or – and this is to be joined at the end of 2018 by the new Daria-I Nor. The 4-star Grandes Rousses is recently renovated and has a brilliant spa.

There are plenty of catered chalets to be had, both from major operators and smaller ones. Crystal's quartet includes one that is awarded its 'Finest' label. Inghams has a chalet hotel here.

In addition to the self-catering options below, Lagrange now operates the Alpenrose hotel as an apartment residence.

Bars and restaurants

This is one of the handful of French resorts that now has an Austrian-style on-mountain après-ski scene, thanks to the local branch at mid-mountain of the famous Folie Douce chain. Table dancing mandatory, unfortunately.

There are countless bars in the town; ones to check out include the Brit-run Underground and Smithy's Tavern, the rum-focused Etalon, Free Ride Cafe and O'Sharkey's – typical Irish bar with screens and games tables.

There are plenty of restaurants, of all kinds. Smithy's is good for casual stuff. A strong candidate for best-in-town is the Chamois d'Or in the eponymous 5-star hotel – superb food, beautiful modern chalet decor. Our roving reporter had her best meal of a short visit at the Espérance in the hotel Grandes Rousses.

Of more modest places, we like the Grenier, the Passe Montagne – a characterful old chalet doing all the old favourites – and the P'tit Creux. The Empreinte, new in 2018, is already getting good reports.

The resort website now lists just one nightclub, Les Caves de l'Alpe; but we believe the Igloo is still going, too.

Off the slopes

The sports centre in the middle of the village offers an impressive range of facilities – indoor and outdoor pools, a big outdoor ice rink, climbing walls, fitness and various ball sports.

The DMC gondola accesses a toboggan run, roughly 2km long and dropping about 250m – designed for fun, with banked curves; free with the ski pass.

The Alpine Coaster is a sled-on-rails, new for 2018, with the bizarre feature that you can rent VR headsets so that what you see is unrelated to what you experience. Enjoy.

Other activities include dog sledding, ice driving and snowmobiling. The widely distributed cross-country loops and cleared paths are extensive and include a lovely quiet area around Lac Besson, beneath Dôme des Rousses.

For families

It's not difficult to find lodgings away from traffic and close to snow, and the range of non-skiing activities is appealing. Two pistes above the village – the very easy Chez Roger and the slightly less easy Marcel – are fun runs dotted with features such as banked turns and tunnels.

Alternatives to Alpe-d'Huez

You have quite a range of alternative bases to consider. Vaujany is a much-expanded old village, detached from the skiing but with a huge cable car to the heart of it. Oz and Auris are small, purpose-built ski stations with some slope-side lodgings – good for families. Just over the minor peak that rises next to the village of Alpe-d'Huez, Villard-Reculas is probably the smallest, quietest resort in these pages. It won't suit everyone, but it might suit you.

Vaujany 1230m

Vaujany is a small farming village that became a ski resort in the late 80s by using income from new hydro-electric dams to finance lifts on the gentle slopes of Montfrais, across the valley, and a gondola to get to them. But its real breakthrough came in 1990 with the opening of an ostentatiously big cable car, crossing the valley and rising 1550m in two stages to the Dôme des Rousses, at the heart of the Alpe-d'Huez ski area.

There are no pistes directly to the village; from Montfrais you can ski a pretty blue run to the mid-station of the gondola at La Villette, to ride the lower stage down. Or from the top of the Montfrais road you can descend the Fare black piste to L'Enversin to ride a short gondola up to the village. There are good nursery slopes at Montfrais, used mainly for children apparently, and at the mid-station of the cable car, Alpette. Lift passes are needed; a local one is available for the

Oz/Vaujany slopes, quite a bit cheaper than the main area pass. Montfrais also offers a fun snow park. At Alpette, at the mid-station of the cable car, paths and cross-country trails go across the mountain shelf towards Alpe-d'Huez.

Of course, the village has developed in many ways. It faces south on quite a steep slope. Above the lift base, close to the old heart of the village, there is now a small pedestrian square with shops, restaurants and new apartments. Below, reached by lift, is an impressively large sports centre with a pool, indoor ice rink, fitness room and bowling. Further up the hill is a second commercial centre, Place de la Fare, surrounded by most of the apartment residences; there are escalators to help you get up there. All in all, there are about eight bar-restaurants.

In the lower part of the village, the Cimes hotel is a fine old spot. There are lots of apartments; nothing stands out, but the 3-star Crystal Blanc is a least fairly new, and has a pool and spa. There are a few catered chalets.

Oz-en-Oisans Station 1350m

Oz Station, the mountain outpost of the village of Oz, is a small, traditionally styled purpose-built resort a lift and a run away from Alpe-d'Huez, in an attractively wooded setting. It's much less of a village than Vaujany, but has all that you need – a handful of bar-restaurants, ditto grocery and food shops.

A lot of the lodgings are on or close to the snow. There's a good nursery slope with a free carpet-lift, also serving a sledging slope, and two short drag-lifts serving green runs. A pass is available for the Oz/Vaujany slopes, quite a bit cheaper than the main area pass.

The funky Moontain Hostel is supposedly a new concept in mountain lodgings. The Chalet des Neiges residence has a pool and spa facilities. There are one or two catered chalets.

The good pool at the holiday 'village' Les Cristaux is open to all, and the tourist office has a climbing wall. There is at least one local woodland walk, and the paths and cross-country trails between Alpette and Alpe-d'Huez can be reached via either gondola.

Auris-en-Oisans 1600m

Auris-en-Oisans is a purpose-built ski station consisting of a few chalet-style apartment blocks spread over a lightly wooded sloping site, 300m and several hairpins up the hill from the somewhat diffuse village of Auris. It offers the necessities of life – two or three shops, a handful of bar-restaurants. The Beau Site is a small, central 2-star hotel. Les Balcons d'Auréa is a 4-star apartment residence with pool and spa, built in 2015, in a ski-in/ski-out location.

The resort suits young families well, with direct access to the snow from many lodgings; there's a sledging slope at the lift base.

The good nursery slope has a free carpet-lift, and there is a cheap beginners' day pass covering three longer local lifts, including the Sures chair-lift; this accesses a long family fun run of blue steepness back to the village. A pass for the whole Signal de l'Homme is available, much cheaper than the main area pass.

Villard-Reculas 1500m

Just over the hill from Alpe-d'Huez, Villard-Reculas is the smallest, least ski-resorty resort we have come across. Life revolves around the one village store/bar/restaurant at the lift base. The only hotel is closed, awaiting resuscitation. Some simple apartments are available to rent.

The village is set on a shelf where the open snowfields of Signal meet the steeper forested slopes below. There are two roads in, one being a narrow, slightly scary traverse from Alpe-d'Huez which is a bit prone to avalanche closure. Small though the village is, some of its chalets are 400m from the lift base and the little shuttle-bus does not lack customers.

To judge by the piste map, this would seem to be a good spot for beginners, but it is not. The green runs at village level are of blue gradient – and the home run from Signal is not the easiest of blue runs. With one of the world's great beginner resorts over the hill, to start here would be perverse.

Annecy Mountains

La Clusaz / Le Grand-Bornand / St-Jean-de-Sixt

These resorts are about 20km (as the eagle flies) east of Annecy, right on the edge of the Alps – in fact, a geographer would put them in the 'prealps', a region distinct from the Alps proper.

La Clusaz sits in a narrow valley beneath the very scenic Aravis mountain range. It is one of the most captivating French villages, rivalling Megève, although it is much smaller and less smart – the resort has recently acquired its first 5-star hotel, but frankly it seems a bit out of place. There are major lifts only yards from the rustic central square.

Le Grand-Bornand is ten minutes away but adds some worthwhile additional skiing – worth a day trip or two during your week.

The mountains in brief

Size On the small side, but nearby Le Grand-Bornand gives a decent boost

Slopes Nicely varied, with lots of woodland as well as open slopes

Snow Gets a lot of weather – good news if it's cold, not if it's not

System, Lift The central flaw: you'll spend most of your days on slow lifts

Sustenance Adequate in general, with a row of good options on L'Aiguille

For beginners A superb high-altitude area of slopes, but a poor pass deal

For true blue skiers You can get around the whole very scenic area

For the confident Some excellent runs, all rather spoilt by slow lifts

For experts Splendid off-piste opportunities when the snow is right

Fancy stuff A good-sized park, and excellent beginner park

La Clusaz – the resort in brief

Convenience Not great in general, but skiing to the door is possible

Lodgings Plenty of mid-market options, with upscale options widening

Bars and restaurants A good range of places, some on the mountain

Off the slopes Lacks a proper toboggan run; top-notch cross-country trails

For families We'd be tempted to stay at altitude

Pass notes

The Aravis pass, covering Le Grand-Bornand as well as La Clusaz, costs very little more than a local La Clusaz pass. Beginners need a lift pass from the start. Regrettably, there are no special passes for beginners, except children in ESF classes.

Key facts

Altitude	1030m
Range	930–2477m
Slopes (see text)	162km

Where to stay, **ideally**
In the heart of La Clusaz, a walk from the main lifts.

Websites
laclusaz.com
legrandbornand.com
saintjeandesixt.com
annecymountains.com

Key ratings

Size	***
Snow	***
Fast lifts	**
Mountain rest's	***
Beginner	****
True blue	****
Confident	****
Expert	****
Convenience	**
Families	***
Village charm	****

The mountains in detail

Although not huge in extent, the mountains of La Clusaz are split into five distinct sectors, four of them arranged in a ring, fully linked for skiing anti-clockwise and partially clockwise. A gondola from the village centre goes up to a great beginner area on Beauregard; easy runs go south from there to the Manigod sector, linked both ways by blue runs to L'Etale; and a cross-valley cable car links this with L'Aiguille, also reached directly from the village by fast chair-lift. The fifth and highest sector, Balme, is out on a limb, but with lift and piste links with L'Aiguille.

The slopes of Le Grand-Bornand are a bus ride away, and much simpler. Lifts from the edge of the village go up to two mid-mountain beginner areas, and on to the peak of Mont Lachat and to lower La Floria at its shoulder. This is also accessible from the satellite village of Le Chinaillon.

Size

La Clusaz's website majors on a figure of 125km allowing for 'necessary turns', but also reveals that proper measurement gives a figure of 96km. That puts the area towards the top of our 2-star category. With the 63km of Le Grand-Bornand, you get a total of 162km, putting the region as a whole at the top of our 3-star category.

Slopes

Variety is the key word, in terms of steepness, in particular. Naturally, at this altitude there is a lot of woodland, but the higher sectors also have many open slopes. Le Grand-Bornand has less woodland skiing than you might expect.

The low altitude of the villages allows some big verticals. The biggest are from Col de Balme – 1200m to the gondola lift base. Le Grand-Bornand makes a lot of fuss about its famous Denivel'Maxx – 1100m from top to bottom. You could put together some quite long runs incorporating the blue or the green from Balme to the village, should you wish to.

The eponymous red piste at the top of L'Aiguille is a proper red, though it perhaps looks steeper than it is

Snow

The area's position in the prealps means that westerly weather can dump a lot of snow, on the upper slopes at least; but it can also bring rain, particularly on the lower slopes. So conditions can be fabulous, but aren't reliably so, despite good snowmaking. The slopes vary quite widely in orientation: many face roughly north, including the high runs at Balme. But some of the runs on L'Aiguille face west, or even south-west – bad news.

System, Lift

There are fasts lifts out of all the valley lift stations, but above that practically everything is slow. (Actually, the mile-long Combe de Juments chair-lift is a detachable double, but runs at half the speed of a modern lift; with its cosy padded sofa seats, it seems to have been designed more for cuddling than speedy uplift.) When doing laps on L'Aiguille and Balme the lack of speed is irritating – the Col de Balme quad is a 15-minute ride.

In Le Grand-Bornand, things are a bit better. As well as gondolas out of the village and one fast six-seat chair out of Le Chinaillon, there are two other six-packs on the hill. But there is also a lot of terrain served by slow chairs.

The pace of change is just too slow. The last replacement of a slow lift in La Clusaz was in 2014.

Naturally, we saw no sign of queues during our recent January visit, and we lack information on how things work at busier times. The area is close to Geneva and Annecy, and in the past it was always day-trip invasions on fine weekends that presented problems.

Sustenance

On L'Aiguille, above the village, you have the widest range of good options: the Relais up at Crêt du Loup, Chez Arthur, the Bercail, the Chalet des Praz, the Vieux Chalet – all decent places. At Balme, the Bergerie is unremarkable. On Beauregard and in the Manigod sector, there are hotel restaurants.

At Le Grand-Bornand, the Terres Rouges above the terrain park is an excellent spot with great views of the Chaîne des Aravis. The Chalet du Maroly does a good job, too. Beginners are well catered for, with a choice of eateries at the Alpage Express area.

More on the slopes

For beginners

There are beginner lifts at village level and at Crêt du Merle at mid-mountain on L'Aiguille, but one of the standout features of La Clusaz is the glorious beginner area at the top of Beauregard – gentle, sunny and extensive, with good snow (usually).

There are no special passes for beginners, except for children attending an Ecole du Ski Français class. This is unusual, and very regrettable.

There are no long green runs, apart from the link from the Balme lift base to the village, but there are easy blues.

For true blue skiers

It's a fair area for building confidence, with few surprises, but the main sector you'll be drawn to is the rather remote Massif de Manigod, supplemented by the fine, wide Joux blue on L'Etale. You can reach Manigod via a blue run from Beauregard, but the run is a bit narrow in parts. The other way is by bus from the village. The blue to the village from Beauregard is a nice run, but a tad steep at the end.

On L'Aiguille, the Dahu from Crêt du Loup is a good middling blue, but the home slope, although correctly classified blue, is not an easy one.

Balme has a nice varied run (Bergerie) at mid-mountain. Below that, Balme to the bottom has some tricky stretches. The 3km Plan blue to the village is steep enough to build up speed a bit; if that doesn't appeal, take the green.

Le Grand-Bornand has plenty of blue skiing, and many long green runs.

For confident intermediates

Within its modest total extent, La Clusaz has lots of good terrain for a competent skier, with worthwhile genuine red runs in all sectors. Highlights include Régine Cavagnoud (named after a local hero) on L'Etale, the top slope on L'Aiguille and the lovely Fernuy below it – once you're past the tedious ledge forming the top part. But the biscuit is taken by the Balme sector – good runs, good snow, good vibe, good chances to play off-piste a bit.

Do bear in mind, though, that all these runs except Fernuy are served by slow lifts – which is one factor that might encourage outings to Le Grand-Bornand.

CHAINE DES ARAVIS
COL DE BALME
2616m
MASSIF DE L'AIGUILLE
2400 m
MASSIF DE L'ETALE
2400 m
ETE DES ANNES
1869 m
COL DES ARAVIS
Vers la vallée
du Mont Blanc
COL DE
MERDASSIER
COL DES ANNES
Lac des Confins
MONT LACHAT
2100 m
MANIGOD
Vallée du Bouchet
LA FLORIA
1800 m
COL DE LA CROIX FRY
Vers Thones / Annecy
par Man god Village
MASSIF DE BEAUREGARD
1690 m
La Clusaz
Vallée du Maroly
col de la Colombière
LE CHINAILLON
LE GRAND BORNAND
ST-JEAN DE SIXT
Vers Thones / Annecy
Ski alpin / Downhill Ski
Ski nordique / Cross country ski
Ski de randonnée / Ski touring
Espace Débutant / Beginner area
Parapente / Paragliding
Freestyle
Piste de luge / Sledge area
Télésiège / Chairlift
Télécabine / Gondolas
Informations
Skibus inter stations
Parking / Parking lots
Secours / Rescue center
REALISATION
Kaleïs
+33 6 83 55 01 35
DONNEES SIG
SAVOIE MONT BLANC

For experts

Short stretches apart, La Clusaz offers only four black runs – one on each of the more serious mountains. La Noire, winding prettily through the woods on Beauregard, has a black stretch in the middle, and Le Tétras on L'Etale has one pitch near the top. Lapiaz on L'Aiguille offers a more sustained challenge, and is properly steep at the top. Vraille on Balme also has good testing sections.

The real appeal for experts, though, lies off-piste. There are routes to be found between the pistes in every sector – on L'Etale, for example, down to the Col de Merdassier pistes. But it's the Aiguille and Balme sectors that hold the aces.

Both combes of the Balme sector, Balme and Torchère, are broad bowls with huge amounts of off-piste terrain outside the two or three pistes. With some hiking to skier's right of Balme, you can access the Combe de la Bella Cha, down to Les Confins. From the Torchère drag with some climbing you can cross over to the south side of the ridge and back over the Porte des Aravis into the Combe de la Creuse.

From the top of L'Aiguille you have access to the west-facing Combe de Borderan. Or you can hike up to the Col la Lana, which leads into the Combe de la Creuse. Lower down, from Côte 2000 and Crêt du Loup there are multiple ways down into the woods of the Combe du Voret or Bois de la Motte.

The whole Aravis range is very popular ski touring terrain, with a long row of snow-filled shady bowls beyond the handful reachable from lifts. These are easily inspected from the top of the slopes at Le Grand-Bornand, which has its own attractions.

On Mont Lachat, the ungroomed Freeride run is genuinely black at the top, and there's a short, sharp black on the upper front face; but the lower Pylones is steep only briefly. There's plenty of accessible off-piste terrain within the lift network, and long, pretty descents outside it to the south, towards the hamlet of Les Plans.

Fancy stuff

The 500m-long LCZ Park is at mid-mountain on L'Aiguille, with features arranged in intermediate, confirmed and expert lines. The LCZ Family Run next door has features in two easy lines either side of the P'tit Loup green run – one for absolute beginners.

Le Grand-Bornand's Snowparkgb is claimed to be among the top ten parks in France. It's 700m long, covers 5ha (over 12 acres), has four lines and some seriously big kickers. There's a big airbag at the bottom, and a boardercross down one side. But it's inconveniently located at the very far end of the ski area, on the Prarian drag-lifts.

A rarity in France: a valley village that has become a major ski resort while retaining its charm intact

La Clusaz – the resort

La Clusaz is a rarity in France – a sizeable resort that retains the ambience of its mountain village origins, notably in the nearly traffic-free Place de l'Eglise, complete with fine stone bell tower.

Convenience

The core is very compact – the main lifts start a short walk from the church square. But it's a resort of two halves, with hotels, shops and restaurants in both halves. A road from the centre leads 250m uphill to meet the bypass road leading to the Col des Aravis; beyond that point is a one-way system which forms the second half of the village. This too is about 250m end to end. The resort spreads widely along the valleys; buses run to all parts.

Lodgings

There are over 20 hotels, practically all 2-star or 3-star. The new 5-star Coeur du Village is indeed in the *coeur du village*. On our last visit we stayed happily in the 2-star Montagne, and we have enjoyed the 3-star Christiania. There are several 4-star places, a couple on the snow; new in 2018 is the St-Alban in 'English club' style. Beginners should note the two simple places at the top of Beauregard – Altitude 1647 and La Piste Bleue.

Bars and restaurants

The mid-January timing of our recent visit wasn't ideal for appraisal of the après scene, but La Clusaz has a good reputation for evening animation. L'Aiguille is the hill to end the day on, with a series of potential pit-stops starting with the lively terrace of the Relais de l'Aiguille at Crêt du Loup. In the village, the Caves du Paccaly is popular; the Salto, the Pressoir and the Grenier, among many other options, get good reports.

There's a good range of restaurants. The Scierie in the upper village is cool but quite pricey; we enjoyed our cheaper dinner at the nearby Fruitière, doing proper cooking as well as Savoyarde stuff. The Vieux Chalet and Chalet des Praz, both on the lower slopes but reachable by road, are among the best. The Ourson gets a toque from the Gault-Millau guide.

Off the slopes

The Aravis Aquatics Centre is an excellent facility, with indoor leisure pool and an outdoor pool including lanes, plus a fun pool for kids and a paddling pool for toddlers; there's a hot tub, a spa and fitness rooms. There's a fair-sized indoor ice rink close to the centre. A four-lane bowling alley was created in 2017.

There's no proper toboggan run – a disappointment in an otherwise well-equipped resort (but read 'For families'). This area is one of the best for cross-country: around Les Confins (at about 1400–1600m), up the valley to the north-east, there are 50km of trails and a link to Le Grand-Bornand, while up at Beauregard there are another 35km at slightly higher altitudes. There are 30km of cleared footpaths, and snowshoe outings are organised. Dog sledding is available, and various equine activities.

For families

There's a sledging area for infants next to the main lift base in the centre of the village, and a longer and steeper one for kids over six at the Nant drag-lift just outside the village.

Alternatives to La Clusaz

We don't see any pressing reason to stay anywhere other than downtown La Clusaz, unless you are set on spending a lot of time skiing the Manigod sector or at Le Grand-Bornand. But they are all pleasant spots. The two cols are peaceful, of course, and we presume St-Jean is economical.

Col de la Croix Fry 1467m

The Col de la Croix Fry is a pass on a back-road route from La Clusaz to Thones. More importantly, it's where you arrive if you ski south off the back of Beauregard to the Massif de Manigod. There's a choice of two good 4-star hotels, both run by the owning families for several generations. The Sapins is right on the snow, and suits families well. The Chalet Hotel de la Croix Fry has a well-regarded restaurant, but is about 2km down from the pass towards Manigod. In Manigod itself is the famous multi-starred restaurant of Marc Veyrat.

Col de Merdassier 1500m

The Col de Merdassier is a pass on a very minor road going nowhere much, in the middle of the Manigod sector of slopes. There are apartment residences on the slopes, but they don't seem to appear on the UK market. On the south side of the col, at the base of the most southerly lifts, is the six-room 3-star hotel la Vielle Ferme.

St-Jean-de-Sixt 960m

St-Jean is midway between La Clusaz and Le Grand-Bornand, a five-minute drive from both. There's a regular shuttle bus service. The village has its own beginner slopes nearby, plus sledging. There are chalets and apartments to rent, and one 3-star hotel, the Beau Site.

Le Grand-Bornand 930m

Le Grand-Bornand spreads up the sunny side of the valley of the Borne, above a curving main street about 1km long, with a centre of activity around the church half-way along, and the lift base at the far end, with gondolas up to two beginner areas.

A road winds up from the village centre to a second lift base below the satellite village of Le Chinaillon (about 1260m) – actually, two lift bases 750m apart. The first has slow lifts serving easy runs, the second a fast six-seat chair serving more challenging slopes on La Floria, with links to the rest of the ski area from there.

The nursery slopes are at the top of both gondolas from Le Grand-Bornand, the larger one a good slope centred on the 230m Alpage Express carpet lift. There are small beginner areas at both lift bases in Le Chinaillon. Long green runs criss-cross the lower mountain – amazingly, you can get around the whole area on green. The skiing as a whole is described under La Clusaz.

There are about a dozen hotels, split between the main village and Le Chinaillon; they're mainly 2-star and 3-star, but there are two 4-stars: Chalet les Saytels in Le Grand-Bornand and the Cimes at Le Chinaillon – a cosy eight-room chalet doing B&B. There are plenty of chalets and apartments to rent. Read 'Pick of the Apartments'. An exceptional standalone chalet is the Ferme de Juliette – a beautiful renovated farmhouse.

There are plenty of bars and restaurants. The Confins des Sens at Villavit, on the southern outskirts of Le Grand-Bornand, is the best around, with two toques from the Gault-Millau guide.

In Le Grand-Bornand there's an aquatic centre with a proper pool plus fun pool, slides etc. The village also has a fair-sized indoor ice rink. There are sledging areas in or near both villages, and on the Alpage Express area at mid-mountain – and the ESF runs weekly 6km descents on ski-bobs at Le Chinaillon. There are cross-country trails up at La Chinaillon and longer ones in (and above) the vallée du Bouchet outside Le Grand-Bornand – you can even ski over to Les Confins near La Clusaz. Dog sledding is available.

Chamonix valley

Chamonix / Argentière / Le Tour / Vallorcine / Les Houches

Chamonix is a lively, historic, characterful town in an incredible setting – literally in the shadow of Mont Blanc, the highest mountain in Europe. It's known for exciting off-piste skiing, but actually offers a good range of options – and its most famous run, the vast Vallée Blanche glacier, can be undertaken with guidance by anyone with basic off-piste competence.

It doesn't suit everybody. The skiing falls in four small, widely separated areas, which can mean a lot of bussing around. And these areas are different in character, so a party of mixed abilities is quite likely to find itself split between them. Far from ideal, you may judge.

But the bottom line is that everyone should give it a try, some day.

The mountains in brief

Size Never mind the width, feel the quality

Slopes Everything from epic glaciers and endless moguls to friendly woods

Snow Good snowfall, but some sectors suffer from sun or low altitude

System, Lift A distressing number of slow chairs and drags remain

Sustenance Hardly a highlight – but a scattering of good places

For beginners Reasonable arrangements in various sectors, but not ideal

For true blue skiers Difficult to recommend – decent runs dotted around

For the confident Plenty to do if you are confident and adventurous

For experts Testing pistes, huge amounts of off-piste from tame to serious

Fancy stuff The biggest park in France, they say

Chamonix – the resort in brief

Convenience Chamonix doesn't really do convenience

Lodgings A good range of hotels, catered chalets and apartments

Bars and restaurants About as good as it gets in the Alps

Off the slopes Great sports centre; no proper toboggan runs though

For families You can have a good holiday here, but it may be hard work

Pass notes
Le Pass covers the main Chamonix areas, but for Les Houches, the top Grands Montets cable car or the Mont Blanc lifts you need the Mont Blanc Unlimited pass also covering Megève, Courmayeur (Italy) and Verbier (Switzerland). Cheap passes are sold for the beginner areas.

Key facts

Altitude	1035m
Range	1035–3840m
Slopes (see text)	173km

Where to stay, ideally
In central Chamonix, or near the lift for your favourite slope sector

Websites
chamonix.com
montblancnaturalresort.com

Key ratings

Size	***
Snow	****
Fast lifts	***
Mountain rest's	***
Beginner	***
True blue	**
Confident	****
Expert	*****
Convenience	*
Families	**
Village charm	****

The mountains in detail

From the edge of downtown Chamonix, a gondola goes up to Le Brévent – two high bowls linked at altitude and on the treeline. A cross-valley cable car links with the more compact area of La Flégère, also accessible via an ancient cable car from Les Praz, a satellite village 2.5km up the valley. These sunny areas give magnificent views of Mont Blanc.

Argentière, 8km up the valley, is at the foot of the Grands Montets, the highest of the piste skiing areas. Another 4km up the valley, above Le Tour, are the lower slopes of Balme – also accessible from remote Vallorcine.

Down the valley, 7km from Chamonix, is Les Houches, at the foot of an area of low wooded slopes that seems out of place here – also reached by rack railway from St-Gervais, in the Megève ski area.

The Mont Blanc road tunnel links Chamonix with Courmayeur in Italy, covered by the Mont Blanc Unlimited lift pass. More than once we have escaped stormy weather here to go skiing in the Italian sunshine.

Size

The resort claims that the main slopes of Balme, Brévent-Flégère and the Grands Montets add up to 118km of pistes. Les Houches claims 55km of pistes, giving a total of 173km. That would put Chamonix right at the top of our 3-star category, along with Serre-Chevalier. We're sceptical about that; we reckon a proper down-the-centre-line measurement would be lower, and close to 2-star territory. We're giving it the benefit of the doubt, and leaving it in the 3-star category.

Slopes

Most of Chamonix's skiing is above the treeline. Each of the higher areas has a single run through woods to the valley, but the south-facing blacks from Brévent and Flégère are notoriously unreliable – not surprisingly. Les Houches is the clear exception, with only a small area of open skiing above the forest, and is the obvious retreat in a blizzard. But also bear in mind Megève, reachable by free buses.

Brévent is a seriously steep hill where even the black runs have to take an indirect route; it does have a spacious balcony at mid-mountain, though. Flégère is a bit less extreme, as is the Grands Montets. Balme is completely different – gloriously gentle, except the very steep slope down to Vallorcine, where the red run cuts across the hillside. Les Houches is essentially an intermediate-gradient hill.

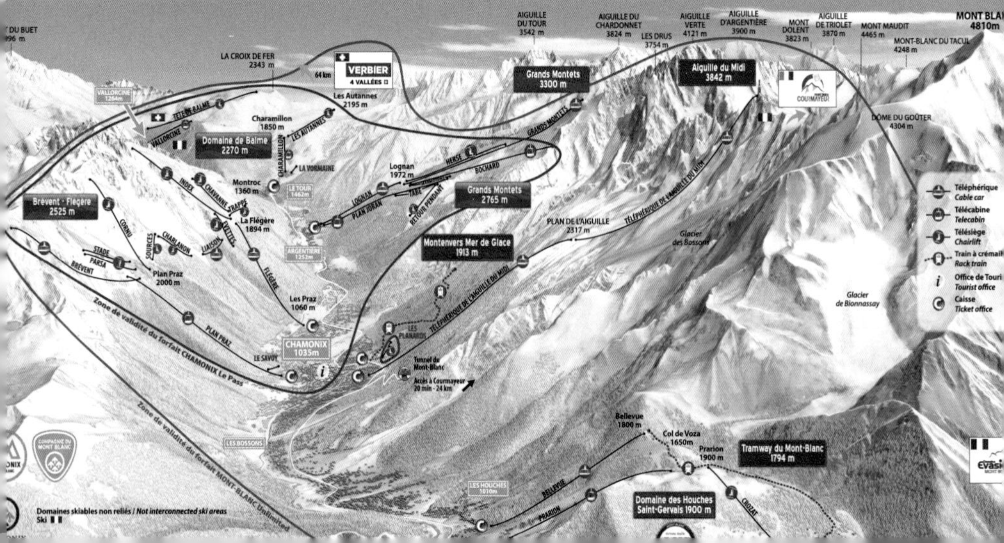

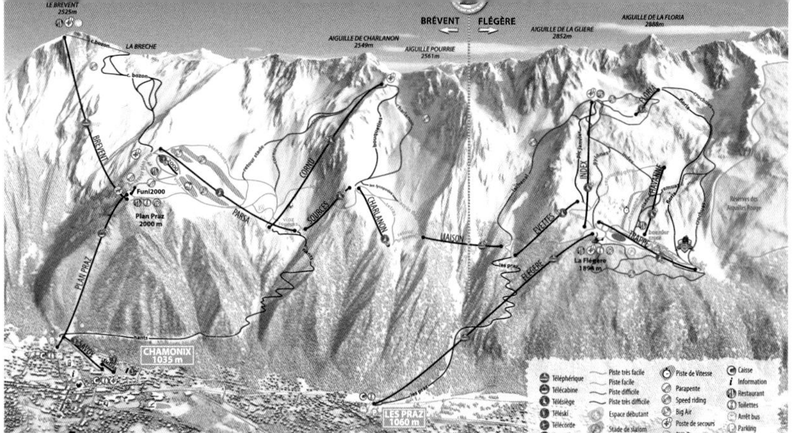

Snow

Altitude and exposure to westerly weather bring plenty of snow. Balme, where winds funnelling up the valley are forced to rise, gets the most snow, but is low and sunny. Brévent and Flégère face generally south-east but are high, with most runs between 1900m and 2400m. The Grands Montets gets it just right – facing north-west, with most runs between 2000m and 2800m. Les Houches is shady, but low.

So Chamonix is a mixed bag; but overall, it rates 4 stars on our snow scale.

System, Lift

It's a bit ironic that the Chamonix lift company is investing in improvements to the Megève lift system: its own lifts could certainly use some investment.

Brévent's two remaining slow chairs are quite short, but Flégère has more problems: three longer slow chairs, and access via an ancient cable car shifting only 1,000 people per hour. This builds queues both up and down. There is talk of a replacement gondola before long.

As we write a major fire at the mid-station seems likely to have knocked out the two-stage cable car to the Grands Montets for 2018/19. Happily there is now a modern 10-person gondola (unaffected by the fire) to mid-mountain. The top cable car here is famously inadequate, and has long operated a booking system (plus a standby queue which can work well). In 2018 the intermediate slopes at mid-mountain are getting a state-of-the-art six pack to replace both the Tabé and Marmottons chairs. So that leaves just one slow chair here, the quite short Retour Pendant.

The 30-year-old access gondola at Balme shifts an inadequate 1,200 people per hour; a replacement was planned for 2018 but has been put off to 2020. All

The famous Vallée Blanche

This long run is a spectacular experience, taking you through stunning scenery. There are various routes, all starting on the eponymous glacier high on Mont Blanc and end at a point below Montenvers, the terminus of a mountain railway from Chamonix which is the usual way home. In exceptional conditions you can ski all the way back to Chamonix (about 19km – less than people say).

The routes vary in difficulty. In good conditions, the easiest require only basic off-piste skills; when snow is poor or is super-abundant, it's not so easy. Take advice on the conditions when you go to book your place in a guided group.

You start by riding the Aiguille du Midi cable car – an experience in itself. Then comes the scary bit: a walk down a long steep-sided ridge to the glacier. Except at the start of the season, steps are cut in the snow, and a rope is fixed for you to hang on to. It's worth having a backpack capable of carrying your skis, and crampons to give your boots some grip; ask about these things when you book.

At the end comes a different challenge – a long, steep stairway up to the gondola accessing the train station (300+ steps).

In good weather, thousands of people do the run every day; to miss the crowds go early on a weekday.

As we write, the cable car is closed for repairs; it may not re-open for 2018-19.

three chairs on the upper slopes are fast, but most runs are served by drag-lifts.

The lifts at Les Houches can get too busy in bad weather. The upper mountain got its first fast chair (Mélèzes) in 2015; the other half-dozen chairs remain slow. The seriously vicious Plancerts drag is worth avoiding, especially by boarders.

Sustenance

There's an adequate range of eating places on the hills. At the top of Brévent, the little Panoramic is worth a visit for the view of Mont Blanc alone. The Bergerie de Plan Praz at mid-mountain is a lovely place, but you must get in early.

On the Grands Montets, the table service section of Plan Joran is adequate. Two smaller options doing satisfying simple food are Refuge de Lognan, off the Variante de l'Hôtel black run, and Crèmerie du Glacier (cheese, mainly) off to skier's right of the home run; service here can be rubbish, however. At Balme, head for the tiny Alpage de Balme.

At Les Houches, the ancient little barn Les Vieilles Luges is an old favourite doing excellent, creative food; booking essential, payment in cash. The Hors Pistes is an excellent alternative.

More on the slopes

For beginners

Close to the centre of town, at the bottom of Brévent, is the Savoy beginner slope – a good slope with a carpet-lift, and two drags, short and quite long. Up at Plan Praz 2000, at mid-mountain on Brévent, the 2000 drag serves a good beginner slope, reached from the cable car by a little funicular. Across the valley in an unfortunately shady position is the bigger Les Planards, with a 640m chair-lift serving a blue run and a slalom course, as well as a choice of drags serving greens. There's a better beginner area at Le Tour.

For true blue skiers

There are blue runs on all four mountains, but they vary a lot in their appeal; all in all, it's not a very rewarding resort.

On Brévent the main slopes served by the fast Parsa chair are fine – gentle and broad. But the pistes linking Brévent and Flégère are quite narrow and off-putting in places. There isn't a lot of blue skiing on Flégère, anyway; don't bother.

The piste set-up on the Grands Montets may change with the new lift

On- or off-piste, the skiing on the Grands Montets gives great views of the glacier d'Argentière

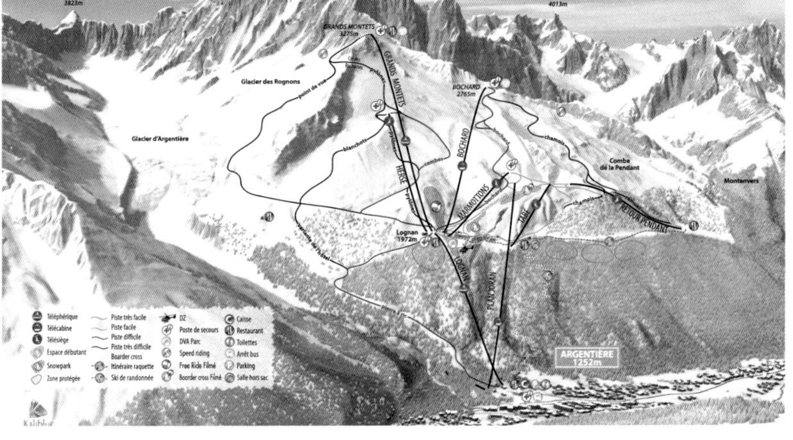

arrangements, but for now there are essentially two quite short genuine blue runs (Coqs appreciably stiffer than Marmottons), plus the slightly longer Arolles – a strange mixture of gentle traverses and steep fall-line pitches.

Balme is very attractive, with a handful of genuine blues on the upper slopes; they don't add up to a lot – the drags are about 1km; but the reds are also worth a look. The longer Esserts blue run to the Tête de Balme chair on the north side of the hill is mostly a rather dull traverse.

At Les Houches there are lovely areas of quite short gentle runs at the top of Prarion (some served by the area's one fast chair), and the long, satisfying Allouds piste from top to bottom – maybe 5km in all. Consider the easier reds, too.

For confident intermediates

For a confident, competent skier the resort has much more to offer. Brévent-Flégère offers a whole row of good, testing red pistes from the top chairs (both with verticals of over 500m), and from the little Floria drag-lift. We particularly like Lachenal.

The Grands Montets is more limited. Bochard is a fine long run of 800m vertical. Combes, though, is a run of two halves – the lower half following a dull track. The home run to the lift base is a lovely broad piste, not steep, but inclined to be badly overcrowded at close of play.

The red runs on the main face of Balme aren't greatly steeper than the blues, but the shady Belle Place down the fast Tête de Balme chair is a bit more testing (and longer). Forêt Verte below it is a tedious track – a way to get home.

There are bits and pieces of red on the map of Les Houches, and most are worth a look, but the highlight here is the top to bottom token black, Kandahar.

For experts

Le Tour has no black pistes, and the one long black on Les Houches is a joke (there's one short steep pitch), but the other two areas have good black runs. Those on the open slopes of Brévent-Flégère are properly steep for short stretches; Charles Bozon is a combination of a gentle track and direct pitches, with variants offering a choice of gradient. With the exception of a fall-line pitch halfway down Les Praz at Flégère, the runs to the valley follow winding tracks, so they are not steep but narrow; and because they are sunny and low, conditions can be dreadful. We ride down, these days.

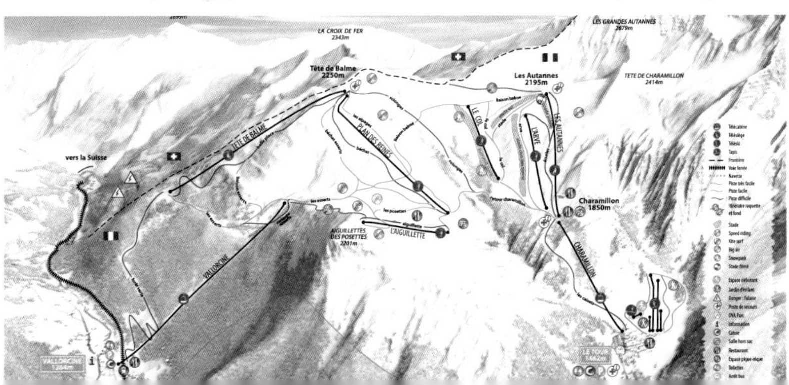

On the Grands Montets the blacks offer more sustained though not severe steepness, plus the best snow in the valley and (in the case of Point de Vue) great glacier views. Pylônes has a seriously steep start. The runs from the Herse chair and Bochard gondola are not in the same league but worth your while – some consolation while the top cable car is out of action. Chamois was groomed last time we skied it – a great blast.

There is a lot of excellent off-piste to be explored close to the pistes, in all four areas. With their gentler terrain, Balme and Les Houches make obvious targets for off-piste novices, but they also offer good tree skiing. The whole face of the Grands Montets is an off-piste playground, steep but not terrifyingly so, with excellent snow. Brévent-Flégère is a great place to head after a dump, when the Grands Montets attracts the crowds. The sun can quickly spoil the snow here, but then there's great spring skiing.

Outside the lift system there are more adventurous routes (some very adventurous) from the top of Brévent and the Grands Montets; from here, some classic runs go towards the glacier d'Argentière, some in the opposite direction ending below the Mer de Glace – the best known being the consistently steep Pas de Chèvre run. There are lots of less dramatic but still challenging and rewarding routes around the Balme sector – from the Aiguillette des Posettes, from the Plan des Reines drag, from the Col de Balme (via the Autannes chair) and from Tête de Balme (some of these ending up in Switzerland to catch a train back).

Fancy stuff

Chamonix's main snow park, with lines for novices and experts, is on the upper slopes of Balme; approaching 1km in length, it is claimed to be one of the biggest in the Alps. There's a big air bag on Brévent, and the piste map shows a boardercross on Flégère, though information about it is scarce. A Summit Cross course has been created on the Grands Montets, with turns, whoops and other features. Les Houches has a snow park and a boardercross course.

Chamonix – the resort

Chamonix was a popular tourist destination before downhill skiing was invented – the first Winter Olympics, held here in 1924, were all about Nordic events – and the town centre is filled with elegant buildings dating from the 19th and early 20th centuries. But away from the centre there has of course been a lot of development more recently, some of it rather brutal.

Chamonix is a big town by ski resort standards, and probably the least conveniently arranged resort in the Alps. The valley road bypasses most of the town, and a large part of the centre is traffic-free, but around that centre the traffic can be heavy.

Convenience

If you're focused on one mountain and you pick your spot carefully (read 'Lodgings'), you can have everything to hand. But for most visitors it doesn't work that way – most days, you need transport at the start and end of the day. Buses, covered by the lift pass, run on several routes – minibuses around the town, proper buses linking to Le Tour and Les Houches. They aren't always up to the job. A train ironically called the Mont Blanc Express runs along the valley and on to Switzerland via Vallorcine, and can be used to reach nearer points.

Lodgings

There's a very wide range of hotels, from three lovely and distinctive 5-star places to half a dozen 2-stars, with dozens in between. The biggest hotel in town, the Alpina, had a radical makeover in 2017 and emerged as the 4-star Alpina Eclectic. As we write in 2018, the Club Med/Savoy Palace, in a great location between the centre and the Brévent gondola, is becoming the first of the Folie Douce chain's hotels, heading for 4-star status (with a 3-star 'hostel' alternative). Nearby is the cool and excellent 3-star Faucigny.

There are plenty of catered chalets,

many run by Chamonix specialists (of which Ski Weekend is one). There are some very swanky places to be found.

Peak Retreats Pick of the apartments

In Chamonix
The 5-star Cristal de Jade apartments are in a great location, right next to the Aiguille du Midi cable car and just 200m from the centre of Chamonix. We love the cool decor using traditional materials and the pool, hot tub, sauna and steam room.
In Argentière
The striking Cristal d'Argentière residence is right in the resort centre, 300m from the Grand Montets cable car.
In Vallorcine
The 4-star Résidence & Spa Vallorcine Mont Blanc is located in the heart of the village, just 100m from the cable car 80m from the railway station for access to Chamonix. We love the indoor pool and the private outdoor skating rink! We also like the comfortable apartments at Les Portes du Mont Blanc in the resort centre.
In Les Houches
Directors' Choice Le Hameau de Pierre Blanche is in a gorgeous setting, surrounded by fir trees, close to the Prarion cable car. There's a pool, hot tub, sauna and steam room.
Other options We also like the convenient location of the brand-new 4-star Elena apartments, in the heart of the resort.

www.peakretreats.co.uk 023 9283 9310

Bars and restaurants

We turned to Chamonix specialists Ski Weekend for pointers in this department. Their resort team came up with ... a lot.

Around the station there's a vibrant après-ski scene. Grab a pitcher from Elevation and sit out to catch the last of the sun. Chambre Neuf requires more energy – dancing on tables to the renowned local band No Limits.

For pre-dinner drinks, Pointe Isabelle has a bustling brasserie feel with funky decor and, like neighbouring Moo Bar, a great cocktail menu. The more sophisticated Cha'Cha'Cha has fab wines by the glass and beers by the bottle.

Le Calèche does traditional Savoyarde meals with a rustic farmhouse ambience – great for large groups and families. Le Caveau is a family-friendly and reasonably priced cellar with fantastic pizzas – open until 1am. For a quiet and intimate meal head to Beurre Noisette – fine French cuisine. Family run L'Impossible has great Italian food with vegan options.

After dinner you could bar-hop along the lively pedestrianised Rue du Moulins. For a quiet digestif try the elegant wine bar Les Caves under the Cap-Horn restaurant, or drink and dance the night away at the fashionable Chamonix Social Club. The stylish Maison des Artistes has live music every night, then a DJ.

The Chamonix Sud square pulls in seasonaires with happy hour deals all night, and nightclubs Amnesia and Le Tof.

The new Folie Douce hotel opening in 2018 will of course add another option.

Off the slopes

The key feature is the big Richard Bozon sports centre, which has an indoor pool, a big outdoor ice rink and an Olympic indoor rink – the Chamonix hockey team has a proud history, and there are regular matches. Other facilities include fitness, weights, tennis, squash, climbing wall and spa facilities. The lift pass includes entry to this and all the valley's ice rinks.

There is a sled-on-rails coaster at Les Planards. Once a week the Evolution 2 school organises descents from mid-mountain on the Grands Montets on single-runner sledges called parets.

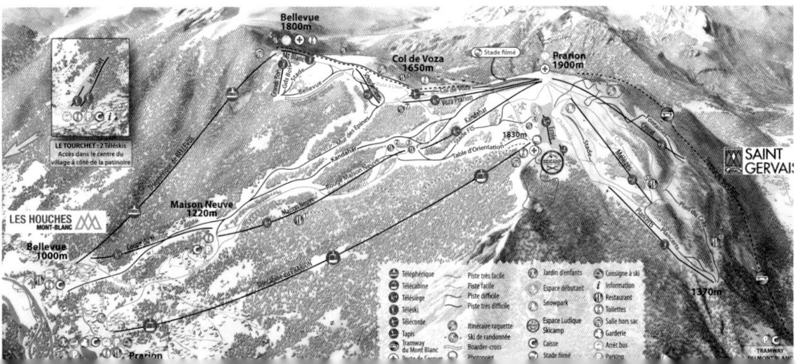

The upper valley has 50km of cross-country trails; one area starts at the edge of the town, and there are further groups of trails around Argentière and Vallorcine. Most of the ski areas have snowshoe opportunities at altitude.

Everyone whose heart/lungs can take it should ride the cable car to the Aiguille du Midi for the views (and the ride); the Unlimited lift pass covers it.

For families

On the Libellules piste at Flégère there's a kids' fun zone with various amusements including a zipline. At the top of Les Houches there is the Ski Camp, with a range of activities including tubing and ziplines. Les Houches strikes us as the most attractive base in the valley for families, though there are many other French resorts that make more sense.

Alternatives to Chamonix

We like staying in towny, animated Chamonix. But if you're planning on spending a lot of time skiing one of the out-of-town ski areas it would make sense to stay in Argentière, Le Tour or Les Houches. You might also like the look of a particular hotel or apartment residence in one of these villages – or in Vallorcine, a quiet backwater that offers an appealing back door to the Balme slopes but has the non-trivial drawback of being separated from the main valley by the Col des Montets. There are recommendations for most of the resorts in 'Pick of the apartments', under Chamonix.

Argentière 1240m

Argentière is a plain but pleasant enough village centred on a 400m stretch of the valley road that goes on to Le Tour, Vallorcine and Switzerland. It has expanded hugely across the valley floor and down the valley around the Grands Montets lift base, about 500m away. The Chamonix ski-bus can be a help in getting to and from the lifts, especially from the village centre and points beyond.

There is a little nursery slope at the lift base, but the main slope is at Les Chosalets, another 500m down the valley. We're told a beginners' area is being fashioned at mid-mountain on the Grands Montets, with two new drag-lifts.

Two central hotels do a good job – the 3-star Couronne and the 2-star Dahu; the 4-star Montana and Grands Montets are out of the centre, nearer the lifts.

There are lots of apartments here (read 'Pick of the apartments') and the Grands Montets attracts a lot of energetic young skiers, so there are plenty of restaurants and bars. The Office Bar, right in the centre, is an old pub-like favourite, particularly with Brits. The Remise is recognised as the top restaurant, with a toque from the Gault-Millau guide, but it's well outside the centre towards Chamonix. The P'tite Verte is central, well-liked and good value.

Le Tour 1465m

Le Tour is a small village with a big car park at the head of the valley and at the foot of the Balme ski area, which rises up to the Swiss border. The excellent Vormaine beginners' area next to the base of the Balme access gondola has a carpet-lift and drag-lifts of various lengths, the longest of them serving a very easy blue run as well as a green. The slopes are sunny but relatively high. And the nearby gondola will take you to some lovely easy longer blues.

The Olympique is a simple (starless) but well-run hotel in a cosy old chalet near the lift base.

Vallorcine 1260m

Vallorcine is a small village in a secluded valley that ought to be in Switzerland – it's beyond the watershed of the Col des Montets. This is not high (1461m) but high enough to be closed sometimes by heavy snow. The valley railway reaches Vallorcine via a 2km tunnel, and when snow closes the col, road traffic uses the tunnel on a one-way system. Right next to the railway station is the base station of the gondola into the Balme slopes. The home red piste is a boring narrow track.

The nursery area is 2km away at La Poya, where there are two drag-lifts serving short blue and red runs, plus rope-tows for beginners. The starless hotel Buet is nearby.

The Café Comptoir is a stylish and excellent little restaurant in a rustic chalet at the foot of the home run from Balme.

There's an artificial outdoor ice rink at the Résidence Vallorcine Mont Blanc.

Les Houches 1010m

Les Houches is an amalgam of hamlets spreading for miles along the foot of its slopes, and beyond. Shuttle-buses link the key points. The central area around the church is about 2km east of the Prarion lift base at Les Chavants. The Tourchet beginner slope is here, with two drag-lifts, but there are also beginner slopes at the top of both access lifts.

There are half-a-dozen 3-star hotels, now including the big, funky Rockypop (way out on the road to Chamonix), opened in late 2016, aiming to be cheap but very cheerful. A more conventional 3-star a bit closer to the centre is the Saint Antoine. The 2-star Campanules is across the valley, but gets good reports.

The Wine Factory is a wine bar and shop combined, offering 40 wines along with Italian mountain meats and cheeses.

There's a big artificial outdoor ice rink in the middle of the village. The Ski Camp, near the beginners' drag up at Prarion, is an excellent facility, with a sledging area, two tubing slopes, ziplines and swings. There are also sledging areas at the Prarion lift base.

Downtown Chamonix has countless bars and restaurants – a buzzing place in season and at weekends

Les Deux-Alpes

Les 2 Alpes 3600, as the place likes to style itself, is an unusual resort. Unlike other big French resorts, it offers lots of modest hotel accommodation, and virtually none that is at all swanky. The main mountain is unusual too. It is exceptionally high – you do most of your skiing between 2100m and 3420m – and long, with some seriously long runs to be done; but it's also narrow, so there's not a huge amount of skiing. In the end, it falls into our unremarkable 3-star size category.

In 2015 the resort took a great step forward: it created an entirely new blue run to the village down the steep mountainside immediately above, at last making a satisfactory way for intermediate skiers to end the day. We'd been asking for this for 20 years, and in 2018 were delighted to ski it.

The mountains in brief

Size Not as big as you might think, given the mountain's overall dimensions

Slopes High, open slopes from the short and sharp to the long and gentle

Snow Some sunny slopes, but all in all excellent, with a big glacier

System, Lift Improvements are needed, but they are coming

Sustenance Not a wide choice of restaurants, but several good ones

For beginners A good set-up at village level and just above

For true blue skiers Excellent – ski from the glacier on 'slow skiing' pistes

For the confident Some very rewarding skiing – but don't expect a lot of it

For experts Not in the first division, but quite a lot to do

Fancy stuff A huge park at mid-mountain, and a half-pipe at the top

Les Deux-Alpes – the resort in brief

Convenience There are ski-in lodgings to be found, and walks are bearable

Lodgings Lots of choice for the budget-conscious, less if looking upmarket

Bars and restaurants A lively resort, and a decent range of restaurants

Off the slopes Lots to do – lacks only a proper toboggan run

For families Fine if you choose your spot carefully

Pass notes
A six-day pass covers two days in Alpe-d'Huez, plus days in Serre-Chevalier, Puy-St-Vincent and Montgenèvre.
The pass covers entry once daily to the ice rink and pool.
There are free drag-lifts on the nursery slopes, and there's a cheap four-hour pass for the higher slopes up at Crêtes.

Key facts

Altitude	1650m
Range	1300–3568m
Slopes (see text)	155km

Where to stay, ideally
Between the main Jandri gondola and the Diable chair-lift.

Websites
les2alpes.com

Key ratings

Size	***
Snow	*****
Fast lifts	****
Mountain rest's	****
Beginner	****
True blue	*****
Confident	***
Expert	****
Convenience	***
Families	****
Village charm	**

The mountains in detail

The two 'alpes' are the pastures above Mont-de-Lans and Venosc on which the resort sits; but the resort does nevertheless have two mountains – the 'alpes' occupy the col between the two sectors.

The smaller hill (450m vertical), curiously branded Vallée Blanche, is on the west side of the village, getting the morning sun. It is accessed via lifts at each end of the village.

The bigger hill on the east side of the village is not branded at all, but is made up of several named sectors. A row of lifts go up over a steep slope to the sloping, rounded ridge called Les Crêtes (or just Crêtes), with a lift at its southern end to the top of the small-but-serious Diable sector. Two lifts go on from Crêtes across a deep bowl to the central junction of the ski area at 2600m. To the right of that is a sector called Toura, which includes Freestyle Land. To the left is another sector called La Fée. The main lifts, meanwhile, go on to the Glacier sector, which peaks first at about 3420m but after a dip reaches 3568m. Hence the 3600 in the resort's branding.

Size

Les Deux-Alpes claims 410 hectares of groomed pistes (which we can't imagine) or 200km of pistes in old money. For decades we've expressed disbelief in such claims, and the Schrahe report puts it at about 155km of marked runs, which places the resort in our middling 3-star size category.

To be frank, that still feels on the high side to us. If you're hungry for mileage, note that a six-day pass covers two days in Alpe-d'Huez (plus days in Serre-Chevalier, Puy-St-Vincent, Montgenèvre and Italian Sestriere). Alpe-d'Huez is only 10km away as the chopper flies, and on certain days helicopter transfers operate – a great adventure, reasonably priced.

Once you are away from the village on the main sector, you're on high, open slopes, usually with good snow

Slopes

There are trees on the slopes above the village, and on the Vallée Blanche side there is one run offering a short stretch of shelter, but the only proper woodland run is the red to Mont-de-Lans. Basically this is all open skiing, and unpleasant or impossible in bad weather. (In the early days of the resort, a long, cold double chair-lift from Bons, on the woody north side of the Vallées Blanche sector, served a piste and some good tree skiing; but it was closed in the noughties after suffering damage in a storm, and removed in 2016. Shame.)

The mountain is quite unusual, with steep slopes immediately above the village and long, easy runs higher up. Runs on the Vallée Blanche side are naturally quite short. In the main area, it's a mixture: the north-facing runs you might do laps on in the Toura, Diable and La Fée sectors are not long – typically in the range 300m–500m vertical. But the runs available along the axis of the mountain, east to west, are epic.

Of most general interest is the descent from the top of the main lift system to the village. The end-points of this sequence of runs are 8km apart, so it probably amounts to 10km+ of skiing – and the vertical is a notable 1600m.

The top-to-bottom run, from Dôme de la Lauze through the resort to Mont-de-Lans on the road up to the resort, amounts to a vertical of 2243m, the biggest in the Alps (but not the world: according to the estimable Christoph Schrahe, a run from the shoulder of Elbrus in Russia offers appreciably more – though the run is serviced by snowcats, not a fixed lift, which doesn't seem quite fair). At 17km this is also one of the longest on-piste runs in the Alps – way longer than the Sarenne at Alpe-d'Huez.

Some of the blue and green runs are designated for slow skiing, though we're not sure they are policed.

Snow

The lower slopes of the main area, below Crêtes, get the afternoon sun and suffer accordingly. They can be brutal in the morning and heavy going in the afternoon. But a lot of the mountain is shady, and a lot of the slopes that are not shady are high enough to keep the effects of the sun within bounds. All in all, we've found repeatedly that you can expect better conditions here than in many other resorts in the region. And then of course you have a glacier at the top offering slopes of 600m vertical. So, despite those icy lower slopes, we've given the resort a 5-star rating for snow.

System, Lift

Practically all the lifts you spend your time on in the main area are fast, and as we write in 2018 two of the remaining slow chair-lifts (Toura and Lac Noir) are being replaced by a powerful eight-seater, with more new chair-lifts planned for 2019.

But the resort is far from queue-free. In the mornings most people head for the big twin-cable Jandri 1 gondola, which looks an impressive beast with its 32-person cabins – but its carrying capacity is actually quite modest, and queues result. It needs to be replaced, and we understand a gondola of triple the present capacity is planned. Meanwhile, it's worth considering other routes up, via the more powerful Diable chair-lift.

Sustenance

The mountain restaurants are not super-numerous, but most of them do table service and are worth a visit. They are marked on the piste map, and on the detailed versions named – hooray! Our favourites are Diable au Coeur (we're suckers for confit de canard) and Chalet la Fée – crowded but doing a good job. Chalet de la Toura is gigantic by comparison, but we've had some good meals there, efficiently served.

More on the slopes

For beginners

There are countless lifts ranged along the length of the village on the gentle lower slopes below Les Crêtes, with three areas designated as beginner zones. There are four free drag-lifts, but only two are in those designated zones; strange. There is also a beginner zone and longer green/easy blue runs up at Crêtes, for which a cheap four-hour pass is available. All in all, a good set-up. Once you've found your feet and are ready to splash out on a proper lift pass, you could consider a trip up to the gentle glacier, to get a sense of what skiing is really all about. Our one reservation: the place lacks the calm cosiness of the ideal beginner resort.

For true blue skiers

It's an excellent resort for building confidence – you can find your ski legs on the runs at Les Crêtes just above the village, then go right to do some laps on the glacier before enjoying the long, easy blue run back down. The Jandri 4 run from the glacier to La Toura is a lovely easy blue, and designated for slow skiing, as are the rather more ordinary Jandri 3, 2 and 1 below it, leading to the village.

Off to the sides of the main axis of the mountain, the Fée blue runs are delightful, although in some snow conditions a bit of skating or poling might be called for towards the end. The blues off the Lac Noir chair-lift are appreciably easier than the Bellecombes 2 blue, which is not greatly different, in fact, from the adjacent reds. Be a bit wary of Thuit 2 – check it out from the chair above it.

The famous new blue run from Les Crêtes to the village has been nicely graded but gets very crowded, and of course is sun-affected in parts. Ride the gondola if in doubt.

On the Vallée Blanche sector there is another slow skiing piste, but if it looks a bit steep, take Super Venosc 1 then Vallée Blanche 1 instead.

For confident intermediates

There are some very rewarding runs here, but they don't add up to a huge amount of skiing. You're likely to spend a lot of your time on just three chair-lifts serving multiple reds and easy blacks – Bellecombes, Fée and Glacier – and the reds from Glacier consist of lovely easy cruising followed by steeper final sections that get sun-affected. The Signal chair on

It's a long, narrow village, broadening at the southern end, above the valley village of Venosc

the north side of the glacier area is worth some laps unless everyone else in the resort has had the same idea.

Don't ignore the Vallée Blanche area if it has decent snow – it has some short but genuine red runs and non-trivial blues.

If you're wanting to get into the black pistes, start with Fée 6, which is barely steeper than the adjacent red. Don't be fooled by the temptingly gentle start of Pierre Grosse 1 – it steepens a lot.

For experts

There are quite a few black pistes, mostly genuine but none of them seriously steep and most on the short side. Runs that don't get groomed are distinguished on the map; they're not necessarily the steeper ones, although the ungroomed Thuit 5 (an itinéraire in the past) is probably the steepest piste in the resort, with a decent vertical. Note that it gets the afternoon sun. Bellecombes 6, Fée 7 and Pierre Grosse 1 are good shady runs that do get groomed. The short but quite serious Super Diable is another sunny run – testing if not softened. The lower Diable slopes are less steep, but miserable as their bumps freeze at the end of the day.

The off-piste has much more to offer. The Bellecombe chair-lift accesses quite a bit of varied terrain, all shady. Traversing to skier's left from here takes you to various routes on the front of Montagne de Rachas. Over on the glacier sector, a favourite offering several routes is the wide combe of Chalance (which had an itinéraire, back in the day), dropping almost 800m to the blue Fée 1 piste. A much more serious project is to traverse around Chalance for access to the steep Pylone Electrique couloir, which delivers you to a wide, sunny, open snowfield, again ending on the blue piste.

The classic major runs outside the ski area are to St Christoph, to the south, for a taxi back to the gondola at Venosc. The Aiguilles Rouges route takes you from the top of the Toura lifts down a broad, varied mountainside facing south-west; the vertical is about 1300m, depending on snow – in spring conditions there's some walking to do at the end. The second route goes from the very top of the mountain, Dôme de la Lauze, down a fine slope facing just east of south, dropping about 1000m to the long Vallon de la Selle, with a further 1000m vertical down to St Christoph at the end of the valley.

Fancy stuff

The resort invests heavily in its impressive terrain park area at La Toura, Freestyle Land. It runs the full 1km length of the Toura lift and is made up of several parts which naturally change over time – and sadly the park website seems to have died – but last time we checked it included a snowcross with fun zone, Easy Park for beginners and families, Slopestyle with a series of jumps, Park Avenue with lots of jibs and Park de l'Envers – kickers and rails, served by a short drag-lift allowing quick loops.

There's also a half-pipe on the glacier, and a kids' park at Les Crêtes.

Les Deux-Alpes – the resort

Les Deux-Alpes is a big, animated, mass-market resort with a young clientele and few pretensions to Alpine charm; it is working to soften the style of its many apartment blocks, but the initial impression isn't helped by the fact that you drive in from the north and all the buildings face south.

Convenience

It's a long, thin village, with most of its shops and restaurants spread along a single garish street a mile long. It widens towards the southern end where a second parallel street (where you find the main lift station, tourist office and sports facilities) allows a one-way traffic system. Right at the southern end, the village spreads more widely to form the Zone du Soleil, around a quite pleasant shopping area. While back at the northern end, at the entrance to the resort, the village has spread up the eastern slopes to form almost a micro-satellite resort, Les Deux-Alpes 1800.

The village is so narrow and its lifts are so numerous that you are unlikely to have a long walk to a lift, but if you want to use a particular one, you might want to use the ski-buses that circulate throughout the resort.

Lodgings

Les Deux-Alpes offers a good range of lodgings of all kinds. It's not a swanky resort, and luxurious pads of any kind are uncommon.

The clear exception is the lovely 4-star Chalet Mounier – run by the same family since its opening in the 1930s, and now blessed with a Michelin star. The tourist office lists eight 3-star hotels and about the same number of 2-stars – a range of budget lodgings unrivalled in the French Alps. We've enjoyed staying in the well-positioned 3-star Côte Brune and most recently the 2-star Chamois Lodge – new owners have kitted out a tired, simple hotel with good new shower rooms and funky urban-retro furnishings and ornaments, and it works well. The restaurant has a good reputation too.

It's not a big resort for catered chalets, but there is a reasonable choice – most of the main operators have a presence. Crystal's trio of properties includes one of its 'Finest' range.

Bars and restaurants

Les Deux-Alpes has not yet been granted a branch of the Folie Douce chain, but has nevertheless developed some afternoon action on the hill at the Pano Bar, at La Toura. Yes, there is dancing on tables, we regret to report. Diable au Coeur makes a bit of an effort too, with an umbrella bar plus DJ and happy hour. Mon Dieu!

Our recent visits have been very hurried affairs, limiting the time available for village après exploration. Our local contact points you towards the hotel Côte Brune's umbrella bar, Motown Cafe and Tribeca; but she is French, and the old favourites are still there – Smokey Joe's, the Red Frog, Smithy's, the Polar Bear.

We have had time to confirm our liking for two restaurants at the south end of town – the cool but friendly Casa Nostra and more traditional Grain de Sel. At the other end, Eli's is recommended.

Off the slopes

The 25m indoor pool in the Croisette building is covered by the lift pass, as is the big outdoor ice rink nearby. There are weekly evening sessions of dodgems on the rink – The Espace 1800 leisure centre has indoor and outdoor pools, fitness and spa facilities, and squash courts. The Palais des Sports is a multipurpose sports hall for tennis and badminton, and a climbing wall. There are sledging areas at three points along the nursery slopes, but strangely no sign of a proper toboggan run. Snowmobiling and dog sledding are available. There are cross-country trails along the face of the Vallée Blanche area, and snowshoe guides are available.

For families

Choose lodgings close to one of the three sledging areas on the vast area of gentle slopes alongside the village, and you're off to a great start. The catalogue of other activities above will help, too.

Espace Diamant

Les Saisies / Praz-sur-Arly / Flumet / Notre-Dame-de-Bellecombe / Crest-Voland / Hauteluce

Espace what? Fear not – you're not alone in failing to recognise the name. A key part of the appeal of this large area, separated from Megève by only one minor valley, is that few people have heard of it, and in particular that it hasn't attracted Parisian riches – quite unlike Megève.

The ski area, naturally, is very similar in character to Megève – low and wooded. But in other respects the two resorts are on different planets. Espace Diamant doesn't do conspicuous consumption; it has few hotels and few mountain restaurants. Happily Les Saisies, our pick of the six villages, has modest numbers of both.

The mountains in brief

Size Plenty big enough, given the speed of the lift system

Slopes Prettily wooded, mostly, and of intermediate steepness

Snow Good snowfall, but altitudes and varying orientation are problems

System, Lift Makes Megève look slick; the central drawback of the area

Sustenance Some good placed dotted around the area

For beginners Les Saisies is close to ideal, other places vary

For true blue skiers Avoid Mont Rond, and you'll love it

For the confident Very enjoyable, if you can live with the lift system

For experts Plenty of off-piste within the lift system

Fancy stuff Mainly kids' stuff at Les Saisies

Les Saisies – the resort in brief

Convenience Could be better, but could be a lot worse

Lodgings Mainly apartments, but also a handful of hotels

Bars and restaurants A reasonable choice, from traditional to cool

Off the slopes Lots to do, notably in a great leisure centre

For families One of the best, given a careful choice of lodgings

Pass notes
There is a local pass for Les Saisies, but it doesn't save much on the cost of an Espace Diamant pass. Beginners in Les Saisies can buy points cards for the short lifts before buying a pass.

Key facts

Altitude	1650m
Range	1000–2050m
Slopes (see text)	192km

Where to stay, ideally
Beginners: at one or other end of Les Saisies; others: near the two six-packs.

Websites
espacediamant.com
lessaisies.com
valdarly-montblanc.com
prazsurarly.com

Key ratings

Size	****
Snow	**
Fast lifts	**
Mountain rest's	***
Beginner	****
True blue	****
Confident	****
Expert	***
Convenience	***
Families	*****
Village charm	***

The mountains in detail

The lifts and runs of Espace Diamant are spread widely over a series of wooded hills, ridges and valleys. We don't know anywhere quite like it.

Many mountainsides are lift-free, and at first it's not easy to grasp which hills are linked, and which not. There are three peaks above Les Saisies. The highest, Mont Bisanne, has the resort's main slopes; La Légette is also accessible from Hauteluce; Chard du Beurre has links with Mont Lachat above Crest-Voland. Both La Légette and Chard du Beurre have links over a low minor peak to the high-point of the area at 2050m (marked on the map as 2069m, the height of nearby Mont de Vorès). We'll refer to this point as Le Sommet.

This high-point is part of a connected ring of peaks. From here you can set off clockwise over Ban Rouge to Crêt du Midi above Praz, or you can set off anticlockwise over Mont Rond to Mont Reguet, above ND-de-Bellecombe and Flumet. You can also take a sunny black run to Les Prés, 3km up the valley from Hauteluce.

Many other connections could be created, given the will and the funds. The one missing link that matters is the one between Mont Requet and Mont Lachat, front centre of the map. An adequate bus service fills the gap.

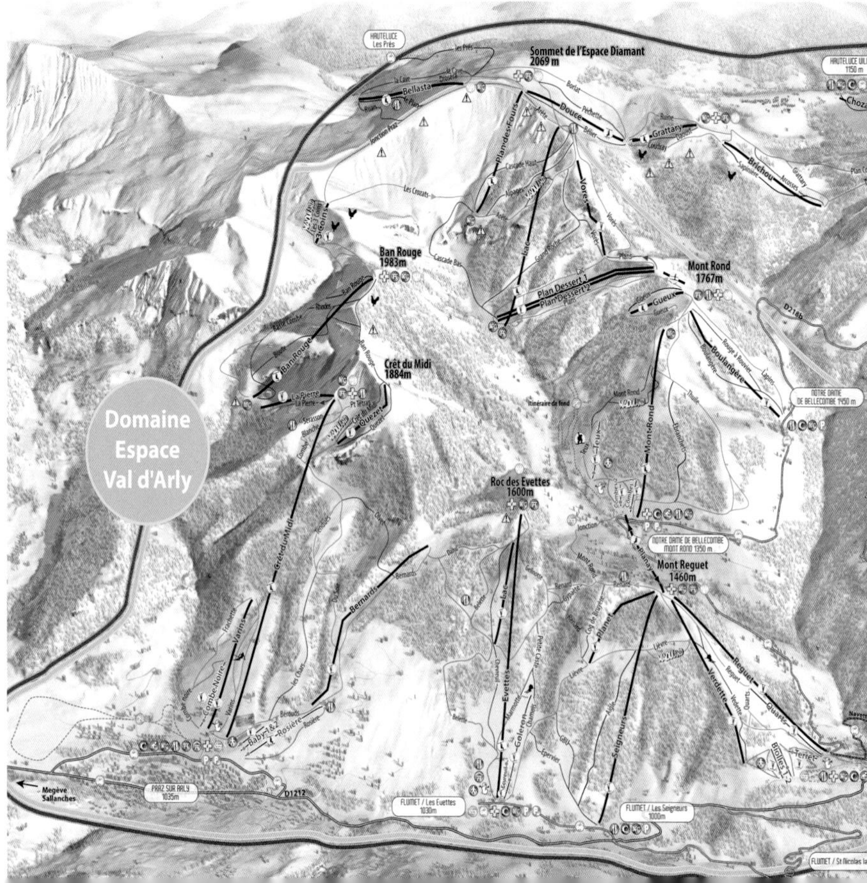

Size

The Espace Diamant pass is claimed to cover 192km of pistes, a figure with which the Schrahe report more or less agrees. This puts the area comfortably inside our 4-star category, alongside the Grand Massif (Flaine) area – but some way behind next-door Megève. If the 2km gap between the two was bridged (the project has long been talked about), they would form the number two area in the world.

Slopes

Most of the slopes are wooded – as we've found on two separate visits, it's a superb place in a snowstorm – although there are quite a few open areas, notably at Les Saisies and on Le Sommet. The mountains offer classic intermediate gradients, rarely approaching black steepness. The slopes at Les Saisies are noticeably gentler than elsewhere.

It is not an area for big verticals or long runs, in general – verticals of about 400m are typical. The clear exception is at Praz: the fast Crêt du Midi chair-lift rises over 700m, and starting from Ban Rouge gets you a descent of over 900m. There is also a beautiful long green run from Mont Bisanne to Le Cernix in Crest-Voland, dropping about 700m over 7km.

Snow

Like the other areas nearby, Annecy Mountains and Megève, Espace Diamant gets a lot of westerly weather, and at altitude quite a lot of snow; but it also gets rain. Les Saisies is at a decent altitude and its main slopes face north-west to north-east, so you can hope for good conditions here. Travelling around the area as a whole involves much lower altitudes and many sunny slopes, though.

You may find the best snow on the east-facing slopes served by the fast Bellasta chair-lift up on Le Sommet, and on the shady woodland runs on the lifts between there and Mont Rond.

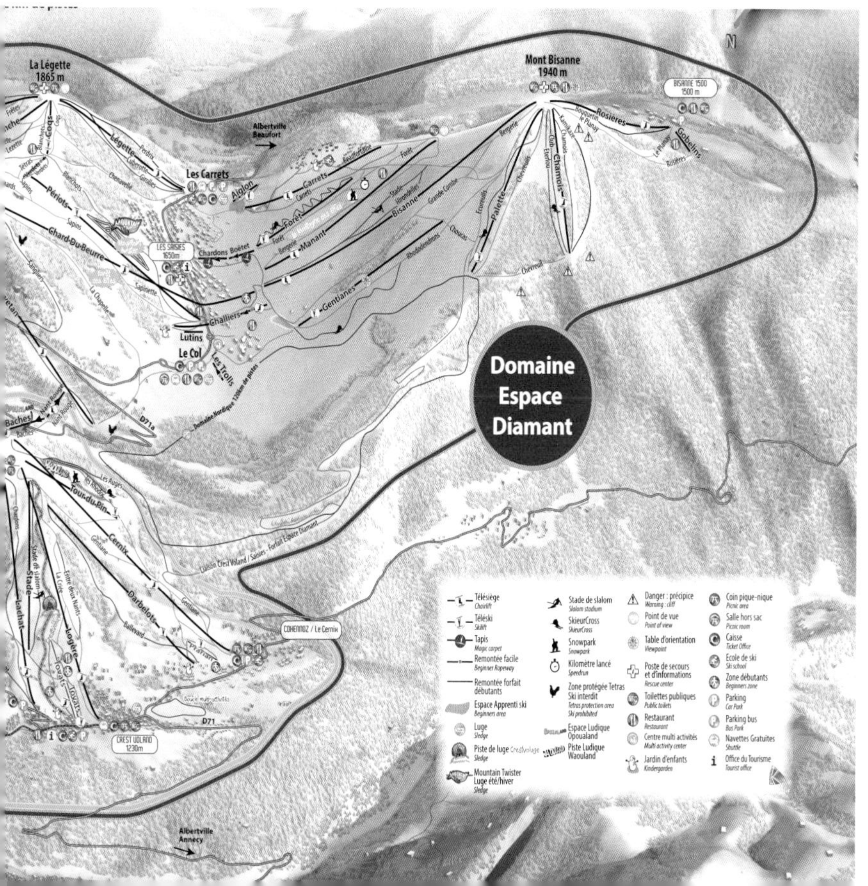

System, Lift

This is the real weakness of the area. Overall, there are eight fast chair-lifts (no gondolas) of which six are six-packs. But three of those are clustered in the Les Saisies sector, and the two quads are in next-door Crest-Voland/Cohennoz. The other three six-packs are dotted about the Espace, lost in a sea of 70+ slow chairs and drag-lifts. New six-packs seem to be installed at roughly two-year intervals, so it's a slow process.

Be warned that the mile-long Seigneurs drag-lift at Flumet is seriously steep – it rises 550m. (Bizarrely, the piste maps understates the altitude of Mont Reguet by about 50m.)

Sustenance

The restaurants here are, in general, noticeably cheaper than in most French areas. They're not super-abundant: above Les Saisies you basically have a choice of three, above Crest-Voland two including the very satisfactory Belle Métairie, above ND-de-Bellecombe just one.

The best we found were near the top of the area – the recently built Au Coeur du Diamant on the Vorès run and Bellasta beside the chair of the same name – an old chalet done up in a cool-rustic style, with great views to Mont Blanc from the snowy terrace, and good food. A narrow choice of dishes is recited not written; the prices are surprisingly high, and may not be volunteered. We also liked the look of two on Crêt du Midi above Praz – the Sarasson and the Petit Tétraz.

More on the slopes

For beginners

At both ends of the village there are drag-lifts serving easy slopes on the gentle mountainside facing the village. You can then move on to longer greens served by the Carrets chair-lift at one end of the village or the Périots drag-lift at the other. Points cards appear to be the method of payment. And then you'll be on to the easy blues, with a lift pass.

For true blue skiers

The home slopes of Les Saisies consist of gloriously easy blues, and once you have found your legs there you can get around the whole Espace Diamant on blue runs – or most of it, at least.

The main problems arise in the neighbourhood of ND-de-Bellecombe. The blue piste down to the village itself

It's a prettily wooded area, with most of the slopes below the treeline; yes, that's Mont Blanc behind

from Mont Reguet is a bit tough, but the ones on Mont Rond down to the higher outposts of ND at 1350m and 1450m are tougher – pretty much indistinguishable from the nearby reds. Avoid Mont Rond, and you should be fine. Mont Lachat above Crest-Voland is much gentler.

For confident intermediates

Provided you can come to terms with the preponderance of slow lifts, Espace Diamant has a lot to offer, particularly if you relish the sense of travel that an area like this can offer. You're not likely to want to spend days on end on the gentle slopes of Les Saisies.

Most of the red runs are genuine, so the piste map gives a fair idea of what there is to do.

Lifts you might plan to spend time on include the Logère fast quad at Crest-Voland – don't miss the Chardons piste down the adjacent slow chair; the Covetans six-pack on Chard du Beurre, for the excellent Sangliers red; the Lac slow chair on Le Sommet, for its row of short but sweet reds; and the Bellasta six-pack on the opposite side of that hill, for its wide open blue/red/black/off-piste slope. These two lifts are also high, shady and close together, making them an obvious target. The slow Ban Rouge chair on the way to Praz is worth a ride or two. The long red to Hauteluce is well worth doing, too.

For experts

There are 11 black runs, dotted all around the Espace, but most barely deserve the classification. Aigle, at Flumet, is a genuine black. Bouquetin, on the back of Mont Bisanne, maybe merits black status; and it's sunny, so have a care. Plan, on the Bellasta chair, is quite steep at the start. And there are a couple of short, sharp mogul slopes you might like to catch – Sapinière on the Brichou chair and Gueux on Mont Rond.

There is a lot of off-piste to be explored within the lift system, both on wooded slopes near the resorts and on the open slopes at the top. As well as the wide slope served by the Bellasta chair, to skier's left of the Douce chair-lift there is a wide and quite shady bowl – but it offers only 200m vertical to the lift.

It's not an area with a lot of *classique* routes outside the lift network. Variants on the black piste to Les Prés are possible, and there must be ways down to Hauteluce from the top of the Brichou chair and from La Légette.

Fancy stuff

Making sense of what's on offer here isn't easy. The piste map advertises six Waouland funslopes dotted around the map – three above Praz, Notre-Dame and Cohennoz, and three on the peaks further back in the area. Some of these seem to be boardercross courses. The one above Crest-Voland and Cohennoz is a boardercross plus terrain park with features at three levels. Just beyond it, Opoualand is a funslope for kids. Les Saisies has no fewer than three boardercross courses – of which Forêt is for beginners.

Les Saisies – the resort

As you can see from our photo, Les Saisies enjoys a lovely sunny setting, at an altitude that's high and snowy by local resort standards. It's mainly modern, but the Alpine chalet style of building has been rigorously maintained, and the many apartment blocks are not too big.

Convenience

It's a small village set on a gentle slope down to the main lift stations. The main street runs diagonally across this slope, dropping 80m in its 1km length, with lodgings set above and below it over quite a wide area. There are lodgings with direct access to the snow, but most require a bit of a walk or use of the ski bus. The excellent Signal leisure centre is right at the north-west extremity of the village. At the south-east end, development has spread up the hill beside the ski slopes to a small suburb in the woods, with direct access to the snow. This suburb, 3km from the centre, needs a name; we're calling it Saisies-Forêt.

At the base of the Rosières chair-lift on the back of the hill is the apartment development of Bisanne 1500, several km from the mother ship by road.

Lodgings

The resort website lists two 2-star places: the Véry is central, the Chalet Hôtel le Caribou is up at Saisies-Forêt. The 3-star Calgary, in a slope-side position at the north-east end of the village, is run by the family of Franck Piccard, super-G gold medallist at the Calgary Olympics in 1988. For 4-star luxury, look to Hauteluce, at the end of the chapter.

Peak Retreats Pick of the apartments

There's a great choice of 4-star places. **Directors' Choice** Le Hameau du Beaufortain is in a peaceful forest setting up at Saisies-Forêt, and offers doorstep skiing. It has a pool, sauna, steam room and hot tub.
Other options Les Chalets d'Emeraude is just 200m from the lifts and has a pool and spa facilities. The Residence des Armaillis has a beautiful spa area, with stunning views. The Chenavelle piste runs within 50m of the residence. We love the location of Les Chalets des Cimes, opening in 2018, which is ski-in/ski-out yet also just 200m from the resort centre. It also has a pool, hot tub, steam room and sauna. We also like the easy access to the slopes from Le Village des Lapons.

www.peakretreats.co.uk 023 9283 9310

Bars and restaurants

This is a quiet, family-oriented resort, but there are bars around the lift base for an end-of-day drink. The Dava is in pole position above the main lift base, and is a satisfactory restaurant too. At the Légette end of the village, Yeti's cafe fits the same bill. There are plenty of other traditional French restaurants dotted along the main street, but the best in town these days may be the cool Table des Amaillis, right at the top of the village, which has a star chef doing Japanese-influenced food. The Calgary restaurant gets a *toque* from the Gault-Millau gastro guide.

Off the slopes

The impressive Signal leisure centre, on the north-west edge of the village, has lots to offer – a pool with jets, a river, a paddling pool, multiple hot tubs, a gym, a sports hall with climbing wall, squash and a proper six-lane bowling alley with attached bar-restaurant, Le 1650. There are spa facilities, too.

This is a great destination for a party

Les Saisies is a pleasant chalet village in a lovely setting on a gentle, sunny slope, with its main lifts below

containing keen cross-country skiers. Les Saisies hosted the cross-country events during the Albertville Olympics. The 17 trails, on skier's left of the downhill slopes between 1600m and 1700m, are claimed to total 120km in length.

The Mountain Twister is a 750m sled-on-rails coaster. The nearest you'll get to a proper toboggan run is a once-a-week thrash down the piste from Mont Bisanne after the lifts close. Or you could schlep over to Crest-Voland to use the run there – daytime only, though.

There are 20km of paths and 65km of snowshoe itineraries (guides available). Or you can be hauled along by horses or dogs; snowmobiling is also available.

For families

Provided you find lodgings with ready access to snow (not difficult) and provided you are content with the nursery-slope sledging (available at each end of the village) plus the Mountain Twister, Les Saisies strikes us as a great place for families. The Montagnes des Elfes on the main slope is a fun zone aimed at families, covering 3ha. The Forêt des Elfes is a woodland trail with a 'fairy world' theme on the Chard du Beurre.

Alternatives to Les Saisies

You have a wide range of options, from towny Flumet on the Albertville–Megève road up the Val d'Arly to tiny, rustic Hauteluce, tucked away at the back of the area in a valley leading up to the back of another area, Les Contamines. If you like the idea of proximity to Megève, Praz-sur-Arly is a much more attractive base than Flumet, with a great access lift. We quite enjoyed a short stay in Notre-Dame-de-Bellecombe, despite its drag-lift, but beginners and apprehensive intermediates are much better off in Les Saisies or Crest-Voland. Les Saisies offers more direct access than any of these alternatives to the high skiing on or near Le Sommet.

Praz-sur-Arly 1035m

Praz is a neat, prosperous village spreading along the Arly valley road for about 2km, only 3km from Megève. The broad, beginner-friendly lift base area is across the river, 400m from the main road. The facilities for beginners are among the best in the Espace – though progression to longer runs is nothing like as easy here as it is in Les Saisies. For keen skiers, the Crêt du Midi access lift is a real plus point – a six-pack rising over 700m in eight minutes.

There are few hotels. One, the 2-star Bernards, has an excellent position at the top of the Rosière beginners' chair-lift.

There's a sledging area at the lift base. This is a well-known centre for flights in hot-air balloons, or *montgolfières*. We see no sign of swimming pools, but it's not far up the road to Megève.

Flumet 1000m

Down in the steep-sided valley where the Arrondine meets the Arly, below ND-de-Bellecombe, Flumet is a little town with few attractions for skiers (except perhaps low prices). But it has higher outposts with ancient lifts into the Espace Diamant system, at Les Seigneurs and Les Evettes. The latter is the main base, with apartment buildings, a chair-lift to Roc des Evettes and a nursery slope at the base.

ND-de-Bellecombe 1100m

Notre-Dame is the quintessential Espace Diamant resort: the two lifts accessing Mont Reguet from here are both drag-lifts. We haven't used a drag-lift as the main/only way out of a resort since ... well, since our first visit to Notre-Dame-de-Bellecombe in 2005.

Still, it could be worse: slow chairs are slower than drags and, in early February at least, the Reguets drag (now over 55 years old) coped with the demand. There are nursery slopes at the lift base, between the two drag-lifts. But beginners have a problem here with progression to longer runs: the blue from Mont Reguet is a tough one.

ND has two outposts further into the mountains, up the road towards Les Saisies, at the foot of Mont Rond – Le Planay at 1350m and Les Frasses at

1450m. The first has some beginner lifts, which could be handy if conditions in ND itself are not good. The Bistrot du Julien is a popular bar-restaurant here.

The 2-star hotel La Mollinière is at the lift base, at the top of the main street which slopes down to the church, 300m away at the bottom. There are a handful of bars and restaurants dotted along the street. We enjoyed a simple meal at the friendly, popular Equipe restaurant. For more ambitious cooking, the Ferme de Victorine is a lovely old chalet up at Le Planay which gets a *toque* from the Gault-Millau guide.

There's an outdoor ice-rink of adequate size in the village. The nursery slopes are used for sledging.

Crest-Voland 1230m

Crest-Voland spreads in an arc around Mont Lachat, with no fewer than seven lifts to the summit area from various points. The nearest thing to a village centre has a slow chair; then, 600m away, the area called Le Crest has a fast quad; and then a further 1km away is another at Le Cernix. (The piste map calls this Cohennoz / Le Cernix, because it belongs to the hamlet of Cohennoz, way down the hill.) There's a nursery slope at Le Cernix, but better facilities at Le Crest.

There are three hotels. The 3-star Caprice des Neiges is at the base of the Reys drag-lift up to Mont Lachat; it has a neat small pool, and its restaurant gets a *toque* from the Gault-Millau guide. The 4-star Mont Charvin is a lovely woody chalet in Le Cernix.

La Crestvoluge is a 2km toboggan run dropping 400m from the top of the fast Logère chair-lift – open daytime only. There's also a mid-sized outdoor ice-rink in Le Cernix.

Hauteluce 1180m

Hauteluce is a charming rustic hamlet out on a limb to the south-east of the main lift system, 7km by road from Les Saisies. There are red and blue pistes down from La Légette to mid-mountain, but only red from there to the village. About 6km up the valley is a gondola that offers a back door into the slopes of Les Contamines (covered in the Megève chapter, although not linked).

La Ferme du Chozal is the place to stay: a 12-room 4-star hotel in a ski-in/ski-out location, with a hot tub and outdoor pool giving views to Mont Blanc.

Early morning mission to the excellent boulangerie in Notre-Dame-de-Bellecombe – a great day ahead

Espace San Bernardo

La Rosière / La Thuile (in Italy)

The name may not be familiar, but newly expanded La Rosière believes it will help to promote the quantity of skiing it can now offer with La Thuile, so we're going along with the area name (sometimes shortened to ESB).

The expansion – an unusual event, these days – is very welcome. Not only does it add five more pistes, but it adds a sector with a worthwhile vertical of 850m – and the steeper upper part adds a bit of character to an area that needs it. Keen, competent skiers will love it, we guess.

The resort is a pleasant, traditional-style village that has grown gently and, like so many other French ski stations, is now adding upscale lodgings of various kinds. It's also sunny (good) but so are its slopes (not so good).

The mountains in brief

Size Mid-sized, taking the bigger Italian sector into account

Slopes Generally open and of intermediate difficulty

Snow A good snowfall record, but the slopes are too sunny for comfort

System, Lift Excellent, with slow lifts confined to the margins of the area

Sustenance A limited choice of restaurants, with more options in Italy

For beginners A good setup, but you need an ESB pass from day two/three

For true blue skiers Good runs locally, but access to Italy is a challenge

For the confident With Italy and the new sector, quite a bit to do

For experts Worthwhile off-piste options, improved by the new lifts

Fancy stuff A reasonable range of features

La Rosière – the resort in brief

Convenience You can find ski-in lodgings, and walks aren't long

Lodgings Improving: a few good hotels as well as chalets and apartments

Bars and restaurants An adequate choice

Off the slopes Best options at the satellite of Les Eucherts

For families A good choice if you pick your spot with care

Pass notes

A local pass is offered for four hours or a day; longer passes are for the whole Espace San Bernardo. There are short free lifts at both lift bases. After that you will need a full lift pass.

Key facts

Altitude	1850m
Range	1176–2800m
Slopes (see text)	152km

Where to stay, ideally

Near a main lift in central La Rosière or Les Eucherts

Websites

larosiere.net
larosiere.ski

Key ratings

Size	***
Snow	***
Fast lifts	****
Mountain rest's	**
Beginner	****
True blue	***
Confident	****
Expert	***
Convenience	***
Families	****
Village charm	***

The mountains in detail

Chair-lifts go up from the top of La Rosière and from the satellite of Les Eucherts towards Le Roc Noir (2330m); the main runs descend from there, including a descent to Le Vaz (1500m) below Les Eucherts, and from another point along the ridge, Col de la Traversette. To spectator's right of this is the skiing newly added to the area in 2018; this revolves around two new six-seat chair-lifts, the upper one going up to a new high-point for the area of 2800m on the shoulder of Mont Valaisan. (All the topo maps have it as Valezan, but we'll use the resort's style, as used on its piste map.)

Col de la Traversette is the point of departure for the slopes of La Thuile in Italy – read the feature panel over the page.

On the left of the map, a solitary red piste descends through woods to the isolated lift station of Les Ecudets, the low-point of the area at 1190m (although in good snow a blue piste operates down to Séez).

Size

To make the most of its 2018 expansion, La Rosière has taken the radical step of becoming the first French resort to have its piste extent certified by Christoph Schrahe, the German consultant who campaigns for clarity and honesty in these matters. The result, for the whole ESB area, is 152km, bang in the middle of our middle 3-star category. We're told about half of this total is on the Italian side (we'd have guessed more), and that half is accessible only to those willing and able to ski the linking red run.

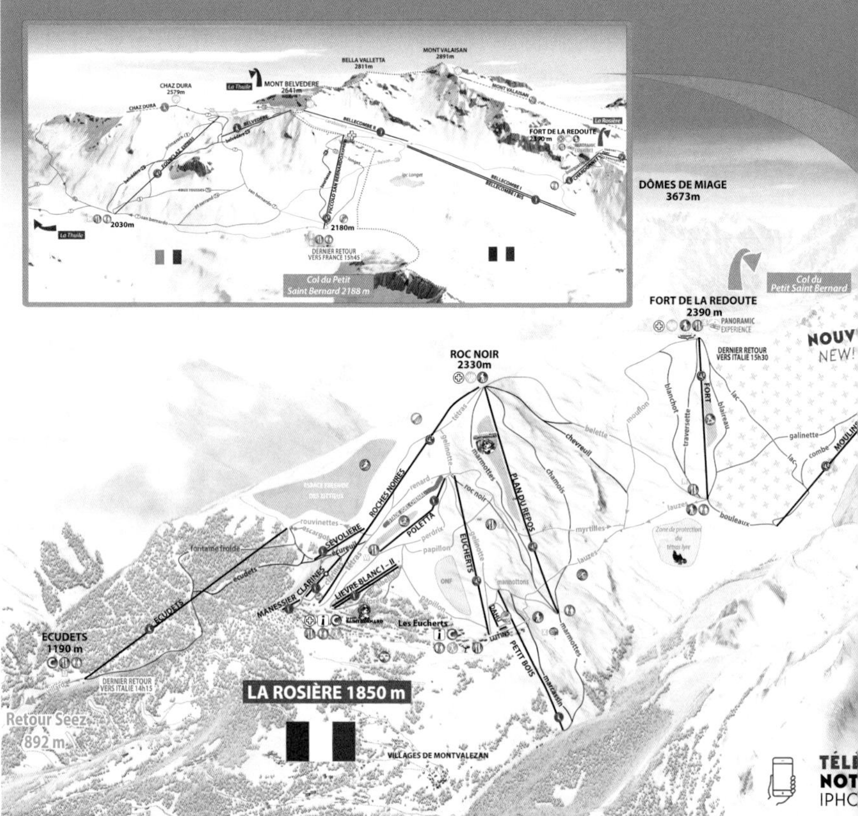

Slopes

Although there are trees at village level, the slopes are mainly open – only the red runs below the resort to Les Ecudets and Le Vaz offer shelter from storms.

The main mountainside is basically of red gradient, with the blue runs cutting diagonally across it (the Eucherts chair is on a gentler slope); only in a few places does the hill reach black steepness. We find these slopes a bit lacking in character. But the lower, woodland runs and the Italian slopes above the pass are more distinctive.

From the existing high-points you can put together descents of up to 5km in length and over 800m vertical down to Le Vaz; the new Mont Valaisan lifts won't add greatly to the length but will add 400m to the vertical. Perhaps more important is that the two new lifts will themselves offer over 850m vertical – twice the vertical of the nearby Fort chair. Roc Noir to Les Ecudets offers a vertical of 1140m.

Near the top of Le Roc Noir is the ungroomed Espace Freeride des Zittieux. Although it is supposed to be avalanche-safe, the resort also says all users should carry avalanche kit. This mirrors the status of the Natur' zones in nearby Ste-Foy. The ski patrol's explanation is that this zone is a training area for off-piste; we think the current advice is confusing and misguided.

Snow

La Rosière has a good snowfall record, thanks to its position on a pass at the end of the Tarentaise valley. But its main mountainside faces south-east, and most of the pistes (the reds in particular) face roughly south – so snow quality can suffer later in the season, especially low down.

System, Lift

The resort has successfully rationalised its lift network in recent years, replacing four slow lifts with two fast chair-lifts. The result is quite a slick system on the main slopes; beginner lifts apart, the only slow lifts now are the long Petit Bois triple chair from Le Vaz and the much longer lifts

from Les Ecudets – a slow 2.2km chair followed by a slightly less slow 1.5km drag; very tedious. Queues are rarely a problem; on blue-sky days in high season there may be a morning rush for the Fort chair towards Italy.

Sustenance

There are two adequate but unremarkable restaurants on the main mountainside (with good views, it must be said), but the options were improved greatly a few years back by the addition of L'Antigel on the home slope just above the village – a light, spacious chalet offering table service of good food. There's more choice (and lower prices) over in Italy – read 'The Italian connection – La Thuile' for some suggestions.

More on the slopes

For beginners

The 200m Manessier drag-lift at the main lift base is free, as are the Lutins carpet lift and the 200m Dahu drag-lift at Les Eucherts. The slopes are gentle and wide. When you are ready to move on to longer runs you need a lift pass – and if you want a pass for more than a day it will have to be a pass for the whole ESB area, including Italy. This is a bit of a rip-off: few people will want to tackle the red run link in their first few days on skis.

Above the nursery slope at the main lift base, a drag-lift serves the genuine green Clarines run. Just across the slope, the twin Lièvre Blanc drags serve a choice of slightly longer greens – about 700m. Then you're on to gentle blue runs.

For true blue skiers

There's quite a bit of blue skiing on the map and it's all genuinely blue. Tétras running the length of the Roches Noires chair-lift is more testing than the others in its middle section, but its great width is helpful. If you're nervous, a better place to start is the blue pistes served by the Eucherts chair-lift, other than Gelinotte.

The creation of the excellent Mouflon blue piste from Traversette a few years ago was a great step forward (along with the conversion from red to blue of Bellete, from Roc Noir). Bellete is the only way from the resort to the Fort chair towards Italy, and suffers from traffic accordingly – in general the slopes are pleasantly uncrowded (being nice and wide helps).

If Italy beckons, beware: check out 'The Italian connection – La Thuile'.

The main local slopes are a bit featureless; the lower runs and the sector above the pass have more character

The linking run towards the pass and Italy is easier than it was originally, but is still properly classified red

The Italian connection – La Thuile

Most intermediate skiers and all advanced skiers should plan on spending time over on the slopes of La Thuile. If you're a nervous true-blue skier ... well, the linking run is a genuine red; it's not very steep, but steep enough to have bumps at times.

There are various rewards. La Rosière isn't noted for crowds, but in French holiday weeks you'll find La Thuile quieter, on weekdays at least. If you find the sunny slopes of La Rosière are turning to slush, the shadier slopes of La Thuile will be a relief. There's a wider choice of restaurants, with clearly lower prices. And the slopes above the San Bernardo pass, west of Monte Belvedere, are varied and interesting, with a mix of challenging red piste and easy blacks (and off-piste).

You'll want to cross to the main east-facing slopes high above La Thuile in search of lunch. Try the eccentrically decorated Off Shore, the tiny Chalet de Cantamont or Maison Carrel – on a good day, our favourite. You may find a map in Italy (or on the La Thuile website) that locates them. The pistes here are mainly motorways (including some very flattering reds) but the wooded runs directly above the village are quite different – seriously steep blacks. If you have time, take the gloriously long red run to the village, away from the lifts, on skier's right.

One word of warning: bad weather can close the link, sometimes for days on end.

For confident intermediates

The red runs offer fun cruising rather than challenges. On the local slopes there are just four lifts or lift combinations you're going to want to spend time on. That's assuming the lovely wooded run to Les Ecudets is skiable despite exposure to the afternoon sun and an uncomfortably low-altitude bottom station.

Both the Plan du Repos and Fort fast chair-lifts on the main mountainside serve a choice of red runs – all genuine reds, but mostly at the easy end of the spectrum. The Marmottes piste on the Plan du Repos chair extends down to the Plan Bois slow triple chair for a total vertical of over 800m.

The fourth item on your local agenda will be the pair of new fast lifts on Mont Valaisan, which are planned to serve red runs advertised as bringing a new, more 'technical' dimension to the skiing. We can't wait to try these new slopes – particularly the one from the top.

And then there is Bella Italia. Get over there early in the week so that you can get a feel for what's on offer and plan the rest of the week accordingly.

For experts

There are three quite short black pistes. Chevreuil has a couple of black pitches, and Ecudets has just one; Marcassin is more sustained. But low, sunny black pistes are a recipe for trouble, and snow conditions on the last two can be very tricky, especially later in the season.

The resort doesn't have a great reputation for off-piste, but there is quite a bit to do, especially with the new lifts in place. For a start, the lightly wooded Zittieux zone above the Ecudets combe is worth a look, particularly in bad weather, and you can carry on down into thicker forest before hitting the Fontaine Froide piste. There's plenty of gentle terrain between the lifts, and you can descend below the main lifts to the lower Plan Bois chair. To spectator's right of the newly developed Mont Valaisan is a wide area of skiable mountain facing the pistes. We're told skiing is allowed in the wildlife protection zone shown on the map. You should be able to drop over the ridge to descend towards the pass, or hike up to ski north-eastwards directly into Italy.

On the Italian side of the area, favourite routes to La Thuile include those from lift-served Chaz Dura and a lovely run (requiring a half-hour hike) east from the shoulder of Bella Valletta to meet the run from Mont Valaisan mentioned above.

Heli-drops are possible in Italy.

Fancy stuff

Off the Poletta drag-lift, just above the main resort, is the snow park. 300m long, it has rails and kickers in lines from green to black. There is a big air bag at the bottom. In parallel there is a mini-boardercross course. The serious boardercross is up on the Fort chair-lift.

The main part of the resort is arranged along the road to the pass, which finishes at the far end of the village

La Rosière – the resort

Although La Rosière is set on the road up to the Petit San Bernard pass, in winter the road terminates at the village, so the resort gets a good access road with no through traffic, and the central area near the main lift base has a pleasantly villagey feel. Although there are quite a few apartment blocks, they are quite small and in traditional Alpine style.

Convenience

The resort plan divides the place into no less than 11 *quartiers,* which seems a bit excessive. The main part of the village is set along a 500m stretch of the pass road leading up to a car park at the lift base. Across the mountainside, and separated by a band of woodland, is the satellite of Les Eucherts, with its own lift into the slopes, about a mile from the main one. Although much less of a village than the main resort, Les Eucherts has the essentials of life. A pleasant floodlit path runs through the forest to the main village, and a shuttle bus links most parts of the resort every 15 minutes. Some of the higher lodgings enjoy ski-in locations.

Lodgings

The original 2-star hotels (eg the Relais du Petit St-Bernard) are now eclipsed by more swanky options in Les Eucherts. The apparently starless Hyatt Centric, opened in 2017, brought a bit of urban chic to the resort (fab outdoor hot tub too); new in 2018 is the 4-star hotel Alparena. Chalet Aiglon is a new departure – a swanky B&B guest house with only five rooms. Chalet Matsuzaka is a Brit-run Japanese-influenced 4-star hotel, but with the feel of a catered chalet. There are quite a few conventional catered chalets here. Mountain Heaven has three, ranging from a fine old stone-built farmhouse to a slick penthouse with picture windows and an outdoor hot tub.

Peak Retreats Pick of the apartments

There is a great choice of 4-star places. **Directors' Choice** Les Cimes Blanches is in a great location in Les Eucherts, close to the slopes and lifts. It has superb facilities including a pool, sauna, steam room and spa. Lodge Hemera is in the heart of the resort; the 30 apartments share a pool. There's also the lovely Chalet les Marmottons (300m from the resort centre and 400m from the slopes).

Other options Le Hameau de Barthelemy (in Les Eucherts) is 200m from the slopes and lifts and has a great spa area. For cosy interiors, we love the ski-in/ski-out Balcons de la Rosière apartments (the larger ones have wood burners) and the luxury apartments at Le Refuge, which have open fires.

www.peakretreats.co.uk 023 9283 9310

Bars and restaurants

There are quite a few bars and restaurants at Les Eucherts as well as in the main resort centre. Nick Williams of Mountain Heaven, who spends a bit of time at the resort, kindly agreed to give us a few pointers. Favourite bar: Le Comptoir. Best restaurant: Le Genepi (we've enjoyed good steaks there, too); good alternatives: Le Flocon, L'Ancolie. He's a man of few words.

Off the slopes

Les Eucherts has the lion's share of the amenities – a hockey-sized indoor ice rink (La Rosière's team plays weekly) and a bowling alley. For swimming, look to your lodgings. There is no proper toboggan run, but there are sledging areas at both lift bases, and the ski schools take groups up as the lifts close to descend the pistes on two special forms of kit: linked sledge snakes or *parets*, sledges with a single runner, a bit like a bike.

There are marked footpaths and short snowshoe trails, and guided outings. There are short cross-country trails from Les Eucherts, with longer ones at the bottom of the Ecudets chair-lift. Dog sledding is also available.

For families

Reached by the Lièvre Blanc drag-lift at the main lift base is an adventure trail on the Foret green run. Off the Marmottes red piste on the Plan du Repos chair is a 1km funcross course with tunnels, jumps and all that stuff.

Grand Massif

Les Carroz / Flaine / Samoëns / Morillon

Extensive, varied terrain with extremely varied resorts

Flaine is the Grand Massif resort that's best known internationally – functional, family-friendly (traffic-free, mostly), uncompromisingly cuboid in its architecture. Perhaps because of Flaine's reputation as a family resort, and maybe because of its modest altitude (the top height is just under 2500m), the area has never really competed with the mega resorts of the Tarentaise (the 3 Vallées and neighbours). But it has good, varied slopes, and plenty of them – it ranks fifth or sixth in France for size, depending on how you deal with Megève's fragmented skiing, and scores a solid 4 stars on our size scale.

We're not great fans of Flaine as a resort village, and, more importantly, in a ski area that has one sector of relatively high, open slopes and another sector of lower, wooded slopes we always tend to favour a base in the latter. When the weather is good, we can ski anywhere; when it's bad, we can stay in the trees, close to home. So we've looked outside the Flaine bowl for our featured resort.

Lovely old Samoëns has hit a rich vein of Brits looking for second homes good for summer as well as winter holidays. Those who have found that second home won't hear a word said against the place – but there are words to be said, as you'll see. Morillon is a rather limited village with very gentle local slopes, which will suit some people, particularly those open to staying up at mid-mountain. But over recent years, as we've spent more time there, we've come to regard Les Carroz as the best base in the area.

There's excellent, varied terrain in the valleys between the Flaine bowl and the other resorts

Les Carroz

You drive through Les Carroz on the way up to Flaine – and there you have its main drawback: on weekends, holidaymakers arriving and leaving, plus day trippers from Geneva, produce heavy traffic through the village. Don't worry – the village is certainly not traffic-free, but for the rest of the week traffic is not a worry.

Les Carroz (unlike Samoëns) is not the stuff of picture postcards, but it is a pleasant village that has been developed in traditional style, set on an attractively wooded, sunny shelf. It's the biggest resort in the Grand Massif, and has the best range of lodgings, but feels quite small-scale – the beds are widely distributed across that wooded shelf. Like Samoëns, it is only three lift-rides from the Flaine bowl.

The mountains in brief

Size Big enough to amuse most visitors for a week
Slopes A good mix of open and wooded intermediate terrain
Snow Good snowfall at the higher altitudes, but some slopes are very low
System, Lift A couple of bottlenecks, and still too many slow lifts
Sustenance Some good places dotted around, but this is not a highlight
For beginners A pretty good set-up, although Morillon is arguably better
For true blue skiers Good runs locally, but links between sectors are tricky
For the confident An excellent, varied area with lots to do
For experts Some proper black pistes, but much more to do off-piste
Fancy stuff Lots of fun zones, but no serious terrain park

Les Carroz – the resort in brief

Convenience Some lodgings on the snow, but most involve bus rides
Lodgings Mainly apartments, but with some other options
Bars and restaurants A reasonable choice
Off the slopes OK swimming and skating – but no proper toboggan run
For families Pick your spot carefully, and it's fine

Pass notes
The Vill4ges [sic] pass which excludes Flaine is slightly cheaper than the Grand Massif pass.
There is a free carpet-lift for beginners at village level, and a half-price day pass covering the gondola and lifts on the easy slopes at the top.

Key facts

Altitude	1120m
Range	690–2480m
Slopes (see text)	175km

Where to stay, ideally
Near the lifts or near the centre, as you prefer.

Websites
winter.lescarroz.com
winter.grand-massif.com
winter.samoens.com
flaine.com
ot-morillon.co.uk

Key ratings

Size	****
Snow	***
Fast lifts	***
Mountain rest's	***
Beginner	****
True blue	****
Confident	*****
Expert	****
Convenience	***
Families	****
Village charm	****

The mountains in detail

This is an area of two halves. Much the bigger half consists of the slopes above Les Carroz, Morillon and Samoëns which peak at Tête des Saix, plus the slopes in the two valleys behind that point, which merge above the lift station previously known as Les Molliets. This is now apparently Les Carroz 1500m – are there plans for a satellite resort here, we wonder? The smaller half of the area is the wide bowl above Flaine. The two are connected at one point, Grands Vans, where chair-lifts arrive and blue runs start.

That simple summary omits two important elements. From the top of the Flaine bowl, on skier's right, runs passing close to the craggy Tête Pelouse link to the experts-only Combe de Gers and to the famously long piste des Cascades, a blue run ending at the micro-resort of Sixt.

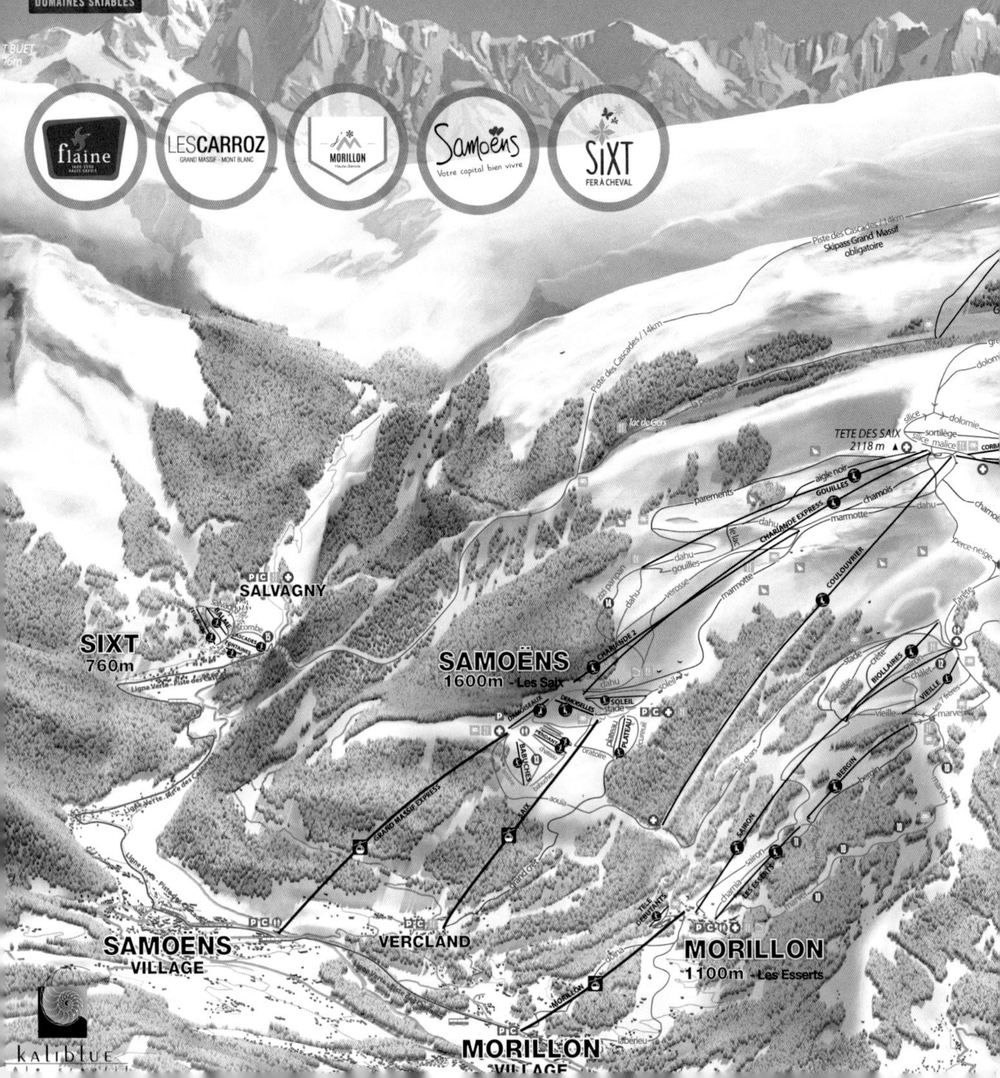

Size

The Grand Massif is one of a handful of French areas falling just outside the premier league but still offering an impressive quantity of terrain. The area claims an overall extent of 40,000 hectares (equal to a 20km square, which is patent nonsense) and seems to have settled on a piste total of 265km – but with an alternative figure of 175km 'réglementés' (ie rule-based, ie genuine). Amazingly, this is slightly less than the figure Herr Schrahe has arrived at in his report, but still is just enough to put the area in our 4-star size category.

Slopes

With the treeline at 1700–1800m, practically all of the skiing above Les Carroz and Morillon is in the trees. With most of its skiing above its mountain outpost at 1600m, Samoëns, like Flaine, has mainly open slopes. The mountains are essentially of intermediate steepness, with black-run terrain in short supply except in the fabulous Combe de Gers.

There are plenty of runs of satisfying if not spectacular length. From the main high point outside the Flaine bowl, Tête des Saix, it's about 6km and 900m vertical to Les Carroz, and 1300m vertical

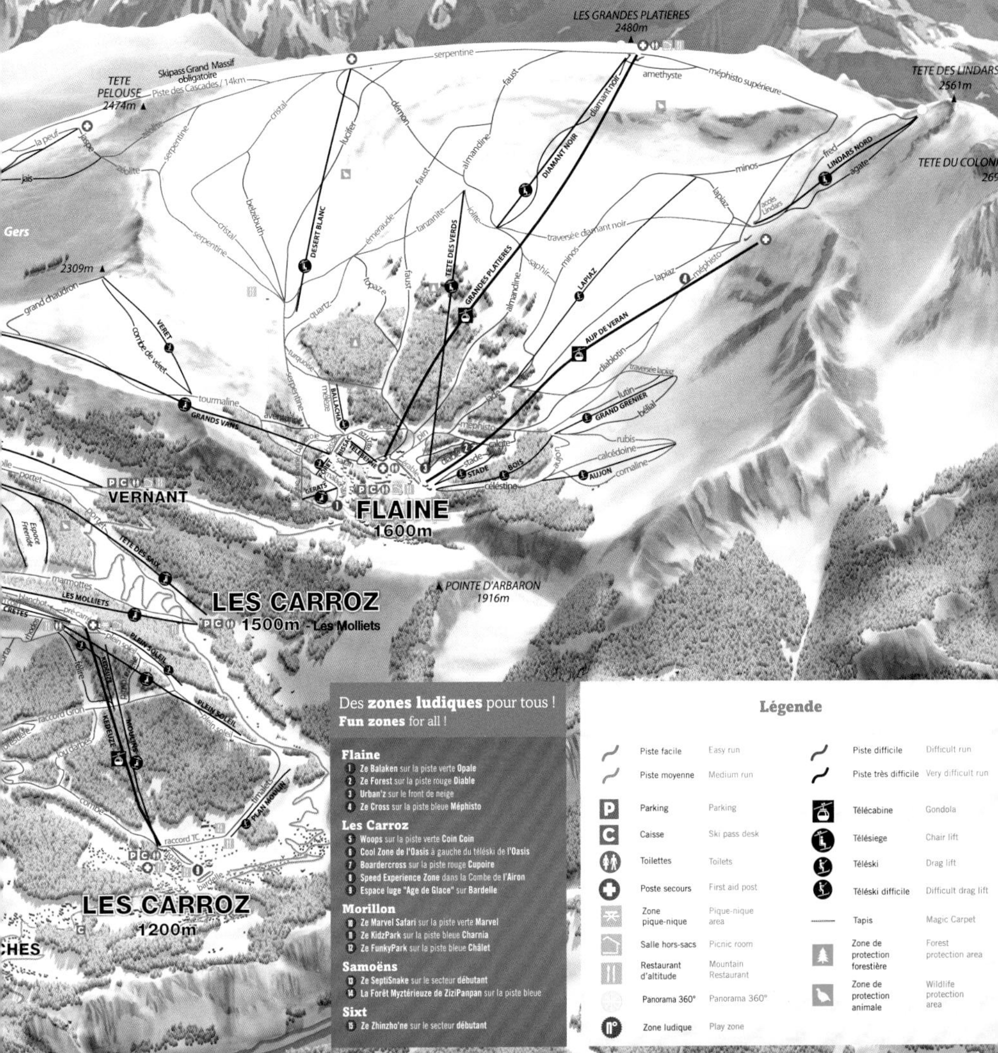

to Vercland, above Samoëns (snow permitting). The 600m descent to Les Molliets is more typical. Flaine's Grandes Platières gondola rises 880m.

The Grand Massif makes a lot of fuss about the Piste des Cascades from the top to Sixt, claiming a length of 14km. We make it just under 12km; still impressive.

Snow

At almost 2500m, Flaine's Grandes Platières is one of the highest mountains on the windward side of Mont Blanc, and as a result has an exceptional snow record. The Flaine bowl faces north-west, so it keeps its snow well, too. Naturally, the lower slopes of the other resorts don't do quite so well, and they are vulnerable to the threat shared with all the low resorts in this part of the Alps: occasional rain. But most of the slopes face roughly north, and the west-facing slopes above Les Carroz are protected from the sun to a degree by the trees. The slopes most vulnerable to sun are those in the Molliets valley, between the two main sectors.

System, Lift

Some big strides have been taken in recent years to address a quite serious problem here – the preponderance of slow lifts on Tête des Saix. In 2017 the giant Coulouvrier chair (almost 3km long) followed the crucial Tête des Saix chair (which created a fast-lift route to the Tête for Flaine skiers) and creates a second fast-lift route for those based in Les Carroz. There are still plenty of slow chairs and drags dotted around, including Corbalanche and Gouilles on Tête des Saix and several lifts above Les Carroz.

In peak season Flaine's Grandes Platières gondola builds queues, but at least it has a singles line, and there are other ways up into the slopes. The links between Flaine and the rest of the area are bottlenecks, and queues form in the afternoon.

Perhaps a bigger problem than lift queues, these days, is crowds on the home runs from Grands Vans and Tête des Saix at the end of the day. Les Carroz and Morillon residents returning from Flaine should avoid Tête des Saix and use the Molliets chair.

Sustenance

There's a fair supply of recommendable table-service places, but they don't constitute a highlight of the area. They are marked on the piste map, but not named – although if you find Lac de Gers

The village enjoys a lovely setting on a sunny, wooded balcony, pretty much on the edge of the Alps

on the Pépinière run you've found one of our favourites, the cosy Chalet de Lac de Gers. Most people reach it from the famous Cascades piste – there is a phone where the two pistes meet, to summon a skidoo tow up to the chalet.

At Samoëns 1600, Lou Caboëns is a friendly and reliable spot near the nursery slopes. We've had good meals at the cosy Luge à Téran, at the bottom of the Gouilles chair. Above Morillon, the Igloo does an excellent plat du jour and is one reader's favourite in the whole GM. Chalet des Molliets, at what is now called Les Carroz 1500m, is a fine cosy place too.

In the Flaine bowl, we have always liked Pente à Jules, but judging by our recent visit it is now too popular for its own good. A bit higher up, Blanchot also does a good job, with better views. Some readers speak highly of L'Epicéa too.

More on the slopes

For beginners

There is a good nursery slope close to the centre of Les Carroz, served by a covered carpet-lift, and at the top of the gondola is a similar set-up, plus a 600m drag-lift serving a gentle green run. There are no longer greens, but plenty of blue pistes, starting with Plein Soleil which runs gently down a wooded ridge below the eponymous chair-lift. There is a half-price day pass covering all necessary lifts.

There is a case for steering nervous beginners towards staying at Morillon: above mid-mountain there is a long green run, appropriately named Marvel.

For true blue skiers

There is plenty of good, easy blue skiing in the woods above Les Carroz (Lou Darbes is an excellent piste winding through the woods) and Morillon, and the links between the two sectors are not difficult; but the piste to Morillon (Arête) follows a quite narrow ridge track – best avoided late in the day when it can be uncomfortably busy. There are also two excellent long runs in the Molliets valley – Portet and Marmottes. Access to the first involves skiing the bottom section of Dolomie; this is blue, but not entirely easy.

If your confidence is fragile, be aware that blue runs from Tête de Saix – the Dahu for Samoëns and the Perce-Neige for Les Carroz – have a start that's uncomfortably steep and busy, at the end of the day in particular. And the Perce-Neige is another narrow ridge run which is intimidating when busy. Avoid it when returning from the Molliet valley or from Flaine by using the Molliet chair. But Dahu is the only way to Samoëns; pity.

Getting to and from Flaine involves, again, skiing the bottom section of Dolomie. Then Tourmaline from Grands Vans down to Flaine is a fine run, although it has a slightly steep start; more importantly, at the end it becomes steeper (often mogulled late in the day) and narrower, and congested with hesitant skiers. If in doubt, go to Flaine by bus.

At Flaine there are some good runs from the top – Cristal avoids the trickier bits of Serpentine. Méphisto is rightly blue, but has some steepish sections (it was red in the past) including the bottom part that you have to ski returning from the lovely short blues on the Aujon drag.

And so to the famous Piste des Cascades, which is very scenic, but has features an inexperienced skier should know about. First, it's very long, and once you've started there is no going back; on the top half there are long flat and even uphill stretches, which can be hard work especially if the snow is fresh and soft; later there are stretches that are not entirely easy, partly because they are narrow; the lower part of the run is really low, and snow conditions can be poor; and the pisteurs can't be relied on to close the run when they should – last time we skied it, we damaged our skis on rocks that looked like ice, and had to walk several stretches. We suggested politely to a pisteur that the run was dangerous and should be closed. Gallic shrug. You're welcome.

For confident intermediates

This is a much better area for confident, competent skiers. Virtually all the many red runs on the map are worthwhile, and quite a few of the blues (eg Méphisto at Flaine and Chars at Morillon) are steep enough to amuse. The reds above Les Carroz are fabulous in falling snow, in particular. Chamois into the Molliets valley from Tête des Saix is excellent. For more of a challenge, take a look at the nearby Corbalanche freeride zone. At Samoëns, Parements is more amusing than Marmotte; in good snow don't miss the neglected Grand Crêt to the base of the old gondola at Vercland.

At Flaine you can hope to find the best snow in the area, and there's lots to do on the three fast chairs, the Lapiaz drag and the Aup de Véran gondola, so you needn't be worried by queues for the Grandes Platières gondola.

For experts

The handful of black pistes above Les Carroz, Morillon and Samoëns are short and not seriously steep, but deserve to be black and have some good off-piste terrain close by. The Corbalanche freeride zone is much longer, and more varied. At Flaine, the Combe de Véret piste is quite steep at the top, and again is surrounded by worthwhile off-piste.

There is plenty of off-piste opportunity from lifts elsewhere in this area. The Véret drag and the Grand Vans chair below it access large areas of sunny off-piste terrain. The Molliets valley also has lots of lift-accessible terrain.

In the Flaine bowl, the Diamant Noir below Grandes Platières is mostly benign, but has a steep pitch halfway down. Agate, on the Lindars Nord slow chair, can present a different challenge after a dump – finding a skiable way down its lumpy terrain. Off-piste in the bowl is complicated by the underlying rock, which has crevasse-like fissures in it – so what looks like the most tame off-piste imaginable is actually very dangerous. But there are short routes to be done, one of which is Pente à Jules, from the top to the Lapiaz drag-lift.

The highlight, though, is the Combe de Gers, at the top left of the piste map. The mile-long Gers drag-lift (labelled *difficile*) rises over 650m to serve the Onyx piste, but also to access a vast north-facing off-piste bowl on skier's left of that, some of it much steeper than the piste. If traversing doesn't get you to the snow or the gradient you are after, you can drop in

The alternative to staying in cute downtown Samoëns: its less cute mid-mountain satellite resort at 1600m

to the bowl from the ridge on skier's left, having ridden the Véret drag-lift.

There are also routes outside the ski area, off the back of Grandes Platières, notably into the Sales valley. Skiing out of this valley to St-Jean-de-Sixt involves abseiling down a cliff; the alternative is to be helicoptered back to Flaine, as a privileged group of us once were. (This 'reverse' form of heli-skiing exploits a loophole in the French legislation.)

Fancy stuff

There is no proper terrain park, at Les Carroz or anywhere else in the Grand Massif, but Les Carroz and Flaine have boardercross courses, and the Oasis drag in the Molliets valley serves the family-oriented Cool Zone L'Oasis, with terrain features and another little boardercross.

There are quite a few funslopes elsewhere in the area (read the individual minor resort entries).

Les Carroz – the resort

Les Carroz was just a hamlet in 1939 when it acquired Europe's longest drag-lift. Since then it has grown into a substantial resort, but has maintained the feel of a traditional village rather than sacrificing that in the cause of convenience for skiing.

Convenience

The core of the village, where all the shops and bars are concentrated, is very compact – no more than 300m across. But the village as a whole is anything but: about 2km long and 1km wide. The lift base and nursery slope are 500m uphill from the centre; there are hotels and apartments located just below the base and on the snow further up the hill. A ski-bus links many parts of the resort to the lift base every 20 minutes, but some parts get a much less frequent service.

Lodgings

Most of the accommodation is in self-catered chalets and apartments. There are one or two catered chalets to be found. The choice of hotels is limited. The very attractive 4-star Servages d'Armelle and the starless but stylish Milkhotel are right at the top of the village and at the foot of the red home piste. The cosy 2-star Airelles is at the lift base. The 4-star Croix de Savoie is in the southern part of the village, up the road to Flaine.

Bars and restaurants

The terrace of the hotel Airelles beckons as you come to the end of the home red run. In the centre, the square is ringed by bars and restaurants; the Marlow and CarpéDiem are old après-ski favourites. Aux Petits Oignons is a reliable, cosy restaurant, and the Bistrot Grill du Gron keeps carnivores happy. The restaurant of the hotel Servages d'Armelle gets two *toques* from the Gault-Millau gastro guide.

Off the slopes

For 2018/19 a new sled-on-rails coaster is being constructed above the village. The Aquacîmes centre has outdoor and indoor pools (the latter with massage jets etc), spa and fitness room. There's a good-sized outdoor ice rink close to the centre of the village, open day and evening. There are 30km of cross-country trails on the plateau d'Agy, 12km away, reached by free shuttle-bus. Snowshoe guides are available. There is dog sledding and snowmobiling up the road to Flaine at Les Molliets.

For families

The Coin Coin green run at the top of the gondola is equipped with whoops. On the Bardelle slope close to the middle of the village there's a sledging space and a tubing jump on to an air bag. There's also a good, steeper slope below the lift base, by the Chalets de Jouvence residence.

Samoëns 720m

Samoëns is a very cute, historic village, but it sits at an exceptionally low altitude on its flat valley floor, so even beginners must ride a gondola – extremely unusual in France – starting a bus ride away from most of the lodgings. The mid-mountain beginner area at 1600m is excellent, and you can cut the hassle by staying up there; but that's not at all cute.

Convenience The core of the village is compact, but lodgings spread quite widely from here, and the main gondola station is 850m from the central square; lodgings on the south side of the village are a five-minute walk from the lift. There are shuttle-buses, of course.

Lodgings There are quite a few catered chalets, many of them individual owner-operated places. There are several hotels, the pick of which is the Neige et Roc, now elevated to 4-star status. The 3-star Gai Soleil has recently developed an all-suite chalet offshoot, Lodge Le Grand Cerf. The new MGM residence Alexane (read on) is following suit, with an all-suite hotel attached. Check out 'Pick of the apartments' under Les Carroz. As we write in 2018, MGM is building a smart central residence, Alexane.

Bars and restaurants It's not a riotous scene. The Savoie is a proper French

Flaine now has quite substantial suburbs up towards the pass – with pitched roofs, we're pleased to note

bar-restaurant in the centre; Covey's is an Irish bar that stays open late. Probably the best restaurant in town is the central 8M des Monts. Au Table de Fifine, out on the road to the lift station, is another good bet.

Off the slopes There's a sports centre and ice rink. Dog sledding is available, and there are snowshoe outings at nearby Sixt.

For families Our first question would be: Where are we going to go sledging? (It's dead flat.) Next: Why not stay somewhere more conveniently arranged? There are funslopes in the nursery area and on the Zizi Panpan blue run.

The Morillon option

Morillon is a few km from Samoëns, at a similarly low altitude but in other ways quite different. It is pleasant enough but not notably cute, and is set at the foot of its gentle home slopes – so it has a sledging area. Like Samoëns, it has lodgings and nursery slopes at mid-mountain, though in this case at the lower altitude of 1100m; snow lower down is unreliable, so staying up here makes sense – check out 'Pick of the apartments', under Les Carroz. The resort website lists just one hotel, the central, woody chalet-style 3-star Morillon.

Flaine 1600m

Flaine is one of the archetypal purpose-built resorts – cuboid apartment blocks on a greenfield site, with a traffic-free centre and direct access to the snow. It has expanded up the road towards the Col de Pierre Carrée – the pass that accesses the Flaine bowl – and in the process has lost the purity of its architect's original vision; some would say it's none the worse for that. The resort has excellent nursery slopes (with free lifts) and short green runs at resort level, but beware: the step up to blue runs is a big one.

Convenience For many years Flaine consisted essentially of two parts, set on shelves on a steep hillside – Forum, set around an open area of snow and ice (a rink), and Forêt, a more linear arrangement of apartment blocks on the upper shelf. Both parts are largely car-free and have lodgings close to the snow, and some that are ski-in, plod-out. They are linked by two little funicular lifts. There has long been a more traditional, chalet-style suburb below the col – Le Hameau de Flaine – but these days there are large apartment developments above and below that point, and the whole area has been labelled Flaine les Gérâts. Only the parts nearer the centre have piste access. A timetabled shuttle-bus links Les Gérâts and Forêt.

Lodgings The 3-star hotel Totem, in an excellent position in Forum, has had several incarnations and after a makeover has now become part of the funky Terminal Neige chain. We found the rooms comfortable, the staff friendly but ineffective, the buffet-style dinners a mistake. There are some very good apartment developments – the CGH Centaure in Forum, two Pierre & Vacances Premium residences in the piste-accessed part of Les Gérâts. There are a few catered chalets.

Bars and restaurants All parts of the resort have some shops and bar-restaurants. Forum has more choice than the other parts, but two of the best restaurants are out of the centre in different parts of Les Gérâts – the Ancolie and the Table d'Helios.

Off the slopes In the middle of Forum is a modest, natural outdoor ice rink. The pool and spa at the Centaure residence are open to the public. There's ice driving (cars and quad bikes) and snowmobiling. There are cross-country loops and snowshoe trails up at the col, and guides are available. There is bowling at Forêt.

For families Pick your lodgings carefully for access to snow and a pool and Flaine works very well for young families. On the front de neige is Urban'z – a kids' freestyle zone with whoops and banked turns. The Opale green run is now Ze Balaken, a family funslope.

La Grave

You'll have spotted that this is not a normal chapter. That's because La Grave isn't a normal ski resort: its only prepared slope is a short one, way up on a glacier, and not easily reached (for the moment, at least). You come here for something else: to ski a serious off-piste mountain, served by a slow pulse gondola of very limited capacity. So our normal ways of describing and evaluating resorts don't really work here.

After a period of great uncertainty, for the foreseeable future the mountain will now operated by the Alpe-d'Huez lift company, which apparently has plans to modernise and extend the main lift to reach that short, high piste (and even more off-piste terrain).

The mountain

La Grave sits in the shade of the highest mountain within France, La Meije (a few metres short of 4000m), but for most of us its skiing starts on the shoulder of the slightly lower peak of Le Rateau (3809m). A pulse gondola (with bunches of cabins fixed to the cable) goes to Col des Ruillans at 3200m, from which point there are some popular runs that are not particularly difficult, and many more challenging routes. A snowcat takes you from the top station to the glacier drag-lift, opening up still more routes.

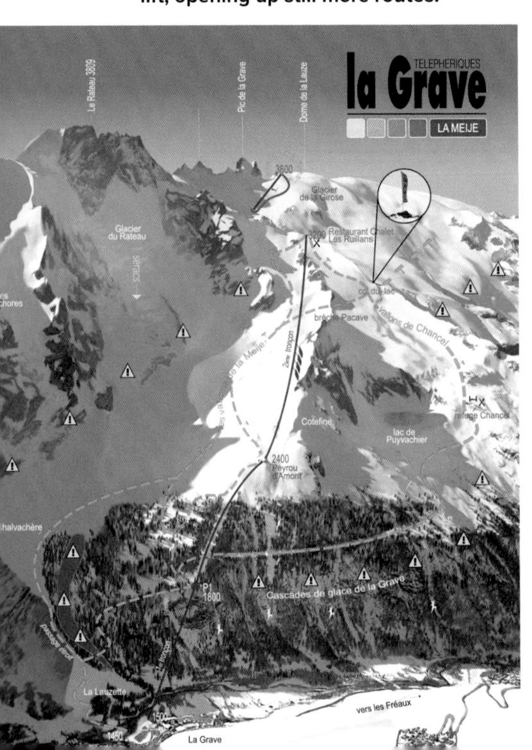

The gondola has two separate stages, with a station at 2400m, and the lower stage has a mid-station at 1800m, called P1 – basically just a pylon with platforms, allowing laps on the upper mountain or rides down the lower mountain.

As you can probably make out from our reproduction of it, the mountain map shows some runs from the top station of the gondola – Vallons de Chancel on skier's left of the lift, and Vallons de la Meije to skier's right, plus several variants. The nature of these runs is unexplained on the map, but a note on the map does make clear that the lift company's responsibilities are limited to the operation of the lifts and the marked pistes on the glacier. So these runs, like the rest of the mountain, are off-piste, and should be skied with appropriate equipment.

If you lack the knowledge and experience to ski high-mountain off-piste terrain on your own, you should go with a guide. The routes are essentially unmarked, mistakes in navigation can be disastrous, the conditions are unpredictable and can be difficult, and

Key facts

Altitude	**1475m**
Range	**1450–3200m**
Slopes	**see text**

Where to stay, ideally
In downtown La Grave.

Websites
lagrave-lameije.com
la-grave.com
skierslodge.com
snowlegend.com

there is no way out other than down. But in good weather, in particular, these runs get skied heavily and lots of people do ski them without guides. They are not very steep – Chancel is the easier of the two runs, but it ends in a traverse through the forest to P1 that can be hard work.

For experts, of course, the draw of this mountain is the more challenging stuff. In both the Meije and Chancel sectors there are much more adventurous ways down, many of them through steep and sometimes narrow couloirs. From the glacier there are very long, very serious descents to left and right of the routes shown on the map, and to the south, as described in Les Deux-Alpes.

The best way to get a feel for these possibilities is to check out the websites of the guiding outfits operating here. At skierslodge.com and snowlegend.com you'll find over 20 'legendary' routes, most rated very serious for difficulty.

The Bureau des Guides, Snowlegend and the ESF run guided groups that you can join at reasonable cost.

Surprisingly, there are three mountain restaurants. Two are adequate places at the lift mid-station and top station, but the real deal is the tiny Refuge Chancel, well away from the lift on the Chancel run.

The resort

La Grave is a small old village set on a steep hillside giving great views across the valley to majestic La Meije. It is bisected by the road from Grenoble towards the Col du Lautaret, Serre-Chevalier and Briançon; traffic can be intrusive, but the village is a pleasant enough place to inhabit, and entirely free of ski resort glitz.

The gondola station is on the edge of the village and slightly below it, about 500m from the 2-star hotel Le Sérac at the top and far end of the village. The best hotel in town, the British-run 3-star Edelweiss, is a bit nearer. Closer still, and in a category of its own, is the hotel des Alpes / Skiers Lodge, packaging 'cosy boutique-style' lodging with mountain guidance. There are plenty of apartments and self-catering chalets to rent, via the tourist office or through EurekaSki based in Serre-Chevalier.

The village has all the necessary shops, a handful of bars which are adequately busy at teatime – the Castillan near the lift base naturally does good business – and several good hotel restaurants, plus one or two independent ones.

The village is a tight huddle, pretty much unspoilt by development; the slopes are across the valley, to the left

Maurienne valley

Les Sybelles (Le Corbier, La Toussuire, St-Sorlin d'Arves etc) / Valloire / Valmeinier / Les Karellis / Valfréjus / La Norma etc

The nearest most British skiers get to visiting the Maurienne valley is dropping over the ridge above Val Thorens, in the fabled 3 Vallées, to ski the 'fourth valley'. The lift base in the bowl they descend into is also the arrival point of an extremely long access gondola up from Orelle, way down in the deep Maurienne. Orelle is dealt with in the Val Thorens chapter, and St-François-Longchamp is similarly dealt with in Valmorel. This chapter covers Maurienne resorts without links to resorts to the north.

The Maurienne is a valley of two halves. Off the western, lower half of the long valley are a string of resorts reached by winding roads climbing from St-Jean and St-Michel on the valley floor. Then, east of the major railway town of Modane, you climb into the Haute Maurienne – only 100m/200m higher than the lower valley, but with a wilder, more remote feel. Up here, some resorts are villages on the valley floor, with no winding climbs involved – notably Val Cenis, which gets its own chapter later in the book, and tiny Bonneval, covered in that chapter.

The Espace Haute Maurienne Vanoise regional lift pass covers the five resorts directly above or to the east of Modane: Aussois, Bonneval, La Norma, Val Cenis and Valfréjus. They claim a total of 350km of piste; more to the point, they are all worth visiting for a day. You must spend your first day in the resort where you buy the pass; then you can do one day in each of the other four resorts. There are free shuttle-buses between the resorts, but those with a car will be better able to make the most of the pass.

Les Sybelles 1100m–1750m

Les Sybelles came out of nowhere in 2003, when half a dozen unknown resorts were linked by a painfully slow network of drags and old chair-lifts to form an area of apparently impressive size. The area used to claim 310km of pistes, which the Schrahe report found to be about the most extreme exaggeration in the Alps – but now it seems to have settled for a meaningless claim of 393ha.

Happily, there is now a sprinkling of fast lifts in key parts of the network, but there are still more slow chairs than fast ones, and more drags than chairs.

The area is south-west of St-Jean-de-Maurienne. The biggest resorts are La Toussuire (1750m) and Le Corbier (1550m). They're also the least attractive – La Toussuire has spacious chalet-style suburbs, but overall both are functional modern blots on the landscape. St-Sorlin-d'Arves (1600m) and St-Jean-d'Arves (1550m), in contrast, are largely unspoiled, traditional villages that have expanded tastefully; and for our money, St-Sorlin has the best local slopes. But, being on the south side of the area, these latter resorts are a long drive from St-Jean.

Given the altitudes and latitude, it's strange that virtually all the skiing is on open slopes. At the centre of the network is the low peak of L'Ouillon (2430m). Reaching this point from the main resorts involves drag-lifts fed by six-packs, so queues can arise at peak times. There are four main sectors radiating from L'Ouillon.

First, a single broad mountainside above Le Corbier, served by a six-pack and a row of slow chairs and drags; this is linked (slowly) over a ridge to a few slopes above St-Jean and via an intervening valley to the second sector, the bowl around La Toussuire. This has an array of six-packs heading over shady slopes for L'Ouillon, while the sunny side of the bowl remains slow-lift territory. The third sector comprises two linked mountains above St-Sorlin, including the area high-point of Les Perrons (2620m); two six-packs depart from the village, and two others make the connection to pivotal L'Ouillon. Finally, there is an unappetising leg stretching down to St-Colomban-des-Villards (1100m), which involves a chain of four slow chairs to return to L'Ouillon.

The slopes are generally easy-intermediate stuff, and a bit featureless;

but the more important weakness of the area is the time it takes to get from one resort to the skiing of another. The St-Sorlin sector has more character and offers more challenge, with some serious reds, the occasional black and abundant, varied off-piste terrain.

Frankly, the main attraction of this area is low prices; but many people would be better off looking to Austria or Italy.

Peak Retreats Pick of the apartments

In St-Sorlin
Les Bergers is well located, just 350m from the ski school meeting point and shops. The residence has a pool.

In La Toussuire
The Hauts de Comborcière residence is in a really convenient location, close to the slopes and only 100m from the centre. It has a pool, hot tub, sauna and steam room, and there's a restaurant within the residence. We also like the Ecrin des Sybelles apartments, which are 200m from the centre and 500m from the slopes and lifts (the free resort shuttle bus stops just 150m away). Leisure facilities include a pool, sauna, steam room and a pool table. The Balcons des Aiguilles residence is in a great location at the foot of the slopes and by the lifts. It has a pool, hot tub, sauna and steam room.

www.peakretreats.co.uk 023 9283 9310

Valloire 1430m

Valloire, south of St-Michel, is the best known of the Maurienne resorts internationally. It is an attractive, polished village with a strong summer trade – the Tour de France normally goes through en route for the famous Col du Galibier. It shares an extensive area of slopes with Valmeinier – the claim is 150km of pistes, which is not unrealistic.

It's a compact village, with its main lifts a short walk from the fine old church and central square. Modern developments spread away from this central area – pretty much all in traditional chalet style.

Gondolas go up to two local sectors of slopes. Sétaz has nursery slopes (with a long covered carpet lift) and restaurants at the mid-mountain junction of Thimel, on the treeline. Sétaz is essentially of red gradient, and blue as well as green runs have to wind their way down. There are a couple of just-genuine blacks served by a six-pack. The second sector, Crey du Quart, has a six-pack to the top height of 2535m above its gondola, making the link with Valmeinier and serving a much broader area of red and blue runs. At the south end of this sector, long and very gentle blue runs loop away from the lifts to take you down into the valleys that separate Crey du Quart from Sétaz and Valmeinier. One flank of Sétaz and most of Crey du Quart face west, and suffer from the sun. There is lots of off-piste terrain, and a terrain park.

There's a range of modest lodgings. The central 3-star hotel Christiania is an old favourite of ours; most of the alternatives are 2-stars. We've also enjoyed staying in a smart and very spacious apartment in the small Chalets d'Adrien residence, in a prime central position. There are lots of traditional restaurants, but for lower cheese content, clearly the best bet is Chez Freddy.

The resort is a pleasant place to spend time, and there is a reasonable range of off-slope activities, including skating and snowshoeing, and tubing up at Sétaz – but we know of no swimming pool.

Valmeinier 1500m–1800m

Valmeinier presents a sharp contrast to linked Valloire: a modern apartment-based ski station – low-rise and in traditional chalet style, so easy on the eye, happily.

That's Valmeinier 1800, where most of the lodgings are to be found – mostly apartments, though there are two modest hotels. Across the hillside is the original village of Valmeinier 1500, plus assorted hamlets dotted around. The home slopes face just south of west. From 1800 a six-pack goes up about 700m serving easy-intermediate slopes, while across the hillside above Valmeinier 1500 slow chairs serve more testing runs below Le Gros Crey (2595m) – there are great views from here. At 1500, a cross-valley chair connects with Valmeinier's side of Crey du Quart, and so with Valloire.

Les Karellis 1600m

Les Karellis seems best known to readers as a good day out from bigger, more rounded Valloire, but it is a proper, small, modern resort consisting mainly of a dozen cuboid apartment blocks in an attractive setting on an open shelf in the forest, south of St-Julien. Practically all the apartments are ski-in, ski-out. The resort claims 60km of pistes, widely spread over three identifiable sectors with a top height of 2520m – one of them above the more traditional village of Albanne. Drags and slow chairs dominate, but a fast chair from the village accesses two sectors. There is something for everyone – easy blues in one sector, wide fairly easy reds elsewhere, and a couple of short but genuine blacks served by a double drag. Cross-country trails add up to 30km.

Albiez 1500m

Albiez is a small, rustic, backwater village in a fine setting on the Col du Mollard, a few km directly south of St-Jean – like Les Karellis, a viable day-trip from Valloire.

The ski area is a modest affair – a network of eight or nine drags and slow chair-lifts from two main lift bases at around 1600m up to a top height of 2100m, with a chair off to one side reaching 2200m. It's a very small area, with no more than 35km of pistes – blue lower slopes with some reds higher up. Accommodation is in apartments and simple B&Bs. There are cross-country trails, cleared paths and snowshoeing.

Valfréjus 1550m

Valfréjus is built over the Fréjus road and rail tunnels from Modane to Italy (there was once fantasy-talk of a link with Bardonecchia). It's a small, purpose-built development in the forest, with most of the skiing higher up on open slopes.

The main access gondola goes to Plateau d'Arrondaz (2220m), where there are nursery slopes and short blue runs (and a kids' park with zipline etc). But the heart of the skiing is the peak of Punta Bagna (2735m), with two six-packs serving slopes on the front and back – direct genuine blacks back to Plateau d'Arrondaz on the front of the hill (500m vertical), less direct reds and roundabout blues elsewhere, including a glorious long blue to the resort, said to be 13km for a vertical of almost 1200m. There are more direct blue and black ways home, too. The pistes total a claimed 70km.

The resort consists mostly of a cluster of chalet-shaped apartment blocks around the lift base, with smaller residences and individual chalets dotted around. There are cleared paths, and snowshoe outings. A chair-lift of 160m vertical serves a toboggan run 3km long, with banked curves and tunnels.

Aussois 1500m

Aussois is on the sunny side of the valley, above Modane. It's a charming old village of stone and wood, complete with central fountain, with quite a respectable little ski area – a claimed 55km of pistes, over half of the total blue and green. There are good nursery slopes next to the village, and a very cheap beginner's lift pass. A fast chair goes up to the treeline, where a six-pack goes on to the top height of 2750m. A slow chair and a drag serve the main west-facing upper slopes, red and blue, and a black goes away from the lifts to drop about 1000m before joining a green run to the village, with plentiful off-piste variants. There are snowshoe trails on the Aussois plateau, and more challenging ones across the hillside near Sardières, where there are also extensive cross-country trails. The village offers a couple of B&Bs and simple hotels, as well as plenty of good-value apartments, some in slope-side locations. There's a kids' sledging area at the base.

La Norma 1350m

Across the deep Maurienne valley from Aussois, La Norma could not be more different – a modern, car-free resort in the shade of its steep, eponymous mountain.

The resort claims 65km of runs (or 700 ha – very fashionable). Most of the skiing, above and below the treeline, is on two flanks of that mountain – a major sector on spectator's right, accessed by a gondola and then two slow chairs to 2750m (giving an impressive vertical of 1400m), and a minor sector reached by a fast chair then two slow ones to 2500m. As you may have gathered, slow lifts dominate. There are excellent nursery slopes at village level and at both mid-mountain areas, with a long winding green track back to the base. But this is essentially a red-gradient mountain, genuinely black in places, so it is not great for timid intermediates. There's lots to do off-piste from the upper lifts.

The resort is compact and family-friendly, with lodgings close to the lifts (though very little is ski-in/ski-out). There are toboggan runs for infants and older children.

Megève

Megève / St-Gervais-les-Bains / Combloux / La Giettaz / St-Nicolas-de-Véroce / Les Contamines

Megève does not come from the standard French resort mould. It was developed as a ski resort to give France its own St Moritz, but it doesn't resemble that high, remote resort either. It is low, easily accessible, prettily wooded, charmingly traditional; it has no giant apartment blocks but lots of chalets, including some deeply comfortable, pricey, boutique hotels. It has a lot of very attractive skiing, although broken up into two or three bits.

St-Gervais is a spa town with a lift into the main Megève slopes. Up the valley from there, famously snowy Les Contamines is not connected, but surely will be, one day. For now, it's a day trip, covered by the lift pass.

The mountains in brief

Size Nowhere near as big as it claims, but plenty big enough

Slopes Friendly, prettily wooded hills of intermediate steepness

Snow Gets plenty of snow, but at these altitudes conditions aren't reliable

System, Lift Upgrades are slow in coming – in due in 2019, another 2020

Sustenance A highlight – lots of restaurants, ranging from simple to superb

For beginners A sensible pass and good slopes – but mostly up the hill

For true blue skiers One of the best, with very few nasty surprises

For the confident A great area, although the slow lifts can't be ignored

For experts Lots of space to play between the pistes, and some adventures

Fancy stuff Reasonable facilities in all sectors of the area

Megève – the resort in brief

Convenience Convenient lodgings can be found, but not easily

Lodgings Lots of choice, including some very lovely boutique hotels

Bars and restaurants From the Folie Douce to the 5 Rues jazz club ...

Off the slopes Great facilities, now including a proper toboggan run

For families Good facilities, but it's not a very child-friendly village

Pass notes

The Megève pass also covers Les Contamines. There is also an Unlimited pass covering Chamonix, Courmayeur (in Italy) and Verbier (Switzerland). The Portes du Mont Blanc pass covers just Le Jaillet. There are free carpet lifts, and a half-price day pass for beginners, covering the lower green-run lifts.

Key facts

Altitude	1100m
Range	850–2353m
Slopes (see text)	230km

Where to stay, ideally

In central Megève, a walk from a main lift.

Websites

megeve.com
tourism.saintgervais.com
winter.combloux.com
lescontamines.com

Key ratings

Size	****
Snow	***
Fast lifts	**
Mountain rest's	****
Beginner	****
True blue	*****
Confident	****
Expert	***
Convenience	**
Families	**
Village charm	****

The mountains in detail

The skiing falls into three sectors. Rochebrune is directly accessible from Megève by a central gondola and a much less central cable car, and has a series of more or less parallel lifts spread across a shady mountainside culminating in Côte 2000. A cross-valley cable car links to the second sector, arriving on the upper fringes of the village, below Mont d'Arbois. That's what we'll call this whole sector (the resort divides it into subsectors that make no sense to us). This sector has lifts and runs in many directions, and peaks at Mont Joly at 2353m – or a bit more, according to some sources. From this part of the ski area, in particular, there are fabulous views of Mont Blanc, rearing up above Les Contamines. There are major lifts into the sector from two other points – La Princesse and St-Gervais – and slow lifts from St-Nicolas.

Across the valley, 800m from the centre of Megève, a gondola accesses the third sector, Le Jaillet. This spreads south-west along a ridge to Le Plan, an outpost of the village of La Giettaz, and north-east to the fringes of Combloux, a village on the road up to Megève from Sallanches.

Size

Megève likes to play with numbers, and in its latest press pack splashes '400km of pistes'. It turns out this claim is made for the Evasion Mont Blanc lift pass area, which includes Les Contamines (unconnected, but easily reached by car, and covered in this chapter). Putting together various bits of data from the Schrahe report wc arrive at a likely genuine total for Megève's two areas of 230km – an impressive figure, at the top end of our 4-star category, only just behind Val d'Isere-Tignes. Adding in a realistic figure for Les Contamines brings us to something like 300km for the lift pass area, rather than 400km. It's enough.

If you take a different view, you can get a pass covering Chamonix (reachable by free shuttle-bus, but more smoothly by car) and Courmayeur.

Slopes

As you can see from the photo over the page, most of the skiing is in the trees. This is a fabulous area to ski in a storm, when most French visitors head for the nearest spa. The mountains are mostly of red/blue gradient, but there's quite a lot of green skiing in the bowl below Mont Joux.

Although it's not an area for epic runs, from Mont d'Arbois there are descents, snow permitting, of 800m to La Princesse and of 1000m to St-Gervais. But these are exceptional – all the lifts we like doing laps on are around the 450m mark.

Snow

Like the Annecy Mountains area to the west and Espace Diamant nearby to the south-west, Megève gets a lot of weather, and the key factor is temperature. The area can get big dumps – and, as we've said, it's a great place to be then. Normally storms bring snow, but they can bring rain. These days, with extensive snowmaking, it's usually not a question of whether runs will be open but of what condition they'll be in (particularly at the start and end of the day), given the low altitudes. But runs that are low and sunny – eg the blue and green to the bottom of Le Jaillet – can be unskiable.

Quite a number of pistes in all sectors are left ungroomed for a time after a snowfall – much better than leaving some pistes ungroomed all the time.

System, Lift

We've been banging on for years about the unacceptable number of slow lifts in this, one of the most affluent resorts in the Alps. In the mid-noughties, the lift companies were managing to install a new fast lift every year, but things slowed down again post-Crash. More recently, in 2015 the Chamonix lift company took a majority stake in the main Megève lift company, with promises of investment. And at long last, some of the slow lifts in the Rochebrune sector are to be replaced by six-packs – in 2020 if all goes to plan. The slow Côte 2000 chairs remain.

Meanwhile, there is more immediate good news from elsewhere. The slow chair-lift at Les Chattrix, an outpost of St-Nicolas, is to be replaced by a fast six-seat chair in 2019. We know of no plans for upgrades at La Giettaz or Combloux.

Queues aren't usually a problem except at absolute peak times; sunny weekends bring in the second-home-owners and day-trippers from Geneva, producing queues for the low-capacity lifts such as those about to be replaced.

Sustenance

The number and range of mountain restaurants here is astounding. If your plastic is in good shape, lunch can be a very serious affair indeed – but happily it can be just fairly serious, or quite casual.

Low, rounded, wooded mountains: Mont Joux then Mont d'Arbois in the foreground, Le Jaillet in the distance

The first thing to know is that our friends at Stanford Skiing continue to produce an invaluable guide to all the restaurants (and their prices), downloadable from their website. Every skier planning on lunch here needs it.

Among our favourite haunts are the following. On Rochebrune: happily the indulgent Alpette is now rising from the ashes to which it was reduced in 2015; on the back of the hill, the Forestier is a lovely old chalet. On Mont d'Arbois: two tiny rustic spots – Gouet, for its famous croûte, and Refuge de Porcherey, a few yards off-piste above St-Nicolas, for simple but excellent fixed meals (reservations essential); for a bit of a blowout, La Fruitière at the Folie Douce faces stiffer competition here than in other resorts. On Le Jaillet: Auberge Bonjournal has everything – rustic style, log fire, top views, great food.

More on the slopes

For beginners

There are excellent beginner slopes above the village; as well as free carpet lifts at each lift base there is a wide range of bigger lifts serving green runs, all covered by the half-price Débutant day pass. At the Mont d'Arbois lift base there's the 130m Débutants drag (and the 1km Petit Vorasset serving an easy blue). At the Rochebrune cable car there's the Petit Roch plus the 800m Grands Champs chair-lift. This goes up to the main lift base of Rochebrune, meeting the Chamois and cross-valley Rocharbois lifts (both also covered by the cheap pass). Here, there's the 270m Cabochon drag and the 400m Moutely. Out of town at La Princesse is the 200m Petit Bois.

Progression to longer runs couldn't be easier. There are green runs down the length of all the main gondolas (including the Jaillet), and on Mont d'Arbois there is an intricate network of greens below Mont Joux – and a long green down to Le Bettex, above St-Gervais.

For true blue skiers

This is a glorious resort for building confidence, with friendly slopes wherever you look. The extensive network of green runs is a good start if you are seriously nervous, but then you can travel over virtually the whole area on good blues.

The main snags arise on expeditions to La Giettaz: the outward blue has stretches that require skating, and there are tricky pitches on both outward and return pistes; avoid. Of course, some other runs are not entirely easy; Clémentines on the Croix du Christ chair-lift is one that has some steep pitches.

Finance, on the St-Gervais side of Mont d'Arbois, is a lovely easy run, as is Prapacot, down the Princesse gondola. On Rochebrune, Jardin is similarly attractive; nearby Mouillettes is a bit more testing, whereas Pré Rosset is mainly a means of getting across to Côte 2000. There's not much choice of blue pistes at Combloux, but they are easy and pretty.

For confident intermediates

There's a huge amount of rewarding red (and easy black) skiing – but bear in mind our reservations about snow conditions, especially later in the season, and the continuing flaws in the lift system.

Practically all of the major red pistes are worth a try. The whole Rochebrune sector is worth exploration, even without its promised fast lifts. Other runs and lifts not to miss include: Mont Joly, for some of the best snow; the Grande Epaule run for stunning views of Mont Blanc, followed by the lovely wooded Petite Epaule (to get a new fast chair-lift in 2019); the shady runs on the Croix du Christ and Mont Rosset chairs, and the Princesse gondola; the slopes at La Giettaz, for a bit more challenge; and the Pertuis and Jouty lifts above Combloux for peace and quiet (though the latter is slow).

For experts

Despite the preponderance of easy skiing there are some genuine black pistes, though others barely merit the classification. Chamois on Mont Joly offers the most sustained challenge. The women's downhill course at Côte 2000, Descente, is often groomed and a great blast, with some short steep pitches. Next-door Marmottes also steepens after a very gentle start, and had a mogulled section last time we visited. Bridans and Voltigeurs, on Mont d'Arbois, have stiff sections near the top.

There is off-piste terrain all over the shop, not least around the steeper pistes described above. Even for this sort of stuff, in our experience it's worth having a guide to get you to the best routes. A bit of hiking to spectator's right of the Côte 2000 drag, for example, gets you to a neglected bowl.

From the Mont Joly chair, below the peak of Mont Joly, you can ski the Bécrey ridge to the hamlet of Le Planay, in the valley between Mont Joly and Rochebrune.

Don't overlook Le Jaillet, both for terrain near the pistes above Combloux and Le Plan at La Giettaz, and longer runs. From the Christomet chair a short hike north brings you to the minor peak of L'Eperon for a shady descent to the lifts at Le Plan. Given good snow, from the top of those lifts there are descents into the broad bowl of La Bonne Fontaine, ending near Praz-sur-Arly, and south-west to the Col des Aravis road.

Fancy stuff

There are several terrain parks. The major one for Megève residents is on Mont Joux, with several lines; there's also a more limited one on Rochebrune (with airbag). Other parks are at the top of the Jaillet gondola, on the upper slopes of Combloux and at the top of Le Torraz, at La Giettaz. Sadly, the Megève tourist office doesn't seem very interested in this sort of thing, so we lack further info.

Megève is one of the most captivating ski resorts in France (once you get away from the traffic)

Megève – the resort

Megève has a charming old core, compact and car-free (shown in our photo), and enjoys a lovely setting on a large flat col with wooded slopes all around. But it's no quaint backwater: its 40,000 visitor beds are housed in thousands of low-rise chalets that spread for miles across that col. Driving in from Sallanches along the arrow-straight D1212, past the supermarkets, gas stations and McDonald's, we're always put in mind of the USA. It's the only resort we know that publishes a 12-page booklet devoted to its parking facilities.

Convenience

Megève is a big resort with lots of component parts. The core, a tight cluster of buildings, is only about 300m across, but the resort has spread for miles along the road from Sallanches to Albertville (which narrowly misses the centre). So choice of location is important – there are various lifts you might opt to be close to (one of them, the newly revamped Chamois gondola, is absolutely central). Above the main village, a road running across the slope at the foot of Mont d'Arbois is lined by expensive properties, including some hotels, that offer the best chance of ski-in convenience. Ski buses link the Rochebrune, Le Jaillet, Mont d'Arbois and Côte 2000 lift bases.

Lodgings

There's an unrivalled range of hotels, with roughly equal numbers (about nine) in the 2-star, 3-star and 5-star categories – plus four 4-star places. An unusual feature of the top hotels here (as opposed to St Moritz, say) is that many of them are small and intimate. A conspicuous exception is the 55-room Four Seasons – opened in December 2017 at the foot of Mont d'Arbois, the first of the chain in the Alps. For value and warmth of welcome you won't beat the 2-star Gai Soleil. We also like the 3-star Coin du Feu and the central 4-star Chalet St Georges.

Catered chalets can be found (through specialist travel agents, for example) – but they tend to be rather upmarket, with multiple flunkies as well as a professional chef. Stanford Skiing has a rather less extravagant 10-bed chalet, but its main offering is two simple but cheerful chalet-hotels – the Sylvana near the Rochebrune cable car and the Rond-Point close to the resort centre. It has a growing portfolio of self-catering apartments, too.

Bars and restaurants

Cool, calm, grown-up Megève got a bit of a shock in 2014 with the construction of a rocking Folie Douce clone (as in Val d'Isère, Val Thorens, Méribel etc) at the top of Mont Joux. It seems to have found a market for noisy afternoon conspicuous consumption, though.

According to local experts Stanford Skiing, you can find life in the village if you know where to look. Tucked away behind the church, for example, is St-Paul – the relaxed locals' bar/tabac, good for a close-of-play beer (and a bit cheaper than most). Some other favourites: Wake Up, a cosy bar with tapas; Cocoon, a big, lively, all-purpose bar with sports TV, resident DJ, live music, theme nights and all that; Nano Caffè, a lively wine bar with tables spreading into the square; Deli's

Club, a dark, trendy bar inside the casino building. Stanfords' management prefers the Bar du M in the cool hotel M. Palo Alto is the main club now that Jumeaux is gone. The jazz club Les 5 Rues is legendary, and a good place for a drink.

You can eat at many of the places mentioned above. There is then a very wide range of restaurants, from the Spaggiari pizzeria to the Michelin 3-star Flocons de Sel. The latter is a few km out, but has a budget branch in the village, Flocons Village – highly recommended.

Off the slopes

The outdoor skating rink has long been a focal point of central Megève, contributing greatly to the festive winter ambience. There is also an Olympic-size indoor rink, at the very impressive Palais, outside the centre, which is claimed to be the biggest sports centre in the Alps. This offers curling as well as skating, and the chance to see hockey matches. The Palais has a 1,000m² fitness area and big spa, as well as an aquatic centre with a 25m pool, a kids' swimming pool and a fab paddling pool with slides etc – and indoor and outdoor mineral water leisure pools. There's also a big climbing wall and a gym/tennis court. Phew!

For the 2018 season the resort opened a new toboggan run through the forest down the upper stage of the Princesse gondola, dropping an impressive 500m over its 3km length. That sounds more our cuppa than the much shorter sled-on-rails coaster at Le Jaillet. Hot-air balloon rides are among many other activities.

There's extensive cross-country skiing up the valley towards Côte 2000, and other trails dotted around. There are plenty of paths, and snowshoe guides.

For families

Lutins des Neiges is a kids play area with inflatable elves, cabins, toboggans etc, at the top of the Rochbrune lifts. (Why up there, we wonder?) Across on Mont d'Arbois is a kids funslope similarly themed, brilliantly named Ludicross.

The fab leisure facilities have their appeal, but in general this doesn't strike us as a natural family resort.

Alternatives to Megève

Megève is the best-positioned base for access to the slopes. St-Gervais can match Megève's access to Mont d'Arbois, but is remote from Rochebrune and Le Jaillet – as is St-Nicolas. Combloux is at one extreme of the separate Le Jaillet sector; but it's only a short bus ride from the Mont d'Arbois Princesse gondola. La Giettaz/Le Plan is at the other extreme, miles from anywhere, with slow lifts into the slopes.

St-Gervais-les-Bains 850m

St-Gervais is a pleasant spa resort, very much a town rather than a village, set above a steep river gorge at the foot of Mont Blanc. The town's chalet suburbs spread up the ski slopes to the mid-mountain lift station of Le Bettex. A gondola goes up to Le Bettex, and another goes on to the shoulder of Mont d'Arbois. The nursery slopes are up at Le Bettex, on the Ecole drag-lift and Pierre-Plate chair-lift. Unless staying up there, you'll need a lift pass; a cheap day pass covering just the necessary lifts is available.

St-Gervais also has access to the slopes of Les Houches, in the Chamonix valley, via a historic mountain railway originally intended to go all the way to the summit of Mont Blanc – the summit (or rather the French half of it) falls within the commune of St-Gervais.

The gondola for Le Bettex is about 1km from the town centre, separated from it by the river gorge. The core of the town is only about 500m across, but its suburbs spread widely. Buses run regularly.

There are seven 3-star hotels and three 2-star ones, with a 4-star one due to open in 2019 – the MGallery. The 3-star Liberty Mont-Blanc is a walkable distance from the gondola. The 3-star Ferme de Cupelin is a charming little chalet up the hill a bit, with a good restaurant. Read 'Pick of the apartments' under Megève.

There are thermal baths with all kinds of miraculous properties, a 25m swimming pool with separate pools for kids and toddlers, and an Olympic-size ice rink (regular hockey matches) offering curling as well as skating. There's a kids' sledging area up at Le Bettex. Snowshoe guides are available.

St-Nicolas-de-Véroce 1170m

St-Nicolas is a small, peaceful village in a balcony setting presided over by its eponymous church, which has a wildly ornate baroque interior. The new lift due to be installed at the outpost of Les Chattrix means much faster access to the slopes, but there aren't many lodging options there. At St-Nicolas itself (about 1km away) there's a three-fireplace Logis de France inn, the Coin du Feu. The big news for 2019 is the opening of a new small hotel in the village that is supposed to get a 5-star rating, the Armancette.

Combloux 1020m

You pass through Combloux on the drive up from Sallanches – a thriving little village. It's obviously affected by the through traffic, but away from the road it is pleasantly rustic and spreads up the hill to the ski slopes. The base of the lifts into the Le Jaillet ski area and the village nursery slopes are at La Cry, about a mile up the hill from the centre and 70m higher, but there is a red piste and a drag-lift below that, at Le Bouchet. A ski bus runs to La Cry from the village. Many of the local blue runs are green in gradient.

There are several hotels. The 4-star Ducs de Savoie is a large chalet near the Bouchet lift. The 3-star Chalet Hotel Aspen Valley is right at the La Cry lift base, with good views. The Megève section has a recommendation in 'Pick of the apartments'.

There is sledging for children up at La Cry. Countless snowshoe itineraries lead through the surrounding woodland.

La Giettaz / Le Plan 1225m

La Giettaz is a small village squeezed into a tight space at the bottom of the winding road over the Col des Aravis, which links La Clusaz to the Val d'Arly. Its skiing starts 3km away at Le Plan, at one end of the long ski area of Le Jaillet. There are nursery slopes there, too.

The 2-star Flor'Alpes is a small hotel in central La Giettaz. There's a small artificial ice rink in the village. Snowshoe guides are available, and cleared paths.

Les Contamines 1180m

Les Contamines, tucked under Mont Blanc, has a reputation for snow. It's a glitz-free rustic village, with a small but very varied ski area (starting a bus ride from the village centre) covered by the Megève pass.

The mountain

It's an unusual area – small, but with four identifiable sectors. Above Le Lay, gondolas rise about 800m along a wooded ridge to Signal, just above the trees. Above this, lifts serve an area of open slopes below a ridge with its low point at the Col du Joly. On the back of the ridge are slopes above Belleville, centred on La Ruelle; down the valley is Hauteluce, in the Espace Diamant. Off to spectator's right of the col are high and mainly steep slopes beneath Aiguille Croche; over that peak is Megève.

Size The resort claims 120km of pistes, but it's obviously nowhere near that. The Schrahe report puts it at a more reasonable 67km, meriting 2 stars.

Slopes The home slopes are wooded; everything else is open. Much of the Aiguille Croche is quite steep; the other sectors are of typical intermediate stuff.

Snow For its very modest height, the resort has an excellent snowfall record, and some of its slopes are shady. But the Ruelle sector is disastrously sunny, and the Aiguille Croche sector faces south-east; at least that part is pretty high, reaching almost 2500m.

System, Lift Unusually for this part of the world, the piste map distinguishes fast chairs and slow, making it easy to spot that fast ones are in the majority. But there are still slow ones in places that matter, and many more drag-lifts.

Sustenance There are quite a few welcoming woody huts. Ferme da la Ruelle is a fine spot on the sunny side; ditto Bûche Croisée on the shady side.

For beginners There are two beginner slopes betwee the village centre and the lift base, and short lifts on easy slopes up at Signal and at mid-mountain. There's a very cheap pass for all these lifts. The long winding green on back of the hill can't be reached by beginners from the Contamines side.

For true blue skiers The runs down the ridge from Signal are easy, and the blues higher up not particularly difficult; the ones over the col above Ruelle are a bit more challenging.

For the confident The reds runs are generally only a bit stiffer than the blues but, again, the Ruelle side is more testing. The Belleville piste to the bottom is excellent when conditions are good.

For experts The black runs are not seriously steep – Rebans offers the most sustained challenge. There is plenty of off-piste terrain between the lifts, and more adventurous routes from the high lifts – the Monument drag offers a 900m sunny descent to the Ruelle gondola.

Fancy stuff The Ludoparc family funslopes in the Aiguille Croche sector seem to be about the extent of it.

The resort

The village spreads for a couple of miles along the valley, but it has a compact, unspoiled centre with a fine old church.

Convenience It's not a conveniently arranged place. The Montjoie gondola base at Le Lay is 1km from the village centre, and many lodgings are further away (although there are also lodgings at the lift base). There is a ski bus, of course.

Lodgings There are half a dozen hotels. The well-run and convenient Chemenaz at Le Lay has made it to 4-star status. The Gai Soleil is a 3-star, the others 2-star. There are chalets and apartments to rent.

Bars and restaurants There are bars in which to round off the day; the Saxo at Le Lay plays blues and jazz while serving rum. Several restaurants serve the traditional range; the cool O à la Bouche is a bit more ambitious.

Off the slopes The Parc Nordique has 25km of cross-country skiing trails of all levels, and they say the discipline of biathlon is close to a religion here. There's a 'semi-natural' outdoor ice rink. We see no sign of a pool, or a proper toboggan run. There are snowshoe guides, and around the village there are cleared paths. Dog sledding is offered, and sleigh rides.

For families At mid-mountain in the Aiguille Croche sector is the Ludoparc zone, with two fun routes for families. There's sledging for tinies in the Nordic Park, and for older kids on the Telebaby drag-lift.

Montgenèvre

Montgenèvre / Claviere (in Italy, just)

Montgenèvre is a work in progress. Since the through-traffic over the pass it sits on was buried in a tunnel, prior to the 2006 Turin Olympics, the resort has moved step by step from being a cheap and not very cheerful backwater towards being a proper international resort. Most recently it has built a smart aquatic centre. But it still has some way to go: to match the increasing range of smart lodgings (and exploit fully its excellent snow record), the resort badly needs investment in its lifts. Especially on the upper slopes, progress around the mountains is just too slow.

Our panel a few pages on explains problems that have been affecting the link with Italy. These may now be over; Montgenèvre must hope so.

The mountains in brief

Size On the small side; happily, the weekly pass covers days elsewhere

Slopes Nicely varied terrain, with trees adding visual interest and shelter

Snow Well placed to catch any snow that's going, and decent altitudes

System, Lift The slowest system we've encountered in a long time

Sustenance Another weakness; a couple of places in Italy save the day

For beginners Excellent slopes, but you need a full lift pass from day two

For true blue skiers Italy is off-limits, but otherwise a good bet

For the confident Few challenges; and factor in the size and the lift system

For experts Excellent off-piste terrain inside and outside the lift network

Fancy stuff Not premiership standard, but the essentials are there

Montgenèvre – the resort in brief

Convenience Some ski-in/ski-out lodgings, and no very long walks needed

Lodgings Not a wide choice, but within that some excellent places

Bars and restaurants Ditto

Off the slopes We'd rather see a proper toboggan run, but we're quibbling

For families A good choice, if you pick your spot with care

Pass notes

The Monts de la Lune pass covers the adjacent lifts in Italy. A six-day pass also covers days in the rest of the Via Lattea, Bardonecchia, Serre-Chevalier, Puy-St-Vincent, Les Deux-Alpes and Alpe-d-Huez.

There is one free carpet-lift, but beginners need a full lift pass after that.

Key facts

Altitude	1850m
Range	1400–2580m
Slopes (see text)	110km

Where to stay, ideally

For most purposes, close to the snow in the middle of the village.

Websites

montgenevre.com
claviere.it

Key ratings

Size	**
Snow	****
Fast lifts	**
Mountain rest's	**
Beginner	****
True blue	****
Confident	***
Expert	****
Convenience	***
Families	****
Village charm	***

The mountains in detail

Montgenèvre sits on a pass with slopes roughly to the north and south of it. The sunny north side, named Chalvet for the peak overlooking it, is reached by a gondola from the east end of the village or a hybrid chondola from a point halfway to Claviere. The south side is more complex.

Lifts from the nursery slopes take you to two points in the Aigle sector, which culminates in the Rocher de l'Aigle chair up to about 2570m on the Italian border. From one of these points you can ski to the separate Gondrans sector, to spectator's right.

Normally you can ski into Italy from the Aigle chair, but not at present (read 'The Italian connection'). Instead you plod to Claviere to access the third sector on this side, the Italian Monts de la Lune.

Size

For the local cross-border area the resort claims 110km of pistes (for Montgenèvre alone, 90km). We reckon these figures are optimistic – but anything around the 100km mark puts the area in our 2-star category. Read our panel on the Italian connection for news on the Via Lattea, which is much bigger; the six-day pass covers a day's access to it, and days in other reachable resorts. Mileage-hungry skiers will want to consider an outing to Briançon, to ski Serre-Chevalier.

Slopes

As at nearby Serre-Chevalier, the treeline here is unusually high, at about 2200m. So there is a bit of woodland skiing, although not nearly as much as in Serre-Che where the lift bases are much lower. The low peak of Prarial is the first place to head in a snowstorm.

There's a good mix of gradients, but the Gondrans sector stands out for genuinely easy skiing on good snow.

This isn't an area for notably long runs, with top-to-bottom verticals limited to about 800m and most individual lifts you might do laps on offering no more than 300m–400m.

Snow

Montgenèvre has a deserved reputation for snowfall; its position on the east-west pass means that it can get weather from the Atlantic or the Med – and the winds dump snow as they rise from the low valleys on each side. The altitude, particularly of the resort, is respectable, and the greater part of the area is roughly north-facing.

Obviously the Chalvet sector is sunnier, but its best slopes (particularly its steepest ones) face east, which isn't nearly as bad as south or west. So, all in all, it's a good picture.

System, Lift

This is a real problem, particularly for mileage-hungry piste skiers who can get down a 300m-vertical piste in no time: the lift system here is the most primitive one we know. All the lifts in the Aigle sector are slow; other than the two access lifts, all the lifts in the Chalvet sector are slow; most of the lifts in the Gondrans sector are slow; half the lifts in the Monts de la Lune sector are slow.

The Chalvet chair is due to be upgraded to a fast quad, and the currently closed Col Saurel chair on the Italian side is fast, so things will improve a bit before long. Until then, the only fast lift a competent skier might want to spend a lot of time on is the Serra Granet, again on the Italian side.

Sustenance

The choice is limited, particularly on the French side – so the Graal in the village does good business. The big Terrasses at mid-mountain on the Chalvet side was new in 2017; great views from the terrace, and satisfying food, but inside it has way too many tables crammed in – a real shame. (They should take a look at Pra Long, above Briançon.) Over in Italy, things improve: we like both Baita la Coche (theoretically self-service, but service is often forthcoming from the cheerful owners) and the smoother Monsoleil.

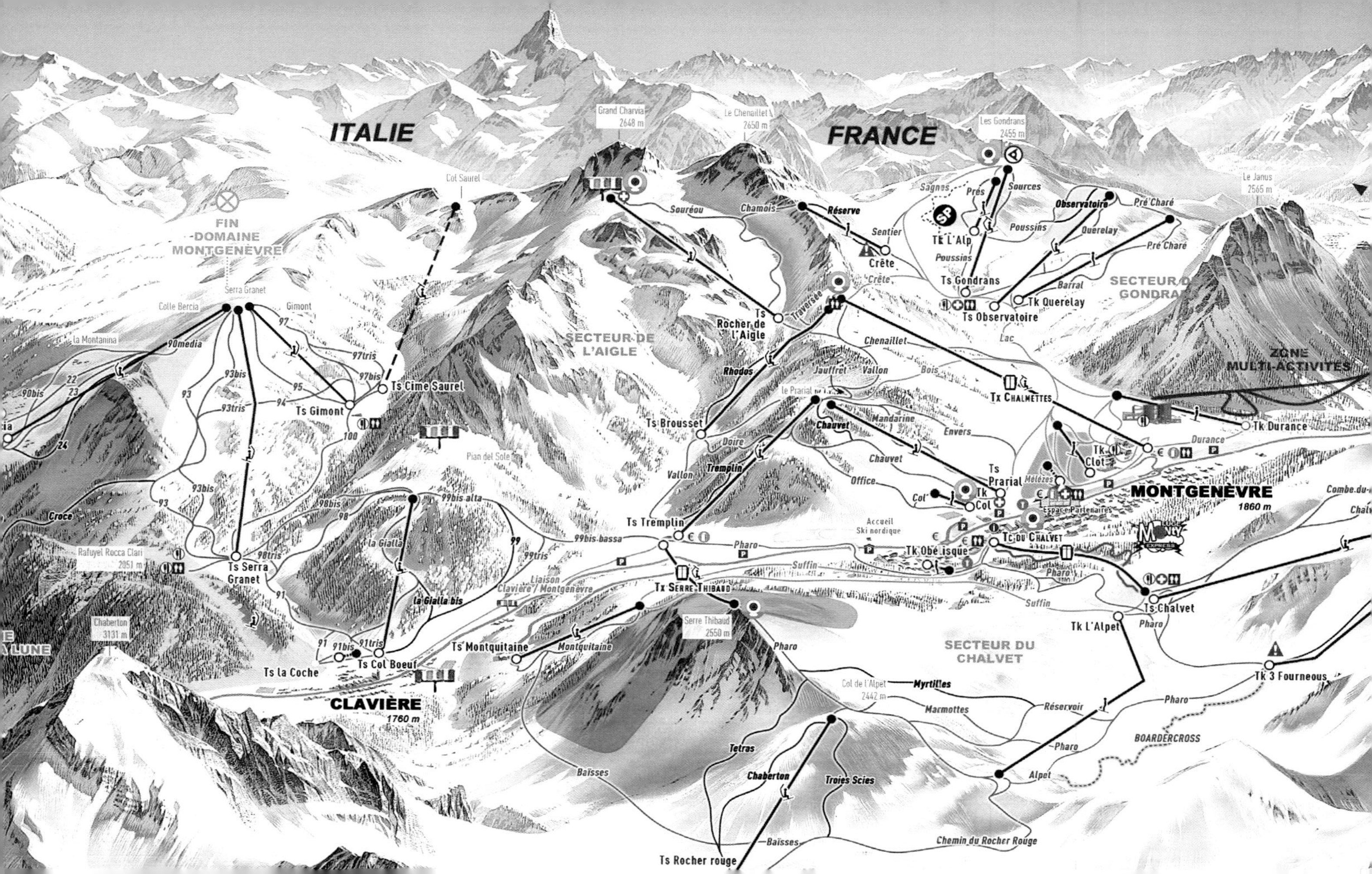
ITALIE
FRANCE
Grand Charvia 2648 m
Le Chenaillet 2650 m
Les Gondrans 2455 m
Le Janus 2565 m
Col Saurel
FIN DOMAINE MONTGENÈVRE
Serra Granet
Colle Bercia
Gimont
La Montanina
SECTEUR DE L'AIGLE
SECTEUR DES GONDRANS
SECTEUR DU CHALVET
ZONE MULTI-ACTIVITÉS
MONTGENÈVRE 1860 m
CLAVIÈRE 1760 m
Chaberton 3131 m
Rafuyel Rocca Clari 2051 m
Serre Thibaud 2550 m
Col de l'Alpet 2442 m
Ts Cime Saurel
Ts Gimont
Ts Serra Granet
Ts la Coche
Ts Col Boeuf
Ts Montquitaine
Ts Tremplin
Ts Brousset
Ts Rocher de l'Aigle
Tx Serre Thibaud
Tx Chalmettes
Ts Gondrans
Ts Observatoire
Tk L'Alp
Tk Querelay
Tk Durance
Tk Clot
Ts Prarial
Tk Col
Tk Obélisque
Tc du Chalvet
Ts Chalvet
Tk L'Alpet
Tk 3 Fourneous
Ts Rocher rouge
Accueil Ski nordique
Espace Partenaires
Liaison Clavière / Montgenèvre
BOARDERCROSS
Pian del Sole
Chemin du Rocher Rouge

More on the slopes

For beginners

The gentle nursery slope is between the two main chair-lifts directly in front of the village, equipped with a carpet-lift and the 400m Clot drag-lift. The carpet-lift is free, but to use Clot or any other lift you must buy a full lift pass. Not ideal.

On the other hand, you'll soon be able to make the most of your pass on the slopes of Les Gondrans. You ride the Chalmettes chondola hybrid then ski a green run to the Gondrans chair, which serves a much longer, beautifully gentle green. Then, when you're ready, you can move on to the blue runs on the Observatoire chair-lift next door. This is all at a fairly high altitude and north-east facing, so the snow is as good as it gets.

For true blue skiers

There is some lovely blue skiing here, and very few blue runs that need health warnings. Whether it amounts to enough skiing for you is another matter – read 'Size' for further observations.

The obvious place to find your ski legs is the Gondrans sector where you can, if you like, start on green runs and end up experimenting with easy reds. From the Chalmettes chondola you can instead ski Vallon to ride a choice of chairs leading to runs back to the village. Over on Chalvet, the Serre Thibaud chondola accesses the long, lovely Pharo blue down the whole Chalvet bowl and back to the bottom; we're guessing it must be over 5km overall. You can do laps on the middle section using the Alpet drag-lift. There is another good blue (Baïsses) back to the valley on the other side of the peak of Serre Thibaud; but this is one run that has a stretch requiring a bit of confidence and energy, particularly if the snow is heavy and only half the width is groomed.

But this is also a resort where you might like to try some reds. Read on.

For confident intermediates

There's quite a lot of red on the map, and if you like cruising in scenic surroundings, the area might suit you well. If you like a bit of a challenge, though, it's a different matter. If the high-altitude link with Italy is re-opened (read our panel on the next page), piste 100 from the border is one of the best. Souréou on the French side from the same point is a lovely run too, but reaches red gradient only briefly. The red pistes on Chalvet are decent runs

Mont de la Plane, seen from Chalvet's Terrasses restaurant, has some fine off-piste, but it's not easily reached

The approach to Claviere, just down the road from Montgenèvre, but just on the Italian side of the border

The Italian connection – being restored, in part?

The Via Lattea (or Milky Way, or Voie Lactée), linking French Montgenèvre with Italian Sansicario, Sauze d'Oulx and Sestriere, has never quite realised its potential. A central flaw is that the link from the big Italian resorts through valley-bottom Cesana Torinese has remained stubbornly slow and inconvenient. But recently other problems have arisen.

The slopes around Montgenèvre spread across the border to those above Claviere (known as the Monts de la Lune). The main link is at high altitude, from the Rocher de l'Aigle chair-lift. Or rather it was: following a fatal accident on an Italian piste (during the 2015/16 season, we are told), this link was closed.

For three seasons, to ski the Italian side of the border you've had to use the village-level link, a flat path past the golf course and cross-country trails to Claviere – extremely tedious, we can confirm. As well as the higher link, both the Cime Saurel and the Gimont chairs on the Italian side have been out of action.

Now, in late 2018, we hear that the high link will be restored for the season ahead, but that the Cime Saurel will remain closed for a fourth season. Nuts.

The six-day Monts de la Lune pass includes a day in the Via Lattea proper, but six-day Via Lattea passes have not recently been offered – just day extensions costing a serious €31.50.

with proper red pitches halfway down. The short Chauvet just above the village is red at the top, and a good place to do laps in a snowstorm; La Gialla above Claviere falls into the same category.

The rest of the reds, though, are either at the easy end of the red spectrum or are blue runs masquerading as reds; on Gondrans, in particular, the reds and blues are barely distinguishable.

Fortunately, the blacks are generally approachable, and are mostly shady so offer the chance of good snow. Rhodos and Tremplin in the Aigle sector are the easiest, the runs on Chalvet the stiffest – Tetras probably stiffest of all.

For experts

The black pistes don't offer much of a challenge – read the previous section. But there is lots of good off-piste, and if snow falls, there's a good chance it will be deep and powdery.

We're dismayed to note that the whole southern end of Serre Thibaud, where we enjoyed an excellent morning a few years back, is now (and possibly was then) a protected zone. So leaving that aside ... north of the top lift station there are some good (though shorter) slopes on the east side of the ridge, down to the blue pistes.

The Rocher de l'Aigle chair-lift opens up several options. As well as off-piste

deviations from the Souréou red piste and descents directly from the col into Italy, there is the obvious and very popular run back to the Brousset chair down the Vallon de la Doire. A 10-minute hike anti-clockwise round the peak of Grand Charvia brings you into the wide, gentle bowl of the Combe de Grand Charvia, down into Italy another way. Heading south instead, there are countless ways down towards Cervières, south-east of Briançon.

There are routes towards Cervières from the top of the Gondrans sector, too. And from the same spot there is a long descent through woods to La Vachette, where the road from Briançon starts to climb to Montgenèvre.

If you're up for some hiking, Mont de la Plane has some good shady slopes towards the resorts – see our photo.

Fancy stuff

There is a 500m-long Snowpark on the Alp drag-lift at the top of the Gondrans sector, with easier and more difficult lines, and next to it is a funslope said to be almost a mile long. Over on the Chalvet sector is a boardercross course, about 800m long.

Montgenèvre – the resort

Montgenèvre is a small, pleasant but unremarkable village offering good-value lodgings in a scenic, usually very snowy setting. Life revolves around one long, sunny street looking on to the snow, which originally was the road from Briançon to Turin but now has hardly any traffic.

Convenience

It's a small village, and no one has to walk very far to reach the snow, to ski or skate to the lifts up the shady side of the pass. But it's big enough to justify minibus navettes running on two routes, along the snow front and up around the village backwaters. You can ski to the door of some lodgings from the Chalvet sector, including some of the new developments in the Hameau de l'Obélisque, at the east end of the village. This area is a bit out on a limb, some distance from the Gondrans lifts but very convenient for the Chalvet one, with a short drag to give you a bit of height when skiing across to it.

Lodgings

Most of the lodgings are in apartments and rented chalets, but there are some catered chalets and some good hotels. We've enjoyed very satisfactory stays in two smart places in the Hameau de l'Obélisque – the cool, relaxed Anova, with pool and spa, and the rather more swanky Chalet Blanc. But for location you can't beat the simple but well run Alpis Cottia, over the focal Graal bar-restaurant, where we've stayed several times.

Bars and restaurants

There are probably a dozen places for a drink or a meal. The central and very popular Graal Café is the all-purpose après bar-restaurant, although its evening menu is more limited than its lunch menu. The back-street Tourmente is a funky vaulted cellar bar where the amusing and amused boss, Maurizio, does a wide range of cocktails and a narrow range of wines (and plays the Stones).

We've enjoyed dinner at La Cave de Montgenèvre, an impressive cheese/charcuterie/wine emporium that also functions as an excellent informal restaurant – good entrecôte au poivre and yes, the charcuterie is very good too. The Capitaine does good pizzas and other Italian staples.

Off the slopes

The newish Durancia aquatic centre has various indoor and outdoor pools, spa and fitness facilities. The Monty Express sled-on-rails coaster is said to be the longest in France, and we don't doubt it – running down the full length of the Chalvet gondola, it has a vertical of a mighty 1400m. There's a big natural outdoor ice rink at the eastern end of the village. None of these facilities is unreasonably expensive. Other diversions include snowmobiling.

There are cross-country loops at village level, but aficionados will want to get a bus down to Les Alberts, on the way to Briançon, to explore the 60km of trails in the unspoiled Clarée valley.

For families

Provided you pick your spot with some care for easy access to snow, this is a fine place for a young family – the slopes have lots to offer, and there is plenty to do after they close (though we'd rather see a proper snowy toboggan run than the sled-on-rails thing).

The Claviere option

Despite the French-sounding name, Claviere is in Italy, just – the border post is right on the edge of the village. Even more than Montgenèvre, it was improved in the noughties by the removal of through-traffic to a bypass – it is now a positively pleasant place to explore.

There is a nursery slope right next to the village, and almost equally close are two chair-lifts – one to the Italian slopes and the other to Col Boeuf for runs in either direction.

There are several modest hotels – a wider choice than in Montgenèvre, in fact. The 4-star hotel Bes is a classic old-fashioned Italian hotel in a very central position. Popular bar-restaurants include the Gran Bouc and the Kilt.

The village has a fine setting on the high pass, facing the sun; the Chalvet slopes are behind, right of centre

Paradiski

Les Arcs / Peisey-Vallandry / Villaroger /Bourg-St-Maurice / **La Plagne** / Montchavin-Les Coches / Montalbert / Champagny-en-Vanoise

Two big ski areas, joined at the hip by a giant cable car

Funny business, the ski area game. Link two ski areas by bus and they remain two areas, even if they share a lift pass. Build a linking cable car, and hey presto! You have one giant area. Thus, in 2003, we got Paradiski.

The Vanoise Express links Peisey-Vallandry (Plan-Peisey, to be precise) on the Les Arcs side to a point some way above Montchavin on the La Plagne side. The link is powerful, with giant double-deck cabins (still the world's biggest, as far as we know), so queues are rarely a problem. It's quick, so it adds very little to your travel-to-lunch time. And it's possible to start from one extreme and have lunch at the other – a satisfying trip.

The combined area claims 425km of pistes, which may be an exaggeration but only a slight one. This puts the area into the exclusive 5-star category for size – on a par with the Portes du Soleil, but some way behind the unrivalled 3 Vallées. It's way ahead of the 4-star pack (led by Val d'Isère-Tignes).

If you're intent on making the most of the whole area, there's obviously a strong case for staying near the link, in Peisey-Vallandry or Montchavin-Les Coches. On the Les Arcs side, it doesn't take long to reach the link from the main resort villages. But on the La Plagne side it's different – if you're thinking of spending days on the Aiguille Rouge above Arc 2000, you don't really want to be starting from Champagny or Montalbert.

As we write in 2018, the local passes include one day skiing the whole area, and a six-day Paradiski pass costs about €35 more than a local one.

Les Arcs

Arc 1800 / Arc 2000 / Arc 1950 / Arc 1600 / Peisey-Vallandry / Villaroger / Bourg-St-Maurice

Les Arcs is a multi-part purpose-built resort, the components of which are increasingly celebrated as classic examples of the species. But from the skier's point of view the original idea of plonking huge blocks of cramped apartments at the lift bases was a lot less successful than the more recent approach of spreading comfortable lodgings, built in Alpine style, beside the pistes, as in the newer parts of Arc 1800 and in Arc 1950.

The slopes here have something for everyone, and include an excellent woodland area above the small resort of Peisey-Vallandry. With the link to La Plagne right there, this makes a compelling base.

The mountains in brief

Size Big enough, with lots more mileage easily accessible in La Plagne
Slopes An excellent cocktail, including very worthwhile woodland sectors
Snow A bit more sunny than is ideal, but pretty good even so
System, Lift There are problems, but most are not usually serious
Sustenance Some good spots, but mainly in the Arc 2000 / Arc 1600 areas
For beginners OK at first, but you soon need a pass; and no green runs
For true blue skiers Easy to get around, but rewarding pistes are few
For the confident Pretty good – but get a Paradiski pass, and use it
For experts One of the best, with more to do over in La Plagne
Fancy stuff A big, bold snow park between Arc 1600 and Arc 1800

Arc 1800 – the resort in brief

Convenience Lots of ski-in lodgings, and no shortage of ski-out ones
Lodgings Good choice of apartments, narrower choice of hotels and chalets
Bars and restaurants A reasonable range – more than in the other Arcs
Off the slopes The Mille 8 zone above the lift base was an inspired idea
For families One of the best, unless you need access to skating

Pass notes
Les Arcs passes cover a day in La Plagne. In 2019 a six-day Paradiski pass costs only €36 extra, and conveys priority at some lifts (read 'System, Lift'). For beginners there are free carpet lifts at Arc 1800 and 2000, but you soon need a pass; in 1600 and Peisey-Vallandry, beginners have to pay from the start.

Key facts

Altitude	1700m
Range	1200–3226m
Slopes (see text)	425km

Where to stay, ideally
In central Arc 1800, or up the slope a bit, eg in Le Chantel.

Websites
lesarcs.com
peisey-vallandry.com
lesarcs-peiseyvallandry.ski
paradiski.com

Key ratings

Size	*****
Snow	****
Fast lifts	****
Mountain rest's	***
Beginner	***
True blue	***
Confident	****
Expert	*****
Convenience	****
Families	*****
Village charm	**

The mountains in detail

Arc 1600, Arc 1800 and Peisey-Vallandry are ranged along a broad mountainside, with lifts up to the ridge from the two Arcs (and over it to Col de la Chal in the case of the gondola from 1800). Beyond the ridge is the high open bowl of Arc 2000, with lifts up to Grand Col (2832m) and the high-point of Aiguille Rouge (3226m), the start of a famously long piste to Villaroger – over 2000m vertical, and said to be 7km long.

Size

Les Arcs is slightly the junior partner in the 400km+ Paradiski area, but still must have something close to 200km of pistes – enough to scrape into our 4-star category on its own. The Paradiski area including La Plagne is one of three areas in the book to merit 5 stars.

Slopes

The main broad mountainside is mostly of red gradient, with blue runs cutting across it. The treeline is about halfway up, so there is a worthwhile amount of woodland skiing, at least above 1600 and Peisey-Vallandry – much of the terrain above 1800 is a summer golf course, with only isolated clumps of trees. The Arc 2000 bowl is mostly gentler; 2000 and 1950 just below it are bang on the treeline, with just a bit of sheltered skiing below the villages and more off to skier's right.

Of course, the aforementioned epic descent from the Aiguille Rouge is not typical – most runs are much shorter. But from the Aiguille to the villages is a healthy 1100m vertical.

While linked La Plagne is curiously short of long green runs, Les Arcs has no greens at all – not even the Cabanes piste, specially created for beginners as part of the Mille 8 zone, is green. Bizarre.

The majority of the black pistes (and several reds) are designated as Natur' runs, which in theory means they are never groomed. We're not keen on this policy: leaving fresh snow ungroomed on advanced runs is a good idea, and leaving some mogul slopes intact is fair enough. But does a resort need a dozen mogul fields with virtually no one using them?

Snow

It's a resort of two halves. The main area above Arc 1600 and 1800 doesn't go super-high – the lifts go to about 2400m – and it faces a tad north of west, which is not ideal. The bowl above Arc 2000 is much more shady, and has higher slopes; there is even a little patch of glacier under

The high, treeless slopes of Arc 2000 – some gentle, but steep (and shady) on the Aiguille Rouge

the top pistes. Some of the blacks, again, face just north of west. So it's good for snow, but not great.

System, Lift

Although the system mainly works well, it has some distinct weaknesses.

In the mornings, the cable car from La Plagne delivers enough people to keep the Peisey chair-lift busy. Higher up, the Derby can't always cope with demand.

The Transarc gondola out of 1800 is not the only way to get to 2000, but it is the obvious one, and builds queues as a result, especially in the afternoons.

The key lifts above 2000 can be busy – the Arcabulle to Col de la Chal, and the Varet gondola and the cable car above it to the Aiguille Rouge. The cable car shifts 1,100 people an hour, the gondola (with lifties efficiently filling the cabins) 2,800 people, and many want to go to the top. We met huge queues recently in March.

As we write in 2018, the slow Comborcière triple chair-lift towards Arc 1600 from below Arc 1950 is being replaced by a fast quad (with a new red piste, parallel to the existing black but in its own 'secret couloir' – Piste du Secret). But there is still no sign of upgrades for the chairs up from Villaroger, nearby.

An interesting step in 2018 is that the Paradiski pass entitles you to use priority lines at half a dozen lifts around the area, including the Varet gondola.

Sustenance

There are decent places spread across the whole area, but few that have sustained our affection in the long term.

Many of the best places are in the Arc 2000 sector. The stylishly traditional Chalets de l'Arc, just above 2000, is one place we've sometimes loved, sometimes despaired of. Below the resort, the ancient Belliou la Fumée is charmingly rustic. On the long run to Villaroger, Chalet du Solliet is a charming chalet with great views, serving excellent food.

We recently had an excellent lunch at the smart, airy Lodge, at the top of the Mille 8 zone – a limited but good menu.

Above 1600, Le Sanglier Qui Fume is a fairly recent addition that we are itching to try – a fine, airy chalet in a great position with a wide-ranging menu, said to include superb *frites*. Above 1800 we like the tiny, simple, good-value Blanche Murée.

More on the slopes

For beginners

The beginner slope at Arc 1800 is at the top of the Mille 8 area, reached from the lift base by the Villards gondola and served by a covered carpet lift, which is free to use and open in the evening. But the Villards gondola costs €5 a ride.

Progression to longer runs is easy enough – the Cabanes piste at Mille 8 is the obvious first step (but at €5 a go).

For true blue skiers

The mountain is covered in blue runs, all of them correctly classified, many very easy indeed and few at the tougher end of the spectrum – Charmettoger and Grands Mélèzes are two that take quite a direct line down the slightly steeper band of terrain above 1800. So you can get around the area quite easily; but many runs are rather tedious tracks, and lots of runs are disappointingly narrow.

On the bright side, some blues we like are Edelweiss down to 2000, Mont Blanc down to 1600 and Renard on the upper mountain above Peisey-Vallandry. The short runs on the St Jacques chair-lift at 2000 are worth a look if you are based there. You can get local day passes for each main sector, but they save very little on the daily cost of a six-day pass.

For confident intermediates

There's a lot of good red skiing, widely spread and varying in character. The wonderful long run from the Aiguille Rouge to Le Pré, above Villaroger, is an obvious highlight. It is classified red for most of its length but black for a stretch in the middle. If you're a confident skier and happy on the top section shared with the Arandelières 2 red piste, you shouldn't be put off by this. That red piste is worth skiing if there is no serious queue for the cable car, and the lower part 1, reached from the gondola, has some good stretches and links to the good trio of reds on the Plagnettes chair-lift.

All the lower resorts have lifts serving a choice of good runs. From the Transarc gondola, Grand Renard and Rêches add up to an excellent long run to 1800. But our favourite sector is the row of long, easy reds winding through the forest above Peisey-Vallandry.

Mont Pourri
Grande Motte
Grande Casse
L'Aliet
Aiguille Rouge
3226 m
Grand Col
2832 m
Glacier Du Varet
Aiguille Grive
2732 m
Col De La Chal
Aiguille Rousse
2488m
Parc National
de la Vanoise
Porte du Parc
National de la Vanoise
Réserve Naturelle
des Hauts de Villaroger
Col du Grand Renard
2425m
L'Arpette
2413 m
Col des Frettes
2384m
AIGUILLE ROUGE 30
GRAND COL 38
VARET 40
ST JACQUES 33
PLAGNETTES 36
ARCABULLE 48
LANCHETTES 45
CABRIOLET
MARMOTTES 32
BOIS DE L'OURS 31
PRE SAINT ESPRIT 35
COMBORCIERE 41
CLOCHERET 8
SNOW PARK 17
ARPETTE 14
CARRELEY 26
PLAN VERT
TRANSARC II 47
VAGERE 24
TRANSARC I 46
VILLARDS
CHARMETTOGER 28
JARDIN ALPIN 29
DERBY 69
FLOCON 65
2300 66
CABRI
GRIZZLY 68
VALLANDRY 74
PEISEY 61
COMBE 72
PARCHEY
LONZAGNE 73
DROSET 52
PLAN DES VIOLETTES 51
REPLAT 50
MONT. BLANC 4
CACHETTE 6
COMBETTES
VEZAILLE 18
TOMMELET 10
FUNICULAIRE 1
MILLERETTE 13
FREESTYLE ZONES
RODÉO LUGE
LA PAUSE
SITE NORDIQUE
Mauve
Arc 2000
Arc 1950
Arc 1600
Arc 1800
Villards
Charvet
Chantel
Charmettoger
Plan Peisey
1600m
Vallandry
1600m
Nancroix
Le Villaret
Villaroger
1200m
Le Planay
RHONAZ
Plan Devin
Courbaton
Les Granges
Montrigon
Bourg Saint Maurice

For experts

Les Arcs has a good range of genuine, though not seriously steep, black pistes (most of them ungroomed Natur' runs), as well as excellent off-piste opportunities.

One group of blacks is on the face of the Aiguille Rouge – all good runs, though not very long. The three reached by the Varet gondola face roughly north, and often have good snow. So does the steeper Robert Blanc, off the Arandelières red run from the top. Three other blacks off the Aiguille Rouge piste get sun in the afternoon; Génépi, the first, is quite steep.

A second cluster of blacks is across the valley, around the minor peaks west of Arc 2000. Muguet and Comborcière (not Natur' pistes) add up to a good run in the morning sun, steepening at the end.

There are also blacks in the woods; Bosses, naturally, offers moguls, but Ecureuil is steeper, longer, more varied.

There is lots of worthwhile off-piste terrain within the lift system, not all of it easy or free of dangers. In good weather, the aforementioned minor peaks have a lot to offer (including short couloirs), as does the Grand Col chair. In bad weather, there are good routes to be done in the woods at Peisey-Vallandry and Villaroger. On the west/north-west faces of the Aiguille Rouges there are several routes.

There are good possibilities outside the lift network in several directions. At the southern end of the area you can ski down into the Nancroix valley or around to the Peisey-Vallandry lifts, starting from Col de la Chal, or with a climb to the shoulder of the Aiguille Grive, or from the Grand Col chair-lift. But the better known option from that chair starts with a short hike up to the col for a lovely long run north-east, behind the Aiguille Rouge to Villaroger. At the start there are

The front de neige at Arc 1800, looking south-west to the slopes below La Plagne's Roche de Mio

two options: one tricky, one not. More challenging routes into the same area – Couloir en S, Grandes Pentes, Combe des Lanchettes, Paravalanches – start from points on the Aiguille Rouge piste.

All these runs to the east of Aiguille Rouge take you through a nature reserve where by law you must ski with a guide.

Fancy stuff

The main snow park – on the upper slopes, a lift ride above both 1600 and 1800, served by its own drag-lift – is about 700m long and is highly regarded by those who know about these things. There's a boardercross course up at Col de la Chal.

Arc 1800 – the resort

This is the best location in Les Arcs: a single lift gets you to Col de la Chal, where a single run gets you to the Aiguille Rouge lifts or to Plan-Peisey, and it has the best amenities – notably the excellent Mille 8 complex.

Convenience

The resort spreads across the hillside for about a mile, with a lot of lodgings that are ski-in/plod-out; the central part is called Les Villards, the southern part Charmettoger, the northern part Le Charvet. There are now a lot of apartment residences up the hill in Le Chantel, above Le Charvet, beside the slopes. Le Chantel is served by a gondola from Les Villards, and shuttle buses link all the parts of the resort.

Mille 8 – a fabulous facility

Created in 2014, the Mille 8 activity zone is a key attraction for Arc 1800. It is open all day and into the evening, later some days than others.

The 600m-long Villards gondola rises 120m over a lightly wooded slope above the main lift base. At the top is Le Lodge, with a good restaurant and snack bar with live music (and a golf simulator). Next to this is the resort's gentle beginner slope (floodlit in the evenings) served by a covered carpet lift (free to use).

The Cabanes piste winds gently down one side of the zone, while a beginner's freestyle course goes down the other side. Between the two is a 900m toboggan run. At the bottom is an excellent aquatic centre with a leisure pool, hot tubs, kids' features, a spa and fitness rooms.

The gondola is free to pedestrians but skiers without a lift pass pay €5 a ride to use it. The pool is reasonably priced, but the rather short toboggan run seems a bit pricey.

Lodgings

There are several hotels. Most interesting is the 4-star Aiguille Grive Chalets Hotel, with six stylish modern units on the snow above Charmettoger, each with four to six rooms. Catered chalets can be found, but are more numerous in Arc 2000 and Peisey-Vallandry.

Ski Collection Pick of the apartments

For ski-in/ski-out convenience it's hard to beat Les Arcs.

In Arc 1800

Edenarc, Les Alpages de Chantel and l'Iseran are all 4-star ski-in/ski-out residences with pools. Edenarc also has an outdoor pool and a children's pool. You can ski to the resort centre easily from Edenarc and Les Alpages or take the Dahu gondola.

In Arc 1950

Le Village is also ski-in/ski-out and has great facilities including an outdoor pool, steam room, hot tub and spa.

In Arc 2000

La Cimes des Arcs is right on the slopes and La Source des Arcs has doorstep skiing. Large groups will like 4-star Chalet Altitude and Chalet de l'Ours – large apartments well placed for the slopes. Les Arolles also has doorstep skiing.

In Peisey-Vallandry

Directors' Choice L'Orée des Cimes offers doorstep skiing and is a short distance (300m) from the village centre. These apartments have a pool, hot tub, sauna, steam room and spa.

Other options L'Orée des Neiges is in a similar location. Guests can use the pool and spa facilities at the L'Orée des Cimes (a 10–15 minute walk away).

www.skicollection.co.uk 023 9289 0960

Bars and restaurants

An on-mountain après scene is said to have developed at the Arpette. A DJ one afternoon a week sounds a bit half-hearted, but apparently you can stay for the evening and then ski home. Wild! There are several lively bars down in Le Charvet and Les Villards. There's quite a wide choice of restaurants, too. L'effet Boeuf steakhouse takes some beating if you like that kind of thing (we do).

Off the slopes

A key facility in 1800 is the Mille 8 zone – read 'Mille 8 – a fabulous facility' on the previous page. Next to the snow park is an airbag on to which you can be launched in a rubber tube.

The Station bar-lounge offers bowling and snooker. There are also short cross-country trails above the resort.

For families

At the top of the Peisey-Vallandry slopes, off the Forêt piste, the Forêt des Pitchouns is a kids' trail that has been created in the woods, with 15 surprises and challenges along the way. Electric snowmobile racing for kids is being introduced for 2018/19 in Arc 2000.

Alternatives to Arc 1800

All the alternative resort villages have their attractions. Each has an adequate range of bars and restaurants, although that's perhaps painting a rather rosy picture of Arc 1600. There are few conventional hotels. Read 'Pick of the apartments' for pointers to the best residences.

Arc 2000 2130m

Arc 2000, named in the 1970s to evoke the distant millennium with little regard for altitude, has an appropriately futuristic design – since diluted by new buildings in traditional chalet style.

Strangely, 2000 is set at the foot of both the easiest skiing in the area and the most challenging skiing in the area. There is a beginner slope on the *front de neige* with a free carpet lift. Nearby is the St Jacques chair-lift serving several blue runs, which you can ride for €5 a go.

It's a compact place, with a lot of the original buildings on a snowy shelf and the later chalet-style places spreading down the hill towards 1950.

The resort now has a hotel, in the shape of the 5-star Taj I Mah, in pole position at the top of the gondola from 1950. Quite a few catered chalets are operated in apartments, some with access to shared pools and other facilities.

There's a toboggan run down the 1.9km length of the Arcabulle six-seat chair above 2000. There's also a fair-sized outdoor artificial ice rink.

Arc 1950 2040m

Possibly the final form of the French purpose-built resort, Arc 1950 was developed in the early 2000s (by the Canadian firm Intrawest) just down the hill from Arc 2000 – hence the idiotic name. The two resorts are linked by a short free gondola, running until 11.30pm. There is no nursery slope here – you ride up to Arc 2000.

1950 is carefully planned to fit a lot of apartments into a quite small space and to combine skiing from the door with something of the feel of a mountain town – the shops and restaurants are dotted around the central streets. We had a delicious dinner recently at Table de Lys.

A few apartments are run as catered chalets – for more choice look at 2000.

Arc 1600 1620m

The original Arc, which opened its doors 50 years ago in 1968, can be reached by funicular railway from Bourg-St-Maurice. It's much smaller than neighbouring 1800.

The 500m Combettes chair-lift serves a choice of blue runs, including a gentle winding one, and you can ride it for €5 a go, but there is no proper nursery slope here. Beginners should go elsewhere.

The 3-star hotel Arcadien is a favourite haunt of one reader, impressed by the location, the food and the prices. Lagrange has one a Prestige residence here, Le Roc Belle Face, with small indoor/outdoor pool, hot tub and spa suite. In 2018, just above the village, a giant Club Med is being built – the largest in the Alps, and perhaps the swankiest.

Peisey-Vallandry 1600m

Plan-Peisey, at the top of a bucket lift from the village of Peisey-Nancroix and site of the lift station for La Plagne, has merged with its neighbour Vallandry and the two are marketed as a single resort alongside Les Arcs. But their lift bases are 600m apart. There are shuttle buses.

From each lift base, a chair-lift takes beginners up to a drag-lift just above the treeline (and brings them down again). The day pass for these lifts costs €20 in 2018. At Plan-Peisey you can also ride the 300m Parchey chair for €5 a go.

Each resort has a 3-star hotel. There are quite a few catered chalets, at the resort level and down in Peisey-Nancroix. Ski Amis' spacious Chalet Sermoz (with 'Premium' service) is in a great position close to the La Plagne lift, with amazing views from the hot tub on the balcony. There's an adequate choice of bars and restaurants, and the necessary shops.

In the valley above Nancroix, reached by bus, there are extensive cross-country trails and cleared footpaths. Guided snowshoe outings are available – and horse-drawn sleigh rides.

Villaroger 1200m

Villaroger is at the end of the famously long descent from the Aiguille Rouge. It has chalets and apartments to rent, and it's reported that many more are to be built, turning the rustic village into a proper mini resort. No doubt the slow chair-lifts up to Arc 2000 will be replaced.

Bourg-St-Maurice 850m

Bourg-St-Maurice is the town where the trains from London, Paris and other points terminate. The base station of a funicular railway up to Arc 1600 is a walkable distance from the main-line station.

Staying here is much cheaper in every way than staying up on the hill, but the real attraction is that from here you could take day trips to a range of top resorts.

La Plagne

Plagne Centre and countless other Plagnes / Montchavin-Les Coches / Montalbert / Champagny-en-Vanoise

The skiing of La Plagne sprawls over a vast area, roughly 12km across, that has enough to entertain most varieties of skier. It links about ten resort villages offering a wide range of options, from rustic villages with orchards around the lift base through low-rise chalet-style developments to monster apartment blocks. Note that our poor charm rating is for Plagne Centre.

When you get down to the choice of lodgings, though, the options are less impressive: there are few hotels, and even fewer with any pretensions to luxury – a handful of 4-star hotels are dotted around the villages (though we hear a 5-star place is planned for Plagne Aime 2000).

The mountains in brief

Size Huge, even if you don't count linked Les Arcs

Slopes Mostly open, with some woods; mostly quite short, with exceptions

Snow Altitude and orientation mean normally good conditions

System, Lift Much improved, but still plenty of slow chairs and drags

Sustenance A wide choice of good table-service options

For beginners Good slopes and a cheap pass; but lacking long green runs

For true blue skiers Plenty to do, but also lots of tricky pitches to avoid

For the confident Some good runs, but they are dotted around the area

For experts Few challenging pistes, but vast off-piste terrain

Fancy stuff A decent main park, a long funslope, and more

Plagne Centre – the resort in brief

Convenience Lots of slope-side lodgings, if you pick the right resort

Lodgings Plenty of apartments and chalets, but only a few hotels

Bars and restaurants Not a highlight

Off the slopes Quite a lot to do, if you're prepared to bus around a bit

For families Pick your village according to your kids' demands

Pass notes
Local passes cover a day in Les Arcs. In 2019 a six-day Paradiski pass costs €36 more than a local pass. There are 'Villages' day passes for the three lower village areas. The CoolSki half-price day pass covers lifts useful to near-beginners around each village.

Key facts

Altitude	1970m
Range	1250–3160m
Slopes (see text)	400+km

Where to stay, ideally
In Centre, the hotel Araucaria. But there are countless other options, all worth considering.

Websites
winter.la-plagne.com
paradiski.com

Key ratings

Size	*****
Snow	****
Fast lifts	***
Mountain rest's	****
Beginner	****
True blue	****
Confident	****
Expert	****
Convenience	*****
Families	****
Village charm	*

The mountains in detail

The heart of La Plagne's area is a high, mainly treeless bowl divided by a low ridge, with the mother resort of Plagne Centre on one side and the apartment-block-wall of Plagne Bellecôte on the other. Dotted around Centre are four satellite resorts – Plagne Soleil, Plagne Villages, Plagne Aime 2000 and Plagne 1800. Above Bellecôte is Belle Plagne.

Lifts go up to half a dozen points on the rim of the bowl including Roche de Mio, the highest at 2700m; above and beyond that are the glacier slopes on Bellecôte itself, approaching 3200m. Outside the bowl are three lower resorts based on old villages. Over the hill from Centre is Montalbert; reached via Plagne Bellecôte is Montchavin-Les Coches; both Centre and Bellecôte have lifts accessing the sunny slopes of Champagny-en-Vanoise.

Size

La Plagne is slightly the senior partner in the 400km+ Paradiski area, and must have something over 200km of pistes – putting it well into our 4-star category. The Paradiski area as a whole is one of three areas in France to merit 5 stars.

Slopes

As the first picture shows, there are trees immediately above Plagne Bellecôte and Plagne Centre, but not enough to offer much bad-weather skiing, and most of the main bowl is open. Outside the bowl, the Champagny slopes are also mainly open; only the runs to the village get into the forest. The other low villages, though, have worthwhile amounts of woodland.

The area has a bit of a reputation for easy skiing, and there is plenty of that, but there are challenging sectors dotted around, some very challenging.

In the main bowl the runs are not notably long – the high-points are 500m above Plagne Centre, and a mile distant. But in an area this size you can of course travel long distances, and much bigger verticals can be achieved. From Roche

The vast main bowl: Belle Plagne to the left, Plagne Bellecôte right, Plagne Soleil and Plagne Centre behind

de Mio there are descents of 1450m to Champagny and via the Crozats black run and rather tedious Routes des Bauches blue to Montchavin, and you can string together a mighty 1830m from the glacier.

Unlike linked Les Arcs, La Plagne does have green 'easy' pistes on its map; but they are few, and short. There are none of the long greens you might hope to find.

Snow

With most of the slopes above 2000m and facing essentially north to north-west, snow conditions over most of the area are normally reliable. The outlying villages are rather low, but snowmaking is pretty good these days. Sunny Champagny of course presents special challenges. Sometimes (eg in March 2018) the sun produces better conditions here than on the shady slopes, but usually it does not. The lovely Mont de la Guerre red run from top to bottom is often closed in warm weather.

Lots of black pistes and quite a few red ones are labelled Natur, indicating that they are never groomed. We hope this is an exaggeration.

System, Lift

The area has not been noted for a slick lift system, but it has gradually improved matters during the 2010s.

As we write in 2018, the 30-year-old, 2km long, slow quad Inversens chair to Roche de Mio is being replaced by a fast six-seater. Sadly this will only make the crowding worse on the blue Levasset piste from the top, which has had a serious problem for many years. Four major lifts meet there, and the only way down (other than an ungroomed black) is that blue. It is often nightmarish.

A lot of slow chair-lifts remain, but they are mainly quite short, and not in locations where they are likely to spoil your day – the lifts out of Plagne 1800, for example. In peak season, queues can build for the lifts out of Plagne Bellecôte for Montchavin and Roche de Mio, but most of the time the problems are not serious – the alternative chair-lift route to Roche de Mio is much more efficient than the 40-year-old gondola.

Sustenance

The choice of good mountain restaurants is a strength of the area. They are marked but not named on the piste map.

Lots of people head to the low villages for lunch, and next time we might be tempted by Union in Montalbert. But normally we stay high, and eat at three favourite places – the purpose-built but warmly welcoming Verdons Sud, above Champagny, or one of two cosily traditional old places: Le Forperet, above Montalbert, or Le Sauget, above Montchavin. All table service, of course. There are lots of good alternatives, too.

One is a notable recent addition, again above Montalbert – Le 360, a glass-walled cube containing a spacious and calm restaurant on the first floor, with excellent food and great views.

More on the slopes

For beginners

All the resort villages have nursery slopes with free drag-lifts or carpet-lifts. Centre also has nearby the Boulevard 450m quad chair-lift serving one of the few green runs in the resort. The CoolSki half-price day pass covers key lifts serving easy blue slopes at Centre (plus nearby satellites), Bellecôte and all three lower villages. All in all, a pretty good set-up.

For true blue skiers

La Plagne has a huge amount of blue skiing, and a confident blue run skier can get around the whole area, including the link to Les Arcs and the Champagny slopes on the back of the mountain. For a nervous skier, though, there are challenges on a number of blue pistes.

Runs that will appeal particularly to less confident skiers include those off the Bergerie and Colorado chairs out of Plagne Centre, the winding runs above Montalbert, the Ours and Lainés blues down to Bellecôte and the lovely trio of runs on the Rossa chair high above Champagny. The CoolSki half-price day pass covers all of these.

Potential problems include Mira, from Grande Rochette, which has a quite long pitch approaching red gradient; some equally tough short pitches on Trieuse, into Bellecôte; the top of Blanchets – keep left on Roc du Diable/Ours instead; the top of Levasset/Tunnel from Roche de Mio – crowded and bumpy as well as a bit steep. On the Champagny side, the blue Bozelet from Les Verdons is really tough

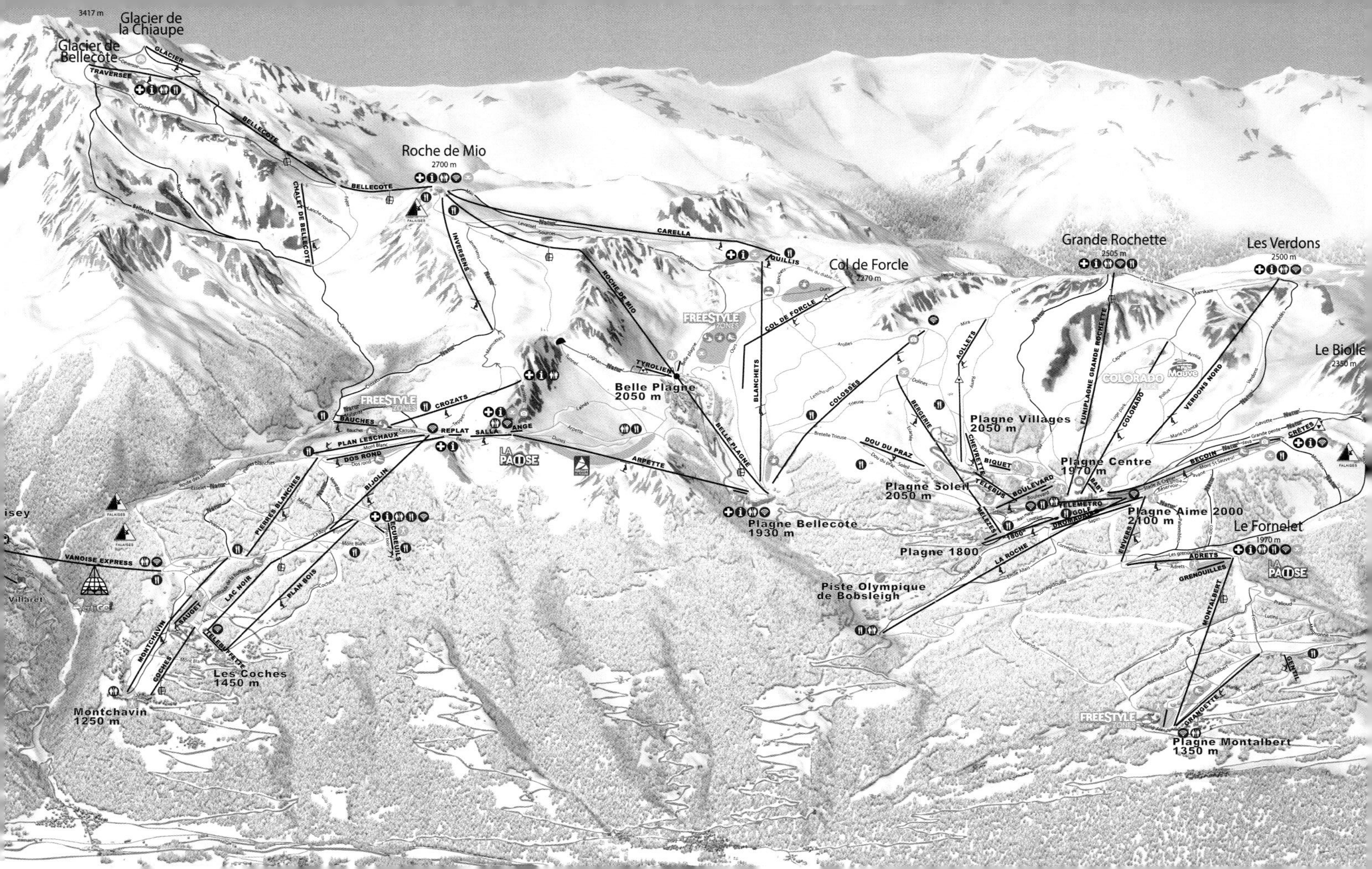

3417 m
Glacier de la Chiaupe
Glacier de Bellecôte
GLACIER
TRAVERSEE
BELLECOTE
CHALET DE BELLECOTE
Roche de Mio
2700 m
INVERSENS
CARELLA
ROCHE DE MIO
QUILLIS
Col de Forcle
2270 m
FREESTYLE ZONES
COL DE FORCLE
BLANCHETS
TYROLIEN
Belle Plagne
2050 m
BELLE PLAGNE
CROZATS
BAUCHES
PLAN LESCHAUX
DOS ROND
REPLAT
SALLA
ANGE
ARPETTE
LA PAUSE
BIJOLIN
PIERRES BLANCHES
ECUREUILS
LAC NOIR
PLAN BOIS
SAUGET
MONTCHAVIN
COCHES
TELEBUFFETTE
Les Coches
1450 m
Montchavin
1250 m
VANOISE EXPRESS
Villaret
Plagne Bellecôte
1930 m
COLOSSES
Piste Olympique de Bobsleigh
DOU DU PRAZ
BERGERIE
AOLLETS
Plagne Villages
2050 m
CHEVRETTE
BIQUET
TELEBUS
Plagne Soleil
2050 m
BOULEVARD
MELEZES
"1800"
Plagne 1800
LA ROCHE
TELEMETRO
GOLF
DROMADAIRE
BABY
Plagne Centre
1970 m
Grande Rochette
2505 m
FUNIPLAGNE GRANDE ROCHETTE
COLORADO
Les Verdons
2500 m
VERDONS NORD
Le Biolle
2350 m
BECOIN
CRETES
Plagne Aime 2000
2100 m
ENVERS
Le Fornelet
1970 m
ADRETS
GRENOUILLES
MONTALBERT
GENTIL
GRANGETTE
Plagne Montalbert
1350 m

in parts, while the link via the Blanchets chair presents two challenges – the short run down the Quillis chair-lift and the first pitch of Levasset below the Quillis/Carella lift station. The easiest way to Champagny is on Geisha from Col de Forcle.

These notes are not comprehensive, obviously; this is an area best skied with someone who knows the runs.

For confident intermediates

There is lots of red-run skiing for the confident intermediate to enjoy, provided you don't mind some long, easy runs on linking blues – the good, challenging runs are all dotted around the map: one long run on the glacier, a couple from Roche de Mio, a couple at Les Coches, a couple at Centre, a couple at Montalbert.

There are some excellent runs over at Champagny, especially when the conditions are right (it's very sunny). The long top-to-bottom, away-from-all-lifts Mont de la Guerre red is fabulous on the right day. Note that this is a Natur run.

For experts

The eye-catchers on the piste map are the two black pistes from the glacier dropping 700m to the Chalet de Bellecôte chair, with the option of a further 500m to the Bauches chair if you're not looking to do laps. They have steep pitches near the top, then become harmless; the longer Bellecôte is less steep than Rochu. These runs get the afternoon sun, so snow conditions can vary, and in the past we've often found them closed. They are not Natur runs, implying occasional grooming.

Similarly the blacks from the peaks between Centre and Champagny have quite steep pitches at or near the top, but soon mellow. The row of runs behind the ridge west of Centre are not long – roughly 300m/400m vertical – but they are genuine blacks, particularly Morbleu. Etroits is less direct but has a short section that is both steep and narrow.

There is a lot of off-piste to be explored between the pistes, both inside the main bowl and outside it – above Les Bauches on the way to Montchavin, for example. The snow doesn't get tracked out as quickly as it does in resorts better known for off-piste terrain.

The Champagny sector has huge areas of skiable terrain, and offers routes to the Verdons Sud chair or on to Champagny itself. From Roche de Mio there are routes down to the Chalet de

The uncompromising blocks of Plagne Centre and, above it, the mess that Plagne Aime 2000 has become

Bellecôte chair or to Les Bauches. A bit of hiking above Aime 2000 or Montalbert opens up some long routes to the valleys.

But the jewel is Bellecôte itself. Its glacier lifts open up countless routes, both within the lift network and outside it, and of course you would hope to find good snow there. Several routes on the front face end up at the Chalet de Bellecôte chair, permitting laps, while others descend through the forest to the Bauches chair. On the splendid, shady north face there are a dozen routes ranging in difficulty from moderate to extreme, some involving climbing. In the opposite direction are routes down to Champagny-le-Haut, including the classic Cul du Nant.

Be aware that the shuttle-bus down the valley to the lifts at Champagny is not open to skiers arriving off-piste.

Fancy stuff

The main freestyle area is on the Col de Forcle drag-lift above Bellecôte, including an air bag and boardercross. There is another boardercross above Montchavin, and a small park with air bag at Montalbert. There's a mile-long funslope on the Arpette chair above Bellecôte.

Plagne Centre – the resort

Plagne centre is very much a first-generation purpose-built resort, although it is on a more human scale than some, with buildings varying a bit in form. And the resort is working hard to make the place more welcoming – the shopping mall had a makeover, and now a 'village' square is taking shape.

Convenience

It's a small place, about 700m end to end, with the access road on one side and the snow and lifts on the other. The ground is essentially level, rising gently at one end as you can see from our photo. All very functional.

Lodgings

Even here, in the focal village of the resort, there are only three hotels. The group behind the high-profile Rockypop hotel in Chamonix gave the Araucaria a 4-star makeover in 2017, with a new 450 m^2 spa and pool, and a kids' pool area.

Ski Collection Pick of the apartments

In Plagne Centre
The 3-star Le Pelvoux apartments are in the centre, 100m from the lifts and only 50m from the slopes. Facilities include a sauna and steam room.

In Plagne 1800
4-star Chalets d'Edelweiss is in a great location, just 20m from the slopes. It has a pool, sauna and steam room.

In Belle Plagne
The 4-star Carlina enjoys a quiet, ski-in/ski-out location; 4-star Les Nereides is also ski-in/ski-out. The popular Balcons de Belle Plagne is at the foot of the slopes with great views over the resort. Le Centaure is also at the foot of the slopes and has a pool.

In Plagne Soleil
Directors' Choice For ultimate convenience, the 4-star Granges du Soleil is in the heart of Plagne Soleil and on the slopes, ski-in/ski-out.
Other options Sun Valley is also on the slopes and offers doorstep skiing.

In Plagne Villages
The Aspen is just 100m from the slopes (it's not difficult to ski back to the door), and is well located for the lifts and shops. We also like the location of the 4-star Front de Neige, which is ski-in/ski-out.

Couples can spend a night high above Bellecôte mountain in a kind of piste-basher-cum-campervan.

Bars and restaurants

The après scene is not great. The British-run Scotty's bar on the front de neige has long been the standard port of call at close of play. For dinner, the unpretentious bar-restaurant rules – this is not a resort for gourmets. About the best restaurant is Le Refuge, doing the usual Savoyard and traditional cuisine.

Off the slopes

There's a sports hall for tennis, badminton etc and a fitness room, but for swimming or skating it's a bus round to Bellecôte.

There's a mile-long toboggan run on the Colorado chair-lift above Centre – 7€ a go in 2018. The Olympic bobsleigh track, at La Roche, below Centre, is open to the public; several options, from a 'slow' self-drive bob (45€ in 2018) to a much more expensive ride behind a pro driver. A 600m zipline links Aime 2000 to Centre, offering speeds of 90km/hr. Snowmobiles are available.

For families

With plenty of traffic-free snow to play on and a toboggan run above the village, Centre makes a good family destination (unless swimming and skating matter).

The other parts of La Plagne

La Plagne manages to accommodate its staggering 55,000 guests by spreading them widely. Sharing the main high bowl with Plagne Centre are no less than six other resort units, most a bit higher than the mother village. Then, outside the bowl, there are three or four further mini-resorts based on old villages; these are at much lower altitudes, below the treeline.

Belle Plagne 2070m

'Beautiful' Plagne is a British favourite, combining a convenient slope-side position (lots of ski-in/ski-out lodgings) with small-scale chalet-style buildings and a choice of bar-restaurants. Up the hill from Bellecôte, it's pretty well positioned for exploration of the whole area. There's a beginner slope at the top of the village, now with a covered carpet-lift.

There are several hotels. The 4-star Carlina is the obvious choice – comfortable, with a pool and spa, well run and in a good slope-side location below the main village. The Belle Plagne and Balcons are 3-stars; the latter has a pool. Catered chalets can be found; Crystal has three chalets that merit its 'Finest' badge. There are lots of apartments; read the Pick panel, above.

There's a reasonable choice of bars – the Tête Inn and Cheyenne Café are popular – and restaurants doing the usual French resort fare. The Matafan has long been about the best of those in the main resort centre. The hotel Carlina has a more ambitious restaurant.

There's bowling at the Bowling Bar. More or less in the middle of the development is a sledging space. Snowmobiling is available. A series of ziplines has been installed across the valley running down to Bellecôte.

In 2018 a new aqua-leisure centre is being developed, with separate outdoor pool areas for families and adults.

Plagne Bellecôte 1930m

Bellecôte is not at all a British favourite, consisting of a giant wall of apartments filling the valley like a dam. Within this monstrosity are half a dozen food shops, maybe 20 other shops, and over a dozen bars and restaurants. We've never had occasion to visit any of them. The Spitting Feathers pub is said to be worth a visit. Bellecôte does have the merit of a good position – arguably the best for exploration of La Plagne's area, with reasonably quick access to the Paradiski link too. There is a decent nursery slope with carpet-lift, an outdoor pool, and a natural ice rink.

Plagne Villages / Soleil 2050m

These two resort units are growing towards one another with each new apartment development. Both are apartment-dominated; read the Pick panel above for pointers to the best residences.

Plagne Villages is essentially a long chain of low-rise apartment buildings running down a gentle hill beside a blue piste to a cluster of residences at the lower end where most of the facilities are – a shop or two, several bar-restaurants (La Spatule is a crêperie run by a couple from Brittany) and a pulse gondola lift down to Plagne Centre.

Just across the hillside, Soleil is less linear and more villagey in layout. It has a hotel, the 3-star Vancouver, and more facilities in general – two food shops, and as many as a dozen bar-restaurants.

Both units have a beginner slope with free drag-lift, and form part of the Plagne Centre half-price CoolSki pass area.

Plagne 1800 1800m

This is chalet-land – a steep hillside below Plagne Centre covered in small chalet-style apartment buildings (read the Pick panel, above) and individual chalets, many of them used by British catered chalet operators. Mountain Heaven has five properties here. There's a beginner slope with free drag-lift, and 1800 forms part of the Plagne Centre half-price CoolSki pass area.

The 4-star boutique hotel Cocoon combines traditional style with modern comfort; it's family run, with one of La Plagne's best restaurants. The Petit Chaperon Rouge is a jolly, traditional place doing the usual specialities. La Cantine does good pizza. The mining-themed Mine bar has live music.

Plagne Aime 2000 2100m

The distinctive mountain-range-shaped apartment block forming the core of this outpost of Plagne Centre has been marred over the years by various additions – not just one Club Med establishment, but two, and an upmarket Pierre & Vacances apartment block. The main block's mall contains a handful of shops and maybe a dozen bars and restaurants; not far away on the slopes, Au Bon Vieux Temps is a cute old chalet, open for dinner. There is also a cable car link to the bright lights of Plagne Centre.

Montchavin-Les Coches 1200m

Montchavin is a restored and much expanded old village, its rustic simplicity well preserved. Les Coches is a sympathetically designed modern satellite a little way up the hill. The two are linked by a gondola. Both have traffic-free centres, and widely spread suburbs served by ski-buses. There is quite a bit of intermediate skiing on the local wooded slopes, beyond which you are on to the open terrain of La Plagne. Both villages have good beginner slopes with free lifts, and dedicated kids' areas. There is a further beginner area at Plan Bois, at the top of the gondola out of Les Coches.

Most of the lodging is in apartments, but in Montchavin there's a 3-star hotel, the Bellecôte, and the cosy mountain restaurant Le Sauget at mid-mountain has neat rooms. There are catered chalets to be found. Ski Amis has two chalets, both with hot tub, one of them recently refurbished with snazzy Italian-style bathrooms. In Les Coches, family specialist Family Ski Company has three piste-side chalets.

There are several bars and restaurants. Locals tip La Bovate for good slow-cooked food. Espace Paradisio is a small pool and wellness centre at Montchavin, which also has a cinema. Les Coches has an ice rink. There is dog sledding up at Plan Bois, and good walks and snowshoe trails across the wooded hillsides (downloadable maps).

The start of the famous Mont de la Guerre red run above sunny Champagny, with a great view of Courchevel

Montalbert 1350m

This is another expanded old village. It has a pleasant front de neige at the foot of its modern gondola, with nursery slope.

Convenience The core of the village, where the essentials of life from tabac to traiteur are concentrated, is tiny, though lodgings spread a bit more widely up both sides of the home run and nursery slope.

Lodgings There's a small, simple hotel, which may or may not have 3 stars, the Aigle Rouge. Ski Amis has a catered chalet here, with hot tub and sauna, a short walk from the lifts and village centre. Mountain Heaven has a wide range of apartments in small chalet-style developments. Some swish new apartment residences are in the pipeline.

Bars and restaurants There are several places. 'For a bit of life it's the White Bear at the lift base,' says Nick Williams of Mountain Heaven, who spends a bit of time here. He also likes the Tourmente – a pub with pool table – and the Skanapia bar-restaurant. The big news in 2018 was the opening of Union by celebrity British chef Phil Howard, proprietor of Elystan Street restaurant in Chelsea. It's not clear how often he will be at the stove. In 2018 dinner cost €55 for three courses, lunch much less. The excellent mid-mountain restaurant Le Forperet is open and accessible in the evening.

Off the slopes There are walking paths, snowshoe trails and cross-country loops across the wooded hillsides around the village. Guides are available. There's a kids' sledging area by the tourist office.

Champagny-en-Vanoise 1250m

Champagny is a traditional-style village on a steep hillside, with its lift base perched right at the top. It's not overtly charming, but pleasant enough; its central square below the lift base is a bit drab.

The nursery slope is at the top of the gondola, so beginners need a lift pass. Its local slopes have something for everybody, including beginners and true-blue skiers – though the blue links with La Plagne present some challenges. The slopes are very sunny, and the home red run (which is in any case narrow and quite steep) suffers accordingly. Courchevel is less than half an hour away by car.

Convenience Although it is a small place with a very compact centre, Champagny consists of small chalets spread widely, and most people need to use private or public shuttles, or their cars (there is just about enough parking at the lift base, in March at least).

Lodgings Catered chalets can be found. There are a couple of simple 3-star hotels a walkable distance from the lift – the Ancolie and the more rustic Glières. Closer still is Club Alpina, an apartment-hotel with a small pool. Most of the lodging is in small apartment buildings and self-catering chalets. CGH has an excellent apartment residence, Alpages de Champagny, with the usual good pool and spa, and a flexible private shuttle service to and from the lifts. MGM has a new development coming on stream – Les Balcons Etoilés, right next to the gondola station.

Bars and restaurants It's a quiet village. There are several places around the little central square below the lift base, and there is sometimes life in one or another. None is notable, but the Timbale has a bit of Alpine style. Your best bet for dinner is one of the three hotels. There is said to be a nightclub, Le Galaxy.

Off the slopes The village put a roof on its pool in 2017, making it usable in winter. Up the valley at Champagny-le-Haut there is cross-country skiing, dog sledding and a big ice-climbing tower.

Portes du Soleil

Châtel / La Chapelle-d'Abondance / Avoriaz / Ardent / Morzine / Les Gets

Lots of excellent skiing in France / Switzerland; but all a bit low

The giant linked areas of the Tarentaise valley are all high-altitude affairs, with resorts that are largely purpose-built. The Portes du Soleil is emphatically different: it is mostly an area of slopes that are as much below the treeline as above it, with resorts based on low valley villages. Avoriaz is a conspicuous exception to the stereotype – a high, entirely purpose-built resort with a greater skiing vertical below it than above it.

It's a huge area. The PdS broadcasts a claim of 600km of pistes. The lift pass covers several small areas that are not connected to the main

network, but even allowing for them, you are left with a figure well in excess of 500km, which would put the area close to the 3 Vallées in size. But is it? The numbers we've assembled from individual resorts over the years add up to more like 400km. This is way behind the 3V but still enough to put the Portes du Soleil alongside the 3V and Paradiski in the exclusive 5-star size category.

The area falls naturally into two parts, which are connected by a short town-train ride at Morzine. Much the bigger part (which we're calling PdS east) is the Franco-Swiss circuit linking French Avoriaz and Châtel with Swiss Morgins, Champéry and other small villages. The smaller part is an area of slopes shared by Morzine and Les Gets (PdS west).

The four resorts mentioned all have their merits, but we would rather be based in Châtel than Avoriaz or in Morzine rather than Les Gets, so Châtel and Morzine get the full resort treatment.

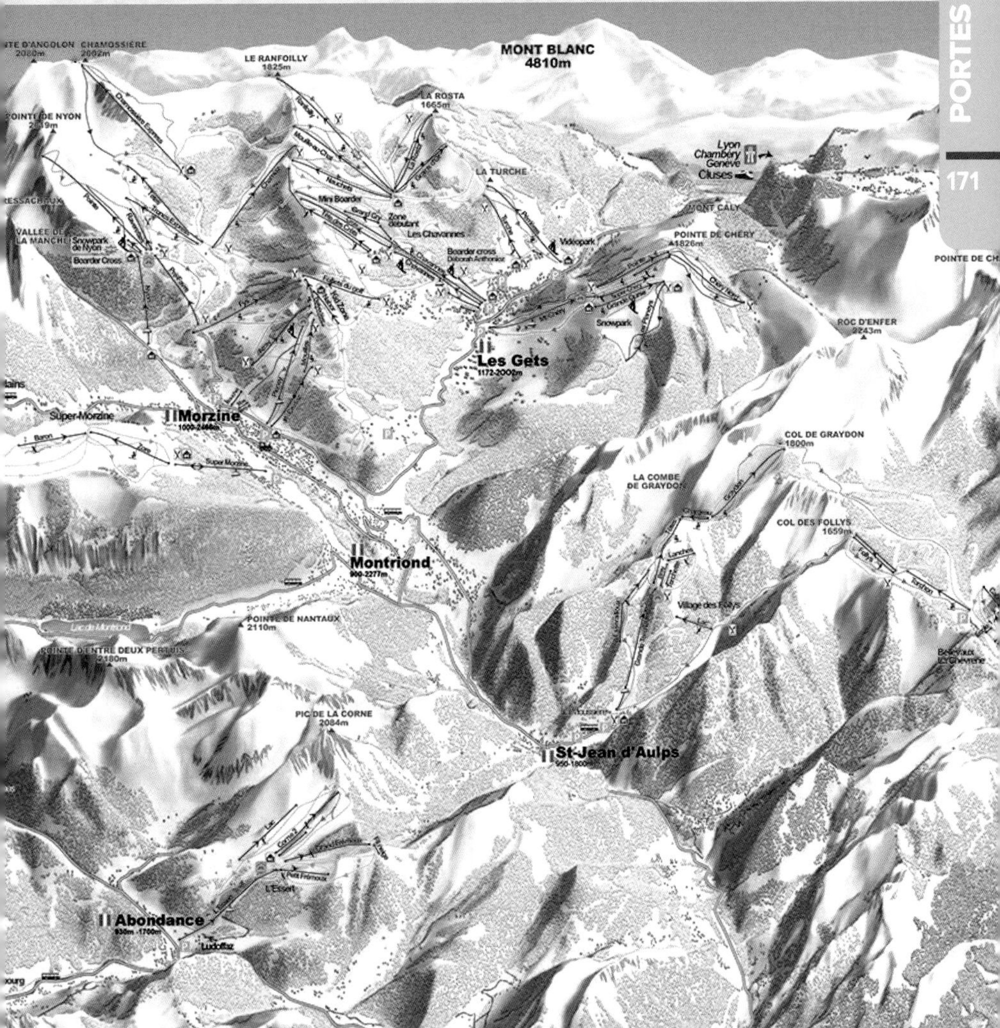

PdS east – Châtel

Châtel / La Chapelle-d'Abondance / Avoriaz / Ardent

The eastern part of the Portes du Soleil – much the bigger sector of the huge Portes du Soleil area – forms a circuit of intermediate slopes linking Châtel and Avoriaz in France with Morgins, Champéry and other smaller villages in Switzerland.

Which of the French villages you prefer will depend on your priorities; for slope-side lodgings (and for the quickest possible access to the western part of the PdS area, shared by Morzine and Les Gets), it's Avoriaz; for traditional ski village atmosphere, it's Châtel. (Alternatively, you can ski the eastern circuit starting from Morzine, or even from Les Gets, but they have the disadvantage that they are not on the circuit itself.)

The mountains in brief

Size Huge, even if you don't stray to Morzine and the PdS west area

Slopes A good mix of terrain, with some decent long runs

Snow Overall, not a strong point, despite the snowfall record of Avoriaz

System, Lift Good in parts, woeful in others (mainly in Switzerland)

Sustenance Plenty of good spots with table service, but at low altitude

For beginners An adequate setup, but could use more long green runs

For true blue skiers Lots to do, including virtually all the clockwise circuit

For the confident Some excellent red runs, but they're scattered about

For experts A good mix of numerous black pistes and plentiful off-piste

Fancy stuff Worthwhile park at Châtel, superb ones at Avoriaz

Châtel – the resort in brief

Convenience Traditional villages do have their drawbacks ...

Lodgings Lots of affordable options, but look elsewhere for luxury

Bars and restaurants An adequate range, but for a Folie Douce it's Avoriaz

Off the slopes Not a highlight, but there's now a good aquatic centre

For families Not an obvious candidate for a family trip

Pass notes
The Liberté pass covers the area shown on our Châtel map, saving €60 against a PdS six-day pass. There is a free moving carpet lift at Pré-la-Joux; other beginner lifts and the Super-Châtel gondola are covered by a special pass for one to three days (no bargain, at €29 for a day in 2019).

Key facts

Altitude	1200m
Range	950–2255m
Slopes (see text)	400+km

Where to stay, ideally
Close to the Super-Châtel gondola, or the Linga one.

Websites
chatel.com
avoriaz.com
portesdusoleil.com

Key ratings

Size	*****
Snow	***
Fast lifts	***
Mountain rest's	****
Beginner	***
True blue	****
Confident	****
Expert	****
Convenience	**
Families	***
Village charm	***

The mountains in detail

This is a large and complex area. A gondola from the village goes up to the plateau of Super-Châtel, where there are links in three directions. Two of the three launch you on to the main PdS circuit – clockwise towards Morgins in Switzerland, or anticlockwise towards Châtel's main local slopes on Linga above Villapeyron, and Cornebois above Pré-la-Joux. The third direction is out on a limb, off the circuit, to Barbossine and Torgon (in a different bit of Switzerland). There are other lifts into the skiing from the northern and southern extremities of Châtel, and from La Chapelle-d'Abondance, as well as major lifts at Villapeyron and Pré-la-Joux.

Beyond Pré-la-Joux on the anticlockwise route are the slopes of Avoriaz – first the Lindarets valley, above the hamlet of Ardent, and then the main Avoriaz valley. Both have lifts up to the Swiss border, for access to broad areas of slopes above Les Croset, Champoussin and the lower valley village of Champéry. The Avoriaz valley has pistes down towards lower Morzine and the western PdS area.

Size

As we've explained in the previous pages, the PdS area is huge – over 400km, and clearly in the 5-star category. The Châtel/Avoriaz/Switzerland sector is very much the senior partner, and well over twice the size of Morzine/Les Gets, putting even this one sector at the top of our 4-star size category, ahead of Val d'Isère-Tignes.

Slopes

There's a good mix of open and wooded terrain, so you can usually find something to amuse on bad-weather days. Gradients, too, are nicely mixed, with steep and gentle sectors. There's also a mix of verticals available. The Avoriaz area consists mainly of runs offering 400–600m, with the excellent

The Pré-la-Joux sector is mainly open above mid-mountain; in the background, the dramatic Dents du Midi

runs from Hauts Forts to Les Prodains giving an exceptional 1000m. At Châtel, both Cornebois and Linga provide up to 1000m, but verticals in the rest of the sector are modest.

It's not an area notable for long runs, but there are exceptions. The French like to say that the Abricotine blue run in the Lindarets valley is the longest piste in the PdS, but of course they haven't looked over the border. The longest run is about 8km from Mossette down a deserted Swiss valley to Morgins. Abricotine plus the Parchets below it probably come second, and the descent from Ripaille to Grand Paradis near Champéry third.

The Avoriaz sector has some features that are eccentric, to say the least. A blue piste and two reds are ungroomed, as well as two blacks. Then these runs are given the label SnowCross, although they are nothing to do with the widely used terms boardercross, skicross or skiercross – or indeed snowcross (a form of snowmobile racing). And finally, the local area is divided into beginner, family, forest and expert zones (which is why our map of Avoriaz looks such a mess). These zones make no sense at all. For example, the one black SnowCross run is in the family zone, while two of the main features of interest to adventurous kids are in the beginner zone. Brilliant.

Snow

For resort-level snow, Avoriaz tops the French table with an average of almost 8m a year; much lower Châtel, of course, doesn't do nearly so well. The piste maps present the heights of surrounding peaks rather than the top heights of the lifts, but they are roughly 2100m at Châtel and 2200 at Avoriaz – only 400m higher than the resort. On the French side, at least, most of the slopes face roughly north-west, which helps; but the Swiss side is very sunny. All in all, it's a satisfactory picture; but it's not great.

System, Lift

The lifts on the main Châtel slopes, at Linga and Cornebois, and at Avoriaz are pretty slick. At Super-Châtel and all points beyond, and on the Swiss side in general, they are anything but; lots of lifts, including many major and inescapable ones in Switzerland, are slow chairs or drags. You have been warned.

Sustenance

You're spoilt for choice, provided you don't insist on altitude. There is an amazing concentration of restaurants on the run to Ardent, in the Lindarets valley between Châtel and Avoriaz, largely because of the summer tourists who flock up here to see the hamlet's

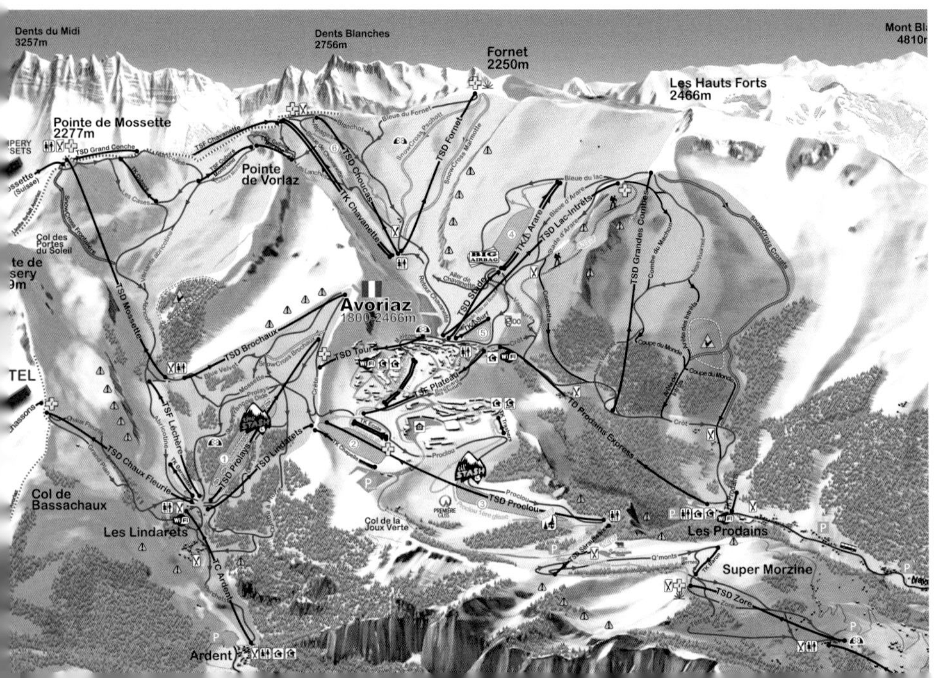

Bec du Corbeau
1842 m
Tête du Géant
2228 m
Cornebois
2200 m
Pointe de Chéser
2251 m
Tête du Linga
2156 m
Morclan
1970 m
Pointe du Midi
1850 m
Tour de Don
1942 m
Tête du Tronchet
1893 m
vers Morgins
vers Avoriaz
SUPER-CHÂTEL
BARBOSSINE
LINGA
PRÉ-LA-JOUX
Smooth Park
Vonnes
Le Crêt
Châtel
L'Oy
Villapeyron
les Combes
1635m
Plaine Dranse
1650m
FANTASTICABLE
Pré la Joux
1310m
La Jorette
Torgon
Barbossine
Petit Châtel
Fun Park
Plan de Croix
Boarder-Cross Braitaz
Limite du Forfait ESPACE LIBERTE
Mont de Grange
2432 m
La Chapelle d'Abondance
Mont Linleu
2093 m
CRÊT BÉNI
BRAITAZ - TORGON
Crêt Béni
1536 m
La Combe
1630 m
Boarder Cross
Mont Chauffé
2093 m
TK DE CULET
TK D'ECOTIS
TS DU CORBEAU
TK DE CHALET NEUF
PRÉ-LA-VIEILLE
TK DE CHERMEU
TS DE MORCLAN
TK ONNAZ
TK DE CHAUX LONGE
TK TOUR DE DON
TS DE BARBOSSINE
TS DU PETIT CHÂTEL
TS DE CONCHE
TC DE SUPER-CHÂTEL
TS PORTES DU SOLEIL
TS GABELOU
TK DE LA LEICHE
TS DE L'ECHO ALPIN
TC DU LINGA
TK DU STADE
TS DES COMBES
TS DE CORNEBOIS
TS DE LA CHAUX DES ROSÉES
TS DES ROCHASSONS
TK DU QUEYSET
TS DE PRÉ-LA-JOUX
TS DE PIERRE LONGUE
TK RUBIS
TK COVAGNYS
TS DU TRONCHEY
TK DES FIGNARDS
TK DIEU DES TÊTES
TK CONCHE 2000
TS DE BRAITAZ
TK DU TROMBY
TC DE LA PANTHIAZ
TS DES FONTAINES
TK PRÉ
TK DAHU
TS CRÊT BÉNI
TK BAMBI
TK LA COMBE
Domaine nordique
Forfait : Espace Liberté
DOMAINES SKIABLES DE CHÂTEL, LA CHAPELLE D'ABONDANCE, TORGON ET MORGINS - SECTEUR CORBEAL
SECTEUR SUPER-CHÂTEL - BARBOSSINE
1 L'Epervier
2 L'Ecureuil
3 Tour de Don
4 Barbossine
5 Folière
6 Panoramique
7 Onnaz
8 Ombrieux
9 Chermillon
10 Chermeu
11 Le Lac
12 Chalet Neuf
13 Bellevue
14 Chermillon
15 Le Corbeau
16 Chanterelle
17 Maxime
18 Le Boude
19 La Combe
20 La Forestière
SECTEUR LINGA - PRÉ LA JOUX
22 Les Pitchounes
23 L'Alty
24 La Leiche
25 La Forgne
26 Françoise Macchi
27 Le Linga
28 Les Combes
29 L'Itinéraire
30 La Perdrix Blanche
31 Les Blattins
32 Pré la Joux
33 Les Renards
34 Les Rennes
35 Le Chésery
36 Les Rochassons
37 La Casse-noisette
38 Les Rhododendrons
39 La Belette
40 Les Rubis
41 Les Covagnys
SECTEUR TORGON
3 Tour de Don
6 Panoramique
7 Onnaz
42 Col de Croix
43 Lac Léman
45 Eusin
47 Stade de Slalom
48 Djeu des Têtes
49 Conche
50 Recon
51 Marmotte
52 Blanchot
SECTEUR LA CHAPELLE
47 Stade de Slalom
48 Djeu des Têtes
49 Conche
50 Recon
51 Marmotte
52 Blanchot
53 Belette
54 Col Vert
55 Lynx
56 Gélinotte
57 Accès Braitaz
58 Dahu
59 Oursen
60 Pingouin
61 Cerf Haut
62 Cerf Bas
63 Le Loup
64 Sanglier
65 Renard
66 Bamby
67 Huski 1
68 Huski 2
69 Hermine
70 Biche haut
71 Biche Bas
Jardin d'enfants
Aire de Luge
Yooner
SnowPark
Stade de Slalom
Office du Tourisme
Parking
Caisses
Poste de Secours
Restaurants
Liaisons Navette
Points de Rencontre
Toilettes
Consigne à skis
Kaliblue

goat population. We've always enjoyed the Terrasse (when sunny) and the Crémaillère (when snowy). The Pomme de Pins is said to do great food.

There's another crazy concentration of places over the ridge towards Châtel at Plaine Dranse. The cosy, kitsch-laden Vieux Chalet is obligatory; its food is said to be excellent, but the real draw is the charmingly eccentric *patronne*, Babeth.

Across the hill a bit, above Le Linga, the Ferme des Pistes is a lovely old barn doing great food. One reader's all-time favourite, anywhere, is the welcoming Passage on the Super-Morzine slopes below Avoriaz – reliable *plat du jour*.

More on the slopes

For beginners

There are beginner areas up at Super-Châtel and out at Pré-la-Joux. The last has a free, long, covered moving carpet-lift plus a couple of drags serving short green runs – and, when you are ready to move on, you can ride the Pierre Longue fast chair to ski a long green run down the *route départmentale* 228a from Plaine Dranse at mid-mountain. The beginner's lift pass covers all these lifts. At Super-Châtel it covers half a dozen lifts, and although there are no long green runs there are some lovely easy blues.

For true blue skiers

There is a good amount of blue skiing in the Châtel area, huge amounts in the wider PdS east area, particularly over in Switzerland, and even more in the PdS west area reached via Morzine.

You can get around practically the whole Franco-Swiss circuit on blue runs, skiing clockwise – it breaks down with the finish in sight, on Linga, where the top red piste is inescapable (and a genuine red). So you need a bus from Pré-la-Joux to Villapeyron, at least. On the way to Morgins go directly for the Chalet Neuf drag-lift; the run to the Pré-la-Vielle drag includes an awkward steep pitch. When you come to return to France, the lovely long Abricotine from Mossette is easier than the run from Chavanette, and also avoids the quite tough descents from Avoriaz into the Lindarets valley.

Some caveats, though. Many of the runs on the Swiss side get full sun, so can be slushy or rock-hard at certain times. And crowds on the runs can be a problem at busy times, notably on the Chésery run to Plaine Dranse, near the end of your day

Châtel has retained its village scale and chalet style with admirable thoroughness, despite expansion

– not the easiest of blues in any case.

Going anticlockwise you can get to the Swiss side (ride the chair-lift down the Swiss Wall, if you can handle that), but not much further – to reach Champoussin, the red Mossettes run is inescapable.

Other areas worth exploring include most of Super-Châtel; the lovely open blue on Cornebois, above Pré-la-Joux; the runs close to the Swiss border above Avoriaz – often the best snow in the area; and the prettily wooded run to Les Prodains, below Avoriaz. Blanchot/Bellette at Braitaz above La Chapelle is a fine blue, but other blues in that sector present challenges.

For confident intermediates

Competent skiers can explore the whole circuit and its offshoots with confidence. As in many such broad areas, there's a lot of relatively easy skiing to do en route to the more challenging stuff.

All the reds around Châtel are worthwhile, with decent verticals when the snow is good. The runs on Linga and above Pré-la-Joux are among the best. There are good slopes in the Lindarets valley, on Hauts Forts (the downhill course named after the legendary Jean Vuarnet) and on both sides of the Swiss border. Further into Switzerland, the long run to Grand Paradis near Champéry is worth doing in good snow.

Beware the long run down a deserted valley to Morgins from the Col des Portes du Soleil, a blue reachable only via reds. It starts well, but then spends 4km dropping 200m. Depending on the conditions, you may fall asleep, or wear yourself out skating and poling.

For experts

There's a better-than-average smattering of steep pistes here. We have to start with the famous 'Swiss Wall', where the slopes of Avoriaz meet those of Champéry – a run of sustained steepness, though not necessarily the precipice it is made out to be. We measured it once, back in the day when we did that sort of thing, and recorded it at 34°; that's a proper black, but not an extreme one. But, crucially, the steepness at the very top depends on the build-up of snow; if snow has been blowing from France, the start can be much steeper, and life may be complicated by moguls the size of VW Beetles. Also, you can find steeper pitches, to skier's left especially.

Directly above Avoriaz the several shady black runs on the Grandes Combes chair-lift are less steep, but still genuine blacks, with the difference that they offer much more vertical. On the French side of Mossette, Frontalière has two steep pitches along its length. Rhododendrons at Plaine Dranse has one steep pitch. Nearby Les Renards doesn't really reach black steepness. Barbossine, way over the other side of Châtel, again has one proper black pitch.

There is lots of off-piste terrain between and close to the pistes – from the Swiss border into the Lindarets valley, for example, or to skier's right of the Brocheaux chair, or through the forest close to the Stash, or on either side of the Chésery ridge – but also more adventurous routes. A classic Châtel route is the valley of La Leiche reached from Tête du Linga by crossing a ridge into the steep-sided, shady bowl leading down to the eponymous drag-lift. At Avoriaz the Fornet chair on the Swiss border goes virtually to the Col du Fornet, start of an epic west-facing run of 1000m vertical into the valley of La Manche, above Morzine, ending at Erigné. From the Grandes Combes chair you can traverse under the crags of Les Hauts Forts to descend north-facing slopes to Les Prodains, 1000m below.

Fancy stuff

Smooth Park at Super-Châtel has features for novices and experts, including a boardercross course. There's also a fun park and boardercross in the Braitaz-Torgon sector.

Avoriaz has always been a leader in the terrain park business. The Arare park is the serious one, and a splendid thing it is. Nearer the village is the easier but similarly impressive Chapelle park. In the forest above Les Lindarets is the famous Stash, with wooden and natural features to attract all kinds of adventurous skiers. On the easy slopes below the village is a version for younger kids, Lil'Stash. There are half-pipes below the village, and up at the Swiss border a skicross course (not to be confused with snowcross, of course).

Over in Switzerland, above Champéry and Les Crosets, is another excellent terrain park.

Châtel – the resort

Châtel is a lively, traditional village on a gently sloping site. It is mainly ranged along the through-road to Switzerland and the dead-end road towards Pré-la-Joux – so it is far from car-free, and very busy at weekends.

Convenience

Slope-side lodgings are not an option here, but the Super-Châtel gondola base is close to the village centre and a red piste (affected by the afternoon sun) comes back down. For most people, most days start and/or end with a bus ride or a drive. The limits of the village are a bit blurry, but it's about a mile long, so après-ski walks are not too bad. Shuttle-buses run on half a dozen routes.

Lodgings

There's a very good range of lodgings, all in traditional chalet style. There are a dozen 2-star hotels, nine 3-star and one 4-star, the smartly modern Macchi close to the centre. Super-keen skiers might want to consider staying at the Villapeyron/Linga lift base, where options include the 3-star Schuss and Dranse. Catered chalets can be found.

Peak Retreats Pick of the apartments

Directors' Choice The 4-star Chalets d'Angèle has a pool and spa area – and a baby pool, making it very family-friendly. The ski-bus stops outside – the Super-Châtel gondola is just 4 minutes away.

Other options The location of 4-star Les Fermes de Châtel couldn't be better – in front of the slopes, next to the Super-Châtel gondola and close to shops. Other good options include Le Grand Lodge, which has a pool and spa, and Le Grand Ermitage, which has an outdoor pool and spa. Both are close to a ski-bus stop.

www.peakretreats.co.uk 023 9283 9310

Bars and restaurants

There are several lively bars; the Chaudron and Godille are natural ports of call on return from Super-Châtel. A locals' favourite bar, the Isba, has changed hands and become the Poste Frontière, still showing sports. We enjoyed dinner at the cool Café Zeph, bang in the centre, and at the more ambitious Vieux Four. For a casual meal, the Hors Piste is tipped.

Off the slopes

Forme d'O is a recently opened aquatic centre with indoor and outdoor pools, spa facilities and sports hall. There's a four-lane bowling alley with other amusements. The Fantasticable is a 1.2km zipline above Plaine Dranse, where you

Avoriaz has a sloping site where you have a good chance of ski-in/ski-out lodgings; and it has a bit of style

may reach speeds of 100km/h. There are extensive cross-country trails in the valley running down to Abondance – and lots of snowshoe trails, with guides available.

For families

Not an obviously suitable place for young families – access to snow isn't easy. There are kids' sledging areas at the top of the village, up at Super-Châtel and out at Pré-la-Joux; no lifts are mentioned.

La Chapelle-d'Abondance

La Chapelle is a small village spread along the valley road at the far end of the Barbossine/Torgon sector of slopes. It is difficult to recommend as a base, being well off the main PdS circuit, but it does have the attraction of a very distinctive hotel, the Cornettes – a 3-star with 4-star facilities, run eccentrically by the same family since the 19th century.

Avoriaz 1800m

Avoriaz (sometimes branded Avoriaz 1800) is one of the more successful purpose-built resorts, designed with a bit of flair and constructed to provide lots of ski-in, ski-out lodgings. More than most, it is apartment-dominated, but at least these days it has a couple of good residences and a single good hotel. It is very good for beginners: below the village is a gentle, prettily wooded mountainside reaching almost all the way to Morzine, 5km away – ideal for progression from the nursery slopes.

Convenience The layout of the village on a steep slope means that many of the lodgings are ski-in, ski-out, but the steepness of the slope presents challenges when you're not skiing, and the fact that cars are absolutely prevented from getting near most of the lodgings means that arrival and departure can be a hassle. Stay near the reception building, and you can drag your bags on a borrowed sled. Stay at the Amara residence and you can park in the basement. Stay elsewhere, and you can queue for a snowcat or a horse-drawn sleigh (and pay, of course).

Lodgings The main alternatives to an apartment are the central 4-star hotel Dromonts, now in the hands of the highly regarded Sibuet group (big in Megève), or a hotel at Les Prodains, at the bottom of the big gondola – the 4-star Neige et Roc is the best bet. Two apartment residences built near the cliff at the resort entrance stand out – Kouria, given a thorough makeover not long ago to create family suites, and the recently built Amara, with a large pool and spa.

Bars and restaurants The unstoppable Folie Douce chain opens its latest branch here for 2018/19; here, as elsewhere, it is going for a broader market (ie dinner sales) by operating at resort level. Existing places popular for both après and eating include Tavaillon and Chapka. The hotel Dromonts' JaJa is a cool wine bar.

Off the slopes The Aquariaz leisure centre is an excellent pool complex with lots of features especially appealing to kids, open afternoons and early evenings; the cost is non-trivial but not unreasonable. There's a fair-sized outdoor ice rink. In lieu of a toboggan run you can descend to Les Prodains on 'yooners' (single-runner things) using head torches.

For families The kids' ski school in the middle of the resort is famously well run. The village as a whole appears to suit young families well, but bear in mind our remarks under 'Convenience'.

The Ardent option

Tucked away down the Lindarets valley between Châtel and Avoriaz is the quiet, rustic hamlet of Ardent. With a gondola up to the main lifts and a blue piste back down, it makes a perfectly sensible base for anyone looking for a quiet time – families, for example. The specialist Family Ski Company has been operating here for many years and has acquired about half the village – nine chalets, at the last count, all more-or-less ski-in and short plod out.

PdS west – Morzine

Morzine / Les Gets

The western part of the Portes du Soleil is not on the same scale as the Franco-Swiss eastern part – and is mostly a bit lower, with only a couple of individual runs starting above 1900m. But it is a lovely woody area shared by two of the most attractive traditional villages in the French Alps.

Most keen skiers choosing a base here are likely to want to spend quite a bit of time in the eastern sector, and this is the main reason our preferred base is Morzine, with much more direct access to Avoriaz on the main circuit. It's a long-established year-round resort, with everyday shops and solid, traditional hotels. But for some people – people happy to stay close to home most days – Les Gets may be the more attractive base.

The mountains in brief

Size Limited local slopes, but the PdS east area is only a few lifts away

Slopes Mostly wooded, but with open areas; nicely mixed terrain

Snow At these altitudes, don't bank on good conditions low-down

System, Lift Good in parts, but not impressive overall

Sustenance Plenty of restaurants, including some excellent ones

For beginners No problems, but not ideal; Les Gets is better than Morzine

For true blue skiers A good choice, with few drawbacks and plenty to do

For the confident Good red runs, with the PdS east also on tap

For experts Great in a snowstorm, and quite a lot to do otherwise

Fancy stuff There are parks, but enthusiasts will look to Avoriaz

Morzine – the resort in brief

Convenience Not bad for a traditional village – it depends on location

Lodgings All the options most of us require; not a place for big spenders

Bars and restaurants All you need, from lively bars to excellent restaurants

Off the slopes Lots to do, though we hanker for a proper toboggan run

For families A good resort given the right location; but Les Gets is better

Pass notes
The local pass offers a non-trivial saving on the cost of a PdS pass. Both Morzine and Les Gets offer cheap day-passes for their beginner lifts.

Key facts

Altitude	980m
Range	950–2255m
Slopes (see text)	400+km

Where to stay, ideally
A walk from the lifts for Le Pléney, or on the snow in Les Gets.

Websites
morzine-avoriaz.com
lesgets.com
portesdusoleil.com

Key ratings

Size	*****
Snow	**
Fast lifts	***
Mountain rest's	****
Beginner	***
True blue	****
Confident	****
Expert	***
Convenience	**
Families	****
Village charm	***

The mountains in detail

A gondola accesses the low peak of Le Pléney, where there are all sorts of facilities. A ridge then runs gently up into the mountains; on spectator's left is a bowl with lifts up to the high-point of Chamossière (which we make slightly under rather than over 2000m) and to Pointe de Nyon; on spectator's right is the broad mountainside above Les Gets, centred on the mid-mountain lift station of Les Chavannes. Beyond that is a slightly higher bowl below Le Ranfoilly (Ranfolly on topo maps), also accessed from Les Perrières, on the fringe of Les Gets, with big car parks for day visitors.

It's a walk or tractor-train across Les Gets to the small but worthwhile Mont Chéry. Back in Morzine, you can similarly cross the resort to a lift up to the area called Super-Morzine, for lifts to Avoriaz – also accessible by taking a bus up the Ardoisières valley to a gondola from Les Prodains.

Some time soon a new gondola is to be built along the valley to Les Prodains to link with the existing one, slashing the time taken to reach the PdS east circuit from Morzine. An underground moving walkway will link the Le Pléney slopes to the new gondola.

Size

As we've explained in the previous pages, the PdS area is huge, with 400+km of pistes, and fully merits our 5-star rating. The PdS west Morzine/Les Gets sector makes up about 120km of the total, which would put the local slopes at the top of our 2-star size category.

Slopes

The photo below gives a fair idea of the nature of the slopes in general – pleasantly wooded and not particularly steep. But there are steeper open slopes at the top, notably on Chamossière. From there you can contrive a descent of 1000m vertical (and several km in length)

Friendly, prettily wooded slopes, shared by Morzine and Les Gets – great in snowy weather

to the Nyon cable car, but verticals in the order of 400–500m are more typical of the area.

Next to the black Creux piste from Chamossière is a freeride area, presumably avalanche-safe although the piste map does not say so. This area is, we are pleased to note, free of the gimmicks that litter the Avoriaz map.

Once a week you can ride the Pléney gondola at 8am to get first tracks with the ski patrol plus breakfast up the hill – free, it seems.

Snow

This area epitomises the skiing in this part of the Alps. It gets the full force of Atlantic weather from the north-west, including a lot of precipitation; but it can take the form of rain – with Morzine below 1000m and the top heights below 2000m, this is one of the lowest areas in the region, alongside the Espace Diamant. There's extensive snowmaking, and the standard plea that grassy runs don't need much snow certainly applies. But overall snow quality is not a strong point.

System, Lift

The main access lifts are fast, and there are some fast lifts on the upper slopes – the Ranfoilly bowl is quite well equipped – but also too many slow chairs, notably below Chamossière, on Le Pléney and on Mont Chéry. All in all, the system is a bit second-division, really.

Sustenance

The slopes are well equipped with over a dozen restaurants. Our favourites are in the Nyon/Chamossière sector – the cosy Chez Nannon and the lovely, spacious Pointe de Nyon (at the foot of the eponymous peak, note, not the top).

High on Mont Chéry, the Grande Ourse, well run by a friendly British family, gives great views across the resort to Mont Blanc; often a barbecue and a band.

More on the slopes

For beginners

At the base of Le Pléney there are nursery slopes served by a gentle (and free) 50m drag-lift and a rather less gentle 125m one. And there is a short moving carpet at the top, plus chair-lifts serving longer easy runs. We're told there is now a cheap pass covering these lifts and the gondola, but lack details. There is also a beginner area at the top of the Nyon cable car.

There are no really long green runs to progress to, but there are gentle blues.

For true blue skiers

There is plenty of blue skiing, and you can get around the whole area without too many unpleasant surprises.

The blues on Le Pléney are generally friendly, but none of them are motorways. Some of the most appealing runs are in the bowl below Chamossière – Choucas and Les Freux. Above Les Gets, Gentianes is a splendid top-to-bottom run dropping 650m, with the option of using Bruyère to steer round the steepest part below Les Chavannes.

The three blue runs from La Rosta at the far side of Les Gets are entirely gentle – a great place to build confidence; Violette, the run to reach the lift base, and Vorosses, the direct run back to the village, are a bit less so in places; but you can avoid both if you like.

For confident intermediates

Most of the red runs on the map are worth your attention – the main exception being Aigle Rouge from Pointe de Nyon,

LE PLAN DES PISTES DU DOMAINE SKIABLE LES GETS-MORZINE

RECHARGEMENT

Afin d'éviter l'attente en caisse, rechargez votre support «mains libres» sur **www.lesgets.com/pass**

To avoid waiting at the ticket offices, reload your «hands free» pass on www.lesgets.com/pass

SECTEUR CHAMOSSIÈRE

E1 : LES FREUX

SECTEUR CHARNIAZ

SECTEUR DES CHAVANNES

B1 : TK BOULE DE GOMME
B2 : TK MOUILLE AU ROY
B3 : TK TÊTE DES CRÊTS
B4 : TS DE LA CROIX
B5 : TK GRAND CRY
B6 : STADE DE SLALOM
B7 : FOUGÈRE
B8 : LES TRAPPEURS
B9 : PISTE MAUVE MILKA
B10 : CYCLAMEN

SECTEUR MONT-CHÉRY

A1 : MT-CHÉRY TRAINING CENTER
A2 : STADE DE SLALOM

SECTEUR NYON

D7 : RAVERETTES
D6 : PÂQUERAGES
D5 : COUTALAYS
D4 : AIGLE NOIR
D3 : AIGLE ROUGE
D2 : TK DES PRÉS
D1 : TK POIREAUX

SECTEUR PLENEY

C1 : TK MAS VERJUS
C2 : TS BELVÉDÈRE
C3 : TAPIS
C4 : LE STADE
C5 : PISTE N
C6 : ZONE ENFANTS
C7 : ZONE DÉBUTANTS

CHAMOSSIÈRE 2002m · LE RANFOILLY 1826m · LA ROSTA 1665m · POINTE DE LA TURCHE · PIC DU MARCELLY 1999m · MONT-CHÉRY 1826m · NYON 2019m · PLENEY 1505m · COL & LAC DE JOUX PLANE · L'ENCRENAZ · LA TURCHE · LES CHAVANNES · LES FOLLIETS · LES LONGUES POSES · ESPACE DE LOISIRS · ZONE FREERIDE · ZONE BIOTOPE · ZONE DÉBUTANTS DES MAPPYS · ACCÈS NYON CHAMOSSIÈRE · PASSERELLE RETOUR PLENEY · TUNNEL · GARE INTERMÉDIAIRE

À DE CETTE LIMITE, VOUS DEVEZ [...]ER LE FORFAIT PORTES DU SOLEIL

CHAMOSSIÈRE EXPRESS · NOUVEAU RANFOILLY EXPRESS · NAUCHETS EXPRESS · CHARNIAZ EXPRESS · MINIBOARDER VIDÉO · SNOWPARK · CHAVANNES EXPRESS · BOARDER CROSS · TS LA ROSTA · GRAINS D'OR EXPRESS · TK LA TURCHE · TK CHÂTEAU · PERRIÈRES EXPRESS · TC MONT-CHÉRY · TS DE LA POINTE · TS GRANDE OURSE · TK DE LA POINTE · TK SUPER CHÉRY · SLALOM PARALLÈLE · TS CHÉRY-NORD · TS PLANEYS · TS DES TÊTES · TRONCS EXPRESS · TS RAVERETTES · TS LA POINTE · TS PRÉ FAVRE · TPH NYON · TS DES FYS · TS FOLLIETS DU GOLF · TC CHAVANNES · TK VIEUX CHÊNE · TK DU STADE · TS NABOR · TS DES MOUILLES · TS D'ATRAY · TS LA CRUSAZ · TC DU PLENEY · TK BOUCHET · ZONES DÉBUTANTS · ZONE ENFANTS · TC SUPER MORZINE

Les Gets · Morzine Portes du Soleil

P	Parking *Parking*
	Restaurant *Restaurant*
	Point de Vue *Point of view*
	Toilette *Toilet*
	Webcam *Webcam*
	Piste de Luges *Ledging slope*
	D.Z. Parapente *D.Z. Pargliding*
	Point Info *Information Poi[nt]*
	Caisse - Forfaits *Sell kiosk*
	Salle Hors-Sac *Picnic room*
	Spot photo *Spot photo*
	Neige Artificiel[le]

TK	Téléski *Skilift*
TS	Télésiège *Chairlift*
Express	TS Débrayable *TS express*
TC	Télécabine *Cable cabin*
TPH	Téléphérique *Cable car*

which is a dreary zig-zag until it reaches blue territory. (Back in the day there was a direct black run here, which made more sense.) Arbis from Chamossière, on the other hand, is a splendid run – long and testing – but too popular on busy weekends. The reds lower down in this sector are rewarding, too. The runs from Ranfoilly would be next on our agenda.

Given good snow, the lower runs are good, too – several on Le Pléney, Chamois at the bottom of Nyon, Mélèzes down to Les Perrières.

The runs on Mont Chéry are short, but sweet, and being numerous they add up to a worthwhile amount of skiing.

So, quite a bit to do, even before you set off to explore the PdS east area, and the famous circuit through Switzerland.

For experts

There are quite a few black runs dotted around the map, and most have something to offer.

Mont Chéry is well worth a visit. On the back, the Mouflon black, on one side of the west-facing bowl, is barely any steeper than the red Marmotte on the other side; Chevreuil down the centre, however, is a proper black, at least at the top. And Bouquetin in the shady bowl on the north-east side becomes genuinely steep after a deceptive start. Gazelle, on the front of the hill, is nicely varied.

The resort is a big, towny place, filling the valley floor between its two sectors of slopes

Over on Chamossière, Les Creux is a lovely shady slope, long and sustained but not as steep as the Mont Chéry runs at their steepest. On Rosta, Myrtilles has one pitch approaching black steepness, but Yéti doesn't even have that. On the home slopes of Le Pléney, the varied Olympique is black in places.

The free ride area on Chamossière is a good thing – an addition to the mountain, in parallel with the piste, rather than a rebranding of an ungroomed piste, as in many other resorts. There are numerous proper off-piste ways down from here and from Nyon, too, including quite a few reached by branching from the two red pistes. There's plenty of off-piste space on the slopes below Ranfoilly, and beside the black pistes on Mont Chéry, too.

The area really comes into its own in bad weather, like most of the low ski areas in this part of the world. For example, the lifts below Chamossière and the lower Fys chair access large areas of safe and sheltered terrain, in and out of the trees.

Of course, you also have access to the PdS east area, including its lifts up to the Swiss border giving access to the classic off-piste run down the Manche valley towards Morzine.

Fancy stuff

There is a snow park for all levels at Les Chavannes above Les Gets, and a 'playful' snow park at mid-mountain in the Nyon sector. There's a boardercross on the Gentiane run above Les Gets. Park enthusiasts might want to make trips to the top-notch stuff in Avoriaz.

Morzine – the resort

In scale, Morzine is more of a town than a village, with sprawling suburbs. But it is all in traditional low-rise chalet style, with the established feel of a year-round resort. It is set right at the foot of the slopes on Le Pléney.

Convenience

It's a big place, well over 2km long, spreading up the side valley towards Les Prodains and its gondola up to Avoriaz, and effectively split in two by the deep gorge of the Dranse de Morzine – crossed by road bridges at the south-east end of town, and by a foot bridge next to the Super-Morzine gondola station. The town is divided into five quartiers: Centre Village is separated from the mountain by Le Pléney; across the river are Super-Morzine and Ressachaux; stretching away down the valley is La Plagne.

Pick the right spot and you'll have a short stroll to one main lift or the other. Elsewhere, you'll be reliant on a multi-route bus service including a clockwise circular route around Centre Village and Le Pléney, and another taking in La Plagne. These services don't have a great reputation for reliability.

Lodgings

Hotels and chalets (catered and self-catered) dominate. There are lots of attractive chalet-style small hotels – about eight 4-star, more like twenty 3-star and a smattering of simpler places. The 4-star Bergerie and Champs Fleuris take some beating (both with pools). And we like the look of the 3-star Equipe.

Morzine is the spiritual home of the single-resort operator running just one or two catered chalets. Host Savoie is slightly bigger, with four properties dotted around the village. Mountain Heaven has two chalets; one a brand-new place that sounds fab. For reasons that escape us, Morzine hasn't attracted the big developers of smart apartments, but the Aiglon de Morzine residence is well up to their standards, with a spa.

Bars and restaurants

Morzine is a lively resort with lots of options, so we turned to Andy Turner of local chalet firm Host Savoie for pointers. He gave us a comprehensive guide; what follows is just the highlights.

If you've been skiing Avoriaz, a great spot to hit as the lifts close is La Grenouille at the top of the home gondola. At the base of the Pléney lifts, the Tremplin is one of several lively bars, with a great DJ and party atmosphere. In the centre, hit Haka for happy hour offers, sports on big screens and a reasonably priced snack menu. Beanies is a favourite for pre-dinner cocktails.

Best restaurants in town are probably L'Atelier in the central hotel Samoyède (which also has the best place for a quiet *digestif*, La Taverne) and the stylish Chamade. Le Coup de Coeur is a crowded wine bar in the same ownership, doing good tapas.

The best mid-priced restaurants are: Le Tyrolien – by far the best pizza in Morzine; La Flamme for a cosy and charming restaurant with great local specialities; L'Etale for a varied menu – good kids' menu and one of the few places open all day; and La Dez'Alp, which has delicious Savoyard specialities, a beautiful interior and friendly staff. Ô Chalet is great for a casual meal any time of day – including gourmet burgers.

Prime late-night bars are Café Chaud and the Cavern, with the resort's one night club next door – Opéra.

Some evenings you can ride the Nyon cable car, dine at the Pointe de Nyon restaurant and ski home with head torches and guides.

Off the slopes

You can descend the piste from Le Pléney on a sledge or 'yooner' in the evening, with head torches and a guide. The Parc des Dérêches leisure centre offers a 25m pool, a half-size learning pool, a paddling pool and a spa. It also has a hockey-size indoor ice rink (weekly matches to watch) and in the town centre is a good-sized outdoor rink.

It's an excellent area for walking, snowshoeing and cross-country, with trails at Le Pléney, up the Manche valley, up at Super-Morzine and in the Ardent valley. There's snowmobiling up at Super-Morzine, too. At the main lift base, the big-air bag is open for tube landings in the evening, for all ages from seven years.

For families

At the top of Le Pléney, Pinguins Parc is a boardercross funslope with woops, tunnels etc. On the Daim blue run to the village is Les Zouzous, a funslope with small terrain features and wildlife info.

There's a good range of off-slope activities for kids, although we suspect for a certain age range the antique carousel outside the tourist office will eclipse most other options.

There is sledging for young kids on the Mas Verjus drag-lift at the lift base, but bizarrely it is open only during the skiing day and not in the early evening. After that, older children can ride the Pléney gondola and descend the piste.

Les Gets 1170m

If you don't insist on slick access to the PdS east circuit, Les Gets is a very appealing destination – an old village, much expanded in traditional style, by-passed by traffic for Morzine and conveniently spread along the base of its slopes. It also spreads up the hill beside those slopes, with lodgings up to 300m above the village at Les Chavannes, where you'll find the main village nursery slopes plus longer green runs (with lifts covered by a cheap day-pass).

Convenience These days Les Gets is not much smaller than Morzine. As in Morzine, the main lifts and pistes are directly in front of the village centre, but in fact the village has a very different layout, offering quite a lot of ski-in lodgings.

Here, on spectator's left of the lifts, the village spreads up the hill to Gibannaz, then to Les Folliets at the foot of the Folliets chair, and finally a road climbs to Les Chavannes. On spectator's right, development spreads up the hill to Lac des Ecoles and the base of the Turche drag-lift. Down the hill from here, at the south-west extremity of the village is a second lift base at Les Perrières, with huge car parks to soak up weekend day visitors. Shuttle-buses link all these parts, plus the many hamlet-suburbs dotted around the hillsides.

Lodgings There are half a dozen 3-star hotels, smaller numbers of 2-star and 4-star places. The 4-star Crychar has a good slope-side location and an excellent restaurant. The 3-star Croix Blanche is up at Les Chavannes – great for the nursery slopes. The Grande Lanière up at La Turche has had a stylish makeover earning it 3-star status.

Peak Retreats Pick of the apartments

The 4-star Annapurna residence, new in 2018, features beautiful, spacious apartments in a top location, just 150m from the Mont Chéry gondola and the village centre. Superb facilities include a stunning pool and a spa with steam room and hot tub. The 4-star Fermes Emiguy is 300m from the resort centre and 400m from the Chavannes gondola. It has a pool and spa area. We also like the Delphine Apartments, just 250m from the slopes and village centre, with a pool and spa.

www.peakretreats.co.uk 023 9283 9310

There aren't as many catered chalet firms here as in Morzine, but there is no shortage, including some family specialists and some swanky options. Ski 2, an established operator to Italy, has taken on a couple of mid-sized chalets here – and offers the unusual option of a two-centre holiday split between Les Gets and Champoluc, in Italy's Monterosa ski area, with a 2hr30 mini-bus transfer between the two via the Mont Blanc tunnel.

Bars and restaurants On the lower slopes, the QG is a natural opportunity to move into après mode on the way home. Favourite drinking spots in the village included the Irish bar and the Canadian Black Bear above it. There are lots of restaurants in the usual French resort mould. The St-Laurent in the hotel Labrador is about the best in town. For cheese dishes, the Fruitière is a must (it's made on the spot). The new Annapurna residence has a cool Vina wine bar-restaurant with a very interesting menu.

Off the slopes For swimming, you'll have to look to your lodgings (or to the excellent leisure centre in Morzine). In the village centre is a big outdoor ice rink. There's also a bowling alley. There are good walks and snowshoe trails up in both ski areas; snowshoe guides are available. The famous museum of mechanical music is worth a look – it now has 750 exhibits.

For families The resort works well for young families: provided you pick your spot, access to snow is easy. There are sledging areas at several points at village level, and up at Les Chavannes. The Grand Cry Territory is a wild-west-themed area at Les Chavannes. Electric snowmobiles are available at Lac des Ecoles. And the oldest merry-go-round in France is back in use in the centre after renovation.

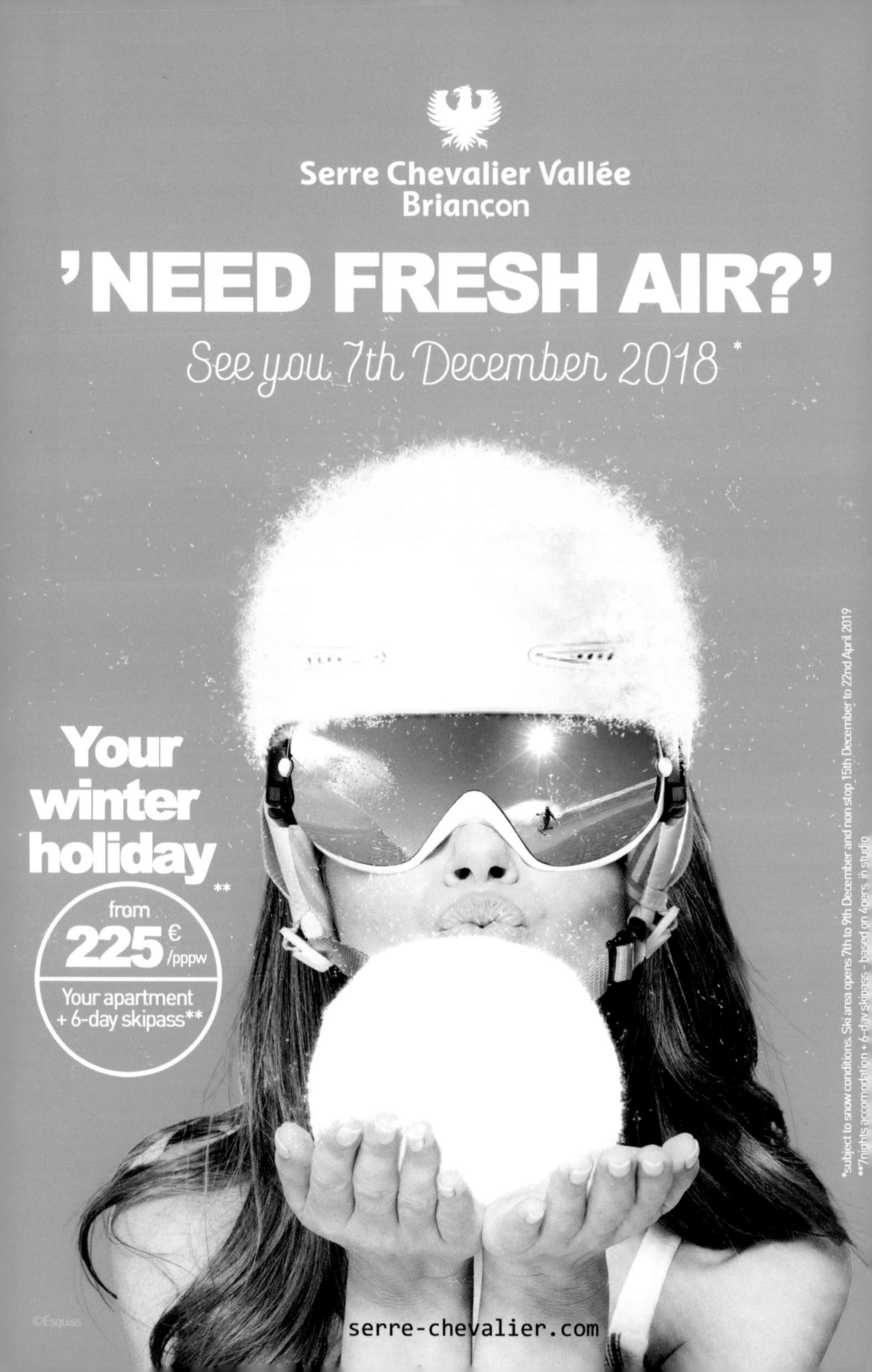

Serre Chevalier Vallée
Briançon
'NEED FRESH AIR?'
See you 7th December 2018 *
Your winter holiday **
from
225 € /pppw
Your apartment + 6-day skipass**
*subject to snow conditions. Ski area opens 7th to 9th December and non stop 15th December to 22nd April 2019
**7nights accomodation + 6-day skipass - based on 4pers. in studio
©Esquiss
serre-chevalier.com

Serre-Chevalier

Chantemerle / Villeneuve / Le Monêtier-les-Bains / Briançon

Serre-Chevalier is one of a kind. Its combination of extensive high slopes and equally extensive woodland skiing is unmatched anywhere else in France, and among the numerous villages dotted along its valley are some charmingly rustic ones, with a distinct Provençal flavour.

It's an extensive area, with four main resort villages. Chantemerle is the one we favour: it's well placed for exploration of the whole area, with a proper little village at the base and a cable car going to a decent altitude. Equally well placed Villeneuve has space to build, and is attracting upmarket developments. We must hope there will be similar investment in Serre-Che's distinctly lacklustre lift system.

The mountains in brief

Size Middling, but feels bigger, with a great sense of travel across the hill

Slopes Nicely varied, with lots of woodland runs, and some good, long ones

Snow Reasonable altitude and shady north-east orientation, so it's OK

System, Lift Not in the premier league; but queues don't seem a problem

Sustenance Some excellent places, spread across the whole area

For beginners A good set-up, but at Chantemerle you start up the hill

For true blue skiers With a bit of confidence you can do a great deal

For the confident Good long red runs in all sectors, and outings possible

For experts Plenty to do, with larch forest to retreat to in a snowstorm

Fancy stuff A range of stuff, including a decent main park

Chantemerle – the resort in brief

Convenience It all depends – but not much slope-side accommodation

Lodgings Apartment-dominated, but with some good hotel options

Bars and restaurants Adequate bars, and several good restaurants

Off the slopes Plenty to do in the valley as a whole (including Briançon)

For families Villeneuve and Le Monêtier are better bets

Pass notes
A six-day pass covers days in Les Deux-Alpes, Alpe-d'Huez, Puy-St-Vincent, Montgenèvre and Sestriere in Italy. Beginners must buy a cheap day pass for the lifts to mid-mountain and the nursery lifts there.

Key facts

Altitude	1350m
Range	1200–2735m
Slopes (see text)	165km

Where to stay, ideally
A walk from the lifts of Chantemerle or of Villeneuve.

Websites
serre-chevalier.com

Key ratings

Size	***
Snow	***
Fast lifts	***
Mountain rest's	****
Beginner	****
True blue	****
Confident	****
Expert	****
Convenience	***
Families	***
Village charm	***

The mountains in detail

The skiing is spread along the front of a long mountain range facing north-east. There are four main lift bases, the outermost ones 13km apart, each with a fairly distinct slope sector above it.

From Briançon at the south-east end, a gondola rises over 1150m to the shoulder of Prorel. Over the ridge is a broad bowl between Prorel and the peak of Serre-Chevalier itself, reached by a two-stage cable car rising 1140m from Chantemerle. Next, with multiple linking pistes, is a more extensive and complex area of bowls above the multiple gondola stations of Villeneuve, dominated by the higher peak of L'Eychauda. And finally, at the north-west end is a more compact sector above Le Monêtier-les-Bains, peaking at the area high-point of Pic de L'Yret (2735m), reached from Le Monêtier by chair-lifts.

Size

Following publication of the first Schrahe report documenting the exaggeration of piste km by many resorts, including Serre-Che, the resort switched from length in km to area in hectares. It now quotes groomed pistes amounting to 410ha and ski terrain as a whole of 3,900ha.

Multiplying by 2.5, farmers may be able to visualise about 1,000 acres of groomed piste, and grouse moor owners may be able to visualise about 10,000 acres overall. The rest of us can refer to the Schrahe report's figure of about 165km of piste, putting the area at the very top of our 3-star category.

It's interesting that the resort ranks right alongside Les Deux-Alpes. Serre-Che feels like it has appreciably more skiing to offer, perhaps because of its four distinct sectors and lift bases, giving a real sense of travel.

Slopes

Serre-Che's combination of villages that are lowish by French standards, an exceptionally high treeline (about 2200m) and mountains of red-to-black gradient results in unrivalled amounts of worthwhile woodland skiing. The top heights are respectable, too – the main peaks are in the 2400m–2800m range – so there is plenty of open skiing above the woods, which is where much of the easier skiing is to be found – the blue runs lower down mostly cut across the mountain rather than going down the fall line. There are some gratifyingly long runs to be done (typically 1200m vertical) in each sector.

Snow

Serre-Che doesn't have a great snow record – it's tucked too far into the Alps for that – but it has reasonable top heights and mostly faces north-east, so it keeps snow well once it arrives (which may be from the south, rather than the west as in the northern French Alps). All in all, it's a reasonable bet.

Various black piste are now branded Brut de Neige runs and are ungroomed.

System, Lift

This is clearly not a resort with money to burn; the lift system is a bit creaky, with multiple slow chair-lifts (above Le Monêtier, in particular) and drag-lifts on many of the higher slopes. So progress around the mountain can be slow in places; but in general queues don't seem to be a problem except at real peak times.

As we write in 2018 the Côte Chevalier chair-lift is being replaced by a six-seater starting at a lower point. The Fréjus chair-lift is being taken out too; this means the Pontillas gondola from the valley no longer connects with any lift at mid-mountain – but a longer replacement gondola is in the pipeline, perhaps replacing the ancient Fréjus gondola, too.

On our last visit (in March 2018) we were pleased to find the Serre-Chevalier cable car, up to 2500m, running until 4.55pm. Austrian resorts that shut down by 4pm please note.

Like many resorts, Serre-Che operates a 'first tracks' scheme, taking up to 30 people up the hill before the standard lift opening time. But here it's free. Weekly, from Chantemerle.

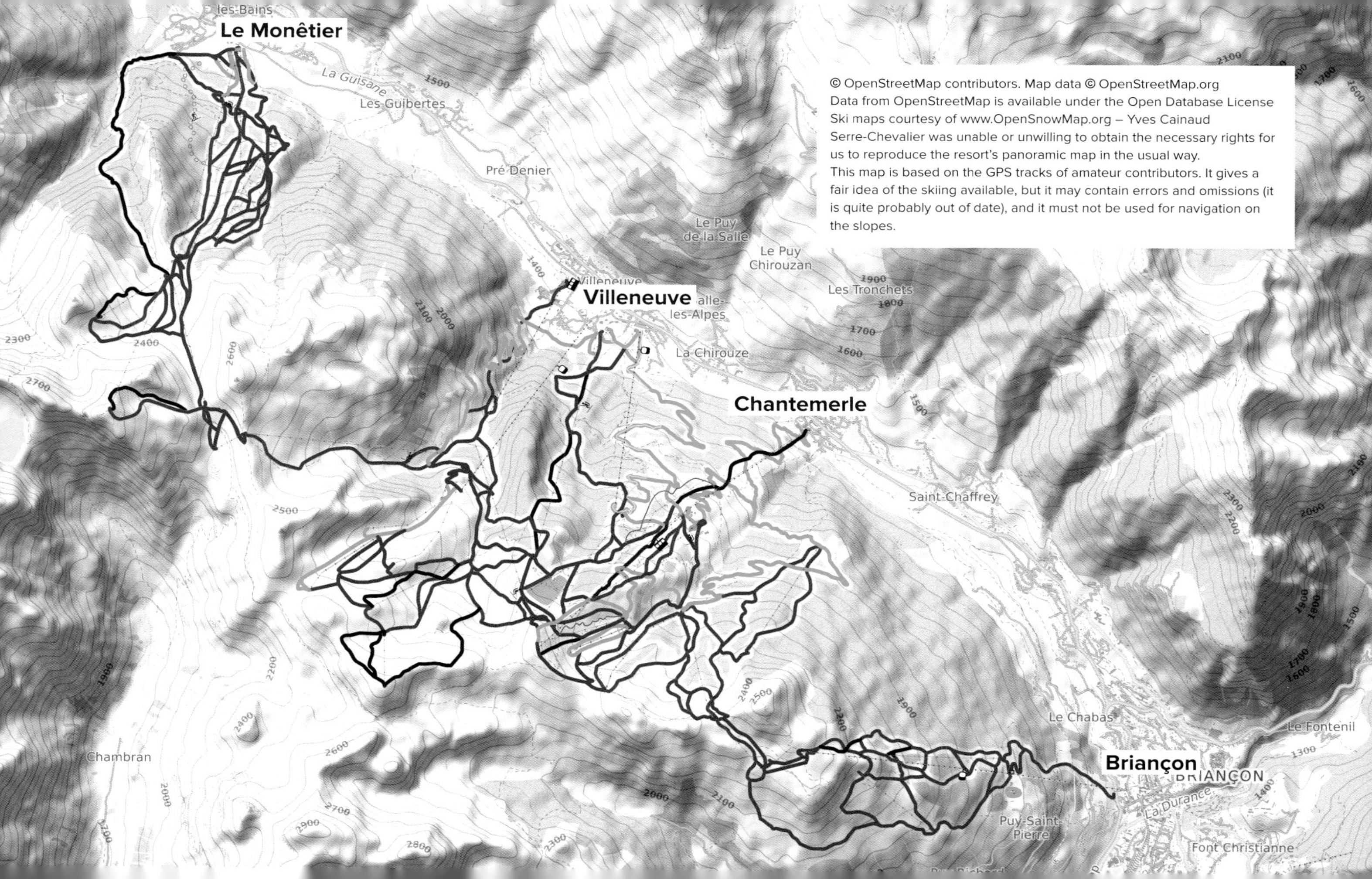

Serre-Chevalier was unable or unwilling to obtain the necessary rights for us to reproduce the resort's panoramic map in the usual way.
This map is based on the GPS tracks of amateur contributors. It gives a fair idea of the skiing available, but it may contain errors and omissions (it is quite probably out of date), and it must not be used for navigation on the slopes.

Sustenance

There are some excellent places here. Restaurants are marked but not named on the piste map.

Above Briançon, Chalet Pra Long near the mid-station has the rare attraction of a table-service restaurant that is not only lofty and light but also spacious and calm; excellent food, too. In the central part of the slopes we have two favourites only slightly less civilsed – Bivouac de la Casse and Pi Maï a bit lower down in the hamlet of Fréjus. The Echaillon is worth bearing in mind, too. At Serre Ratier, Le White is a cool, pricey table-service place that has replaced the Troll. Above Le Monêtier we like the Flocon, and it is endorsed by our local scout. And we love the tiny, cheerful Peyra-Juana lower down – the plat du jour is great value.

More on the slopes

For beginners

The Chantemerle nursery slopes are at mid-mountain, at Serre Ratier (1900m) – good for snow conditions, but requiring a day pass covering the access lifts; it is cheap (18€ in 2019), but an irritant.

From there you can progress to long, winding green runs to the lift base or across to Villeneuve, where you can ride the Aravet gondola and ski back across to Serre Ratier. Confession time: we haven't skied these runs, but they look like genuine greens, and don't have too many flat bits. Then the Orée du Bois chair from Serre Ratier accesses another long green. The next step would be quite a big one – up the cable car to the top for the long, not entirely easy Vallons blue.

For true blue skiers

To really enjoy Serre-Che you do need a little bit of bottle – there is hardly any motorway skiing. But if you can summon it, this is a fabulous mountain. You can travel over the whole area on pretty, rewarding runs, with just two caveats: there are no blue runs to the valley at Chantemerle and Briançon, and there is no blue run back to the central sectors from the Le Monêtier slopes – so you're in for a 2€ bus ride home if you go over there (which you really should).

Many blue runs fall into the same category: rewarding to ski, mostly straightforward but with the occasional testing stretch. Examples include Myrtilles from Prorel, Marteau down to Villeneuve, Vallons from the Serre-Che cable car;

Good skiing on and off-piste from Pic de l'Yret, the area high-point at 2735m, above Le Monêtier

the one run that has a proper red section in it – quite short, near the end – is the otherwise lovely Fangeas.

You should have no difficulty skiing to Pra Long above Briançon – the long Chemin has some nice skiing at the start and end, with a mile of cat-track in the middle. Enjoy some quiet laps on Yeti, if you can find your way to it. Similarly, above Le Monêtier the Eychauda run is a delight, as is Pas de l'Ane; the Rochamout run to the valley from there is a lovely, long, varied blue, but it's not a doddle.

For confident intermediates

Provided you have not been spoilt by the areas further north that rate 5 stars for size, you should have a great time here.

Many of the blue runs have their rewards, and practically all the red you see on the piste map is worth skiing. Lifts we head for are the Prorel gondola, with lovely rewarding red runs on the top stage and a great scenic run to the valley when snow is good (these runs get the morning sun); the slow Aiguillette chair, with two cracking reds; the Serre-Che cable car, serving the long Draye run; the two lifts beneath L'Eychauda; and all the lifts above Le Monêtier – Yret is a great run (pity about the slow chair-lift), and the several lower runs in the woods are as good as it gets in a snowstorm.

If you're wanting more, start playing off-piste (eg on the Cucumelle chair-lift) or try some blacks – they're not super-tough – or go and have a day in Montgenèvre, covered by the lift pass.

For experts

The black pistes provide challenges more because of snow conditions than steepness. The short, open runs at altitude that are labelled Brut de Neige, and are therefore not groomed, can offer moguls. The longer runs in the woods, mostly descending to the valley, can be testing if hard, but are a great thrash if soft (and dreamy if under fresh snow). The Tabuc run at Le Monêtier is one on its own, in more ways than one – an easy cruise apart from a couple of genuinely steep short pitches.

There is a lot of off-piste to be explored, much of it close to the pistes and relatively safe – the Eychauda, Yret and Cibouit chairs are particularly good spots; there are lots of areas in the well-spaced larch forests to retreat to in bad weather; sadly, one favourite area at Fréjus above Villeneuve is less easy to exploit now that the Pré du Bois drag-lift has been removed.

More adventurous stuff away from the lifts includes the Montagnolles valley, north-west from Pic de l'Yret, down to Le Monêtier; traversing /hiking from Col de la Cucumelle towards Tête du Grand Pré for various routes to Le Monêtier or Villeneuve; and epic, beautiful runs off the back of L'Eychauda or the peak of Serre-Chevalier south-east to Puy-St-André, for a taxi to Briançon.

Fancy stuff

The resort has a full set, mainly concentrated above Chantemerle and Villeneuve. The main Snowpark served by the Alpage drag at the top of Villeneuve (also easily accessed from Chantemerle) is a good size – about 500m long – and has four zones of different difficulty. Just across the hill at Grande Alpe above Chantemerle is a Boardercross course. Lower down in the larch (mélèzes) forest is Mélèzone – a fun freestyle course with snow and wooden features. Funnycross is a family funslope on the Rocher Blanc chair-lift at the top of Prorel, above Briançon.

Chantemerle – the resort

The valley road rather splits Chantermerle in two, but the traffic isn't heavy except on peak weekends. The part at the foot of the slopes forms a neat mini-resort, with bars around the lift base and the restaurants of the old village only a few yards away. Note that Chantemerle is in the commune of smaller St-Chaffrey, just down the valley, and that name is widely used to locate hotels and the like (eg on the resort website).

Convenience

This is not a ski-in/ski-out resort, but some of the best lodgings are at the lift base or close to it. Other lodgings spread up the hillside, across the valley from the skiing, to the hamlet of Le Villard-Laté, about 600m from the lift base. A free ski-bus links these areas to the lift base.

You might want to start skiing in one place and end up in another (particularly if starting from Briançon or Le Monêtier). There is a valley ski-bus to allow this, but it now costs an irritating 2€ per ride. Here and at Villeneuve it stops quite near the lift bases, but not quite at them.

Lodgings

Serre-Chevalier as a whole has always been a resort with a low swank factor, and 3-star and 2-star places still dominate the hotel scene. But more 4-star hotels are appearing, notably up the valley in Villeneuve and Le Monêtier; and in Chantemerle the Grand hotel, perfectly positioned a few yards from the lift base, has recently had a very successful 4-star makeover. With the closure of the Balme Alphand, the best 3-star bet in Chantemerle is the cosy Boule de Neige, in the old village centre.

Catered chalets are not widely available, but they can be found. Zenith offers various chalets, with catering available. EurekaSki does tailor-made packages here of all kinds, but mainly self-catering in apartments or chalets. The people who run it are based in the resort, ready to look after you; co-owner Gavin also runs the local branch of the excellent New Generation ski school,so they have all the bases covered.

The old villages are pleasantly rustic; this is the old part of Villeneuve; Chantemerle has a similar bit

Peak Retreats Pick of the apartments

In Chantemerle
The 4-star Hameau du Rocher Blanc apartments are a good option: they are in a prime position close to the slopes and lifts and only 200m from the centre. They also have a pool and spa facilities. The 4-star Adret apartments are just 300m from the village centre and 400m from the lifts. They have an indoor/outdoor pool with a sun terrace.

In Villeneuve
The Aquisana apartments are in a quiet setting 500m from the Pontillas gondola, and have a pool and steam room.

In Briançon
We like Aigle Bleu apartments for their location right by the gondola but only a short walk from the centre. They have a sauna, hot tub and steam room.

www.peakretreats.co.uk 023 9283 9310

In Le Monêtier
Check out the apartments and chalets that EurekaSki has to offer.

Bars and restaurants

There are several bars around the lift base that do good business at close of play, the Royal probably the liveliest (the Station seemed to have closed, last time we visited). Later on you'll find us in Le Maurice, a very civilised wine bar (also doing food) reached by lift from the little square in front of the cable car station.

We've had good meals in several restaurants in the old village right next to the lift base. Despite changing hands in late 2017, our favourite is probably still the funky Triptyque. The Loup Blanc does good food, but it's more expensive, and the plush decor seems somehow a bit out of place. We like the cool 34 too. For a pizza, we'd head across the valley road to La Cabassa, in the little shopping precinct.

Off the slopes

At Chantemerle there isn't a great deal to do. At the top of the Serre-Chevalier cable car you can descend a 2km/300m vertical course by luge or wheeled 'mountain kart', but this stops at 3pm. There's bowling at the lift base, and ice karting not far away.

Villeneuve has a proper 4km toboggan run through the woods on the Aravet gondola, running into the early evening – but only during French school holidays.

Villeneuve has an outdoor ice rink, and there's an Olympic-size indoor rink on the edge of Briançon with regular hockey matches to watch. At the same venue (Parc 1326) there is an aquatic centre with indoor and outdoor pools. There is now an indoor pool in Villeneuve, too, and the thermal spa at Le Monêtier is impressive, with indoor and outdoor pools.

There are cross-country trails of differing standards running up the valley to the Col du Lautaret, and snowshoe routes too (a guide booklet is on sale). There's an ice-driving circuit at Villeneuve, although the current site is due for redevelopment. Other options include dog sledding and horse riding.

The fortified old town of Briançon is a world heritage site, and more generally this is an area with an unusual amount of historic and cultural interest.

For families

Chantemerle doesn't strike us as the ideal basis for a family holiday. Le Monêtier and Villeneuve have the advantage of space for village-level nursery slopes (with sledging opportunities), and lodgings on or very near the snow. Villeneuve has other advantages too – a swimming pool and ice rink. Wherever you go, you do have to pick your spot for quick and easy access to the snow.

Alternatives to Chantemerle

All the alternatives have their attractions. Briançon is a real town with a historic core, while Le Monêtier offers village-level nursery slopes, considerable charm and good boutique hotels with excellent restaurants. But Villeneuve has a better position, good off-slope amenities and the attraction of its rustic old village just across the river.

Briançon 1200m

Briançon is not a village, but emphatically a town, with sporting, cultural and historical dimensions you don't normally find in a ski resort. The town is quite compact – the central area is about 1km across, with the fortified Cité de Vauban on the far side away from the lift base. It seems to have no special ski-bus arrangements.

The nursery slope is up at Pra Long, at mid-mountain, the necessary day pass costing 15€ in 2019. The home run from Prorel is an excellent red, but not entirely reliable for snow.

There are two 3-star hotels, the Vauban and Chaussée, about 300m from the gondola) and more 2-star ones. Read 'Pick of the apartments' for self-catering pointers. There are some catered chalets.

There are several bars around the lift base, so you won't die of thirst. Best restaurant in town is the pricey Michelin-starred Pêché Gourmand near the lift base. There are half a dozen good places up in the old town; our girl on the spot Mel reports L'Etage (French with influence from Italian family owners) to be fabulous. Au Plaisir Ambré is highly regarded.

Villeneuve 1400m

Just as Chantemerle is part of St-Chaffrey, Villeneuve is in the commune of smaller La Salle-les-Alpes, and the names are used interchangeably – all very confusing.

The resort consists mainly of apartment developments spreading widely around the lift stations (of which there are several) without any kind of focus; but not far away are the characterful old village, over the river, and another village, Le Bez, right at the foot of the hill. Free navettes run on two routes linking all parts, while a little train links the lift bases and the old village.

There are several nursery slopes at valley level, and an area with two moving carpets at mid-mountain, at the top of the Aravet gondola. There is a day pass for all of this, costing €20 in 2019. Sledging takes place on the nursery slopes.

The range of lodgings is quite wide, and getting wider. The Grand Aigle is a cool 4-star on the fringe of Le Bez. The 4-star Rock Noir is a small 'design' hotel just a few yards from the Aravet gondola. The company behind that is also heavily involved in the plans of the famous Folie Douce group to build a big new lodging/restaurant/bar/activity complex at the north-west end of the resort. Zenith's offerings include a 10-bed catered chalet close to the Aravet gondola. Read 'Pick of the apartments' for self-catering pointers.

At the Aravet lift base, La Grotte is a live music/sports bar that also does good-value food until 6pm. In the old village of La Salle, Mojo is a welcoming Brit-run bar-restaurant doing good value food. Le 1420 is a cosy-but-stylish wine bar sometimes with live music. For a mid-priced proper restaurant, you won't beat Eau Petit Pont (yes, by the river).

Le Monêtier-les-Bains 1500m

Le Monêtier could be the most captivating of the villages if it didn't have the valley road traffic squeezed into its narrow main street. The lift base and nursery slopes are on the edge of the village, about 500m from the centre. A free ski-bus runs on a circular route. The carpet-lift on the nursery slopes is used for sledging. For the longer drag-lifts such as the 500m Pré Chabert you need a cheap day pass.

The hotel de l'Europe is a nice old 2-star in the back streets. The 3-star Alliey has an excellent restaurant, as does the 4-star Auberge du Choucas. As we write in 2018 a new central 4-star Le Monêtier is being built, in mountain lodge style. Try EurekaSki for good apartments.

The Alpen is the main bar, with sports TV and live bands. We have a soft spot for the bar of the hotel de l'Europe. There are quite a few restaurants. As well as the hotels mentioned, the more modest Kawa is also excellent, and very friendly.

Ste-Foy-Tarentaise

Ste-Foy is a small village on the road up from Bourg-St-Maurice to Val d'Isère-Tignes. Its mountain outpost, variously known as Bon Conseil or Ste-Foy-Station, started life in 1990 with a chain of three chair-lifts and little else. Since development took off at the turn of the century it has grown to become a proper little resort; but it has added only one chair-lift and upgraded another.

The slopes offer a decent 1100m vertical and a good mix of pistes. But most people staying here, children apart, will want to ski off-piste inside and outside the lift network, for which there are good opportunities, or to head off for days in other nearby resorts. As well as Val d'Isère-Tignes, Les Arcs and La Rosière are easily reached by road.

The mountains in brief

Size The ski area is small; most people will want to ski outside it, somehow
Slopes Pleasantly varied, with a high proportion of woodland runs
Snow Mainly west-facing, which is not great
System, Lift Half fast, half slow, but pretty much queue-free
Sustenance In an area this size, three options are plenty
For beginners Good slopes, but you need a full pass from day two
For true blue skiers Excellent slopes, and no nasty surprises
For the confident Very limited unless you are up for exploration off-piste
For experts Some sunny off-piste within bounds, varied long runs outside
Fancy stuff No terrain parks as such

Ste-Foy – the resort in brief

Convenience Lots of ski-in/plod-out lodgings set at the foot of the slopes
Lodgings Some good chalets and apartments, but no hotels
Bars and restaurants An adequate range, including some good spots
Off the slopes There's sledging, and your apartment may have a pool
For families They don't come much better than this

Pass notes
With a six-day pass you can buy day passes at a worthwhile discount in Les Arcs/Paradiski, Val d'Isère-Tignes and La Rosière – 30€ in 2018. The carpet-lifts at village level are free, but to move on you need a full pass.

Key facts

Altitude	1520m
Range	1520–2622m
Slopes (see text)	25 pistes

Where to stay, ideally
On the snow.

Websites
saintefoy-tarentaise.com

Key ratings

Size	*
Snow	***
Fast lifts	**
Mountain rest's	***
Beginner	****
True blue	*****
Confident	***
Expert	****
Convenience	****
Families	*****
Village charm	***

The mountains in detail

A fast chair-lift followed by two slow ones form the backbone of the lift system, rising 1100m to 2622m on the ridge near Col de l'Aiguille. To skier's right of that chain is another fast chair-lift finishing about 200m lower.

Size

Ste-Foy makes occasional reference to its 25 pistes but otherwise doesn't draw attention to the size of its ski area. Having measured a couple of them, we'd guess the total is 30–40km, and certainly less than 60km, putting the resort firmly in our 1-star category. It's seriously small.

Slopes

The treeline on this west-facing hill is quite high – about 2100m – and a good part of the area is below it. As you can see from the photo-based piste map, the first two chair-lifts are in the trees, the third above them, with the Marquise on the left about 50:50. The middle part of the hill is basically of blue gradient, the lower and upper parts steeper.

You can ski 1100m vertical from the top to the bottom, a run of maybe 5km, but the snow on the lower slopes is not always appealing. The fast Marquise chair serves a decent vertical of 575m.

Three black pistes are left ungroomed, and they and their surroundings are designated as Natur' zones (as are a short red and a short blue). The resort says the zones are avalanche-safe when open, but its *Guide Pratique* says that avalanche kit is required for the black zones; when asked, the resort explains that this is because people might go on from these zones to real off-piste. We think this policy is confusing and makes no sense.

Snow

The resort gets reasonable snowfall, and the upper slopes on the Aiguille chair face north-west, but everything else is essentially west-facing, so things get affected by the sun, especially in late season. The main off-piste runs face basically north or south.

System, Lift

Queues are rarely a problem here; if one appears briefly, it will be at the second chair-lift. In warm weather you're likely to want to spend time on the best snow high up, which means a choice between the slow Aiguille and fast Marquise chairs.

Sustenance

There are three restaurants on the hill. At the top of the first lift are the cramped but cosy Brevettes and the more spacious Chez Léon. Les Marquises, at the bottom of the Marquise chair, has great views and is highly recommended.

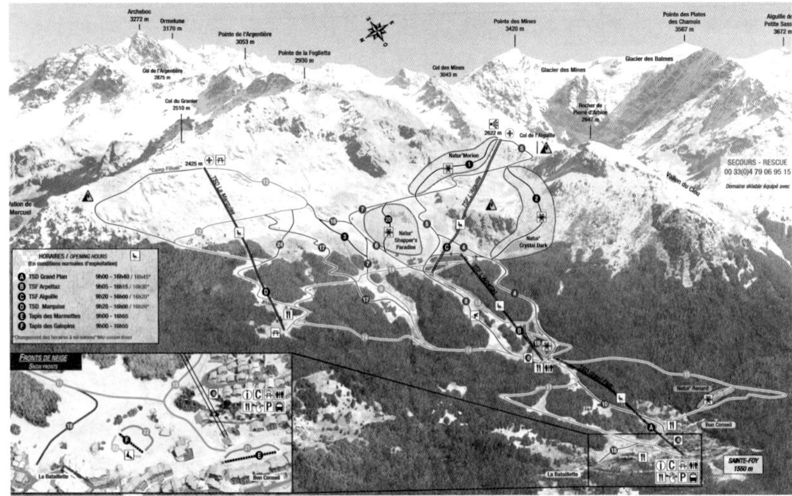

More on the slopes

For beginners

There are two carpet-lifts on the gentle nursery slopes directly in front of the village centre – you can probably make them out on the photo on the next page. These are free; when you're ready to move on, you need a full lift pass.

There are no green runs, but the transition to blues is painless – Combes down the first chair-lift is very gentle.

For true blue skiers

Given the small size of the area, there is quite a lot to do. All the blue pistes are genuine blues, and it's pretty clear from the map which ones are easier and less easy – leave the more direct 13 and 9 alone until you have found your feet on the more roundabout runs.

For confident intermediates

To be happy here, a competent, keen intermediate needs to be interested in skiing off-piste, in which category we include the Natur' zones around the main black pistes – Shaper's is relatively gentle, and a great place for novices to build confidence. The red runs don't add up to much, and most of the blues are very easy. A plus point is that the runs are uncrowded, so you can indulge in some fast carving without endangering anyone.

The resort makes a lot of sense, though, as an economical base for outings to the giant areas nearby.

For experts

Ste-Foy has a deserved reputation for off-piste opportunities. The three Natur' zones within the piste network are well worth exploration – and there are large areas of proper off-piste reachable from the Marquise chair. But the real draw is that both the high lifts access longer routes, some quite serious.

From the same chair you can traverse to skier's right via Col du Granier for a 1000m descent to Le Crot, ending up in the hamlet of Le Miroir. For a longer and more serious descent in the same direction you can hike up from the top of the Aiguille chair to Pointe de la Foglietta for access to the whole 1500m of its famous north face. For the less brave and energetic, that lift also accesses the very popular runs down the bowl of Lac du Clou to the historic deserted village of Le Monal, ending in a long ski-out back to the resort or (with some hiking) a descent to the road to Val d'Isère.

The resort is close to the Italian border, and heli-skiing can be arranged there.

Fancy stuff

Shaper's Paradise, one of the Natur' zones, has natural terrain features, and sometimes people build their own.

Ste-Foy – the resort

Ste-Foy has been developed in a traditional style, with pitched roofs and wood cladding. Although development continues, it now feels quite established; but its shops and restaurants are widely spread, so the place lacks the central focus of a village.

Convenience

The resort is set on a red-gradient hillside facing west. At the south end, to skier's left of the chair-lift is one cluster of apartment buildings, shops and other amenities, with chalets spreading up and down the hillside, the highest about 100m vertical above the lowest. The village has expanded across the hillside from here, and the apartment buildings to skier's right of the chair now contain most of the bars and restaurants. Further right still, the apartment developments of La Bataillettaz are slightly detached from the rest of the resort, but the gap is sure to be filled.

Much of the accommodation is ski-in/plod-out, and most of the walks are short. But overall the village is now about 750m end to end, and La Bataillettaz is 400m from the lift base – far enough to warrant a shuttle-bus service. There is also a shuttle serving the village of Ste-Foy and the hamlet of Le Miroir.

Lodgings

There are quite a few catered chalets, and lots of good modern apartments, but for a hotel you have to look to the 3-star Monal in the centre of Ste-Foy itself, an 8km drive down the hill.

Bars and restaurants

There's a handful of bars and restaurants. The Après, in the little commercial area at the south end, is as you might hope a good spot for an après beer, with live music some evenings. At La Bataillettaz, the relatively new Black Diamond has become very popular as both a bar and a non-traditional restaurant. More traditional favourites are Maison à Colonnes by the home piste and L'à Coeur, next to Après.

Off the slopes

The shorter carpet-lift at the base is used for sledging. There are guided snowshoe outings, daytime and evenings, and there are four signposted routes, shown on a free map. There are walks, too.

For families

The resort suits young families very well, provided the limited range of activities isn't a problem.

Small but perfectly formed; well, quite sensibly formed, at least, with nursery slopes on the front de neige

Val Cenis

Lanslevillard / Lanslebourg / Termignon / Bonneval-sur-Arc

Val Cenis is a small ski area in the Haute Maurienne – the high, remote part of the Maurienne valley – with the three quiet, traditional villages of Lanslevillard, Lanslebourg and Termignon ranged along the foot of the slopes. The first of these is the obvious place to stay, unless you are looking for a smart hotel (in which case it's Lanslebourg for you).

Bonneval is a quite separate and tiny resort at the head of the valley which adds a bit of variety, particularly for off-piste skiers; it's described at the end of the chapter. And there are three other resorts a little way down the valley, covered by the lift pass, which add more in the way of piste km – described in the Maurienne valley chapter earlier in the book.

The mountains in brief

Size On the small side, but with good options for outings by car or bus
Slopes An excellent mixture of open and wooded slopes
Snow Unusual weather patterns, but pretty reliable on the whole
System, Lift Not a strong point – many slow lifts, some bottlenecks
Sustenance You won't starve, but you might wish for a more varied diet
For beginners Pretty good arrangements, with lots of green runs
For true blue skiers Not as good as the map suggests, but not bad
For the confident A slightly frustrating mountain, not brilliantly planned
For experts Quite a bit to do, but less in the woods than you might hope
Fancy stuff Several boardercrosses in the area, and an 'easypark'

Lanslevillard – the resort in brief

Convenience A spread-out place, but ski-in lodgings are not hard to find
Lodgings A reasonable choice, but don't expect luxury
Bars and restaurants Quiet après-ski; a good choice of simple restaurants
Off the slopes The key bases are covered
For families The beginner terrain is great for young children

Pass notes
The Haute Maurienne pass permits a day in each of Bonneval, Aussois, La Norma and Valfréjus. Free shuttle-buses link the resorts. Several lifts on the good beginner terrain at Lanslevillard are covered by a cheap day-pass.

Key facts

Altitude	1460m
Range	1300–2800m
Slopes (see text)	100km

Where to stay, ideally
Near one of three main lifts out of Lanslevillard, or at Les Champs.

Websites
haute-maurienne-vanoise.com

Key ratings

Size	**
Snow	****
Fast lifts	***
Mountain rest's	***
Beginner	****
True blue	***
Confident	***
Expert	***
Convenience	***
Families	****
Village charm	****

The mountains in detail

The skiing falls into three sectors. Lifts go up from three or four bases around Lanslevillard into the main sector below Plan Cardinal at 2520m and Col de la Met at 2800m. From the latter there are links across the mountainside to slightly lower slopes around Col du Mont Cenis, directly accessible from Lanslebourg. The third sector, peaking at 2465m, is above Termignon, which is 6km from Lanslebourg; it's reached by a long fast chair from Lanslebourg, followed by a slow one. There is a blue piste back to Lanslebourg, but it's a pretty tedious affair, and many people opt to ride the fast chair back down.

Size

Val Cenis claims 125km of pistes, but the Schrahe report puts it at 100km, squarely in our 2-star category. But even that assessment overstates what the area offers in practice, because of the exceptional length of three runs of little interest to most skiers: the famous green road from the Col and the two tedious blue forest tracks from the Termignon upper slopes to the valley add up to something approaching 25km. Knock those off, and you're getting towards the bottom end of our 2-star category.

Keen skiers will want to make the most of the lift pass and visit some of the other resorts it covers (read 'Pass notes'). It's much more easily done with the aid of a car.

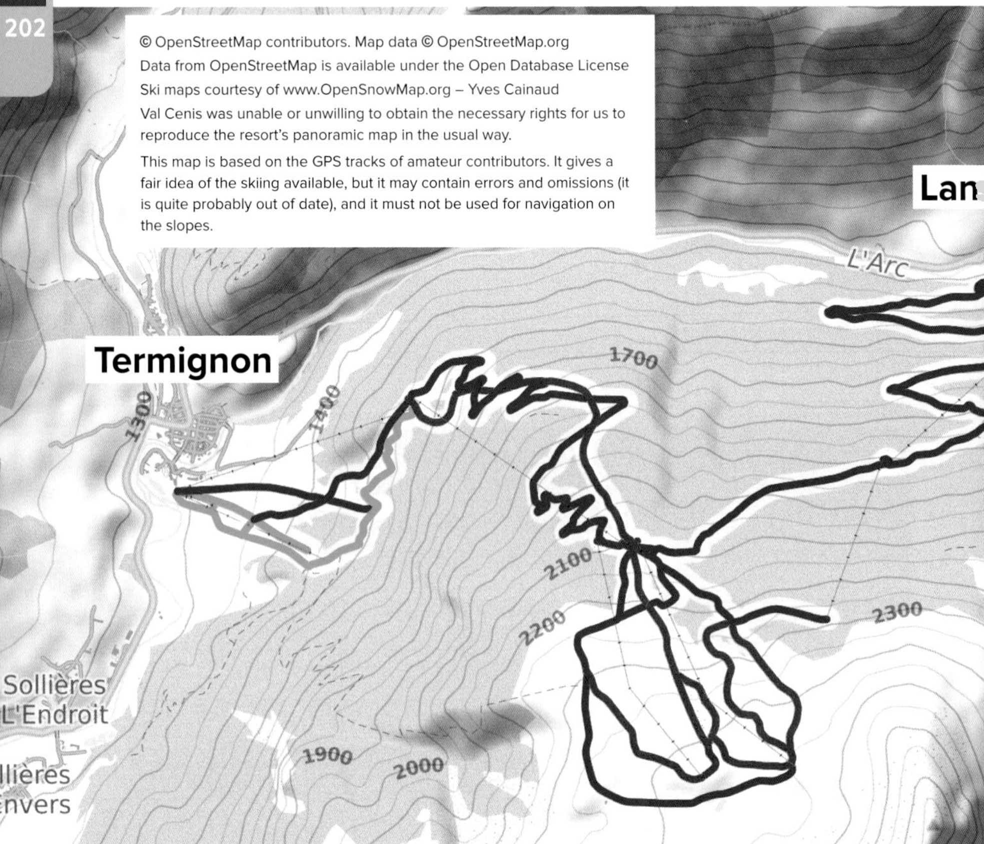

Slopes

With a relatively high treeline, the mountain offers a good mix of open slopes and woodland runs. It's essentially a red-gradient hill, with blue runs mostly cutting across the slope, and the few blacks rarely achieving genuine black steepness. There are plenty of descents of over 1000m vertical to be done, in all sectors, with a maximum from the high-point of 2800m to Lanslebourg racking up 1340m; it's about 5km as the eagle flies, so probably something like 7km along the pistes. A distinctive feature is the famous Escargot green run, dropping 600m over its 10km length from the Col du Mont Cenis – it employs the *route départmentale* 1006, closed in winter.

Snow

The Haute Maurienne has unusual weather patterns. Snow arriving from the north-west is likely to fall on the Tarentaise resorts and not get this far, but big dumps can materialise from the south-east when there is low pressure in the Mediterranean – a phenomenon known as the Retour de l'Est. The sheltered setting, highish altitudes and shady orientation of the slopes are helpful. All in all, the snow is pretty reliable.

Another factor, though, is the famous and fairly frequent Lombarde wind, again from the south-east – not necessarily bringing snow, but bringing chilly chair-lift rides, possibly fog and probably lift closures, particularly in the Col du Mont Cenis sector.

System, Lift

The lift system is not a strong point of the area. Basically, most of the access lifts are fast, but most of the upper lifts are slow chairs (at Lanslevillard) or drags (elsewhere), so in good weather you are likely to find yourself on slow lifts much of the time. The one very welcome exception to the first rule is the fast six-

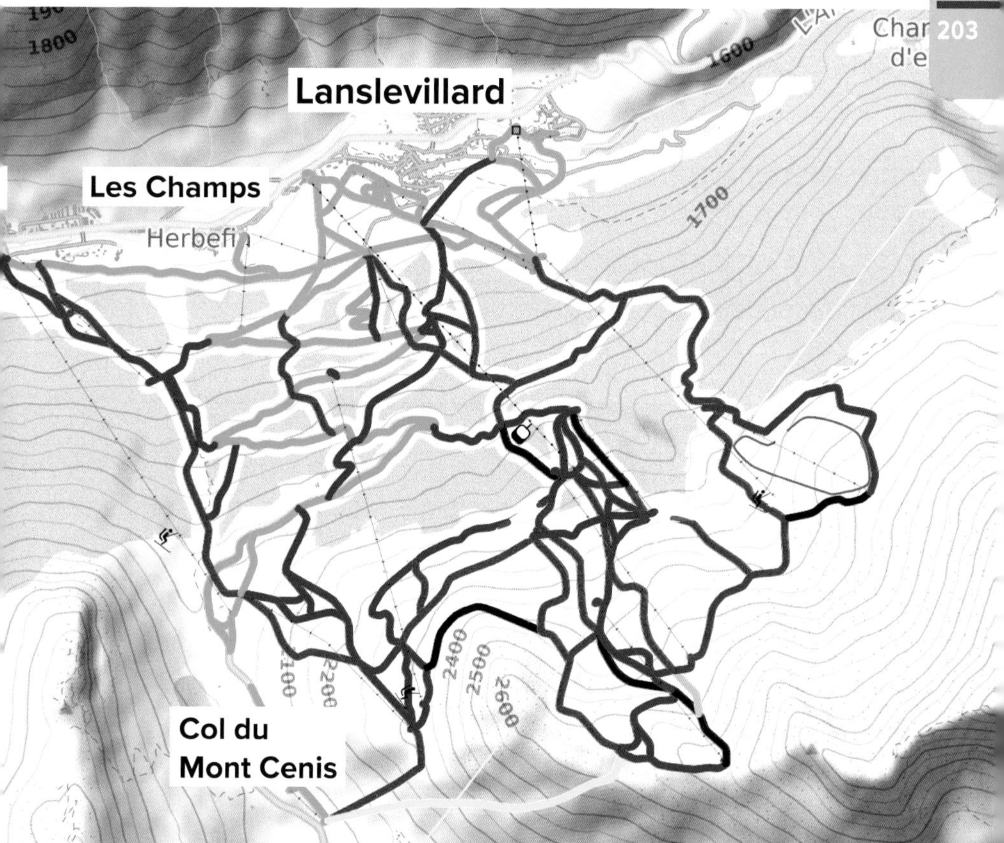

seat Solert chair, bang in the middle of the Lanslevillard slopes, while the main exception to the second rule is the slow Roches Blanches quad chair to mid-mountain above Termignon.

There are some theoretical bottlenecks in the network. Above Lanslevillard, the Arcelle six-pack is accessed by two powerful lifts, either of which could keep it busy. And at Mont Cenis the Mont Cenis drag-lift is fed by a six-pack from Lanslebourg (plus several pistes). We're short of evidence, but we'd be surprised if these points are queue-free in peak season.

As we write in 2018, a new drag-lift (there's a rare thing) is being installed at Les Champs to give residents of the apartments there painless access to the main Vieux Moulin gondola (and to serve gentle green runs).

Sustenance

The choice of mountain restaurants is adequate, but no more than that: two at mid-mountain above Lanslevillard, one above each of the other villages, plus one at the Col du Mont Cenis. La Ranova, near the Plan Cardinal chair at Lanslevillard, is our favourite – a cosy place with a wood stove, doing good, simple meals.

More on the slopes

For beginners

There are magic carpet lifts on the *front de neige*. Between Lanslevillard and the mountain proper is an excellent area for beginners – extensive gentle slopes served by a short drag-lift and by two longer lifts, the Val Cenis le Haut gondola and the Colomba fast chair-lift. There's a half-price day-pass covering all these lifts.

The obvious next step is to ski down the long green run to Lanslebourg, ride the fast Ramasse chair and ski the long green Escargot all the way to the village.

For true blue skiers

There is a reasonable amount of blue run skiing here, though not as much in practice as the map suggests at first sight: the long forest tracks from the upper slopes of Termignon are tedious. The Cupules piste, on spectator's left of the whole area, would be a fine run if you didn't have to ski red runs to reach it and to leave it. There is a fine easy run at the top of the Termignon sector, but it's a bit of a schlep to get there and back.

So you're looking at the runs in the heart of the area, accessed via the Vieux

There are some nice easy runs at village level, served by efficient, novice-friendly lifts

Moulin gondola from Lanslevillard and the Ramasse chair-lift from Lanslebourg. There are good runs above these lifts on the Solert chair, the Met chair, the Arcellins chair and the Mont Cenis drag – and Chamois is a good linking run, too.

For confident intermediates

Within the limits of the smallish area (read 'Size'), there's quite a bit to do, with the merit of worthwhile amounts of skiing in the trees as well as on the higher open slopes. But it has to be said that the red piste network is a bit fragmented, and not brilliantly served by the lifts.

For example, to ski the whole of Arcellin above Les Champs you'd have to ski a lot of blue and green runs to get to the start, and to ski Bec Rouge and Tomba you have to ride two lifts.

Much better for that purpose are the runs on the Arcelle and Solert fast chair-lifts, Met on the Met slow chair, Fort on the Mont Cenis drag near the Col and Ramasse below that to Termignon.

Beware the Ecureuil linking run in the woods: in icy conditions it is a nightmare.

The trip out to Termignon is worth the effort for red-run skiers, with several runs on the open upper slopes plus the excellent Bois des Coqs in the woods.

For experts

There is hardly any steep piste skiing. The main black piste, the Michèle Jacot Met from the Col de la Met, earns its status from a steepish start, but soon mellows. The much shorter Moraine has a black pitch half-way down. The short lower blacks may have trickier snow. As you might guess from the map, the piste labelled 'vers le Mont Cenis' is black not because of steepness but because it's a narrow track crossing a steep slope.

The lifts serve quite a lot of viable terrain between and outside the pistes, on the higher slopes but also in parts of the forest. We've enjoyed playing on the slow Plan Cardinal chair on a day when the otherwise inviting, higher, Met chair was closed by wind. The resort doesn't attract experts, so the snow lasts well.

Sadly, some of the most attractive terrain – gladed slopes above Termignon, for example – is off limits in the interests of protecting plants and animals.

Some of the other resorts covered by the lift pass are well worth a visit – Bonneval in particular.

Fancy stuff

There is a gentle boardercross course on the slopes above Lanslevillard and a more serious one at mid-mountain, reached from the Solert chair-lift. On the *front de neige* there's a fun zone with big-air bag (used with skis or tubes). At Lanslebourg there is a long boardercross on the Bleue du Lac blue run, apparently getting stiffer as you descend, and an 'easypark'.

Lanslevillard – the resort

Lanslevillard is a quiet, solid old village with modern but traditional-style apartment developments nearby and further away – notably part-way to Lanslebourg (Les Champs) and above the main village at Le Haut; both of these outposts have their own lifts into the slopes.

Convenience

It's not difficult to find ski-in, plod-out lodgings around the main part of Lanslevillard, at Le Haut or out at Les Champs, beyond the main gondola. Equally, there are plenty of places that involve walks. But you have a choice of four lift bases, and it's not a huge place – the village is about 1km end to end, and Les Champs is about 1km from the centre. There are frequent shuttles between Lanslevillard and Lanslebourg running into the early evening.

Lodgings

The swank factor in the whole valley is strikingly low. The only hotel we know of in Lanslevillard is the 3-star Etoile des Neiges – there are more in Lanslebourg.

Peak Retreats Pick of the apartments

Directors' Choice The location of the 4-star Chalets de Flambeau couldn't be much better – in Les Champs, at the foot of the slopes, by the Pré Novel chair-lift and ski school meeting point. It has a pool, hot tub, sauna, steam room and spa – and a children's pool.

Other options In a similar location at Les Champs are the Alpages de Val Cenis apartments. We love their outdoor pool – plus they have a hot tub, sauna and steam room. The Criterium apartments are also in the same spot; in the Criterium building (and easily accessible from the other two) are a mini-market, a friendly restaurant and a bakery. On the other side of Lanslevillard, a short walk from the centre, the 4-star Balcons de Val Cenis Village features generous-sized apartments at the foot of the slopes and less than 200m from the Val Cenis le Haut gondola. The 3-star Balcons de Val Cenis le Haut (with sauna) is in Le Haut, 100m from the end of the Terres Grasses green piste and the same gondola. Guests at these two residences get free access to the pool at the Glières leisure centre. Also great for location are the Bonheur des Pistes apartments, which are next to the Vieux Moulin gondola, with great views.

www.peakretreats.co.uk 023 9283 9310

Bars and restaurants

It's a quiet place, but the Creperie des Glaces at on the front de neige and Tata'Tine at the main gondola base dispense après beers, and food if required. There are maybe a dozen restaurants. We've had a good meal at the Arcelle, bang in the middle of the village. The Terroir Savoyard also gets good reports (and no, it's not limited to Savoyard specialities). Howard's pub has a good name for burgers. At Les Champs, the Peau de Vache is said to be great. Down the valley at Sollières (beyond Termignon) is the lovely Erablo, in a spacious farmhouse vault – charming service, very good food.

Off the slopes

There's a fair-sized artificial outdoor ice rink and a leisure centre with 25m pool,

Of course, most of the lodgings are in modern chalets, but Lanslevillard has a traditional old core

kids' fun pool, hot tubs and spa facilities. Bowling 1480 is a six-lane alley with attached bar-restaurant.

The gondola from Le Haut (700m long, rising 140m) has a toboggan run down its length, and snake-sledging down a piste from mid-mountain is organised. Snowtubing is offered after skiing at village level and three afternoons a week at the top of the Solert chair-lift, at 2500m – not an ideal arrangement.

There are seriously extensive cross-country trails at various points along the valley, notably down-valley at Bramans and up-valley at Bessans – said to be one of the biggest areas in the French Alps.

Alternative bases

Lanslebourg is bigger than Lanslevillard, with a reasonable choice of hotels, more shops and maybe slightly more restaurants, but we find it less appealing. Termignon is a long schlep from the main slopes above Lanslevillard; who it might suit is not immediately obvious to us.

Lanslebourg

Lanslebourg is spread along the die-straight RN6, with no central focus. There are several 3-star hotels (look first at the Clé des Champs), and a 4-star hotel opened here in 2015 – the Saint Charles. It has a particular appeal to families, thanks to its 24 family suites and ski-in location. There is a nursery slope at one end of the village, but it is nothing like as good as the other village slopes.

Termignon

Termignon is a pleasant village set in a bend in the river Arc, with its skilifts and excellent nursery slopes across the river, where a mini-village for skiers has grown up consisting mostly of apartments. The Balcons de la Vanoise apartments are well placed for the ski lifts and village amenities. La Turra is a central 2-star hotel. There's a good nursery slope, and a 2km green run above that.

Bonneval-sur-Arc 1850m

Bonneval has the classic ingredients of a cult resort – very high slopes, few pistes, a remote and snowy location at the head of the valley, few lodgings, entirely slow lifts. Not for the average skier, then.

In the unlikely event that you want to stay here, you have a choice between Tralenta, the modern development just above the lift base, or the fringes of the famously lovely old village, 600m away.

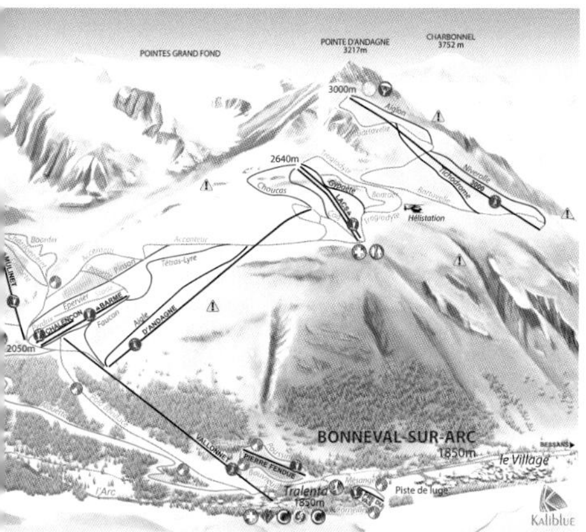

There's a small but well-formed lift and piste network with something for everyone, including a long green piste at the bottom which is getting a funslope makeover. So piste skiers could happily spend a day here while experts in the party get to grips with the off-piste.

The lift-served off-piste falls into three main sectors. To skier's left of the top lift (which doesn't actually reach 3000m, sadly) is a broad area of mainly gentle terrain, facing west, allowing a return to the lift. Below the main piste area are much steeper routes to the valley; some in trees, some not. Often the best skiing is in the third sector, reached by a traverse across a steep slope to skier's right from the Lacs drags. Extend this traverse and you reach a glorious, wide, north-east-facing slope; cut it short for steeper, narrower and more dangerous descents.

Val d'Isère-Tignes

Val d'Isère and satellites / Tignes in various forms

Not the biggest French area, but in many eyes the best

Espace Killy was one of the first attempts to brand a ski area, and now the name has at long last been cast on to the bonfire of marketing cock-ups. J-C Killy (born in Paris but brought up in Val) was the spectacularly successful hero of the Grenoble Olympic Games. But the name was never promoted with any real energy, it never caught on, and, as the memory of Grenoble (50 long years ago) fades, it has become clear that it never will.

So now, at a time when area names are finding some traction, this area has no name. The two resorts just string their names together in various ad hoc ways, in either order. Our chosen label rolls off the tongue better than 'Tignes and Val d'Isère'. 'Val-Tignes' seems the obvious handy short form.

Famously, experts are drawn to this area by vast amounts of off-piste, multiple guiding outfits and a good snow record. But it also has lots of long, easy pistes, and enough to amuse the keen intermediate. The area is nowhere near the size of the 3 Vallées or Paradiski, but with about 240km of piste (according to the Schrahe report) it comes at the top of our 4-star category, just ahead of Megève, Grand Massif etc.

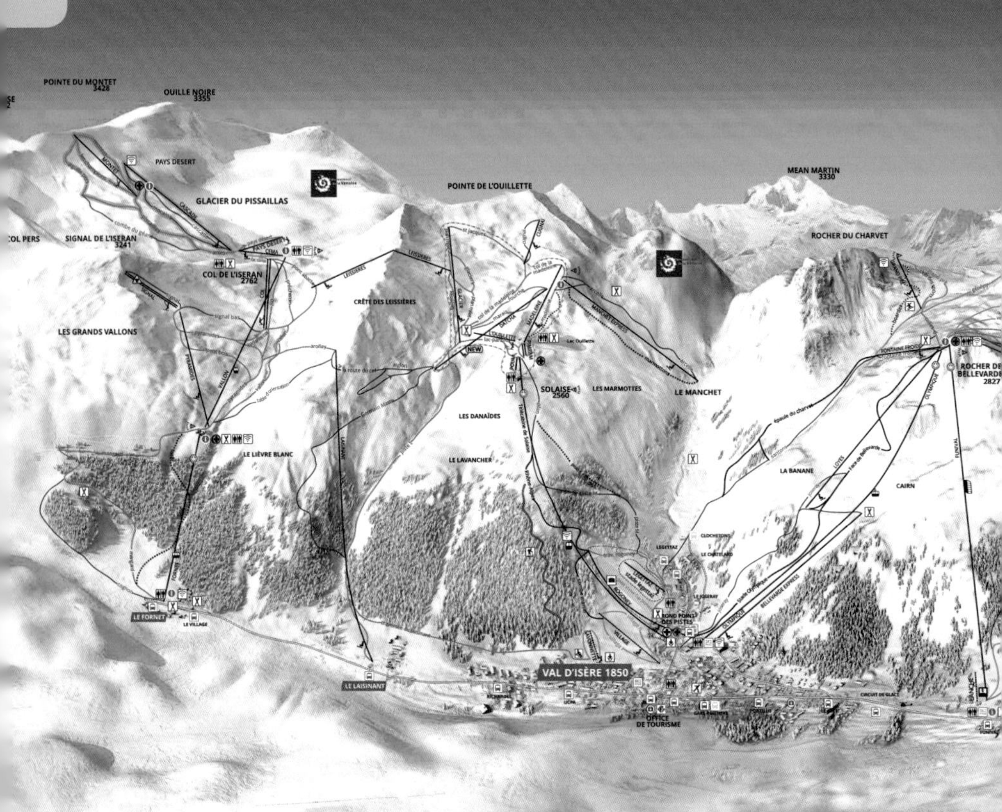

YSE
Val d'Isère
Twenty chalets ranging from comfortable to sumptuous
Exceptional food
Easy Sunday travel
www.yseski.co.uk
01935 816550

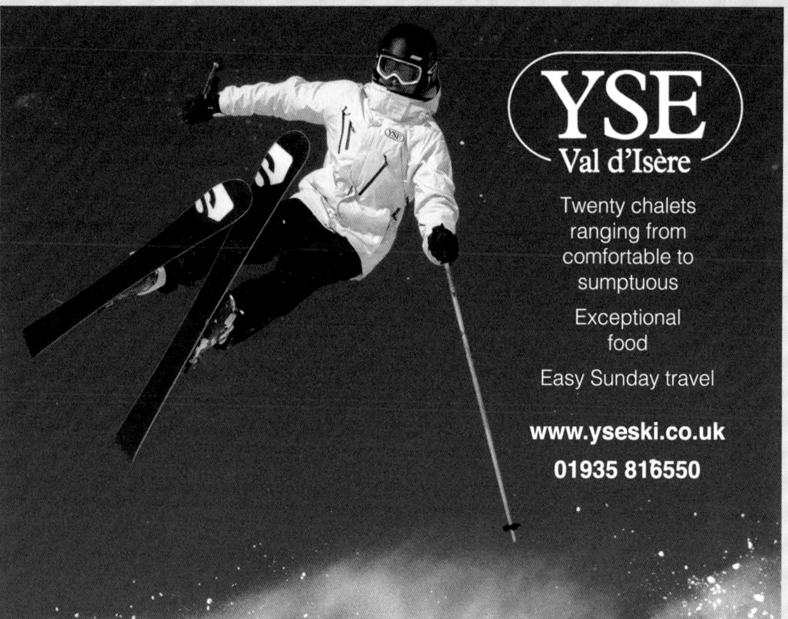

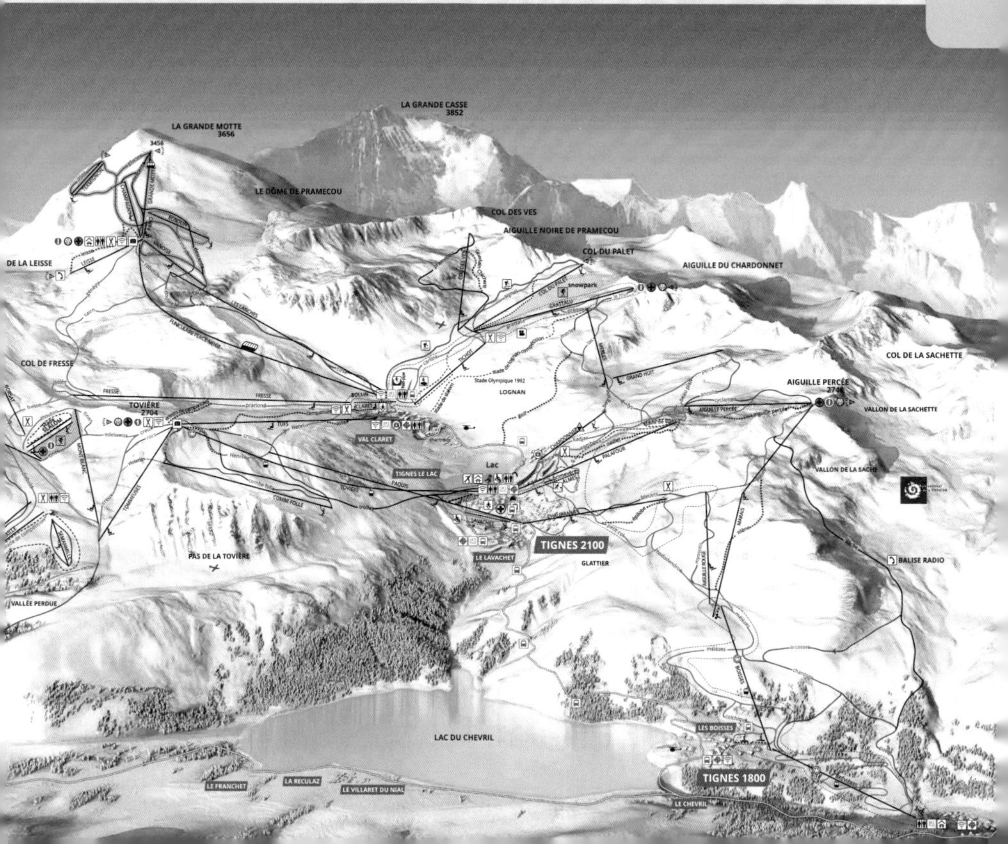
LA GRANDE CASSE
3852
LA GRANDE MOTTE
3656
3456
LE DÔME DE PRAMECOU
COL DES VES
AIGUILLE NOIRE DE PRAMECOU
COL DU PALET
AIGUILLE DU CHARDONNET
DE LA LEISSE
COL DE FRESSE
COL DE LA SACHETTE
AIGUILLE PERCÉE
VALLON DE LA SACHETTE
TOVIÈRE
2704
Stade Olympique 1992
LOGNAN
VAL CLARET
TIGNES LE LAC
Lac
VALLON DE LA SACHE
TIGNES 2100
LE LAVACHET
GLATTIER
BALISE RADIO
PAS DE LA TOVIÈRE
VALLÉE PERDUE
LAC DU CHEVRIL
LES BOISSES
TIGNES 1800
LE FRANCHET
LA RECULAZ
LE VILLARET DU NIAL
LE CHEVRIL

Val d'Isère

Val d'Isère / Le Fornet / La Daille

Val isn't perfect, but it has a range of attractions that few other resorts can match. Tignes, 250m higher, may draw the snow connoisseur or ski-bus-phobe, and is arguably better for our true blue skiers. But Val is more rewarding for the keen, competent intermediate skier and, crucially, is a much more pleasant place to inhabit.

Before the 1992 Olympics, Val catered for people who just wanted to ski, drink, eat and sleep. In 1991, editor Gill's *Good Skiing Guide* noted that Val was 'beginning to invest in its appearance, and seems to be moving upmarket'. Today's resort is stylish and vibrant, and continuing to improve, notably via the central Coin de Val development currently underway.

The mountains in brief

Size The shared area is big enough for anyone, though not the biggest
Slopes Mostly gentle open slopes high up, steep wooded slopes low down
Snow About as good as it gets, with the bonus of a worthwhile glacier
System, Lift The few flaws are not serious; big new lift due for 2018-19
Sustenance Some good places, and improvements continue
For beginners Now a good place to start, though not convenient
For true blue skiers Lots to do high up, but no easy runs to the resorts
For the confident Some cracking runs, though they don't add up to a lot
For experts Simply the best
Fancy stuff A good park, and multiple boardercrosses; Tignes has a pipe

Val d'Isère – the resort in brief

Convenience Probably the best ski resort bus service in the world
Lodgings All styles available, at all levels of the market; some fab chalets
Bars and restaurants A top place for après action, and good restaurants
Off the slopes An excellent sports/aquatic centre, and other diversions
For families Fine if you pick your spot and can handle the inconvenience

Pass notes
There is no pass for Val d'Isère alone.
There are two free lifts on the village nursery slopes (but read the main text).
There is a Solaise pass covering the nursery slopes and green and blue runs at the top and the Rogoney blue run at the bottom – no great bargain, at 37€ in 2019.

Key facts

Altitude	1830m
Range	1550–3456m
Slopes (see text)	300km

Where to stay, ideally
A walk from the main lifts to Bellevarde and Solaise.

Websites
valdisere.com
valdisere.ski

Key ratings

Size	****
Snow	*****
Fast lifts	****
Mountain rest's	****
Beginner	****
True blue	*****
Confident	****
Expert	*****
Convenience	**
Families	****
Village charm	***

The mountains in detail

Val's main lift base is a little way out of the centre, in the side valley of Le Manchet. The lifts go west to Bellevarde and roughly east to Solaise.

Bellevarde has runs (including famous downhill race courses) back to the lift base, and to the brutal satellite mini-resort of La Daille, where there are two more access lifts, one of them a super-efficient underground funicular to the very top of Bellevarde. Above La Daille are lifts to Col de Fresse and Tovière, linking with Tignes.

Solaise, always an excellent area for near-beginners, has now been made into an equally good area for absolute beginners, too. It has runs to the main lift base, and to isolated lifts at Le Manchet and Le Laisinant, and has links (described later) over the Leissières ridge to Col de l'Iseran.

Col de l'Iseran (Europe's highest paved road pass, closed in winter) is above another (not at all brutal) satellite village and lift base, Le Fornet. On the far side of the col are lifts up on to Val's glacier, Pissaillas – not as impressive as Tignes' Grande Motte, but a worthwhile area.

Size

The shared area claims '10,000 hectares and 300km of slopes'. The Schrahe report puts it at about 240km, which places the area at the very top of our 4-star category, although well behind the three areas in the exclusive 5-star group (3V, Portes du Soleil and Paradiski). The area is 15km across as the eagle flies.

Slopes

As our picture shows, the lower slopes here are wooded, and range from the fairly gentle to the practically unskiable. The open upper slopes vary a bit too, but they are predominantly gentle. Naturally, the lifts on those upper slopes offer limited verticals, but there are some good long runs to the valley – 1000m vertical

A lot of what you see here is within the lift network – Solaise and Pissaillas to the left, Bellevarde to the right

from Bellevarde, rather less from Solaise. There are no strikingly long runs in terms of km, but several in the 4–5km region.

Unlike Tignes, Val has adopted the Naturide concept with restraint: most blacks get at least occasional grooming.

Snow

Like Tignes, the main sectors of slopes here (glaciers apart) go high but not super-high – roughly in the range 2800–2900m. The resort, at 1830m, is similarly high without rivalling Tignes and Val Thorens. These heights are enough to give confidence that whatever snow falls will stay a while. Tignes and Val d'Isère also benefit from a geographical position that delivers snow from Mediterranean storms as well as Atlantic storms. Most of the runs are quite shady, the notable exception being the west-facing runs from Solaise into the Manchet valley. Add in a glacier area (even if it is remote from the village), and this is clearly a 5-star resort.

System, Lift

There are few slow lifts, and none is in a key position – unless it's the Mont Blanc chair. This is one of two lifts at the top of the powerful new gondola being installed at La Daille in 2018, and one route to the Col de Fresse, the more reliably pleasant way to Tignes.

Queues are not usually a problem;

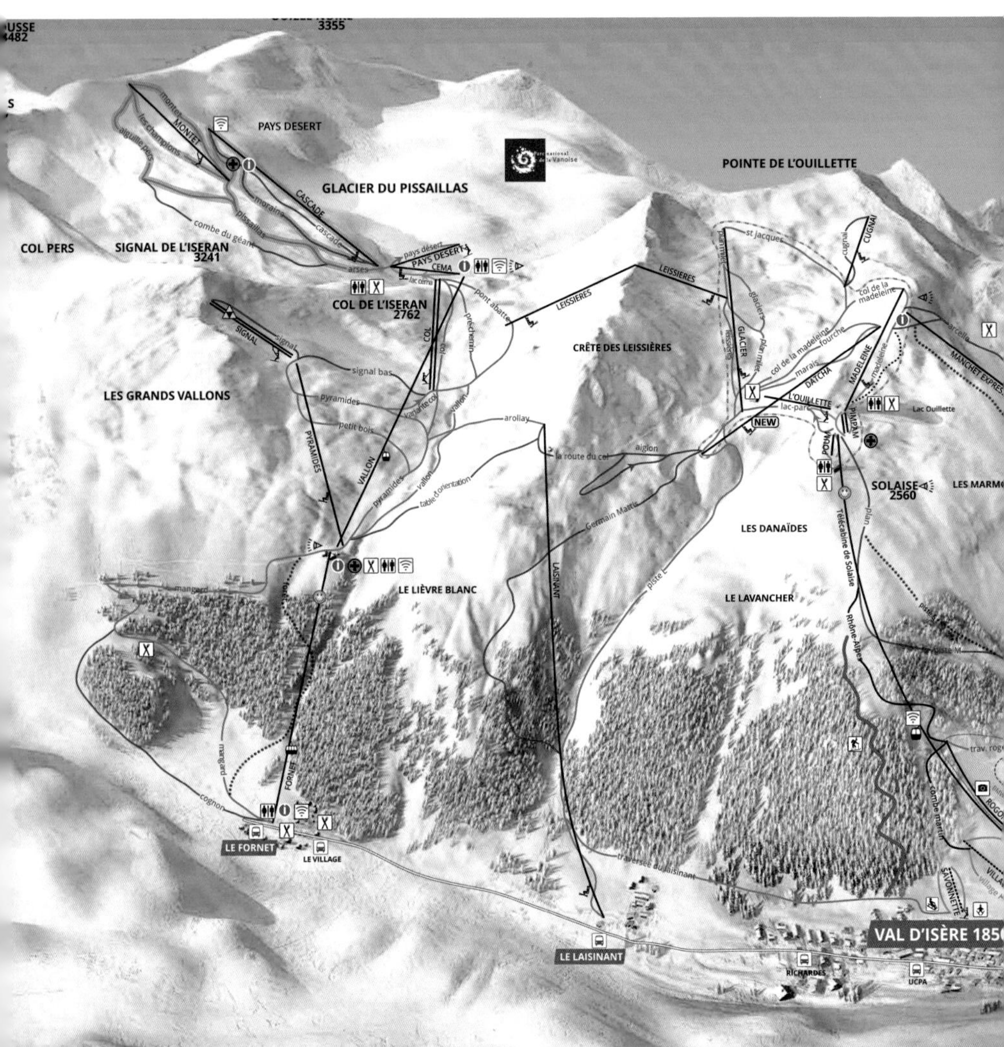

MEAN MARTIN
3330

POINTE DE LA SANA
3436

3456

ROCHER DU CHARVET

COL DE LA LEISSE

COL DE FRESSE

ROCHER DE
BELLEVARDE
2827

TOVIÈRE
2704

LA BANANE

CAIRN

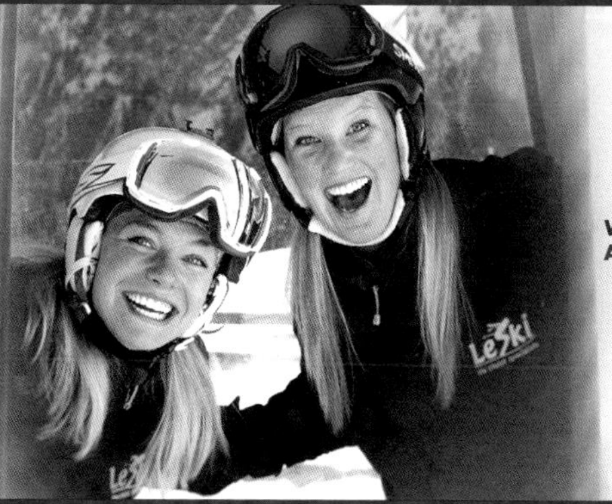

LA SPATULE

VALLÉE PERDUE

CIRCUIT DE GLACE

FUNIVAL

LA DAILLE 1785

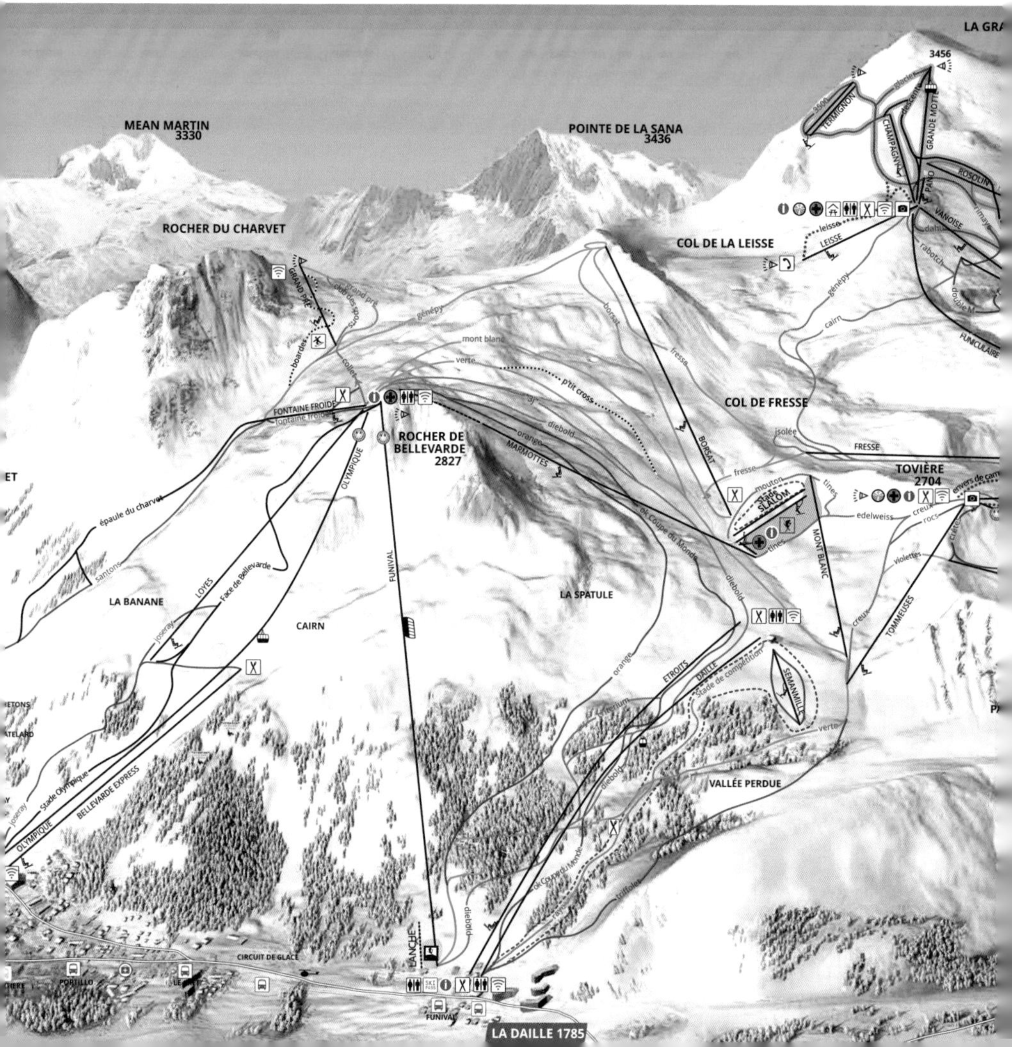

any pressure on the funicular at La Daille will presumably be relieved by the new gondola there, offering a slick way up for Tignes-bound skiers. If a peak-time queue does form for the Olympique gondola from Val to Bellevarde, the parallel chair-lift route is usually queue-free.

Solaise and Col de l'Iseran are linked by a very unusual up-and-down chair-lift over the ridge; some people find the ride unnerving, but for most of us it's probably less unnerving than the alternative: for the 2018-19 season the téléski des 3000 is re-opening and will again serve a steep slope on the Solaise side and another, said to be steep and gnarly, on the Col side, reached through a tunnel.

Sustenance

There aren't many good mountain restaurants, but there are some. We have a love-hate relationship with two of them – the Edelweiss above Le Fornet and the Fruitière above La Daille, part of the famous Folie Douce institution. Both have interesting menus and excellent food, but both have too many tables crammed together inside (the Fruitière in particular). We're much happier on the terraces.

Other places to bear in mind on Bellevarde are Peau de Vache at the top of the Bellevarde chair and the Trifollet (upstairs) halfway down the OK run to La Daille. On Col de l'Iseran, we also like the Signal at the top of the cable car.

On Solaise, the Bar de l'Oulliette is a place for a sunny day – great barbecue at reasonable prices. And we're expecting great things of the restaurant at the new Refuge de Solaise hotel.

More on the slopes

For beginners

Although there are beginner slopes next to the village, with free lifts, they are a bit too steep for comfort at the top, and all the emphasis now is on the recently developed and much more extensive beginner area 700m higher on Solaise, with three covered carpet-lifts on gentle slopes. Some parts of these slopes get through-traffic – it's worth avoiding those parts – but Solaise as a whole is now close to being an ideal beginner area. The main flaw is that the longer Madeleine green run is a tad steep at the top, but it's bearable. The blue runs nearby make ideal progression territory. And at the top of the area is the Lounge – an exceptionally civilised picnic room/ coffee bar with panoramic windows and good free loos (a rarity in these parts).

Of course, you have to buy a lift pass – a day pass for all the Solaise lifts. This costs 37€ in 2019 – hardly a bargain.

With a full pass, you could go from the nursery slopes to the long gentle green runs at the top of Bellevarde – Verte and Mont Blanc. The very top of the hill is a bit steep – use the chair-lift route up for the easiest way to the pistes. Be sure you don't descend Verte beyond the Marmottes chair, or you will find yourself on the steepest, narrowest, gnarliest green run in the Alps. The greens from the Borsat chair have a very steep start.

To get home, ride the Marmottes chair and take the funicular or gondola down.

For true blue skiers

A glance at the piste map reveals the first flaw in Val's skiing: there are no blue runs down to Val itself; and no, the reds are not easy. Until 2017 the Santons run from Bellevarde into the Manchet valley and down to the main lift base – a gun-barrel run that's a nightmare at the end of the day – was classified blue, but is now rightly a red. At La Daille there are blue and green runs to the valley, but these are not easy – not even the infamous Verte, which by the end of the day is both crowded and mogulled. The blue to the valley at Le Fornet has a steep pitch near the start, too. The best way to the valley is the lovely Piste L below Solaise to Le Laisinant; but it is not a motorway – ski down to the Datcha chair and take a look at the start; the rest is easier.

But the piste map also shows a great deal of blue (and green) skiing at altitude. Happily, this is all easy skiing; it doesn't much matter where you head. We haven't detected any nasty surprises anywhere on these higher slopes, but the runs from Tovière are a bit tougher than most. Tignes is also easily accessible – go via Col de Fresse for an easy life.

For confident intermediates

Not surprisingly, given what we say above, it's the descents to the valley that offer the most rewards for the competent skier. Ski them early in the day, as far as possible, when they are less crowded and less mogulled than later on. Even Santons and Piste M from Solaise can be very enjoyable in the right conditions.

The classic runs are the Orange and OK Coupe du Monde reds to La Daille – wonderful rolling cruises when groomed, 1000m vertical to the bottom. The reds from Col de l'Iseran and from Solaise to Le Laisinant also offer worthwhile genuine stretches. Don't overlook the excellent Arcelle on the Manchet chair (bearing in mind that it gets the afternoon sun). Or Triffolet, away from the lifts and crowds down to La Daille.

All of which doesn't add up to a huge amount by the standards of Courchevel, say; just as well there is Tignes to explore.

For experts

There are black pistes and Naturide runs dotted around the map, most of them descents to the valley which are genuine blacks but not seriously steep. The famous and excellent Face de Bellevarde, for example, is a great blast when groomed, with only one steep pitch half-way down. Epaule du Charvet, another way down from Bellevarde, is nowhere near as long, but offers a more sustained challenge in its middle section. Rhône-Alpes and Combe Martin from Solaise are little steeper than the red option (and often more pleasant late in the day). At Le Fornet, Forêt is a good, direct, shady woodland run touching black gradient.

The Marmottons Naturide run down the Manchet chair is basically a run of sustained red steepness with a stiffer pitch near the end.

But then there is the off-piste: the mountains were clearly designed to maximise opportunities outside the lift network. There's an unrivalled range of routes, and an unrivalled range of guiding outfits to help you make the most of them.

Back in the day, the piste map had discreet orange arrows indicating the start of the recognised runs. These days only unexplained labels survive to hint at many of them – La Banane and Le Cairn, long runs with great views on Bellevarde, Le Lavancher and Les Danaïdes down through the woods on the north face of Solaise, Les Marmottes down the east face, Le Lièvre Blanc again through woods between Le Laisinant and Le Fornet, Les Grand Vallons from the Signal drag-lifts at Col de l'Iseran, the epic 1200m vertical Col Pers and Pays Desert from the Pissaillas glacier and La Spatule, a long and varied run above La Daille. Among many routes with no hint on the map are the easy, lovely and therefore very popular Tour du Charvet, from the Grand Pré chair; and the Cugnaï bowl from the eponymous chair at the top of the Solaise sector.

Fancy stuff

The snow park is on the slopes of Tovière, above La Daille – 500m long, with lines from beginner to expert, and other features including a mini-pipe. Up on the Grand Pré chair-lift at the back of Bellevarde is a long and quite serious boardercross, and on Solaise is another aimed at beginners. Bear in mind that over the hill in Tignes is a bigger park, and a super-pipe.

Val d'Isère – the resort

These days, Val is a polished, stylish, rounded resort where it is a positive pleasure to arrive. What has long been one of the best ski areas in France now has one of the best villages, too.

Convenience

It's a big resort – about a mile long, and reaching about half a mile up the Manchet valley past the main lift base. There are plenty of lodgings within easy walking distance of the lift base, but more that are not. More to the point, the structure of the skiing is such that you're quite likely to want to start or end your day somewhere other than that main lift base.

The shuttle-bus services, connecting the main lift base with La Daille, Le Fornet and points up the valley of Le Manchet, are pretty reliable, and the main service runs every five minutes during the day.

Lodgings

There are lots of hotels at all levels of the market, including six 5-star places. There are more 3-star than 4-star places, and a few 2-stars. Two central 3-stars would be on our shortlist – the Auberge St Hubert and the Kandahar.

In December 2018, France's oldest cable car station at the top of Solaise re-opens as France's highest hotel, the Refuge de Solaise, offering a big penthouse suite and a traditional refuge dormitory; next season it will open fully with 18 rooms and more suites. It looks lovely on the plans, with a spa and a 23m pool. Access is by gondola or on skis.

Along with Méribel, Val is Planet Chalet, with more catered chalet options than anywhere else. All the big operators are here, of course, plus numbers of mid-sized companies, some running very swanky properties indeed. The original Val specialist firm is YSE; it now offers 19 chalets from small and simple to some of the grandest in town. Le Ski has ten chalets including a couple at La Daille, a group of six units in a little complex off the main street and one chalet up the side valley beyond the lift stations. There are several chalet hotels; YSE has the very central Les Chardons, notable for its wide range of rooms; the Ski Total/Inghams/Esprit group has the unusually swanky Savoie – a regular 5-star hotel until they took it over in 2015.

Bars and restaurants

Val now has more après-ski options than we can cope with, so for guidance we've turned to Fiona Easdale, of Val specialist operator YSE. Her response follows.

Over the years, Val has applied wood and stone to transform itself into a welcoming, traditional-style resort

Famously, the après-ski kicks off at the original Folie Douce, above La Daille. Down in Val, Cocorico at the bottom of Solaise is a similarly loud, wild rival, with less ostentation. Bananas is also great fun. The young and fit also tend to stand in the Baraque or outside the Coin des Amis, whereas grown-ups head for the comfortable hotel bars (eg Blizzard, Tsanteleina and Savoyarde). The Rosée Blanche (aka Rosie's) in La Daille is a perennial favourite.

For dinner, the pricey starred L'Atelier d'Edmond is the best in town (or out of town – up at Le Fornet). Other good restaurants are Table de l'Ours (in the hotel Barmes de l'Ours), L'Etincelle, the Blizzard, the Table des Neiges in the Tsanteleina and the Taverne d'Alsace. Good-value places include Le Barillon, Le Lodge, Le 1789 and La Casserole.

After dinner, the options are wider than ever. Dick's Bar, a lone pioneer in the early 80s, still survives but now has competition from the Doudoune, Le Petit Danois, Fall Line, XV, Blue Note and Pacific to name a few.

Off the slopes

The Aquasportif centre near the Bellevarde lifts is an excellent facility, with lane and leisure pools (including river etc), spa, gym, climbing wall, squash courts and a multi-purpose sports hall. The lift pass gets you one free entry. Closer to the centre is an outdoor artificial ice rink, open afternoon and evening.

There's an 800m ice-driving circuit equipped with BMWs (plus a smaller karting circuit). Other activities include snowmobiling, dog sledding and snowshoe outings.

For families

Stay near the snow and it makes a good family resort, thanks not least to the facilities listed above. Up on Solaise you'll find the Sunny Ride funslope and ValKids – a funslope, playground, sledging area and boardercross. Le Lounge up there is handy for picnic lunches. There's also a sledging area on the village nursery slope. In a natural gully off the upper Verte run on Bellevarde is the P'tit Cross course, including mini-jumps.

Alternatives to central Val d'Isère

These satellites of Val, a mile or so from the resort centre, aren't marketed as separate resorts, but they do offer distinct options.

Le Fornet 1940m

Le Fornet is an unspoilt old village at the foot of the Col de l'Iseran sector. It extremely quiet in the evenings. As noted above, it benefits from a seriously good restaurant, L'Atelier d'Edmond. A very interesting development in 2018 is the opening this winter of the new hotel du Fornet – a 12-room hotel housed an old building 200m from the lift base, with a spa, and set dinners available.

La Daille 1800m

La Daille is well placed for exploration of the shared Val-Tignes area. It is dominated by monstrous apartment blocks, but does not lack life. Read 'Pick of the apartments' for a recommendation. The hotel la Tovière is re-opening for 2018-19 after a complete makeover lifting it into the 4-star category alongside the Samovar, renovated a while back. There are catered chalets, too.

Tignes

Tignes-le-Lac / Val Claret and various other forms of Tignes

Once upon a time, high and bleak Tignes attracted skiers wanting little other than skiing on good snow. These days, it's quite a rounded resort, with good off-slope amenities and a good range of comfortable lodgings. Still, given the choice, we would always opt to stay in lower, comparatively captivating Val d'Isère.

But of course we can see and understand the contrary view. The high villages of Tignes, at least, are more conveniently arranged for skiing than Val is, and have large areas of good intermediate skiing immediately on hand; and the Grande Motte glacier is only one lift ride from Val Claret. Your call.

The mountains in brief

Size The shared area is big enough for anyone, though not the biggest
Slopes Essentially treeless, with lots of easy terrain and some not so easy
Snow About as good as it gets, with the bonus of a serious glacier
System, Lift Powerful village lifts, but too many slow ones higher up
Sustenance Not a lot of choice, but two places we like a lot
For beginners A good set-up at Le Lac and Tignes 1800, in particular
For true blue skiers A great resort, and yes, you can get to Val d'Isère
For the confident The local slopes are a big limited, but then there's Val ...
For experts A huge range of possibilities off-piste, from the high lifts
Fancy stuff A serious park, and a very serious half-pipe

Tignes-le-Lac – the resort in brief

Convenience Expect to do a bit of plodding, but not a lot
Lodgings Chalets, hotels, apartments: the choice is yours
Bars and restaurants Plenty to choose from
Off the slopes Lots to do; sadly, we accept the plastic rink makes sense
For families A good choice – easy access to snow, lots to do

Pass notes
There are local passes for a day or half-day, but they cost more per day than a six-day pass for the whole shared area.
There are free lifts for absolute beginners, but no special deals beyond that.

Key facts

Altitude	1550–2100m
Range	1550–3456m
Slopes (see text)	300km

Where to stay, ideally
Close to the Tovière lift base – except freestylers, who should definitely stay in Val Claret, close to the Tichot chair-lift.

Websites
tignes.net

Key ratings

Size	****
Snow	*****
Fast lifts	***
Mountain rest's	***
Beginner	***
True blue	*****
Confident	****
Expert	*****
Convenience	****
Families	****
Village charm	*

The mountains in detail

The mother village of Tignes-le-Lac and its offspring Val Claret are set in a valley that curves around the peak of La Tovière, where lifts from both villages converge to meet the key linking lift from Val d'Isère. Across the valley, on the outside of the curve, is a huge expanse of east-facing skiing, accessible, again, from both villages.

Above Tignes-le-Lac, these slopes spread into the main Isère valley above the big Lac du Chevril and down to two lower outposts sharing a chain of lifts back up to Le Lac – Tignes 1800 (previously known as Les Boisses), right next to the dam that contains the lake, and Tignes-les-Brévières. From Val Claret, at the head of the valley, an underground funicular accesses the Grande Motte, and one of the great skiing glaciers of France. A run from the glacier and a lift from Val Claret access another lift linking with Val d'Isère via the lower Col de Fresse.

Size

The shared area claims '10,000 hectares and 300km of slopes'. The Schrahe report puts it at about 240km, which places the area at the very top of our 4-star category, although well behind the three areas in the exclusive 5-star group (3V, Portes du Soleil and Paradiski). The area is 15km across as the eagle flies, from Les Brévières to the Pissaillas glacier.

Slopes

The slopes are treeless, so it's good that the resort now has quite a broad range of indoor off-slope activities. Tovière, putting Le Lac in the shade for much of the morning in midwinter, is steep; the Grande Motte sector is less so; and the broad, rolling mountainside on the west side of the valley is classic intermediate terrain, blue in places and red in others.

Val Claret and high above it the glacial Grande Motte, seen from the distinctive Aiguille Percée

In general, it's not an area for particularly big verticals: the top heights are mostly about 600m above the villages, and the red and black runs are mostly above mid-mountain. But there are some major exceptions: 1300m vertical from the top of the glacier (900m from the top of the access lift) and 1200m from the Aiguille Percée to Les Brévières. Much the longest run is from the glacier down the Génépy blue piste, past Col de Fresse to Val Claret – about 10km.

Ten black pistes – that's most of them – are left ungroomed and branded Naturide. We're not fans of this approach when applied on this scale; once they are mogulled, these runs don't get much use.

Snow

The slopes immediately surrounding Tignes don't go super-high – to 2700–2800m, rather like La Saulire between Courchevel and Méribel. But the Grande Motte sector is different – the main lift station is above 3000m, and the cable car above that goes almost to 3500m. Add in the fact that the main resort villages are at about 2100m, and you can see that altitude is one of the attractions of the place. Tignes and Val d'Isère also benefit from a geographical position that delivers snow from Mediterranean storms as well as Atlantic storms. The slope orientations range from dead south to dead north, with the main area facing generally east, which is not at all bad. The runs on Tovière and Col de Fresse suffer from the afternoon sun. But all in all, for a seriously large ski area, the snow here is about as good as it gets.

System, Lift

The Tignes lift system has been playing catch-up for many years, and still has some way to go before people like us will stop whingeing. Most of the key lifts are now fast, but irritating slow ones that remain include Col des Ves (almost 2km long), Grand Huit, Chardonnet and Aiguille Percée on the main east-facing area and Aiguille Rouge and Marais (2.3km long – a 20-minute ride) above Tignes 1800. As we write in 2018, the chair-lift from Les Brévières to Tignes 1800 is being replaced by a gondola (with a different arrival point).

Queues are not generally a problem unless poor snow on the lower slopes drives people towards the Grande Motte. Whatever the conditions, the cable car at the top of the Grande Motte almost always has a serious queue. It has now been revamped, with cabins that have an open viewing platform on top – part of a bigger project to develop summer tourism here (and to make winter queues worse).

Crowding on the pistes into Val Claret can be more of a problem – the shady Double M red from the glacier and the blue Henri from Tovière, the main way home from Val d'Isère.

Sustenance

With such easy access to the villages from the slopes, it's no surprise that the mountain restaurants are not a highlight. We've even been known to eat in Le Lac ourselves, at the hotel Montana, piste-side in Les Almes. But there are some good places higher up. Lo Soli, at the top of the Chaudannes chair, is our clear favourite, combining a relaxed, spacious setting with excellent food and friendly service – the terrace has a great view, too. We've also had good meals at the sheepskin-themed Panoramic, at the top of the funicular, run by local celebrity chef Jean-Michel Bouvier; it gets a toque from the Gault-Millau gastro guide. Neither is cheap, sadly.

More on the slopes

For beginners

The Lavachet slope between Le Rosset and Le Lavachet is admirably gentle and is served by a detachable chair-lift – that is, one that virtually stops to let you on and off. The Rosset slope in front of Le Rosset is classified blue, but really it could be green. The lifts on these slopes and the Almes chair serving a longer, looping green run on the main east-facing slopes are all free, as are the Claret carpet-lift and Bollin chair at Val Claret. This whole set-up is exemplary. As for progression – read on ...

For true blue skiers

Several blue runs on the lower slopes are identified as progression zones – mostly above Le Lac, but also at Val Claret and at Tignes 1800. This is a fine idea in principle – it would be even finer if accompanied by a half-price lift pass, as in many other

LE DÔME DE PRAMECOU
COL DES VES
AIGUILLE NOIRE DE PRAMECOU
COL DU PALET
AIGUILLE DU CHARDONNET
DE LA LEISSE
COL DE FRESSE
COL DE LA SACHETTE
AIGUILLE PERCÉE
2748
VALLON DE LA SACHETTE
VALLON DE LA SACHE
TOVIÈRE
2704
LOGNAN
Stade Olympique 1992
snowpark
VAL CLARET
Lac
TIGNES LE LAC
TIGNES 2100
GLATTIER
LE LAVACHET
PAS DE LA TOVIÈRE
VALLÉE PERDUE
BALISE RADIO
LAC DU CHEVRIL
LES BOISSES
TIGNES 1800
LE CHEVRIL
LE FRANCHET
LA RECULAZ
LE VILLARET DU NIAL
TIGNES 1550 LES BRÉVIÈRES
GRANDE MOTTE
CHAMPAGNY
TEMIGNON
PANO
ROSOLIN
VANOISE
LEISSE
LES LANCHES
FUNICULAIRE PERCE NEIGE
FRESSE
BOLLIN
CLARET
TUFS
TICHOT
COL DU PALET
GRATTALU
MERLES
GRAND HUIT
AIGUILLE PERCÉE
CHARDONNET
PALAFOUR
PALMES
CHAUDANNES
ROSSET
LAVACHET
PAQUIS
TOVIÈRE
COMBE FOLLE
TOMMEUSES
MONT BLANC
SLALOM
SEMANMILLE
AIGUILLE ROUGE
MARAIS
BOISSES
BRÉVIÈRES

resorts; but the runs are not entirely easy. At Le Lac, Kadjar and Combe have a stiffer pitch halfway down, as does Carline at Val Claret. These stiffer pitches are not seriously steep, and shouldn't cause problems once your confidence is established. But if you're feeling fragile, start on Almes and Petit Col above Lac.

The main east-facing slopes offer a lot of genuine blue skiing higher up – some of it easier than the 'progression zone' runs, and it all connects nicely. Note that there is no blue piste down the top part of the Aiguille Percée chair-lift – a pity, but you can steer round it. From that same lift, Corniche down the Marias lift is a fine run, as is Lac in the middle of the area.

The Henri piste from Tovière is not the easiest of blues, but enjoyable in good conditions – most likely in the middle of the day; it can be miserable at the end of the day, though, when it gets crowded and mogulled (and even icy). If in doubt, return from Val d'Isère via Col de Fresse and the Prariond blue. This is joined by the lovely Génépy from the glacier, which ought to be on your agenda. It has a slightly steeper section shortly after the start, but nothing serious. You might also take a look at the glacier itself: start with the easy red down the Champagny chair.

For confident intermediates

The Tignes area isn't great for the intermediate who wants to stick to groomed red pistes. There is some good terrain – generally the red runs are genuine, at least in part – but there's not very much of it, and it is scattered around.

Ancolie, Cyclamen and Myosotis are all worth getting to. In principle, the long, shady run to Val Claret from the glacier is a highlight – a classic red at the top, easing on the bottom half, with two powerful lift options. Sadly, the two lifts deliver more people than the run can handle, particularly late in the day – so ski it early, and go home another way (eg on the lovely blue). All the glacier runs are worth a look – the blacks are not steep.

Don't miss Combe Folle, on Tovière – with luck you'll enjoy a delightful cruise on good snow with few people, and the drag is faster than the chairs elsewhere.

If the snow conditions are good and you're a strong skier, don't shy away from the shady, secluded Sache black run to Les Brévières, which would probably be red were it not so splendidly isolated. Peel off on the red Arcosses if you want to avoid the slightly tricky bit at the end. Pramecou is another black to put high on your agenda – back in the day, the red

Tignes-le-Lac, centre, with Le Lavachet left, Les Almes front right; in the distance, Val Claret again

Ves run followed much the same route, and apart from one very short pitch in the middle it could almost be blue. But also read the following section.

For experts

As we've explained, practically all the black pistes are never groomed, so it's common for them to get heavily mogulled and then ignored for quite long periods. Many are short and quite sharp, and those that are not short are sharp only in short pitches. The runs from Tovière offer the most sustained challenge.

But of course it's the famous off-piste that draws experts here. Space permits us to do no more than scratch the surface of what's available in this department.

The broad east-facing mountainside between the lifts of Val Claret and Le Lac known as Lognan (helpfully labelled on the piste map) has numerous easy ways down. From the nearby Grattalu chair, a short walk under the Pointe du Chardonnet brings you to the famously shady and sheltered eponymous couloirs, for short and sweet descents to the lake below. The Col du Palet chair brings you to the start of the classic, beautiful and easy route towards Champagny, on the back of La Plagne (taxi required); ideally, you'll leave time to ski the Paradiski pistes to Villaroger, for a second taxi home.

From the Grande Motte glacier there are countless possibilities to skier's left of the piste to the valley; well-known routes are Petite Balme and Tour de Pramecou (aka Tour de la Grande Balme).

Heading south from Tovière there are multiple ways down beside the Envers de Campanules Naturide run. Heading west you have the tricky couloirs des Tufs down to Val Claret. Heading north there are very steep descents to Le Lac, or you can hike on to the peak of Le Lavachet, for the descents known as Mickey's Ears, to Le Lac, or the Lac du Chevril, or La Daille in the Val d'Isère area.

Finally, there are various routes from Aiguille Percée, or thereabouts. Among them are off-piste ways down the Vallon de la Sache, parallel to the Sache piste, and easy descents to Le Lac.

And then there's Val d'Isère next door.

Fancy stuff

Tignes takes freestyle very seriously. There's a big snow park running the length of the Col du Palet drag-lift and the Grattalu chair above Val Claret, split into four levels of difficulty; a boardercross runs down beside it. Down at Val Claret is the famous XXL super-pipe, unmatched in France – 190m long with 7m walls. Given the energy, you can just walk up and ride it for free.

Tignes-le-Lac – the resort

Le Lac is a resort of parts, separated by pistes, lifts and the access road. Central Le Rosset, at least, has something of the feel of a village, having acquired a welcome veneer of traditional style in the last decade or two. Le Lac also has the lion's share of the resort's off-slope diversions.

Convenience

Le Lac, more than most resorts, has identifiable parts. The core is Le Rosset, built on a low hill next to the nursery slope and the gondola for Tovière. Across a snowy plaza (with the valley road buried beneath it) is monstrous Bec Rouge, no doubt by now a historic monument. Over that low hill beyond another nursery slope is the slightly less hideous apartment development of Le Lavachet. And across the access road is the jumble of chalet-style lodgings called Les Almes. Each of these parts is quite compact and easy to get around – Le Rosset is no more than 400m across. In each part there are lodgings on the snow, but also plenty involving a short walk to reach it. Shuttle-buses run around Le Rosset and Le Lavachet, and past Le Bec Rouge and Val Claret to the Grande Motte lift base.

Lodgings

This is the main village in Tignes for catered chalets, with several major operators represented. It also has the widest choice of hotels – a few 3-stars, fewer 4-stars and the 5-star Suites du Montana in Les Almes. The 3-star Arbina is in an ideal location, with a popular bar and restaurant, and we've stayed happily in the Gentiana. The newish 4-star Taos is a cool spot.

Bars and restaurants

Our friends at Skiworld know the evening scene in Tignes back to front, so we took their advice in compiling this and the Val Claret section.

We didn't need any help in identifying the key place in the late afternoon – the infamously lively Folie Douce, over the hill above La Daille. Be warned: the vital Tommeuse chair-lift to get back to Tignes closes before the music stops.

There are plenty of places in the village for a restorative beer, some with live bands to enjoy. Loop Bar on the main drag is one such place. Cave du Loop beneath it is a cooler wine/cocktail bar opened in 2018. In Lavachet, Queue de Cochon is a great gin bar, often with live bands; it also does delicious French/English fusion food, reasonably priced. We like the bar of the hotel Arbina, and among the best places for a serious dinner is its upstairs restaurant (superb seafood); also consider La Ferme des 3 Capucines in Lavachet (but it gets booked out). The late-night scene can vary, with the best parties happening on alternate nights. You'll find some of the best live bands at Underground.

Editor's note: the cool new Kaya restaurant is on our agenda.

Off the slopes

The Palafour chair-lift accesses a 'very sporty' 3km toboggan run, open most days 5pm to 7.30pm. The Bun J ride ingeniously combines a ski jump, a bungee jump and a zipline; consultant editor Watts can't wait! Tignespace is an impressive sports centre with various courts including squash and tennis, a climbing wall, fitness and weights rooms. There's now an indoor synthetic skating rink. Nearby is the Lagon aquatic centre, with a 25m main pool, a fun pool with a slide etc, a paddling pool, hot tubs and spa facilities. Entry to both the skating rink and Lagon is free with the lift pass. Other activities include snowmobiling and dog sledding.

For families

Le Lac makes a good family resort, with easy access to snow. There are kids' sledging areas near the Tovière lift base and at Le Lavachet. Gliss'Park is a kids' snow park at the bottom of the Palafour chair, with mini boxes and a boardercross.

The other parts of Tignes

Val Claret has the advantage of two blue home runs from Val d'Isère (Le Lac has only a black), and instant access to the Grande Motte. The two lower villages enjoy a less moon-like setting below the tree-line, but are a long way from Tovière and the skiing of Val d'Isère. The two are linked by a free gondola, and shuttle buses run from Tignes 1800 to Le Lac.

Val Claret 2215m

Val Claret is a big village consisting almost entirely of apartments, built in a more palatable form than Le Lavachet or (particularly) Le Lac's Bec Rouge quartier. It's built on a hill, and, depending on your location, you may find yourself making much use of elevators to get around.

Read the 'Pick of the Apartments' panel for pointers to apartments. The village now has good hotel options too – the 5-star Les Suites and the 4-star Ski d'Or and Ecrin du Val Claret.

The fire pit outside Grizzly's draws people as the lifts close; cosy interior, too, with bears. The classic bars (with happy hours) are Saloon and the slightly smoother Couloir, also a good restaurant with a varied menu. Pépé 2000 is a traditional mid-range restaurant. For late-night dancing it's Blue Girl or Melting Pot.

There's an impressive tubing hill with three different courses and a big-air bag – all served by a carpet-lift.

Tignes 1800 1800m

Previously known as Tignes-les-Boisses (and with a part still labelled Les Boisses), Tignes 1800 is now dominated by smart apartment residences built in the last few years (read the 'Pick of the Apartments' panel). It also has a couple of simple small hotels. There are small nursery slopes with free carpet-lifts, and an easy blue run to Les Brévières.

Tignes-les-Brévières 1500m

The low point of the Tignes skiing, and a popular lunch destination, Les Brévières offers lodgings mainly in individual self-catering chalets and simple apartment buildings. There's ice driving, in some very powerful machines. There's a short free drag-lift for beginners.

Valmorel

Valmorel / St-François-Longchamp / Celliers / Doucy

When Valmorel was created, in the mid-1970s, it was revolutionary, and it remains very unusual – a purpose-built, car-free and conveniently laid out resort built in a highly traditional style. What's not to like?

Well, the mountain is a bit underwhelming, the altitudes are modest by local standards (high-points roughly in the 2000–2400m range) and the lift system needs investment. For years, we feared that the resort was slipping into terminal decline; but then, in 2012, Club Med opened a smart new 'village' here, and a couple of years later CGH opened an upscale apartment residence. We dared to hope for an upturn. It may be happening, slowly: one new six-pack is due in 2018, and another in 2020.

The mountains in brief

Size Not in the same league as neighbouring areas in the Tarentaise
Slopes Wooded and gentle low down, open and steeper higher up
Snow Altitudes are low by local standards, and Longchamp is sunny
System, Lift Improving, but very slowly; still lots of slow lifts
Sustenance Not a highlight, but you won't starve
For beginners Good arrangements, apart from a lack of long green runs
For true blue skiers Good skiing; but links with Longchamp not very easy
For the confident Good genuine red runs, but not many of them
For experts Off-piste within the lift network is good
Fancy stuff Serious and kids' parks, and multiple boardercross courses

Valmorel – the resort in brief

Convenience Few places are better for ski-in lodgings
Lodgings Apartments, plus the odd hotel and an impressive Club Med
Bars and restaurants Not a highlight, but you'll find something to suit
Off the slopes Not an impressive range of activities
For families In many respects, as good as it gets

Pass notes
Beginners need a day-pass (rather more than half-price) covering the beginner lifts at village level and at mid-mountain, plus the gondola to get there.

Key facts

Altitude	1400m
Range	1250–2514m
Slopes (see text)	165km

Where to stay, ideally
In Valmorel, with access to a piste down to one of the two main lifts.

Websites
valmorel.com
saintfrancoislongchamp.com

Key ratings

Size	***
Snow	**
Fast lifts	**
Mountain rest's	**
Beginner	***
True blue	****
Confident	****
Expert	***
Convenience	*****
Families	****
Village charm	****

The mountains in detail

The optimistically named Grand Domaine is a quite complex affair. Its two resorts are separated by the Celliers valley, at the head of which is the Col de la Madeleine, a pass used by the Tour de France but closed in winter.

Lifts from Valmorel go up to the ridge above, whence runs go into the Celliers valley and down the long ridge to Doucy, the area low-point at 1250m. There is also a lift up to this ridge from Celliers, but no return piste.

Back in Valmorel, to spectator's left a gondola goes up to the key mid-mountain area of Pierrafort, and above it a chair goes on to Col du Mottet. Further left again is an isolated drag-lift to Col du Gollet.

Beyond the intervening Celliers valley, the slopes of St-François-Longchamp are spread across a broad, gentle bowl above Longchamp 1650. An isolated chair-lift goes to the shoulder of La Lauzière, the area high-point at 2514m (a good 300m lower than the piste map implies).

Size

Le Grand Domaine claims 165km of pistes, but the Schrahe report puts it at a more modest 140km – not a huge discrepancy. There is some sensation of travel available – Doucy is an impressive 13km from St-François. Keen, competent skiers should note that these quite decent figures (putting the area in our 3-star category) reflect a lot of green and easy blue skiing, especially at Longchamp, which may not amuse you much.

Slopes

Given the modest altitudes, it's no surprise that there is a healthy amount of woodland skiing, particularly in the Valmorel half of the area (Longchamp is a good 250m higher than Valmorel). It's a good resort for a bad day. The terrain offers a good mix of gradients, but easy slopes dominate.

The fact that the altitudes are modest doesn't mean the runs are necessarily short. From the Col du Mottet to the

The village is lower than most resorts in this region (1400m) and has quite a bit of woodland skiing above it

village is 1000m vertical, and from the area high-point of La Lauzière you have descents of over 850m vertical on both sides of the Col de la Madeleine. But verticals of 500–600m are more typical.

Three black pistes and one red are designated as Free Ride runs, which we presume means they are never groomed.

Snow

The altitudes here are on the low side for a French area. At least the Valmorel bowl is essentially north-facing, but the runs into the Celliers valley get the afternoon sun, as do the slopes of St-François-Longchamp. It's not a great picture.

System, Lift

The system is not impressive. Most of the main access lifts and links are fast. But there are exceptions, and over the area as a whole there are still lots of slow chairs and drags. Things are now improving, but it's a slow business. As we write, in 2018, the old double Mottet chair-lift accessing the most challenging slopes is being replaced by a six-seater, and another six-pack is planned to replace the Biollène slow quad and the two parallel Arenouillaz drag-lifts in 2020.

Sustenance

There are relatively few mountain restaurants. The Prariond on the lower slopes of the Pierrafort sector served us efficiently while lounging on its terrace sofas last time we visited.

More on the slopes

For beginners

There are two main nursery areas, each with a carpet lift and a drag-lift: near the base of the Pierrafort gondola, and up the gondola at mid-mountain. Then there is a third area down the access road, between the hamlet of Le Crey and the chalet-suburb of La Charmette. A cheap day-pass covers the lifts.

These are all good arrangements, but it's a disappointment that there are no longer green runs to progress to. There are easy blues, though – read on.

For true blue skiers

The main lifts out of Valmorel access terrain that is almost entirely blue in steepness, and yes, blue-run skiers can (and should) get over to the wide, gentle slopes above Longchamp, but not before you have built up a bit of confidence for the linking runs.

The place to head for confidence-building is the lovely, gentle bowl served by the Biollène chair and Arenouillaz drags (all to be replaced by a fast chair-lift in 2020). For the easiest way home from here, take Retour Valmorel followed by Traverses. Of the options on skier's right (for Club Med etc), Froide is easier than Combe du Morel. The runs from Pierrafort are good middling blues; Oratoire is a bit steeper in places than Lanches.

The countless sunny blues over at Longchamp are gloriously gentle. As we've suggested, the linking runs into the Celliers valley are not the easiest of blues. Outbound, bear in mind that the runs get the afternoon sun, so can be rock-hard in the early morning; Mucillon is particularly sunny, but less steep than Valette. The return pistes also have short tough bits; probably the easiest route, just, is Retour du Col then the lower part of Madeleine.

For confident intermediates

There are some good, rewarding runs for competent skiers, but you may well judge that there aren't many of them.

All the reds dotted around the Valmorel sector are worthwhile. The most satisfying, combining gradient and length, are Planco on the Madeleine lift and the runs down the Mottet chair. The Gollet slope is about the steepest.

Longchamp is certainly worth visiting, although the red runs tend to be blue with just a short red stretch somewhere. But the testing runs on the isolated Lauzière chair-lift are in a different league; bear in mind that the steep Reverdy, in particular, is affected by the afternoon sun.

For experts

All the black pistes (practically of which are ungroomed Free Ride runs) merit the classification with the curious exception of the short Riondet. Combe du Riondet

from the same point is a shady long run away from the lifts but is steep only for a short central stretch. The Mottet, Gollet and Procureuse runs offer more sustained challenges, though nothing extreme. The blacks at Longchamp are just about genuine; Lauzière is the most rewarding.

There is lots of off-piste within the ski area from the high lifts, notably from the Riondet and Côte 2305 drag-lifts and the Lauzière chair into the Celliers valley. The resort is not known for off-piste, so the snow lasts well.

The classic route outside the ski area is from the Col du Gollet down the Orgentil valley to Deux Nant then, after a substantial climb, down to La Flachère in the Belleville valley below St-Martin.

Fancy stuff

The main snow park is at Pierrafort, with lines classified as difficult and very difficult. The kids' Pirates adventure zone is across the mountain on the Combe de Beaudin run. There are boardercross courses in roughly the same spots.

Valmorel – the resort

The original mountain-town simulation at the foot of the main lift, Le Bourg, remains a pleasant and relaxed place for après-ski and shopping, but has declined in importance as lodgings have spread widely up and across the Valmorel bowl. These are mainly in traditional Alpine chalet style.

Convenience

The resort's low-rise apartment buildings are split into half a dozen *quartiers*. On skier's left of the home slope approaching Le Bourg are La Forêt and Fontaine (at the foot of the Lanchettes chair); on skier's right are Le Mottet and Planchamp – the Telebourg gondola links these to Le Bourg. Just across the hill is the base of the second main lift, the Pierrafort gondola, at one end of a broad development called Creve-Coeur. Then, up the hill some way is the Club Med development at Le Bois de la Croix. Practically all the lodgings are ski-in, or nearly so, but there may be a bit of plod-out, depending on location.

The centre of Valmorel looks better than most modern resorts – but don't bank on snow in the street

Lodgings

There are two 3-star hotels: the Bourg is a simple, central B&B place while the Oxygène is down the access road at La Charmette. There is also an upscale Club Med 'village' on the slopes well outside the centre. But practically all the lodgings are in apartments. In addition to the apartment residences picked out below, MGM is now opening a swanky residence close to the village centre, the Anitéa.

Peak Retreats Pick of the apartments

In Valmorel
Directors' Choice The location of La Grange aux Fées is pretty spot on – it's in a quiet sunny position, with ski-in/ski-out convenience, adjacent to the Lanchettes chair-lift. The resort centre is a 10-minute walk away. There is a pool, plus a smaller baby pool, hot tub, sauna and steam room, as well as a spa.
In St-François-Longchamp
We like the 3-star ski-in/ski-out 4 Vallées residence (at 1650m). It's just 150m from the Mollaret chair-lift and has a pool.
www.peakretreats.co.uk 023 9283 9310

Bars and restaurants

Le Bourg is the natural place to end the day, and there are several bars at the foot of the pistes. There are quite a few eateries, too, of which the rustic Petit Prince is about the best.

Off the slopes

You can descend the piste from Pierrafort to the village on an inflatable sledge/ body board. The spa and pool at the CGH Grange aux Fées residence may be open to the public.

For families

There is a new Pirates adventure zone, with a boardercross course and various terrain features. Next to the village is a sledging area, floodlit in the early evening. The resort's childcare facilities are famous, but they are French.

Alternatives to Valmorel

St-François-Longchamp is accessed from the south, via the Maurienne valley. The hamlet of St-François makes little sense as a base; higher Longchamp is much more convenient for skiing, and a wider choice of lodgings. Doucy is out on a long limb of the lift network. Celliers offers a way of getting access to skiing without staying in a ski resort.

Longchamp 1650m

Sunny Longchamp is a modern village with the attraction for beginners and nervous novices of acres of easy skiing right above the resort. There are two 3-star hotels: the Lac Bleu is in a good central position; the Pérelle is at the top of the village, on the Route du Tour green run. For self-catering, read 'Pick of the Apartments' under Valmorel. There's a 900m sled-on-rails coaster, La Comète, and snake-sledging is organised. The spa centre has a good leisure pool and various other amenities, including fitness – and an attached bowling alley.

Celliers 1300m

Celliers is an unspoilt mountain village with a gondola up to the ridge above Valmorel, but no run back down. The Grand-Pic is a simple hotel in the centre.

Doucy 1250m

Doucy is an apartment development of surprising size, given its inconvenient location at the end of a long ridge separating Valmorel from the Celliers valley. To connect with the Valmorel skiing you ride a 2km fast chair then two drags totalling a further 2km – a great start to your day.

Published in the UK by
Guide Editors

Editor **Chris Gill**
Consultant editor **Dave Watts**
Editorial assistant **Mandy Crook**
Design and production **Graham Wells**
Ad manager **Dave Ashmore**

Printed in the UK
by Pureprint Group Limited

ISBN-13: 978-1-9997708-2-2

A CIP catalogue entry for this book is available from the British Library.

Enquiries and feedback to:
publisher@wheretoski.uk

Trade orders to:
Central Books Ltd
50 Freshwater Road, Chadwell Heath,
London RM8 1RX
020 8326 5696
contactus@centralbooks.com

This first edition published 2018

Map credits

3 Vallées
Overview – l'Association les 3 Vallées
Courchevel – OT Courchevel
Méribel – OT Méribel
Menuires – OT Les Menuires
Val Thorens – OT Val Thorens
Alpe-dHuez – SATA Alpe-d'Huez
Annecy Mountains – Syndicat Intercommunal du Massif des Aravis
Chamonix valley – Compagnie du Mont Blanc
Les Deux-Alpes – Deux Alpes Loisirs
Espace Diamant – Val d'Arly Labellemontagne
Espace San Bernardo – SAS DSR Domaine Skiable de La Rosière
Grand Massif – Grand Massif Domaine Skiable
La Grave – OT La Grave-la Meije
Megève – Megève Domaine Skiable
Les Contamines – SECMH Les Contamines
Montgenèvre – Régie autonome des remontées mécaniques de Montgenèvre
Paradiski
Les Arcs – ADS
La Plagne – SAP
Portes du Soleil
Overview – Association Internationale des Portes du Soleil
East – SAEM Sports et Tourisme Châtel; OT Avoriaz 1800
West – SAGETS
Serre-Chevalier – OpenSnowMap
Ste-Foy-Tarentaise – Sainte-Foy Loisirs Developpement
Val Cenis – OpenSnowMap
Val d'Isère-Tignes
Val d'Isère – Val d'Isère Tourisme
Tignes – Tignes Developpement
Valmorel – Domaine Skiable de Valmorel

Photo credits

The copyright in photos listed here belongs to the photographers or entities credited below. Other photos are the copyright of Chris Gill.

page	chapter	
6	About this book	C Cattin / OT Val Thorens
9	Introduction	Megève Tourisme / JP Noisillier
32	Shortlists	Val d'Isère Tourisme
40	3 Vallées	Courchevel Tourisme / David André
42	3 Vallées	Courchevel Tourisme / David André
47	3 Vallées	Méribel Tourisme / Sylvain Aymoz
50	3 Vallées	Méribel Tourisme / Sylvain Aymoz
52	3 Vallées	Méribel Tourisme / Sylvain Aymoz
56	3 Vallées	Les Menuires Tourisme / P Lebeau
58	3 Vallées	Les Menuires Tourisme / G Lansard
65	3 Vallées	C Cattin / OT Val Thorens
68	3 Vallées	C Cattin / OT Val Thorens
74	Alpe d'Huez	Laurent Salino / Alpe d'Huez Tourisme
76	Alpe d'Huez	Laurent Salino / Alpe d'Huez Tourisme
84	Annecy Mountains	Pascal Lebeau
90	Chamonix Valley	OT Vallée de Chamonix
95	Chamonix Valley	Salome Abrial / OT Vallée de Chamonix
100	Les Deux-Alpes	B Longo / OT Les Deux-Alpes
114	Espace San Bernardo	OT La Rosière
116	Espace San Bernardo	Julien Eustache / OT La Rosière
122	Grand Massif	OT Les Carroz
129	La Grave	OT La Meije
138	Megève	Megève Tourisme / Simon Garnier
153	Paradiski	KAB / OT Les Arcs
156	Paradiski	C Stramba-Badiali / OT Les Arcs
161	Paradiski	Elina Sirparanta / La Plagne Tourisme
164	Paradiski	P Augier / La Plagne Tourisme
173	Portes du Soleil	JF Vuarand / Avoriaz Tourisme
176	Portes du Soleil	JF Vuarand / Avoriaz Tourisme
178	Portes du Soleil	Thibaut Loubère / Avoriaz Tourisme
180	Portes du Soleil	N Joly / OT Les Gets
184	Portes du Soleil	OT Morzine / Jarry Tripelon
194	Serre-Chevalier	Zoom
200	Ste-Foy	Philippe Royer / OT Ste-Foy
204	Val Cenis	Haute Maurienne Vanoise / Andres
206	Val Cenis	Haute Maurienne Vanoise / Andres
211	Val d'Isère	OT Val d'Isère
216	Val d'Isère	OT Val d'Isère
219	Tignes	Andy Parant / OT Tignes
222	Tignes	Andy Parant / OT Tignes
227	Valmorel	Scalpfoto / OT Valmorel
230	Valmorel	Scalpfoto / OT Valmorel

Resort index / directory

This is both an index to the 100 or so resorts covered in the body of the book and a quick guide to about 50 other resorts you just might come across. Page references are to the start of the relevant chapter; minor resorts are generally covered towards the end of the chapter.

Albiez – Maurienne valley – 130
Backwater village a few miles south of St-Jean, with a very small ski area.

Les Allues – 3 Vallées – 46
Rustic village below Méribel, with a station on the gondola up from Brides-les-Bains.

Alpe-d'Huez – 71

Alpe-du-Grand-Serre
Small resort close to Grenoble, off the road to Alpe-d'Huez and Les Deux-Alpes. 800m vertical, split between a broad open bowl above the treeline and a worthwhile sheltered sector below it. Mainly blue and red slopes served by drag-lifts.

Les Angles
A small but charming stone village in the Pyrenees (near Font Romeu), complete with an old church. The slopes are limited but relatively snow-sure and family-friendly, with good beginner terrain, both at village level (1650m) and up at 1800m. There are good cross-country trails and walks, but otherwise off-slope diversions are few.

Les Arcs – Paradiski – 152

Ardent – Portes du Soleil – 172
A small, quiet, family-friendly village at the foot of the gondola in the Lindarets valley between Châtel and Avoriaz.

Arêches-Beaufort
Secluded village south of Beaufort and the Espace Diamant, with mostly intermediate terrain on two areas 3km apart, with a red piste link one way and a blue piste link the other. A chain of lifts rises from Arêches at 1080m to Col de la Forclaz at 2320m, with intermediate pistes on open slopes at the top and a lone black through the forest to the village. Above Le Planay at 1200m is a more compact, mixed area of red and blue runs below Col des Combettes at 2130m, mostly below the treeline. We're sceptical of the claim of 50km of pistes.

Argentière – Chamonix Valley – 87
Unremarkable old village beneath a remarkable mountain – Les Grands Montets.

Auris-en-Oisans – Alpe-d'Huez – 71
A series of wood-clad, chalet-style apartment blocks forming a tiny ski station.

Auron
A pleasant, family-oriented resort in the far south of the Alps, near Isola 2000, claiming an impressive but wildly exaggerated 135km of pistes. The resort sits on an open shelf at 1600m, with varied intermediate slopes, practically all wooded. Lifts from the village go up to the main Las Donnas sector, with a top height approaching 2500m, where various runs connect with the other sectors – Sauma Longue, Demandols and Lieuson, which also has gondola access from the lower village of St-Etienne-de-Tinée. There is a good choice of mountain restaurants.

Aussois – Maurienne valley – 130
Charming rustic village near Modane in the Maurienne valley. Small but interesting south-facing ski area.

Avoriaz – Portes du Soleil – 172

Ax-les-Thermes
A sizeable spa village in the Pyrenees, near Font-Romeu and Andorra. There is gondola access from the village to the ski area above Bonascre. The mainly intermediate slopes are mostly served by fast chair-lifts.

Barèges
A shady spa village set in a narrow, steep-sided valley. It's the second oldest ski resort in France and shares with La Mongie one of the biggest ski areas in the Pyrenees – 100km of pistes collectively known as Grand Tourmalet. The distinctively French village is quiet, with one main street and a few basic hotels. The lift base is at Tournaboup, 4km up the valley and served by ski bus, but in good conditions you can ski back to the village. The slopes spread widely across four major sectors, with contrasting woodland runs above Barèges and open bowl skiing towards La Mongie. The whole area is best suited to intermediates, but there are some gentle greens for novices and decent unexploited off-piste. There are several interesting descents from the Pic du Midi observatory cable car, which has opened to off-piste skiers.

Le Bettex – Megève– 133
A cluster of lodgings near the mid-station of the gondola from St-Gervais into the slopes.

Beuil
Alpes-Maritimes resort closest to Nice. Medieval village with a lift into the quite extensive Valberg ski area.

Bonneval-sur-Arc – Val Cenis – 201

Les Bottières – Maurienne valley – 130
Hamlet at the edge of Les Sybelles, with limited infrastructure and poor access to the main network.

Bourg-St-Maurice – Paradiski – 152
Pleasant valley town, terminus of the TGV trains from London and Paris, at the base of a funicular to Les Arcs; also useful as a base

for visiting various nearby resorts.
Briançon – Serre-Chevalier – 188
Historic town at one end of the long Serre-Chevalier area.
Brides-les-Bains – 3 Vallées – 46
Quiet spa town in valley below Méribel, and connected to it by a long, slow gondola.
Les Carroz – Grand Massif – 118
Cauterets
A charming old spa town at 935m, at the head of a wide, sunny valley in the Pyrenees. Many of the central buildings are well-preserved examples of 19th century France, with the grand spas the main attraction. A gondola takes you up to a high, open bowl 850m above the town – you have to ride it down as well as up. Lifts radiate around the bowl, serving a limited range of mainly red and blue runs with a vertical of about 700m. There is a good nursery area by the top station, making this a popular weekend destination for local families. Cauterets' jewel is its cross-country terrain, a long drive or bus ride from town at Pont d'Espagne and served by a gondola. It is the start of the Pyrenees National Park.
Celliers – Valmorel – 226
Rustic village in the valley up to the Col de la Madeleine, with a lift to a limb of the slopes.
Chamonix – 87
Champagny-en-Vanoise – Paradiski – 160
Pleasant, unremarkable village with back-door access to La Plagne's slopes – and quite quick access by road to Courchevel.
Chamrousse
A functional family resort near Grenoble, with good, sheltered slopes. Chair-lifts and a cable car from three bases (1650, 1700 and 1750) serve largely beginner and intermediate slopes.
Chantemerle – Serre-Chevalier – 188
One of the main valley villages making up the big resort of Serre-Chevalier.
La Chapelle-d'Abondance – Portes du Soleil – 172
Roadside village down the valley from Châtel, with a lift into a limb of the ski area.
Châtel – Portes du Soleil – 172
Le Chazelet
Tiny hamlet 5km up the Col du Lautaret road from La Grave, useful on bad-weather days.
Le Chinaillon – Annecy Mountains – 80
Spread-out ski station, more convenient for skiing than mother resort Le Grand-Bornand.
La Clusaz – Annecy Mountains – 80
Les Coches – Paradiski – 160
Small, quiet, modern mini-resort, up the hill from Montchavin on the northern side of the La Plagne area, near the link to Les Arcs.
Combloux – Megève – 133
Spread-out village at one end of Megève's Le Jaillet sector of slopes.
Les Contamines – Megève – 133
Unspoiled but sprawling chalet resort close to Megève and covered by the same lift pass, with a good snow record for its height.
Le Corbier – Maurienne valley – 130
Purpose-built tower-block resort centrally placed in the Sybelles area.
Corrençon-en-Vercors
Charming, rustic village at foot of Villard-de-Lans ski area. Good cross-country, too.
Courchevel – 3 Vallées – 36
Crest-Voland – Espace Diamant – 103
Traditional village spread around the base of its ski hill in the Espace Diamant.
La Daille – Val d'Isère – 210
Satellite of Val d'Isère, dominated by big apartment blocks.
Les Deux-Alpes – 96
Dévoluy
Commune in the southern Alps which contains and markets the ski area shared by Superdévoluy and La Joue-du-Loup.
Doucy – Valmorel – 226
Quiet apartment development out on a limb at the foot of long easy pistes.
Espace Lumière
One of the bigger areas in the southern Alps, south of Barcelonnette, shared by La Foux d'Allos and Pra-Loup. It claims a ludicrous 180km of pistes (it's half that size). Each resort has a decent amount of mixed intermediate skiing on the lower slopes, with stiffer stuff from the top heights in the 2500–2600m region. But the two/three little valleys between the resorts have no blue runs, limiting the appeal for many.
Flaine – Grand Massif – 118
Flumet – Espace Diamant – 103
Valley town on the Albertville-Megève road with lifts from an elevated outpost into the Espace Diamant slopes.
Font-Romeu
A delightful old village set high up (1775m) in woodland in the Pyrenees, to the east of Andorra. You ride a gondola to and from the slopes, but you can alternatively stay at the foot of the slopes in purpose-built Pyrenees 2000. The intermediate pistes spread across three partly wooded hills, with a limited vertical. The resort is popular with families, and very busy on fine weekends. There are large amounts of cross-country skiing.
Le Fornet – Val d'Isère – 210
Rustic old hamlet 3km up the valley from Val d'Isère, with cable car up to the Col de l'Iseran slopes.

La Foux-d'Allos
Purpose-built resort also referred to as Val d'Allos that shares a good intermediate area (Espace Lumière) with Pra-Loup.
Les Gets – Portes du Soleil – 180
La Giettaz – Megève – 133
Small village with lifts at its higher outpost of Le Plan into Megève's Le Jaillet slopes.
Le Grand-Bornand – Annecy M'tains – 80
Sizeable village with a worthwhile area of slopes supplementing those of larger La Clusaz, nearby.
La Grave – 128
Guzet
Nicely varied area west of Andorra in the Pyrenees, with a claimed 40km of pistes between 1400m and 2100m, mainly open but some in woods. Lodgings in self-catering chalets in the forest.
Hauteluce – Espace Diamant – 103
Rustic hamlet offering a back door into the Espace Diamant area and, with the aid of buses, into the slopes of Les Contamines.
Les Houches – Chamonix Valley – 87
Spread-out village at the base of a low, wooded area of slopes in the Chamonix valley, dominated by high, open slopes.
Isola 2000
A compact purpose-built resort a mere 90km from Nice, which makes it great for short breaks. The doorstep snow, high slopes and an improving range of amenities make it equally appealing to families and beginners; there are some excellent nursery slopes near the base. But the core of the resort village isn't pretty: mostly block-like and tatty apartment buildings. The slopes spread across three main sectors, with varied runs suiting confident intermediates best; most are above the treeline and often sunny, but the resort's southerly location means that the area can have masses of snow when it is in shorter supply elsewhere in the French Alps. And most slopes keep their snow well.
La Joue-du-Loup
Slightly stylish little purpose-built resort a few km north-west of Gap, in the southern Alps. Shares a fair-sized intermediate area with Superdévoluy. A ski-in/ski-out, family-oriented resort; all accommodation in good-value apartments and chalets, with a good choice of affordable restaurants.
Les Karellis – Maurienne valley – 130
Purpose-built resort in the Maurienne valley, a viable day trip from Valloire.
Lanslebourg – Val Cenis – 201
The middle village of the three that make up Val Cenis.
Lanslevillard – Val Cenis – 201

Le Lavancher
Village between Chamonix and Argentière.
Le Lioran
Auvergne village near Aurillac with a purpose-built satellite above and a claimed 60km of runs. Spectacular volcanic scenery.
Longchamp – Valmorel – 226
Modern apartment resort forming the main ski station of St-Françoise-Longchamp, sharing a ski area with Valmorel.
Luchon Superbagnères
The ski area belonging to Bagnères de Luchon, aka Luchon, a thermal spa town in the Pyrenees with plenty of amenities, and a gondola up to purpose-built Superbagnères, which it claims is the oldest in the Pyrenees. There are good beginner slopes on one side of the resort, more serious skiing on the other side in two sectors linked by a fast chair-lift and blue pistes. The main sector has a top height of 2125m and a bottom height of 1465m, and the pistes are claimed to total 32km.
Luz-Ardiden
Spa village below its ski area. Cauterets and Barèges are nearby.
Manigod – Annecy Mountains – 80
Small village detached from its skiing at the Col de la Croix-Fry, an extremity of La Clusaz's slopes.
Megève – 133
Les Menuires – 3 Vallées – 55
Méribel – 3 Vallées – 46
Le Monêtier – Serre-Chevalier – 188
Charming but traffic-dominated village at one end of the long Serre-Chevalier ski area.
La Mongie
Modern purpose-built resort set in a large, treeless bowl and sharing (with Barèges) one of the biggest ski areas in the Pyrenees, best suited to intermediates. There are 20km of cross-country trails.
Montalbert – Paradiski – 160
Quiet backwater village at one extremity of the La Plagne ski area, far distant from the Vanoise Express link with Les Arcs.
Montchavin – Paradiski – 160
Charming rustic village turned car-free ski resort on northern side of La Plagne and close to the link with Les Arcs.
Le Mont-Dore
Attractive traditional small town, the largest resort in the stunningly beautiful volcanic Auvergne region near Clermont-Ferrand.
Montgenèvre – 143
Morillon – Grand Massif – 118
Unremarkable neighbour of Samoëns in the Grand Massif area, but more conveniently arranged for skiiing.

Morzine – Portes du Soleil – 180
Mottaret – 3 Vallées – 46
Slightly higher modern satellite of Méribel, centrally placed for exploration of the 3 Vallées area.
La Norma – Maurienne valley – 130
Modern, car-free compact resort on the shady side of the Maurienne valley.
Nôtre-Dame-de-Bellecombe – Espace Diamant – 103
Quiet, simple village near Flumet with an antique lift into the Espace Diamant.
Orcières-Merlette
High, conveniently laid-out family resort a few km north-east of Gap in the southern Alps, Merlette (1850m) being the ugly, purpose-built ski station above the village of Orcières (1450m). Snow-sure beginner area. Slopes have a mix of difficulty spread over several mountain flanks, peaking at 2725m.
Orelle – 3 Vallées – 64
Ski station outpost of a farming village with a long gondola offering a back door into the slopes of Val Thorens, at one end of the 3 Vallées area.
Les Orres
Friendly but somewhat inaccessible modern resort east of Gap in the southern Alps, with great views and varied intermediate terrain. The slopes run up to about 2700m, with lift bases at 1550, 1650 and 1800 set amid larch forest reaching well over 2100m (so some good verticals to be had). There's a mixture of mainly blue and red skiing in the forest, more red and black higher up. A total of 100km of pistes is claimed – a wild exaggeration.
Oz-en-Oisans – Alpe-d'Huez – 71
Modern ski station satellite of lower old village, well placed in the Alpe-d'Huez ski area.
Peisey – Paradiski – 152
Small village (often referred to as Peisey-Nancroix) below its outpost of Plan-Peisey, with a lift into the slopes of Les Arcs.
Peisey-Vallandry – Paradiski – 152
Overall name for the modern ski stations of Plan-Peisey and Vallandry, at one end of the Les Arcs slopes.
Peyragudes
Small resort in the Pyrenees, straddling the Col de Flamme (perhaps better known as a feature of the Tour de France cycle race). The resort appeals mainly to day visitors from Toulouse and Pau. Two small, purpose-built base villages consisting mainly of apartments sit at 1600m on either side of the ridge. Peyresourde, the larger village, is on the afternoon-sun side of the col, with splendid views to St-Lary-Soulan; on the morning-sun side is smaller Les Agudes. The slopes offer quite a lot of variety, including good beginner areas. A highlight is the remote 6km-long and 1000m-vertical Vallée Blanche red run. Down the valley is the splendid multi-theme Balnea spa complex.
Piau
A small but varied and quite high area in a remote, scenic spot in the Pyrenees, near the Spanish border, which claims to have been the world's snowiest resort in 2015. The 'village' at 1850, is barely that: three semi-circular apartment buildings, with little else. There is a chair-lift up from a valley parking area at Piau 1420, a mile or two from the hamlet of Aragnouet, a few km from St-Lary. There are lots of gentle cruising pistes to suit novices. Highlights for experienced skiers are the uncrowded runs into the Vallée de Badet, and an off-piste route that descends to the Vallée de la Gela with a walk out to Piau at the end.
Pla-d'Adet
Limited purpose-built complex above St-Lary, at one end of the ski area.
La Plagne – Paradiski – 160
Plan-Peisey – Paradiski – 152
Small development above Peisey with lift into the slopes of Les Arcs and a cable-car link to La Plagne.
Pralognan-la-Vanoise
Unspoiled traditional village tucked up a remote valley between Courchevel and Val d'Isère, south of La Plagne, overlooked by spectacular peaks. It has a small sunny ski area, but is better known for Nordic activities and ski touring.
Pra-Loup
Convenient, purpose-built family resort that shares an extensive, varied intermediate area with La Foux-d'Allos (Espace Lumière).
Le Praz – 3 Vallées – 36
Lowest part of Courchevel, with wooded slopes linked with those of La Tania.
Praz-de-Lys
Small family resort close to Geneva with slopes fanning out in all directions. Short runs and old lifts, but nicely varied skiing, and a snow-pocket location.
Praz-sur-Arly – Espace Diamant – 103
Traditional, spacious village on the Albertville-Megève road, with one of the major access lifts of the Espace Diamant.
Puy-St-Vincent
Modern apartment complex above an old village south of Briançon (Serre-Chevalier); it gives convenient access to an area of slopes that are limited in extent but offer a decent vertical and a lot of variety, including a bit of steep stuff. Most accommodation is

in self-catering apartments at the foot of the slopes. It is relatively inexpensive and makes an attractive choice for a family not hungry for piste miles.

Pyrenees 2000
Tiny resort built in a pleasing manner at the foot of the pretty area of short runs shared with Font-Romeu. Impressive snowmaking.

Risoul
Risoul is a quiet, purpose-built apartment-based resort, popular with families and in a pleasantly woody setting, sharing with Vars the slopes of the Forêt Blanche – a quite extensive area in the southern Alps (about 30km south of Serre-Chevalier) that attracts very little international attention and therefore retains a very French ambience. The slopes are, as the name implies, attractively wooded, and nicely varied; but the lift system is one of the most antiquated in the Alps. The compact centre has a small range of shops and restaurants, with sunny terraces facing the slopes. We visited a few seasons ago for a couple of days and loved it; a week might be too much for a keen skier or boarder, though.

La Rosière – Espace San Bernardo – 111
Les Saisies – Espace Diamant – 103
Samoëns – Grand Massif – 118
Le Sauze
Neat little area near Barcelonnette, claiming 65km of pistes between 1400 and 2200m, sadly remote from airports.

Le Seignus-d'Allos
Close to La Foux-d'Allos (which shares large area with Pra-Loup) and has own little area, too.

Les Sept-Laux
Family resort near Grenoble with pretty slopes and a modern lift system, these days promoted more often as Les 7 Laux. The main resort, with quite a bit of accommodation, is Prapoutel in the woods at 1350m; across the mountainside is another lift base at Pipay, at 1550m, and on the back of the hill is a third entry point at Le Pleynet. There is easy skiing at resort level, but the mountain as a whole is challenging. We're very sceptical of the resort's claim of 120km of pistes.

Serre-Chevalier – 188
Sixt-Fer-à-Cheval – Grand Massif – 118
Small, traditional village near Samoëns, at the end of the famous Piste des Cascades from Flaine, with its own small ski area.

Sommand
Purpose-built base that shares area with Praz-de-Lys.

St-Colomban-des-Villards – Maurienne valley – 130
Small village on periphery of the Sybelles area, with an endless chain of slow lifts to access the core of the network.

Ste-Foy-Tarentaise – 197
St-Etienne-de-Tinée
Small valley town at 1500m with gondola access to the fair-sized Auron ski area in the southern Alps.

St-François-Longchamp – Valmorel – 226
Sunny half of the Grande Domain shared with Valmorel – this half accessed from the Maurienne valley.

St-Gervais – Megève – 133
Handsome spa town sharing Megève's main Mont d'Arbois ski area and offering a back door into the slopes of Les Houches in the Chamonix valley.

St-Jean-d'Arves – Maurienne valley – 130
Small, scattered resort on the back of the Sybelles area, with a lift link with Le Corbier.

St-Jean-de-Sixt – Annecy Mountains – 80
Small village mid-way between La Clusaz and Le Grand-Bornand.

St-Jean-Montclar
Small village at the foot of thickly forested slopes. Good day out from nearby Pra-Loup.

St-Lary
An attractive, traditional village which has good value restaurants and hotels, combined with one of the largest ski areas in the Pyrenees. If you stay in the old village, you have to ride an access lift both ways, as there are no runs to resort level. For more convenience you can stay up at purpose-built St-Lary 1700 (Pla-d'Adet) right on the slopes. The slopes spread west across a broad valley and three main sectors, not notably challenging but with some good off-piste. Intermediates will be most at home here, though. The resort claims 100km of pistes, a clear exaggeration.

St-Martin-de-Belleville – 3 Vallées – 55
St-Nicolas-de-Véroce – Megève – 133
Hamlet with lifts into the Megève slopes, between St-Gervais and Les Contamines.

St-Sorlin-d'Arves – Maurienne valley – 130
Small traditional village with the most interesting slopes in the Sybelles area.

St-Véran
Said to be the highest 'real' village in Europe, and full of charm. In the southern Alps, close to Serre-Chevalier and the Milky Way. Snow-reliable cross-country skiing.

Super-Besse
Purpose-built resort amid spectacular extinct-volcano scenery. Shares area with the spa town of Mont-Dore. Limited village.

Superdévoluy
A purpose-built, friendly family resort in a remote spot near Gap, in the southern Alps. There is a mix of huge tower blocks plus traditional chalets. The slopes offer a sizeable intermediate area shared with La Joue-du-Loup, and reach a respectable height. Most slopes are above the treeline, but there are some long blues and wide open green runs for confidence building.
La Tania – 3 Vallées – 36
Termignon – Val Cenis – 201
Traditional rustic village 6km down the Maurienne valley from Lanslebourg and the main slopes of Val Cenis, to which it is linked.
Tignes – 218
Le Tour – Chamonix Valley – 87
Small village at the head of the Chamonix valley and the foot of the Balme slopes.
La Toussuire – Maurienne valley – 130
One of the main resorts of Les Sybelles, with a core of dreary apartment buildings plus chalet suburbs.
Valberg
Large Alpes-Maritimes resort (bigger than better-known Isola 2000) close to Nice. The area claims a wildly exaggerated 90km of slopes served by 7 chair-lifts and 23 drag-lifts, and a sea view from the top height of Dreccia (2011m). The village, mainly in chalet style, spreads widely over a col at 1700m, and the skiing extends over a series of low wooded peaks – a good mixture of pistes, but with limited verticals.
Val d'Allos
Currently favoured name for La Foux-d'Allos.
Val d'Isère – 210
Valfréjus – Maurienne valley – 130
A small, quiet and unusual modern resort in the Maurienne valley – built in the woods, with most of the slopes higher up above the treeline.
Vallandry – Paradiski – 152
Ski station forming part of Peisey-Vallandry at one end of the Les Arcs slopes, with a cable-car link to La Plagne.
Valloire – Maurienne valley – 130
Vallorcine – Chamonix Valley – 87
Quiet backwater village on road between Chamonix and Switzerland, with a gondola into the Balme area above Le Tour.
Valmeinier – Maurienne valley – 130
Quiet, old mountain village with a modern, purpose-built satellite sharing with Valloire the most extensive slopes in the Maurienne.
Valmorel – 226
Val Thorens – 3 Vallées – 64
Vars
Vars and nearby Risoul share the slopes of the Forêt Blanche – a quite extensive area in the southern Alps (about 30km south of Serre-Chevalier) that attracts very little international attention and therefore retains a very French ambience. The slopes are, as the name implies, attractively wooded, and nicely varied; but the lift system is one of the most antiquated in the Alps. Vars includes several small, old villages on or near the road running southwards towards the Col de Vars. But for winter visitors it mainly consists of purpose-built Vars-les-Claux, higher up the road. The resort has convenience and reasonable prices in common with Risoul, but it is bigger and has far more in the way of amenities; less English is spoken though. There are a lot of block-like apartments, but Vars-les-Claux is not a complete eyesore, thanks mainly to surrounding woods. There are two centres: the original, geographical one – base of the main gondola – has most of the accommodation and shopping; Point Show is a collection of bars and shops, 10 minutes' walk away. Vars-Ste-Marie makes a more attractive base now that fast chairs take you to the top of La Mayt, but is dead in the evenings.
Vaujany – Alpe-d'Huez – 71
Small but much expanded village with a big cable car into the heart of the Alpe-d'Huez ski area.
Venosc – Les Deux-Alpes – 96
Rustic village with a gondola nearby up to Les Deux-Alpes.
Villar-d'Arêne
Tiny area on main road between La Grave and Serre-Chevalier. Empty, immaculately groomed, short easy runs, plus a couple of hotels.
Villard-de-Lans
Unspoiled, lively, traditional village west of Grenoble. Snow-sure, thanks to snowmaking.
Villard-Reculas – Alpe-d'Huez – 71
Micro-resort on the back of Signal, the hill above Alpe-d'Huez.
Villaroger – Paradiski – 152
Rustic hamlet with slow lifts nearby into the slopes of Les Arcs.
Villeneuve – Serre-Chevalier – 188
One of the central villages making up the resort of Serre-Chevalier.

We hope you like ***Where to Ski in France***. If you do, maybe you should get hold of ***Where to Ski in Austria***, published in autumn 2017. Like this book, it covers all the resorts you're likely to be interested in, and it covers them in just the same thorough, uncompromising way.

You can buy both books at discount prices through our new online shop at skibooks.uk. Given that you seem to have France already, you'll be able to buy Austria at a very special discount.

In 2019 we plan to publish
Where to Ski in Italy and
Where to Ski in Switzerland.

A book on North America may follow those.

If you'd like to keep up to date with these publishing plans – and be among the first to know about discount pricing offers – sign up for our email newsletter on our well established website. Go to www.wheretoskiandsnowboard.com